NARCOLAND

NARCOLAND

The Mexican Drug Lords and Their Godfathers

Anabel Hernández

Foreword by Roberto Saviano

Translated by Iain Bruce

VERSO

London • New York

*To all the sources who shared with me
a wealth of knowledge, testimonies and documents,
despite the risks involved. Today some of their
names feature in the appalling catalog of
the executed and the disappeared of Mexico.*

*To Héctor, my children, my family,
and my friends, for their boundless understanding
while I carried out this investigation.*

This English-language edition published by Verso 2013
Translation © Iain Bruce 2013
First published as Los *señores del narco*
© Grijalbo 2010
Foreword © Roberto Saviano 2013
Foreword translation © Paolo Mossetti 2013

1 3 5 7 9 10 8 6 4 2

Verso
UK: 6 Meard Street, London W1F 0EG
US: 20 Jay Street, Suite 1010, Brooklyn, NY 11201
www.versobooks.com

Verso is the imprint of New Left Books

ISBN-13: 978-1-78168-073-5

British Library Cataloguing in Publication Data
A catalogue record for this book is available from the British Library

Library of Congress Cataloging-in-Publication Data

Hernández, Anabel.
[Señores del narco. English]
Narcoland : the Mexican drug lords and their godfathers / Anabel Hernandez ;
foreword by Roberto Saviano ; translated by Iain Bruce.
pages cm
Includes index.
ISBN 978-1-78168-073-5 (alk. paper)
1. Drug traffic—Mexico. 2. Organized crime—Mexico. 3. Drug control—Mexico. 4.
Corruption—Mexico. I. Title.
HV5840.M4H4713 2013
363.450972—dc23
2013011559

Typeset in Minion by Hewer UK Ltd, Edinburgh
Printed in the US by Maple Press

Contents

Foreword
by Roberto Saviano

A nabel Hernández's Narco*land* is essential for understanding the power dynamics inside the Mexican economy—the economy's deep, often concealed, links with politics. This is a book that exposes how everything in Mexico is implicated in the "narco system." And yet, Anabel's work is hard to describe. She doesn't just write about drug trafficking or drugs or Mexico. Her storytelling becomes a method of revealing an entire world.

Anabel's writing has a scientific, clear, rigorous, almost martial rhythm. She does not give in to lazy descriptions, nor does she give in to anger or disgust. She is a journalist who never loses focus on the mechanisms of power. Her method makes her a rarity in Mexico, and because of this, her voice is a precious resource. She wants to know how it was possible that one of the great democracies of America became a narco-democracy. With her investigation of the "first government of change" of Vicente Fox (which brought an end to seventy years of one-party rule under the Partido Revolucionario Institucional), she showed how that "change" was fictitious. She was one of the first reporters to talk about economic corruption, long before the crisis exploded, and she did that by tracking seemingly endless political expenditures. She could already see the system becoming a black hole of bribes and payoffs. Hernández was one of the first to talk openly about El Chapo Guzmán, and one of the first reporters to talk about El Chapo's connections to politics. Because of this, she became a target of organized crime and now lives a life filled with danger.

Anabel was threatened in a way that might seem bizarre to those unfamiliar with political intimidation. The secretary of public security in Mexico, Genaro García Luna, declared that Anabel had refused protection. Actually, she had never received any protection offers from the state, nor had she refused them. So the message was ominous and clear. What they were saying was: We *could* protect you, we *could* grant you this protection, but not to defend your words: rather, only if you stop writing. And this invitation won't come again. Anabel, when put in this corner, demonstrated her courage by saying she didn't want to die.

The role of the journalist is often a difficult one. Journalists often hate each other, or envy each other. This is perhaps one of the jobs in which these feelings are most common, and it can lead to isolation. It happened to Anna Politkovskaya after she said she was poisoned while on a flight. Many journalists accused Anna of having made it up, saying that she had become a sort of delirious writer who believed in 007-style poisonings. The honesty of her words became apparent when she was murdered. Anabel said: "I want to live. I do not want to be murdered. I don't want my name to be added to the list of reporters killed every year in Mexico." And this is courage. The strong, profound courage that I have always admired.

Narco*land* is not only an essential book for anyone willing to look squarely at organized crime today. Narco*land* also shows how contemporary capitalism is in no position to renounce the mafia. Because it is not the mafia that has transformed itself into a modern capitalist enterprise—it is capitalism that has transformed itself into a mafia. The rules of drug trafficking that Anabel Hernández describes are also the rules of capitalism. What I appreciate in Anabel is not only her courage—it is this comprehensive view of society that is so rare to find.

The value of Anabel's work is also, perhaps above all, scientific. She managed to get information that had been held by the CIA. She was the first to collate police investigations in several different countries, and she did that by making use of her inheritance: the stories of journalists who came before her. One example is the case of journalist Manuel Buendía Tellezgirón, who had collected information on the relationship between the CIA and the narcos of Veracruz. He got this information from the Mexican secret service and paid for it with his life.

Anabel also had the courage to ask questions about politicians. And to pose these questions does not mean to defame. Her strength was in questioning how it could have been possible for politics to become so powerless or corrupt, justice so incompetent or reluctant. In a situation like this, asking questions becomes an instrument of freedom. A hypothesis can give us insight into the meaning of clues and force politicians to give answers. When those answers are not given, when politicians do not deny allegations by providing evidence, one can justly suspect their complicity. In the case, for example, of the escape of El Chapo Guzmán, Anabel proved the official version to be false while giving a political interpretation of it: politicians may have released El Chapo because it was convenient for them to do so. In a country like Mexico, which has a deeply compromised democracy, reporters proposing interpretations like these are acting to save their democracy. It is an attempt to bring responsibility back into politics. While nailing politicians to their responsibilities, Anabel transforms her pages into an instrument for readers—an instrument of democracy.

Narcoland describes a disastrous "war on drugs" that has led to more than 80,000 deaths since its inception in 2006. A war that has been nothing more than a blood battle between feuding fiefdoms. A war between one, often corrupt, part of the state against another corrupt part of the state. Hence the war on drugs has not been a war on criminal cartels, nor did it weaken the strength of the cartels. On the contrary, it boosted it. The war redistributed money, weapons, and repression—and eventually provoked counterattacks. Counterattacks by a government itself infiltrated by criminal organizations. Add to this the disastrous policies of the United States, which for years has claimed to be challenging drug trafficking in Mexico, with no positive results.

Anabel recounts all of this with the detachment of an analyst, but the pages themselves exude tragedy and drama. The drama of those who know that if things keep going this way, democracy itself will be destroyed, crushed. Anabel Hernández sketches a map for her readers, so they can navigate the state of things today. This is a map for all those who understand that the current economic crisis is not only the result of financial speculation without regulations, but also a total impunity for limitless greed. Anabel describes the geography of a world in which political economy has become criminal economy.

Introduction

M y introduction to the life of Joaquín Guzmán Loera began at 6:30 in the morning of June 11, 2005. That is when I boarded a bus that would take me and photographer Ernesto Ramírez to Guadalupe y Calvo, a small, storm-prone municipality in the northern Mexican state of Chihuahua, deep in the "golden triangle" spanned by the towering Sierra Madre Occidental. It was the start of a five-day voyage to the land of drug kingpins: Ismael El Mayo Zambada, Eduardo Quintero Payán, Ernesto Fonseca Carrillo, Rafael Caro Quintero, Juan José Esparragoza Moreno, a.k.a. El Azul—and Joaquín El Chapo (Shorty) Guzmán, the man *Forbes* magazine has called "the biggest drug lord of all time" (and in their latest ranking, the fifty-fifth most powerful person in the world). I still have the notebook in which I recorded the journey. It was one that was to change forever my view of the drug trade, which is today the backbone of organized crime in Mexico.

Most of the road to Guadalupe y Calvo runs through a dreamlike landscape of serried pinewoods. The sky was that intense blue you can sense in a black-and-white photograph by Manuel Álvarez Bravo. At 10:50 in the morning we arrived at the town of Rio Verde, where they hang meat on the line like washed socks. Unfortunately it's no longer just beef, but also the bodies of victims from the "war on drugs."

The winding road began to climb as steeply as a big dipper. The driver was an old hand. He threw the bus round the bends entrusting our fates to Pope John Paul II, the Virgin of Guadalupe, and St. Juan Diego, whose pictures were stuck on the windscreen. At one stop a newspaper vendor called Federico Chávez got on. The youngster exchanged greetings with almost all of the passengers; we were the only outsiders. Before we left Mexico City, Iván Noé Licón, a Chihuahua education official, had warned me on the phone to be discreet about our identity. "People are cagey with strangers, because they think they're police," he told me. So when some of the travelers took Ernesto for a priest, we didn't say anything. It seems teachers and priests are the only outsiders who are greeted without suspicion in those parts.

After eight hours, we finally reached our destination: the municipal capital of Guadalupe y Calvo. From there we planned to tour the surrounding villages—although that is a manner of speaking, because on the bumpy tracks that link these hamlets it takes five or six hours to get anywhere. We met up with Chava, a local official who would be our guide and friend in this world we knew so little of. It was impossible not to be moved by the majestic beauty of the place, and the tragedy of its inhabitants. They were five unforgettable days.

As a journalist I had come to investigate the story of child exploitation in the area, where minors are put often to work by their parents on the poppy and marijuana harvests. These are kids who become criminals without even realizing it. Many, from the age of seven upwards, die of poisoning by the pesticides used on the plantations. Those who survive into adolescence are already carrying AK-47s, or "goat's horns" as these weapons are popularly known.

We entered this mountain world along its narrow dirt tracks and cattle trails, learning of its customs, dreams, and legends, as well as its poverty. We visited remote places like Baborigame, Dolores, El Saucito de Araujo, and Mesa del Frijol, where more than 80 percent of the population grow drug crops. In these communities, long forgotten by federal or state social programs, you nonetheless see four-wheel-drive Cadillac Escalades, satellite dishes, and men with walkie-talkies and a pistol in their belt.

Here I met Father Martín, a Peruvian priest with a dark, glossy complexion, an extraordinary sense of humor and a great heart, who had chosen to stay in Guadalupe y Calvo rather than accept a transfer to the safety of El Paso, Texas. He carried out his pastoral work with matchless energy, even if his sermons against the wrong kind of seeds fell on deaf ears. Talking to him helped me to understand the human dimension of the problem, as opposed to the perspective of military and police operations.

People have been doing this for decades. They don't know any other way of life, and no one has shown them an alternative. No doubt in these humid ravines you could grow guava, papaya, or other fruits, but the lack of decent roads makes it impossible to transport such produce. To make matters worse, residents say some places here, like Baborigame, didn't get electricity until 2001. Many illegal plantations have been supported by the Mexican and US governments. But the authorities don't understand that being nurtured here are not just drug crops, but future drug traffickers. Kids don't want to be firemen or doctors when they grow up; they want to become drug barons. That's the only measure of success they know.

Stories abound of El Chapo roaming the streets of Guadalupe y Calvo, flanked by bodyguards dressed in black. People have embraced the myth of the generous godfather figure, the sponsor of baptisms, first communions, and weddings.

I climbed to the top of Mohinora, in the south of the Tarahumara range. At 3,307 meters, it's the highest peak in Chihuahua. Below, in season, you can see the green valley flooded with red poppies. Its beauty is enough to make you cry—and so are the consequences of this trade. I had gone to research a story about child labor, but I came back with much more: the knowledge of a way of life which for these people is as necessary as the blood that runs in their veins—and that now increasingly runs in the streets.

At the end of 2005, the lawyer Eduardo Sahagún called me at the Mexico City offices of *La Revista*, the magazine of El *Universal*, the newspaper where I was working. He wanted to know if I'd be interested in the story of a client of his, Luis Francisco Fernández Ruiz, the former assistant warden of the Puente Grande maximum security prison, in the state of Jalisco. Fernández wanted to talk to me about his case. He was being tried along with sixty-seven other public employees who had been working at Puente Grande's Federal Center for Social Rehabilitation Number 2 on the night of January 19, 2001, the night El Chapo Guzmán went missing from the prison. They were all accused of taking bribes and facilitating El Chapo's escape. Fernández had already spent nearly five years in jail, and he still hadn't been sentenced. "The state prosecutor's office has always refused an on-the-spot inspection and a reconstruction of the escape, to establish how El Chapo got away and who was responsible," the lawyer told me. All I'd heard about the affair were the Hollywoodesque stories circulating afterwards, of how the drug baron had fled in a laundry cart. This improbable version of events was repeated so often in the domestic and international media that it had become an unquestionable truth; the same thing happened with many other stories of Mexico's drug trade.

I finally met Fernández in the visiting rooms of Mexico City's Reclusorio Oriente detention center. It was a short encounter, during which he expounded his innocence. The former assistant warden of Puente Grande told me of his dealings with the drug baron, and gave me his impressions of the man: "He was introverted, with a serious, withdrawn manner, not at all overbearing or rude, and he was intelligent, very intelligent." There was no admiration in Fernández's words, but a certain respect for the drug trafficker, who was in his custody from 1999 until the day he was sprung from Puente Grande.

"After the alarm was raised following the escape, the Federal Police took control of the prison, we were all shut into the hall, and armed personnel in balaclavas moved in," recalled Fernández. Two years later this fact would prove crucial.

Soon after I published my interview with Luis Fernández in *La Revista*, he won his appeal and was released. Today there is almost no one still behind bars for what the authorities call "El Chapo's escape." Even the warden of the maximum security prison, Leonardo Beltrán Santana, whose path I crossed a couple of times in the VIP dormitory of the Reclusorio Oriente, was freed in 2010.

In May 2006, at the Nikko Hotel in Mexico City, I met a DEA agent who confirmed my growing conviction that Joaquín Guzmán and the drug trade were essential to understanding a key aspect of corruption in Mexico, perhaps the most important aspect of all: the one that involves top government figures putting prices on the country's millions of inhabitants, as if they were head of cattle.

According to this agent, DEA informers infiltrated into the organization of drug lord Ignacio Coronel Villarreal had told him that El Chapo Guzmán left Puente Grande penitentiary after paying a multimillion-dollar bribe to the family of President Vicente Fox, of the National Action Party (PAN). And that the deal included systematic protection by the federal government of him and his group, the all-powerful Pacific cartel. Fox is now a leading advocate for the legalization of not only the consumption, but also the production, distribution, and sale of every class of drug.

This book is the result of five grueling years of research. Over this time I gradually became immersed in a shadowy world full of traps, lies, betrayals, and contradictions. The data I present is backed up by numerous legal documents, and the testimony of many who witnessed the events first-hand. I met people involved in the Mexican drug cartels. I spoke to police and army officers, US government officials, professional hit men, and priests. I interviewed figures who know the drug trade inside out, and have even been accused of protecting it, as happened with General Jorge Carrillo Olea—a former governor of the state of Morelos and secretary of the interior, who gave me an exclusive interview for this book.

I read avidly the thousands of pages of evidence in the case of "El Chapo's escape." Through the dozens of statements given by cooks, laundry workers, inmates, detention officers, and prison police commanders that make up the proceedings of penal case 16/2001, I learned of Guzmán's passion for painting landscapes, how much he missed his mother, his "romantic" side, his brutality as a rapist, his need for Viagra, his taste for candy and volleyball, but above all his infinite capacity to corrupt everyone and everything in his path. Similarly, hundreds of sheets of official documents allowed me to confirm that in 2001 El Chapo did not escape from Puente Grande in that famous laundry cart: instead, high-ranking officials took him out, disguised as a policeman.

I also obtained recently declassified CIA and DEA documents on the Iran-Contra affair—something nobody seems to remember anymore—which is what turned Mexican drug traffickers from humble marijuana and poppy farmers into sophisticated international dealers in cocaine and synthetic drugs. I retrieved files eliminated from the archives of the federal prosecutor's office, referring to the businessmen who, in the early 1990s, sheltered in their hangars the planes of El Chapo, Amado Carrillo Fuentes, and Héctor El Güero Palma. Today, these eminent entrepreneurs are the owners of hotel chains, hospitals, and newspapers. I found a different account of the air crash that killed the former interior secretary, Juan Camilo Mouriño, on November 4, 2008, which suggests that the crash was not an accident but an act of revenge by drug barons for agreements not kept.

In similar fashion, I discovered the identity of the businessmen who appear as the owners of a company supposedly run by Ismael El Mayo Zambada, which operates out of a hangar in Mexico City International Airport and transports drugs and money, with both the knowledge and consent of the Communications and Transport Secretariat and the airport administration.

The story of how Joaquín Guzmán Loera became a great drug baron, the king of betrayal and bribery, and the boss of top Federal Police commanders, is intimately linked to a process of decay in Mexico where two factors are constant: corruption, and an unbridled ambition for money and power.

Semi-illiterate peasants like El Príncipe, Don Neto, El Azul, El Mayo, and El Chapo would not have got far without the collusion of businessmen, politicians, and policemen, and all those who exercise everyday power from behind a false halo of legality. We see their faces all the time, not in the mug shots of most wanted felons put out by the Attorney General's Office, but in the front-page stories, business sections, and society columns of the main papers. *All these are the true godfathers of Narcoland, the true lords of the drug world.*

Often the protection given to drug barons continues until they commit a major blunder, are ratted out by others anxious to take their place, or simply cease to be useful for business. Now there also exists the option of voluntary retirement, like that taken by Nacho Coronel or Edgar Valdez, La Barbie. There will always be substitute candidates for support to continue the criminal enterprise. Many have seen their time come in this way: Ernesto Fonseca Carrillo, Rafael Caro Quintero, Miguel Ángel Félix Gallardo, Amado Carrillo Fuentes. Joaquín Guzmán Loera alone will quit when he feels like it, not when the authorities choose. Some say he is already preparing his exit.

The current war on drugs, launched by the government of Felipe Calderón, is just as fake as that undertaken by the administration of Vicente Fox. In both cases, the "strategy" has been limited to protecting the Sinaloa cartel. The continuity of such protection has been underwritten by the shady police chief and Calderón's secretary of public security, Genaro García Luna, and his team of collaborators: the previously unpublished documents presented here are irrefutable proof of this. García Luna is the man who aimed to become, with Calderón's support, the single head of all the country's police forces. He has even stated, with complete impunity, that there is no option but to let El Chapo operate freely and "bring to heel" the other criminal organizations, since it would be easier for the government to negotiate with just one cartel, rather than five. The bloody results of war between opposing cartels we know only too well.

Currently, all the old rules governing relations between the drug barons and the centers of economic and political power have broken down. The drug traffickers impose their own law. The businessmen who launder their money are their partners, while local and federal officials are viewed as employees to be paid off in advance, for example by financing their political campaigns. The culture of terror encouraged by the federal government itself, as well as by the criminal gangs through their grotesque violence, produces a paralyzing fear at all levels of society. Finishing this book demanded a constant battle against such fear. They have tried to convince us that the drug barons and their cronies are immovable and untouchable, but this book offers a modest demonstration of the contrary. As citizens or as journalists, we must never allow the state and the authorities to give up on their duty to provide security, and simply hand the country over to an outlaw network made up of drug traffickers, businessmen, and politicians, allowing them to impose on all Mexicans their intolerable law of "silver or lead." Pay up or die.

*   *   *

On December 1, 2012, Felipe Calderón's government came to an end. His presidency bears the burden of more than 80,000 people killed in the "war on drugs," over 20,000 disappeared, around 200,000 driven from their homes by the violence, and hundreds of thousands of victims of kidnappings, extortion, and general violence. Mexican society and the international community will not allow the terrible events of these last six years to be forgotten.

Calderón's time in office has left Mexico ablaze. There is only one victor in his so-called war on drugs: Joaquín Loera Guzmán, El Chapo, who remains free, and more powerful and ubiquitous than ever. The US Drug Enforcement Administration says that during Calderón's six-year term, Guzmán became the most powerful drug trafficker in history, while his enemies were decimated. El Chapo's empire is Calderón's chief legacy.

Now it is December 2012, and the Institutional Revolutionary Party (PRI) is back in power in Mexico. Many of the politicians and businessmen that you will come across in the pages of this book are not mere specters of the past. They are figures who still hold positions of power, both in public office and private enterprise. As long as they remain in place, Mexico will continue to be Narcoland.

CHAPTER ONE

A Poor Devil

It was nearly eleven in the morning. The two generals were standing in the baking June sun, at an isolated spot on the road to Caca-hoatán, Chiapas, five or six kilometers from the Mexican-Guatemalan border. The atmosphere was as taut as a violin string. The army had deployed a rifle squad in a security ring a hundred meters across. Closer by, there was a smaller circle of paratroopers. All were armed to the teeth.

The minutes seemed to last forever. They'd already heard on the radio that the convoy had crossed the Mexican border without problems. The handover had been perfectly planned and agreed. But there was always the possibility an ambush might damage the package before it arrived.

Standing on a mound of earth beside the road, General Jorge Carrillo Olea finally made out a small dust cloud in the distance. They were all astonished when an old pickup truck drove up, flanked by two more in an equally battered state. In the lead truck there was just the driver, a young co-driver, and in the back the valuable cargo.

A young Guatemalan army captain, aged no more than twenty-six, got out of the old wreck and greeted them with elaborate gallantry: "My general, I have been entrusted with a sensitive consignment that may only be delivered to you in person," he announced ceremoniously to General Carrillo, who was overall coordinator of the Fight Against the Drug Trade for the government of President Carlos Salinas de Gortari, and the man responsible for this important mission.

Looking at the captain, Carrillo Olea couldn't help feeling a little ridiculous. The Mexican government had sent two generals—Guillermo Álvarez Nahara, head of the Military Police, and himself—plus two battalions to support the operation.[1] Guatemala, on the other hand, had made do with a young officer to hand over someone who was still practically unknown, but who was being accused, along with the Arellano Félix brothers, of killing Cardinal Juan Jesús Posadas Ocampo, in the course of an alleged shoot-out between the two sides. Less than a month earlier, on May 24, 1993, the cardinal had died in a spectacular hail of bullets in the parking lot of Guadalajara International Airport.

Without more ado, the Guatemalan captain opened the back of the pickup and pointed to his precious cargo. On the blistering metal deck, tied hand and foot like a pig, lay Joaquín Guzmán Loera. His body had been bouncing around like a bale of hay during the three-hour trip from Guatemala to Mexico.

At the time, El Chapo Guzmán—a member of the criminal gang led by Amado Carrillo Fuentes, better known as El Señor de los Cielos, the Lord of the Skies—was pretty much a nobody in the drugs world. He'd been just fleetingly in the limelight after a shoot-out at the Christine Discotheque in Puerto Vallarta in 1992, when he tried to kill one of the Arellano Félix family, former friends and partners with whom he'd fallen out.

The disputes between the Arellano Félix family, El Chapo Guzmán, and his friend Héctor El Güero Palma were like schoolboy squabbles with machine guns. They'd already featured on the crime pages of Mexican newspapers, but without much prominence. Guzmán had a lot of money, like any other drug trafficker of his ranking, but little power of his own. What power he did have came by using the name of Amado Carrillo Fuentes. Maybe that is why the Guatemalan government had sent him back to Mexico not as a high-risk prisoner. Nonetheless, El Chapo seemed to offer a vital political opportunity to the Mexican government of President Carlos Salinas de Gortari. That bruised figure in the back of the pickup provided an excellent pretext to explain the murder of Cardinal Juan Jesús Posadas Ocampo.

Supposedly, the Arellano Félix brothers and El Chapo Guzmán had had a shoot-out, and the cardinal had been killed in the crossfire. The story, as already reported in the press, was undoubtedly plausible, but a later post-mortem of what happened at Guadalajara airport cast doubt on this version. Forensic experts reported that there had been no crossfire, and that the cardinal had been hit by fourteen bullets at close range.

To look at him in that sorry, helpless state on June 9, 1993, nobody would have imagined that this short, uncharismatic thirty-six-year-old, with barely three years of elementary schooling behind him, would within sixteen years have become the head of the Sinaloa Cartel, the most powerful criminal organization in the Americas— much less that *Forbes* magazine would rank him as one of the richest, and therefore most powerful, men in the world. No one would have imagined either that sixteen years later Jorge Carrillo Olea, vilified and publicly demoted for his alleged protection of drug traffickers during his time as governor of Morelos state (1994–98), would be describing his detailed memories of El Chapo's capture in an affable interview at his home in Cuernavaca, where he lives almost forgotten by all those he once served.

El Chapo Guzmán, with a hood over his head, and Carrillo Olea, impressed by the young Guatemalan captain, never suspected that from that day on their destinies would be forever linked. Carrillo Olea took the credit for successfully arresting the drug trafficker. But seven years, seven months, and ten days later it would be one of his closest protégés, virtually his alter ego, that would help El Chapo to escape from the maximum security prison of Puente Grande on June 19, 2001, according to the trafficker's own account and the investigation into the escape. In Mexico, the worlds of the drug traffickers and the police are quite similar. Maybe that's why they understand each other so well. Complicity and betrayal go hand in hand. One day your closest friend is your accomplice, the next he is your worst enemy.

Capture

Carrillo Olea said that thanks to the Planning Center for Drug Control (Cendro), set up by him in 1992, they were able to follow the route taken by El Chapo from Guadalajara to Guatemala after the shoot-out at the airport. As he recalled it,

After he got into an unknown vehicle on the Chapala to Guadalajara highway, I say unknown because we never knew if it was ready and waiting, if it was to protect him, or it was a private car, I don't know, he disappeared. But the system picked him up in Morelia and we started tracking him. He reached Mexico City, we half lost him, he reappeared. He had a radio and I don't know how many credit cards, four, five, six, and we had [their numbers]. So we hear of a card being used in Coyoacán, in Puebla. . . . Sometimes he'd make mistakes, or he had no choice but to use the phone. That's how we followed him all the way down to San Cristóbal.

Carrillo Olea said that the Cendro notified the Guatemalan government that Guzmán had crossed the border and was headed for El Salvador, which he probably reached via Honduras. "We got in touch with [the authorities in] El Salvador, and their legs turned to jelly. They told us: 'Yes, we've detected him here.' We said, 'Arrest him.' But they didn't, they just scared him off, like a rat. They made it obvious he'd been spotted, so he went back to Guatemala."

Here he was arrested. Carrillo Olea gave the news to the then Attorney General, Jorge Carpizo McGregor, and to President Salinas, to whom he'd had a direct line ever since he took office. It was excellent news. The cardinal's murder was still a burning issue and public opinion wanted a head on a plate. "Now he has to be brought from Guatemala without all the legal hurdles of an extradition," Salinas told Carrillo Olea. That's how it was agreed to hand the prisoner over at the border, without any diplomatic niceties to get in the way.

Carpizo, a former rector of the National Autonomous University (UNAM) and president of the National Human Rights Commission, was the third attorney general in just five years of Salinas's presidency. The first, Enrique Álvarez del Castillo, had been mostly renowned for allowing the Guadalajara (later Sinaloa) Cartel to thrive under his nose while he was the governor of Jalisco state. He was replaced as attorney general by Ignacio Morales Lechuga, who resigned abruptly in 1993. As a result, Carrillo Olea was the one constant factor in Mexico's drug policy under Salinas.

*   *   *

Still in bed and acting on instructions from the president and Carpizo, Carrillo Olea dialed Antonio Riviello Bazán, the secretary of defense.

"I'm calling to trouble you with a rather strange matter. If you're in any doubt, please call the president," said Carrillo Olea.

"So, what's it about?" Riviello asked anxiously.

"I need a 727, a rifle squad, and for the military commander in Chiapas to do what I tell him."

"It's that sensitive?"

"Yes, general, and I'm sorry I can't say any more at this moment in time."

"Don't worry," said the secretary, "we'll see it's done."

Carrillo Olea arrived at 5:45 a.m. at the military gate of Mexico City airport. The paratroopers were already there; General Guillermo Álvarez Nahara turned up shortly afterwards.

"The general told me to go with you. Is that ok?" Álvarez asked Carrillo.

"On the contrary, the more witnesses the better," answered Carrillo.

A few hours later, El Chapo Guzmán was in their custody.

When he saw El Chapo tied up in the truck, Carrillo felt sorry for him: "After all, he was a human being," he recalled. The paratroopers lifted up the hooded figure and dumped him in one of the Mexican army vehicles.

"Captain, thank you," said Carrillo, giving the Guatemalan officer an embrace. "I wish we could have gotten to know each other better. I don't even know your name or where I can call you."

The Mexican convoy moved off swiftly towards the barracks. There a doctor and a lab technician were waiting to examine Guzmán. General Carrillo ordered the prisoner be given a bath and something to eat.

Next, the president's trusted associate tried to call Attorney General Carpizo, to tell him about the operation, but in vain. Carrillo had left things in Mexico City in the hands of his young apprentice, Jorge Enrique Tello Peón, who had first worked with him at the state-owned United Shipyards, as his bag carrier. Now he was the head of the Cendro, but not always efficient: he hadn't followed the instruction to leave three lines free for this very call. Carrillo had to dial his office direct.

"Jorge, didn't I tell you?"

"Sorry, I forgot."

"Put me through to the attorney general."

"Hello, what's up? How are things going?" asked Carpizo at the other end.

"The package is in our hands, and we're on our way to the capital," General Carrillo Olea told him.

"Wonderful, I'll tell the chief."

El Chapo's boss

On March 7, 1999, José Alfredo Andrade Bojorges,[2] a thirty-seven-year-old trial lawyer with a master's degree in criminology, gave public prosecutor Gerardo Vázquez a very different account to that of Carrillo Olea of how the Attorney General's Office (PGR) had learnt of El Chapo Guzmán's whereabouts.

Andrade is key to understanding the details of the drug business at the time. He was a close friend and worked with Sergio Aguilar Hernández, lawyer to El Señor de los Cielos. In 1989, when Aguilar was sub-director of the PGR in Sinaloa state, he was sacked and imprisoned. However, released thanks to Andrade, his childhood friend, he soon went to work for the drug trafficker.

Later, Andrade enjoyed a direct relationship with El Señor de los Cielos when he took up the defense of Sósimo Leyva Pérez, the drug baron's brother-in-law who was in Morelia prison in Michoacán, in 1994 and 1995. He was an unusual lawyer. His clients included not only drug traffickers but members of the Zapatista National Liberation Army (EZLN) captured in 1995, as well as members of the UNAM's trade union (STUNAM). Those who knew him say he was a good lawyer, a brilliant man, and also an accomplished informer. In 1993 he was drawing a modest retainer from the PGR.

Andrade's account was recorded in the investigation into Cardinal Posadas's murder. His testimony shed light on what had happened on May 24, 1993, at Amado Carrillo Fuentes's house, when the cardinal was killed.

In 1993, Guzmán was working for Carrillo Fuentes in the Guadalajara area. In those days, El Chapo was a liability. Carrillo Fuentes was fed up with his subordinate's chaotic ways, his liking for alcohol, drugs, scandal and violence. He was particularly irritated by the amount of time he spent with his bodyguards, taking over entire floors of luxury hotels and causing a stir. Working with El Chapo was more hazardous than handling gunpowder. Carrillo Fuentes's concerns were not misplaced. The discretion traditionally sought by organized crime groups was in jeopardy.

As a result, Carrillo Fuentes decided to remove El Chapo from the Guadalajara patch and send him to Nayarit state, under the supervision of Héctor El Güero Palma, Guzmán's friend and partner. However, El Chapo did not obey the order. He had other plans. In his place he sent his crony and accountant Martín Moreno to Tepic, the capital of Nayarit. At the same time he sent another henchman to Guatemala, to buy some farms. Central America was from around that time seen by the narcotics traffickers as just an extension of their own territory.

Carrillo Fuentes was deeply upset to hear that Cardinal Posadas had been killed in a shoot-out between drug gangs in Guadalajara. He immediately began to call military and police authorities, and summoned El Güero Palma. El Señor de los Cielos could not believe his own men were involved. He was furious.

When El Güero arrived, looking completely unperturbed, he calmed down. El Señor de los Cielos knew that the Arellano Félix brothers came from a very religious family, which had cultivated personal links with Cardinal Posadas since his time in Tijuana. What's more, their mother admired the cardinal and would never forgive her sons such a thing. (Indeed, she stopped talking to them for as long as doubts remained.) As for Carrillo Fuentes, he had no connection with the Catholic hierarchy. The closest he got to the Church was when he built a temple at Guamuchilito, in Navolato, Sinaloa, his home town.

"El Chapo was being followed, it can't have been him," El Güero said reassuringly.

"Who's got the guns, and the balls, to do this?" asked Carrillo Fuentes.

"And a motive . . ." added Palma.

After getting answers to his calls, Carrillo Fuentes informed his people that neither the Arellano Félix brothers nor Guzmán had taken part in the shoot-out. It was a third group, whose members were not from the north, although they were dressed as northerners: "They had short hair, and were wearing jeans, plaid shirts and new boots they could hardly run in," he said, adding that he had gotten this information from General Jesús Gutiérrez Rebollo[3] and his son-in-law, Horacio Montenegro.

"Let the witness say who told him that Amado Carrillo Fuentes found out about the shoot-out at Guadalajara airport at 16:40 on May 24, 1993," was one of the public prosecutor's requests to Andrade Bojorges, as he made his sworn statement in March 1999.

"On that day, Mr. Sergio Aguilar [a friend of Andrade's] was with Amado Carrillo at one of his houses in Morelos state. Jesús Bitar Tafich, the 'Arab,' was there too," answered Andrade.

Jesús Bitar was known as the brains behind Carrillo Fuentes's financial operations in South America. He was arrested in July 1997 after his boss's death, and entered a witness protection program. Today he is a wealthy cattle rancher, with a franchise for Pemex gas stations, in Durango state. He also supplies a government-funded program called the Countryside Alliance. Four years after Cardinal Posadas's murder, Bitar testified to the PGR that General Jorge Carrillo Olea was a friend of Amado Carrillo Fuentes. When I asked him directly, the general denied it.

At 3 a.m. on May 25, 1993, Carrillo Fuentes's staff answered the phone at one of his homes in Cuernavaca, Morelos, where he was staying.

"Is the gentleman awake?" asked Javier Coello Trejo—no less than the former drug czar under Attorney General Enrique Álvarez del Castillo. "Ask him if I can visit tomorrow!"

"Tell him to come over right away," responded Carrillo Fuentes.

Meanwhile, El Señor de los Cielos ordered El Güero Palma to suspend a shipment of two tons of cocaine that was due in by train from El Salvador, and to contact the people who were keeping an eye on El Chapo. At 5 a.m., Coello arrived, alone. Amado was still accompanied by his lawyer Sergio Aguilar, Jesús Bitar, and El Güero Palma.

"I've just talked to the deputy attorney general of the PGR in Jalisco [Antonio García Torres]. You must hand over El Chapo with the utmost urgency," said Coello.

For Carrillo Fuentes, there couldn't be a better opportunity to get rid of El Chapo without bloodshed. But he knew that Guzmán had not killed the cardinal or had anything to do with it, according to the information he had obtained. He wanted to know just one thing before surrendering his man:

"Who killed the cardinal?" Amado asked Coello.

There was no answer, just a suggestion that it was better not to ask.

"So tell me, is it yes or no?" insisted Coello.

El Chapo's fate was sealed. He would be the scapegoat, and not a shot would be fired in his defense.

Amado, El Chapo, and El Güero

Amado Carrillo Fuentes entered the narcotics business in the 1970s thanks to his uncle, Ernesto Fonseca Carrillo, the notorious Don Neto. Don Neto was a friend and partner of the Sinaloan Pedro Avilés Pérez, the first Mexican to smuggle cocaine from South America into the United States.

When Avilés was murdered in 1978, his replacement was Miguel Angel Félix Gallardo, the overall coordinator of the organization. The main members of this criminal group were Félix Gallardo himself, Don Neto, Manuel Salcido El Cochiloco, Juan José Quintero, Pablo Acosta, and Juan José Esparragoza El Azul. At a lower level were Amado Carrillo Fuentes, Rafael Caro Quintero, and Ismael Zambada El Mayo. Well below them, as small-scale growers, dealers, and gunmen, were Héctor Palma, Joaquín Guzmán, the Arellano Félix brothers and the Beltrán Leyva brothers. Although almost all the members of the organization led by Félix Gallardo were natives of Sinaloa, it became known as the Guadalajara group, because that city was their operational and residential base.

At that stage the term "cartel" was not widely used, nor had the drug traffickers carved up the country into areas of control as if it were their private property. The Federal Judicial Police (PJF) and the Federal Security Directorate (DFS) identified them as "cliques" or gangs. There were two main organizations: one that smuggled drugs on the Pacific coast (the Guadalajara group) and another that worked along the Gulf of Mexico (the Gulf group). At the beginning of President Miguel de la Madrid's mandate (1982–88), the growing activity of the traffickers in Jalisco state and its capital, Guadalajara, was reflected in the big investments pouring into hotels, restaurants, housing developments, foreign exchange agencies, and car dealerships. But it was concealed by the state governor, Enrique Álvarez del Castillo, and tolerated by society. No lights were shone on it, nor was there any violence.

In 1981, Amado Carrillo Fuentes was working closely with his uncle Don Neto and Félix Gallardo in Guadalajara. However, it became impossible for him to remain in the state capital because of tensions with Rafael Caro Quintero, also a protégé of Don Neto's. The conflict was over a woman. Caro Quintero sought the favours of an attractive seventeen-year-old called Sara Cosío. For her part, the young woman—from one of the most eminent political families in Guadalajara—flirted with Carrillo Fuentes at every opportunity. Before his protégés could come to blows, Don Neto decided to remove his nephew from the scene: he sent him north to Ojinaga, a border town in Chihuahua, to work with Pablo Acosta. Without realizing it, Don Neto was doing Carrillo Fuentes a favor.

The rise of Amado Carrillo Fuentes

On April 24, 1987, a federal police officer called Guillermo González Calderoni arrived in Ojinaga. He was one of the most corrupt cops in Mexican history. His mission was to arrest Pablo Acosta, who as it happens had been paying him a fortune for protection. But the drug baron didn't get out alive; they say he burned to death in his bunker. Some colleagues of the former policeman say the killer was González Calderoni himself. For drug traffickers there's one thing worse than death, and that's prison.

After Acosta's death, Rafael Aguilar Guajardo, another former DFS commander—the Federal Security Directorate was then the Mexican equivalent of the CIA—took over the regional franchise, still with the support of Carrillo Fuentes, who was steadily climbing the ladder of the drug hierarchy.

Amado had a vision. In 1987 he left Ojinaga and moved to Torreón, where he began to assemble a fleet of aircraft, including Sabreliners, Learjets and Cessnas. His boyhood dreams of being a pilot were realized in the strangest of ways, but he still had a long way to go before becoming the legendary Lord of the Skies.

On August 21, 1989, Carrillo Fuentes was arrested by officers from the Ninth Military Zone based in Culiacán, Sinaloa, under the command of Jesús Gutiérrez Rebollo, whose military career was just taking off. Years later, fate would again bring these two together, the drug dealer and the three-star general. Appointed to prepare the case against Carrillo Fuentes in the PGR was the deputy attorney general, Javier Coello Trejo—Amado's loyal servant as a result of the money periodically showered on him.

A few months earlier, in April, Commander Guillermo González Calderoni had arrested his own compadre, Félix Gallardo. Nobody could trust anyone.

It was the first year of Carlos Salinas's presidency. Given the publicly-known relationship between his father, Raúl Salinas Lozano, his uncle, Carlos, and Juan Nepomuceno, the veteran leader of the Gulf Cartel, some writers on the drug trade in Mexico have seen these arrests as an attempt to favour the criminal organization closest to the president's family. But the events of later years were to show that, in spite of their good relations with the Gulf traffickers, Salinas's family were more inclined to do business with those on the Pacific side.

Too fat to be a bad guy

When in 1988 Salinas named Enrique Álvarez del Castillo as attorney general, he in turn appointed as deputy attorney general for drug control a man called Javier Coello Trejo. Coello's most striking characteristic was his extreme corpulence, of similar dimensions to his corruption.

During the first two years of Salinas's mandate, Jorge Carrillo Olea was at the Secretariat of the Interior under Fernando Gutiérrez Barrios, reorganizing the state intelligence systems according to direct instructions from the president. Carrillo was highly experienced in this field; indeed he could be called the father of Mexican "intelligence," if such a thing exists. He and Miguel de la Madrid dismantled the Federal Security Directorate, and set up in its place the Research and National Security Directorate (Disen), later the Center for Research and National Security (Cisen).

Carrillo was well placed to observe Coello's chaotic mutations. In 1989, several of the deputy attorney's bodyguards were arrested and charged with belonging to a gang that was plaguing the streets of southern Mexico City, snatching and raping young women. Only after intense pressure from Congress did the capital's prosecution office, under Ignacio Morales Lechuga, find itself obliged to act, and finally some of Coello's men were put behind bars.

In the final months of the Salinas administration, Carrillo frequently phoned Coello in order to pass on the complaints he was getting. Coello would typically protest, as he recalled:

"Of course not, Mr. Under Secretary, pure fairy tales. I'm too fat to be a bad guy!"

"Well, they're saying you sit on the detainees, that's the third degree," Carrillo Olea would reply sardonically.

In 1989, Coello's full weight was brought to bear on his friend Amado Carrillo Fuentes, who found himself imprisoned in the Reclusorio Sur along with Félix Gallardo and El Azul Esparragoza. But after the disgrace of his bodyguards, Deputy Attorney Coello had lost clout. He knew his days at the PGR were numbered, and that he'd need friends when he was ousted. Therefore he helped to get Carrillo Fuentes acquitted and released, to the surprise of his jailmates.

In 1990, President Salinas summoned Carrillo Olea and told him: "Jorge, Coello is severely undermining our image abroad. Enrique [Álvarez] has had enough. Help him out. He needs somebody he can trust." As Carrillo Olea hadn't trained as a lawyer, he could not take over the exact post occupied by Coello. Salinas created a job for him out of thin air: General Coordinator of the Fight Against the Drug Traffic.

Álvarez welcomed Carrillo's arrival at the PGR, and practically invited him to take it under his control, which little by little he did.

In 1991, Carrillo appointed Rodolfo León Aragón, El Chino, as chief of the Federal Judicial Police (PJF). According to the general, relations between them were always good, despite El Chino's high corruption ratings. León also got along very well with the equally corrupt police commander, González Calderoni. It's in the light of this closeness to the command of the Mexican prosecutor's office that Benjamín Arellano Félix's recent declarations about the Cardinal's killing are important.

Readjustments

When Carrillo Fuentes left prison, the structure of organized crime had broken down as a result of the arrest of Félix Gallardo. The only man strong enough replace him was Salcido, El Cochiloco, who ruled in Sinaloa, and who had the support of Benjamín Arellano Félix and his brothers, ensconced in Tijuana.

For their part, Juan and Humberto García Ábrego, leaders of the Gulf organization and the protégés of Juan Nepomuceno, were not interested in the others' territory. Their own vast territory was quite enough. Besides, at that stage all of them were cooperating. There was a kind of tacit peace agreement. At the time, El Mayo Zambada—always an independent force—and El Azul Esparragoza had no influence beyond Sinaloa, and had not built up their organizations into what we know them as today. As for El Chapo Guzmán, El Güero Palma and the Beltrán Leyva brothers, these were just emerging leaders who picked up the crumbs. Indeed, some of them—like El Chapo, El Güero Palma and the Arellano Félix brothers—had certain shared interests that encouraged them to do business together. Nonetheless, these links were too weak to withstand the blows of betrayal, and mutual hatred developed. It was a hatred that was to be measured in the hundreds of deaths they have contributed to the cruel war waged among the cartels over the last decade in almost every part of the country.

El Chapo and El Güero were ambitious, violent characters, who sought ever more money and power. They weren't as strong but they fought El Cochiloco and the Arellano Félixes for control of the Guadalajara "franchise."

Amado Carrillo Fuentes hatched a more ambitious plan. In alliance with Rafael Aguilar Guajardo, he decided to seize control of the drug trade all along the northern Pacific coast. El Chapo Guzmán and El Güero Palma joined him, to build up their own strength.

El Cochiloco was executed in October 1991. Guzmán claims he was killed by his own followers, the Arellano Félix brothers. The war for the prize territory had begun. Those who had previously coexisted in the same area now engaged in a fight to the death. The dwarfs wanted to grow bigger, so they began to fight for control of Guadalajara. That was when El Chapo began to create problems for the Carrillo Fuentes organization; his lack of experience led him to commit serious mistakes.

Your closest friend betrays you

From 1990 until June 1993, the mafiocracy gave the same protection to El Chapo Guzmán as they had given to Carrillo Fuentes, El Señor de los Cielos—who could never have created such an empire without the help of illustrious businessmen, bankers, military chiefs, police officers, and politicians, including former presidents of the Republic and their relatives. This web of connections is inextricable. All are united around one single goal: money and power.

Aguilar Guajardo, the leader of organized crime in Juárez, the border city where drug trafficking was most intense, was murdered in Cancún in April 1993. Carrillo Fuentes was his natural successor. In mafia circles it was said that the person who ordered the killing of Aguilar was he who benefited most from it.

Carrillo Fuentes began to become a legend. One of his first decisions was to clean out the organization. El Chapo Guzmán was top of the list; he'd fallen out of favor with his boss. Carrillo Fuentes handed him over to the PGR, not because he thought he was involved in the murder of Cardinal Posadas, but because it was now or never. On March 9, 1999, during his interrogation, Andrade Bojorges revealed the traitor's name.

"Let the witness say if he knows who was the intermediary whereby Amado Carrillo Fuentes provided the information that led to the capture of Joaquín Guzmán Loera," the public prosecutor asked point-blank.

"El Güero Palma," answered Andrade, without hesitation.

Four months after making his statement, Andrade vanished. The earth swallowed him up. His last appearance in public was at the International Book Fair held in Mexico City in February 1999. The lawyer showed up dressed in black, accompanied by a mariachi dressed in white, who went through the corridors singing "The Man from Sinaloa," Carrillo Fuentes's favourite song. Andrade was there to launch his book on the "secret history" of drug kingpins and their respectable protectors.[4]

The friends of his I spoke to had different theories about how Andrade got hold of the information for his book, but all agree on one thing: everything he wrote about Carrillo Fuentes was true—so true that, one friend claimed, Carrillo's own mother was up in arms over the publication. She was very upset with him.

Nothing more was known of Andrade's whereabouts. His acquaintances think he is dead.

Carrillo Olea denied in the interview that he, Coello, and Álvarez del Castillo were ever involved in drug trafficking.

The prisoner on the 727

On the way back to Mexico City, with his explosive cargo on board, General Carrillo Olea ordered four paratroopers to guard the cabin. Two others kept El Chapo handcuffed in a seat at the back. The rest of the battalion guarded the exits, while General Guillermo Álvarez Nahara, head of the military police, sat next to Carrillo.

The Boeing 727 landed at 7 p.m. at Toluca airport, in the State of Mexico. The head of security was there to meet it. El Chapo got off the plane with a hood over his head.

"Here is your prisoner," said Carrillo.

"Quite a responsibility you have there, sir."

"Don't say a word . . . and don't mention my name."

Carrillo got into the waiting car and phoned the attorney general, Jorge Carpizo: "The plane is on its way back to base, and our friend is on his way to his cell." The operation was finally over.

There are some, like José Antonio Ortega, lawyer for the Guad-alajara archdioceses, who say the murder of Cardinal Posadas was the work of the state, with Carrillo Olea presumably taking part as the brains behind the logistics. Although the Arellano Félix broth-ers and El Chapo do appear to have been at Guadalajara airport that day, summoned by the head of the Federal Judicial Police, Rodolfo León, none of them took part in the shoot-out. According to this account, the cardinal's death happened just as Carrillo Fuentes told his people it did.

Eighteen years later, Benjamín Arellano Félix would provide a different account of the cardinal's death. In testimony given on April 15, 2011, to the PGR at the Altiplano prison in Almoloya de Juárez, the former leader of the Tijuana Cartel made the following declara-tion: "Rodolfo León Aragón told me he and a federal police commando unit killed Cardinal Juan Jesús Posadas Ocampo because he was supplying weapons to the guerrillas."

On May 25, 1993, Benjamín Arellano Félix received a disturbing phone call in Tijuana. The previous day, an old family friend had died: Cardinal Posadas. The Salinas government was blaming him and his brothers for the crime, along with their former partner, Guzmán. Their mother was furious and refusing to speak to them, a very serious matter for any self-respecting drug baron, who regards his mother as sacred.

The phone call was from the federal police chief, León Aragón, El Chino. He told Benjamín they needed to meet urgently at Tijuana airport, and the drug trafficker promptly agreed.

The Arellano Félix family had a long-standing relationship with León. Carrillo Fuentes introduced him to Ramón Arellano Félix at one of his houses in Mexico City in 1991, just a few months after Carrillo Olea had appointed León head of the Federal Judicial Police. By 1993, the police chief and Ramón were close friends. Amado had recommended León highly. He told the Arellano Félixes they could rely on him whenever they wanted to travel somewhere in the coun-try unmolested. So Benjamín trusted his brother's friend, enough to decide to attend the meeting at the border airport. It was 4 p.m. when he met León, who told him flatly:

"You're in big trouble: they're blaming you for the cardinal's murder."

"It wasn't us. I was here in Tijuana, and my brother Ramón had already boarded his plane when it happened," answered Benjamín.

"I know it wasn't you," replied the police chief. "The perpetrators were members of a federal police commando under my command at Guadalajara airport. If I'm to help you, you have to give me ten million dollars and six addresses we can raid, because I have apprehended two of your men who traveled with Ramón to Guadalajara."

"All right, let me see what I can do. I'll look for the addresses, just give me time for the money."

"Ok," said León, and immediately made a call. "Done. All well," he said into the phone.

León told him he'd been calling the attorney general, Jorge Carpizo, who instructed him to "go ahead with the plan."

That night Benjamín met his brother Ramón, who told him he'd already given the money to León. The following day the police chief called Benjamín just to tell him that he was searching some addresses and that he'd received the money from Ramón. Ramón had told Benjamín that while he was in Guadalajara, before the cardinal's murder, León had called to tell him that he could travel without a care on the 24th. So, at the police chief's suggestion, Ramón arrived at Guadalajara airport at almost the same time as the archbishop.

The Arellano Félix brothers and El Chapo Guzmán had fallen into a trap carefully set by the PGR.

After making his statement in April 2011, Benjamín Arellano Félix asked the witnesses from the Guadalajara archdioceses to pray for him, because he would soon be killed.[5] On April 29, however, Benjamín was suddenly extradited to the United States without his lawyers apparently knowing that this was about to happen.

In Mexico, the murder of Cardinal Posadas remains one of the most controversial episodes of recent decades, and one that has marked the country's history.

Days before El Chapo Guzmán was captured, Attorney General Carpizo announced a $1 million reward for information leading to his arrest. Officially, it was Drug Control Center (Cendro) staff and authorities in El Salvador and Guatemala that supplied the information.

Carrillo Olea proposed sending some of the money to the foreign authorities who had participated in the capture. In El Salvador, $300,000 in cash was delivered to the then president Alfredo Cristiani, to be shared out among those who had forced El Chapo to flee from there to Guatemala.

General Carrillo himself took another $300,000 to the new president of Guatemala, Ramiro de León Carpio, and that young captain who had made such an impression on him.

By 2010, the reward on Guzmán's head had increased sevenfold. The US government was offering $5 million for information on his whereabouts, and since 2009 the Mexican government had been offering $2.5 million. El Chapo had ceased to be a two-bit trafficker and convenient fall guy, to become the CEO of a global business. Today he is the best-known face of Mexico's crime industry.

On that two-hour flight from Chiapas to the State of Mexico, El Chapo Guzmán learned the first big lesson of his prodigious criminal career. A few minutes after the 727 took off, the head of the military police and two other officers sat down beside him.

"Well?" said General Álvarez to El Chapo.

The time had come to confess.

CHAPTER TWO

Life or Death

When General Guillermo Álvarez Nahara, head of the Military Judicial Police, joined the operation to capture El Chapo Guzmán, he had one precise brief: to interrogate him.

At fifty-four years old, Álvarez was used to dealing with obdurate criminals. He would never have expected the reaction he got from the drug trafficker when he went to the back of the plane and sat down beside him to begin the session.

"Do you mind if I question the prisoner?" Álvarez asked Carrillo Olea, soon after the plane took off from Tapachula on its way to Toluca.

"Let's see," thought Carrillo to himself. "He's expected to deliver a report. On what, on how the journey went? He deserves a bit of meat." Even so, being formally responsible for the prisoner, Carrillo couldn't ignore Álvarez's past history and the methods he'd used in the 1970s to interrogate left-wing guerrillas.

"Remember that whatever you say he can use as evidence," warned Carrillo. "If he detects any sort of threat, the least mistreatment or bad language, he'll use it to his advantage. He'll say anything you want, but it could mean that tomorrow you have to resign. So take it easy."

"Thanks for the advice!"

About an hour later, the military police chief returned to his seat next to Carrillo.

"I've spoken to him."

"Good."

If he felt at all nervous, Carrillo never mentioned it. Nonetheless, he must have been pretty concerned over the amount of information

El Chapo possessed about his protectors. Among them were senior officials in the PGR who were very close to Jorge Carrillo Olea.

The general of the White Brigade

Guillermo Álvarez Nahara is from Mexico City. He's a tough man, strongly built with dark skin and prominent cheeks. At first sight, his CV is misleading. He seems to have been just another bureaucrat in Mexico's Secretariat of National Defense (Sedena).

His last post, in 2004, was as Sedena's head of human resources. Since then he's been retired.

But Álvarez is much more than this. In the 1970s he was part of the so-called White Brigade, which gained notoriety for its role in the Mexican government's "dirty war" against left-wing opposition groups. The White Brigade was credited with exterminating several armed social movements of the day, such as the Revolutionary Armed Movement, the People's Armed Revolutionary Front, and the Peasants' Brigade Against Injustice.

At the time of the White Brigade, Álvarez was a colonel in the Federal Military Judicial Police. By the time he took El Chapo's statement, he was head of that same police force.[1] They say you never forget a lesson well learned, but on this occasion Álvarez was in luck: El Chapo Guzmán, very inexperienced in the ways of police detention—it seems this was his first time—proved to be highly cooperative, without the general having to apply the least pressure.

One of the passengers on the Boeing 727 noted that the Guatemalan military had not only stolen $1.5 million from El Chapo—as he himself complained in his first statement to the military police—they had also given him a good beating. According to this account, El Chapo was so grateful for the treatment he received, compared with what he got in Guatemala, that he offered no resistance to General Álvarez's questions.

"On the contrary, we had to kick him to shut him up, he wouldn't stop, he wanted to spill all the beans," recalled the passenger.

El Chapo spilled rather too many. It was undoubtedly the most spontaneous declaration of his whole criminal career. He wouldn't be so indiscreet again until fifteen years later, in 2008, when he had another conversation with a general, this time at the pinnacle of his power as Mexico's top drug baron.

El Chapo's confessions

The declarations made by El Chapo Guzmán on June 9, 1993, were recorded in dossier 1387 of the Military Attorney General's Operational Subdivision, under the title "Report on the interrogation of Joaquín Guzmán Loera (alias) El Chapo Guzmán."

Four pages long, it was addressed to the then military attorney general, Brigadier General Mario Fromow García, written by General Guillermo Álvarez Nahara and witnessed by the two cavalry officers present.

As he listened to what Guzmán had to say, Álvarez understood that this testimony was pure dynamite and would send shock waves through the government. Guzmán began with the story of what happened on May 24, 1993, at Guadalajara International Airport, and ended up telling on all his accomplices.

El Chapo said that on that day he went to the airport with his bags packed to go to Puerto Vallarta, one of his favorite towns to party in.[2] In the airport parking lot his blue Century stopped, blocking the way of other cars, while he calmly alighted. Suddenly, the accountant Martín Moreno, who was traveling with him, warned that there were armed men getting out of various vehicles. With extraordinary presence of mind, Guzmán threw himself to the ground and crawled all the way into the terminal building.

Of the eight people with El Chapo, two were killed, two were arrested in Guatemala, and four others were captured by the Federal Judicial Police a few days after the incident. "None of my men fired because their weapons were in the bags that had already been checked in," El Chapo explained to Álvarez. With this account, the trafficker blew apart the story that Carpizo and Carrillo Olea had tried to sell to the public, namely that Cardinal Posadas had been the victim of crossfire between the Arellano Félix gang and that of El Chapo Guzmán.

A few days after the murder, the evening news on Televisa—which always toes the official line—showed a reconstruction of the events by way of a slick animation prepared by Cisen and Cendro. Those involved in this production were all close to Jorge Carrillo Olea.

According to the account given by Guzmán in the Boeing 727, after escaping from the airport he went to Mexico City and lay low in Martín Moreno's house. There a certain commander "Gómez" fixed him up with a false passport and drove him to San Cristóbal de las Casas, capital of the southern state of Chiapas, where a contact "put me in touch with Lieutenant Colonel Carlos Rosales of the Guatemalan army, who was going to help us there." However, El Chapo continued, the Guatemalan officer didn't help him but instead handed him over to the Mexican authorities, after relieving him of $1.5 million.

In his confession to General Álvarez, El Chapo Guzmán admitted working for the Colombian Cali Cartel, then led by the Rodríguez Orejuela brothers—even though his real links were with Pablo Escobar's Medellín Cartel in the same country. He also stated that he and Héctor El Güero Palma had been responsible for the shooting at Puerto Vallarta's Christine Discotheque in November 1992, as well as the Iguala killings, "but I had nothing to do with the other things the press accuse me of." It seems that the apprentice drug baron felt a moment's reticence. Yes, he was a bit of a murderer, but not *that* bad. A little later this reticence would evaporate, like water on a stove.

As the minutes passed, El Chapo's confessions stepped up a gear.

El Chapo's first payroll

On board the plane, Guzmán revealed that he enjoyed protection from the Mexican government's Attorney General's Office (PGR) at the highest level. He confessed that about three years earlier, in 1990, during one of his visits to Miguel Ángel Félix Gallardo in Mexico City's Reclusorio Sur prison, he met a "gentleman" who was now working in the PGR. El Chapo said it was through this gentleman's contacts that he obtained the false passport to enter Guatemala.

When Guzmán got cozy with this gentleman, whose name was Federico Ponce Rojas, the latter was in charge of the Initial Inquiries department at the Mexico City Attorney General's Office (PGJDF), which was headed at the time by Ignacio Morales Lechuga. Ponce was one of Morales's most trusted assistants.

"I gave Federico Ponce $1.5 million every couple of months, when there were cocaine or marijuana deliveries, for him to protect me," declared Guzmán. At the Reclusorio Sur, according to El Chapo, Ponce also introduced him to the commander "Gómez" who would become his contact. In the report drawn up by General Álvarez, the drug trafficker didn't say how long he continued to pay bribes to Federico Ponce, nor exactly what kind of "protection" was provided.

Ignacio Morales was attorney general of the Federal District (or Mexico City) from 1988 to 1991. In May 1991, after the departure of Enrique Álvarez del Castillo, President Salinas appointed him attorney general of the Republic, a post he held until January 1993. When Morales moved to the PGR, Ponce moved with him.

Carrillo Olea and Morales never got along. The former Mexico City attorney general has stated publicly that all drug control issues were dealt with directly between Carrillo and President Salinas—so he had very little to do with it. There is little doubt that Ponce's rapid exit from the PGR (after a bloody and still unclear confrontation between police and army on a secret airstrip in 1991) did nothing to smooth the relationship between Carrillo and Morales.

At the time when El Chapo Guzmán made his statement, Federico Ponce was no longer officially working for the PGR but for one of the country's main banks, Banamex, privatized by Salinas in 1991. However, according to El Chapo, Ponce was not his only contact in the PGR.

"I had dealings with the head of the Federal Judicial Police in Sonora. On one occasion I gave him $500,000 to let me grow a marijuana crop." El Chapo also told Álvarez that he had paid for protection from federal police commander Guillermo Salazar Ramos, who was posted in Guadalajara at the end of the 1980s.

El Chapo's last significant revelation during the flight was that the first-ever state governor from the PAN,[3] Ernesto Ruffo Appel of Baja California, was living proof that a change in the party in power didn't imply any change in the well-oiled machinery of complicity with the drugs trade: "The Arellano Félix brothers get protection from the governor and the attorney general of Baja California state. One of the governor's brothers is their partner in a business," declared El Chapo indignantly at the end of his statement.

It took him some time to realize that, with this fulsome confession on the long journey from Tapachula to Toluca, he had been gambling not with his freedom but with his life.

El Chapo from top to bottom

Joaquín Archivaldo Guzmán Loera—his full name, although he only likes to use his first given name—was born on April 4, 1957, in the hamlet of La Tuna in Badiraguato, Sinaloa. It's a place deep in the Sierra Madre Occidental, in an area known as the "Golden Triangle," made up of a group of municipalities spanning the borders between Sinaloa, Durango, and Chihuahua states. Around there, the most popular profession is that of drug trafficker.

Joaquín is the son of Emilio Guzmán Bustillos and Consuelo Loera Pérez, the oldest of seven children with barely a year between each of them: Armida, Bernarda, Miguel Ángel, Aureliano, Arturo, and Emiliano. He had three older siblings, but they died of the diseases of poverty when he was very young; he cannot even remember their names. For generations, his family have lived and died in La Tuna.

El Chapo, as they affectionately call the more stunted boys in those parts, is five and a half feet tall, shorter than average for the local men. He attended school only as far as the third grade of elementary, something he's always been ashamed of. In some of his formal statements he claimed to have completed high school in prison, but that is not true.

It is not surprising that Guzmán never managed to finish elementary school. Every year, hundreds of children in the region drop out when their parents send them to work on the marijuana and poppy harvests. When they go back, they repeat the year until they get fed up and decide there is only one certainty about the future: "Either you become a narco, or you get killed."

Guzmán began his criminal career at the bottom, following the family tradition of growing cannabis and opium poppies in the gullies and hillsides of the Sierra Madre Occidental. At that point he embodied the most vulnerable link in the criminal chain.

Some say that he went on to join the police, where he met Miguel Ángel Félix Gallardo—whose job was to guard the then governor of Sinaloa, Leopoldo Sánchez Celis, a political patron to drug traffickers. Félix Gallardo went into the business in the mid 1970s. We first hear about Guzmán as his driver, in the period when Félix Gallardo, Pedro Avilés, Manuel Salcido, Emilio Quintero Payán, Ernesto Fonseca Carrillo, and Rafael Caro Quintero were running the Guadalajara-based gang later called the Sinaloa Cartel.

Guzmán obtained rapid promotion because he was full of ideas for expanding the business. At the same time, as we've seen, he was distrusted for being violent and impulsive, and too fond of living it up. When Félix Gallardo was arrested in April 1989, Guzmán teamed up with El Güero Palma. Carrillo Fuentes was arrested the same year, and when he came out in 1990, El Chapo and El Güero joined him. Of the three, Guzmán was the weakest: he was thirty-three, physically less than imposing, and almost illiterate.

Amado Carrillo Fuentes was born in Guamuchilito, Sinaloa. He, by contrast, was an impressive figure, tall and fit, charismatic, methodical, and smart. At thirty-four, a long delinquent life stretched ahead of him. With an uncle like the legendary Don Neto, Amado was never going to be a bottom feeder in the crime world.

Héctor Palma was twenty-eight, tall and blue-eyed, and he had finished high school. Despite his youth, he outranked El Chapo in the hierarchy.

El Chapo was only protected as long as Carrillo Fuentes willed it. Upon arrival at Almoloya de Juárez maximum security prison, in the State of Mexico, he realized that the protection had come to an end.

Under threat

Once the Boeing 727 landed at Toluca airport, Álvarez Nahara immediately got in touch with the secretary of defense, Antonio Riviello, and gave him a summary of El Chapo's statement, which a few hours later he formally recorded in document number 1387.[4]

The secretary of defense rushed to tell the president—fast enough for El Chapo Guzmán to find an unexpected welcome as soon as he arrived at the prison. A senior government official was there, who threatened Guzmán with death unless he altered the statement he'd made in the plane. El Chapo was given no other option: cooperate or die.

At 8 p.m., the start of the long night of June 9, 1993, shaven-headed, dressed in the regulation khaki, and visibly exhausted, Guzmán gave his first formal statement to Leticia Gutiérrez, from the federal public prosecutor's office. Henceforth, for the Mexican justice system, this new statement was the only one that would count.

"My name is Joaquín Guzmán Loera, I am thirty-six years old and they call me El Chapo," began the trafficker's agreed confession. He spoke with the strong northern accent he never lost. "I am married, I studied to third grade, I am from Culiacán, Sinaloa, I am Mexican and I make my living from farming and commerce," he went on. I am a Catholic and the father of four children," and "my monthly income is 20 thousand new pesos [$6,400 in 1993] without any extras."

At the time, he was married to Alejandrina Salazar Hernández, although the incorrigible womanizer was picked up in Guatemala not with her but with a "girlfriend," María del Villar. His children with Alejandrina were César, Giselle, Iván (El Chapito), and Alfredo, respectively aged fourteen, eleven, ten, and seven years old. It was also established that when apprehended El Chapo was carrying a passport in the name of Jorge Ramos Pérez, his travel name, while the name he used as a farmer and tradesman was Raúl Guzmán Ruiz—that of a partner of his who was shot coming out of a grocery store in 1992.

El Chapo wasn't educated enough to ensure that his statement made consistent sense. He said that one of those arrested with him in Guatemala, Antonio Mendoza Cruz, was his bodyguard and driver, and that he paid him 10,000 new pesos a month. Math wasn't his strong point. If he really made 20,000 pesos a month clear, how could he be paying his employee half of his entire income? Guzmán continued his statement to the public prosecutor:

"I have spent my whole life as a farmer. I always lived in Culiacán, Sinaloa, until I moved to Guadalajara in 1984. I lived there until 1992, when I returned to Culiacán because a family by the name of Arellano Félix had tried to kill me."

The assassination attempts

It was early November, 1992. At just after 3 p.m., Guzmán was driving peacefully through Guadalajara in a latest-model black Cutlass, with Mexico City license plates, when a white Ram pickup truck with five people in it crashed into the back of him. Three men jumped out and began to spray his car with bullets, in broad daylight. The noise of the AK-47s was deafening. Like a cat with nine lives, El Chapo survived the attack without a scratch, even though there were twelve bullet holes in his Cutlass. He managed to identify the attackers: Ramón Arellano Félix, Lino Portillo—his gunman—and Armando Portillo, the latter's brother.

El Chapo sought refuge and later called Benjamín Arellano, Ramón's brother, to angrily protest at the shooting. Benjamín denied having anything to do with it. That day a war began between the two that would claim dozens of lives.

"Before that, the Arellanos and I were good friends," recalled El Chapo almost wistfully in his formal statement.

He also testified that the Arellanos had killed Manuel Salcido, El Cochiloco, his partner Armando López, El Chapo Caro, Onofre Landey, and Jaime Payán.

"My differences with the Arellanos and with Félix Gallardo came from their killing Armando López. He was like a brother to me."

The second attack against him took place on May 24, 1993, at Guadalajara airport, said the drug trafficker, in keeping with the PGR's official script. He was accompanied by his cousin, Héctor Guzmán Leyva and his friend, Pancho Beltrán.

"Everything that happened with that shooting occurred exactly as the PGR explained it on TV," said the obedient drug baron, avoiding getting into knots over the details. Now at last his formal statement fitted perfectly with the Nintendo version provided by the government of Carlos Salinas.

Guzmán claimed to know Emilio Quintero Payán—the co-founder of the Juárez Cartel—and Rafael Caro Quintero—a big player in the Guadalajara organization—by sight, from restaurants and local fiestas. "I had no idea what they did for a living, until I read the news." He recited these ludicrous lies with aplomb.

With regard to his relations with Héctor Palma, El Chapo did not repeat his confession on the plane to General Álvarez. This time he said: "I don't know El Güero Palma. I know he lives in Culiacán, Sinaloa, but I don't know what he does."

And of course he denied his involvement in the narcotics business, as well as his first killings: "I do not have any connection with anyone in Colombia, and it's not true that I'm a drug trafficker," he repeated several times. "I do not know what happened in the Iguala massacre where nine people died; they say El Güero Palma was responsible, well that's what the newspapers said, not me, but it made a big impression on me because so many people died," he lamented hypocritically.

"I don't know what happened at the Christine Discotheque either, I found out from the news, although people say El Güero Palma did it. I read the papers every day and that's how I know what is going on."

The most difficult part of his interrogation was still to come.

El Chapo caves in

When Defense Secretary Riviello told the president what Guzmán had revealed on the plane, alarm bells sounded not only in the Los Pinos presidential palace, but also in the PGR and the Federal Judicial Police (PJF). If El Chapo really wanted to tell all, the filth would splatter the white-collar participants too—especially the brothers who had begun their brilliant business career during the sexennial of President Luis Echeverría, and were now doing better than ever under Salinas, thanks to their proximity to the president's family.

A study undertaken for the PGR had revealed, almost accidentally, the connection between these businessmen brothers and Carrillo Fuentes, Palma, and Guzmán. If El Chapo retracted the statement he'd made en route from Tapachula to Toluca, it should help to whitewash all of them, once and for all.

At the end of a list of people, all of whom Guzmán denied knowing, the public prosecutor asked the questions that would exonerate the brothers who were so pally with the Salinas de Gortari family .

"Are you a shareholder in or owner of any of these companies: Galce Constructora, Aerobastos, or Servicios Aéreos Ejecutivos Poblanos?"

"No."

"Do you know anyone by the names of Miguel, Carlos, and Laura Segoviano Barbosa [sic]?"

"No."

El Chapo Guzmán had caved in completely. He no longer maintained any of the accusations he'd made against PGR officials, those he'd named on the Boeing 727 as receiving payments to protect him. Nor did he continue to affirm their participation in his front companies or others that provided him with services.

After hours of testimony, Guzmán carefully signed the twelve double-sided pages of the confession he'd dictated at the Almoloya de Juárez penitentiary. He had kept his side of the bargain. And with this he had not only saved his own life; he had also shown that he was a criminal you could do business with.

El Chapo's first confession disappears

"That document exists," stated Jorge Carrillo Olea in our interview at the end of 2009, referring to General Álvarez Nahara's record of his airborne interrogation of El Chapo Guzmán. At first he said he hadn't been present at the interrogation, and didn't know what Guzmán had said. But in the end he admitted he had held the vital document in his hands. He had given, he recalled, a copy to Jorge Carpizo.

One day, when he was no longer attorney general, Carpizo went to see Carrillo at home. The latter could guess why.

"Now, Jorge, I've heard tell of a document . . ." Carpizo began.

"Here it is," Carrillo said, and handed it over.

"But why didn't he get a copy at the time? That's the strange thing," commented Carrillo, as if hinting at some murky motive.

The former attorney general referred publicly to the document drawn up by the head of the military judicial police, nine years after El Chapo's interrogation. In 2002, Carpizo, along with journalist Julián Andrade, wrote a book called *Murder of a Cardinal*.

"The military tried to contact El Chapo in prison to confirm what he'd said on the plane, which could have caused a catastrophe. The cold at Almoloya and its high concrete walls made him change his mind: in the end he said a former official had read him the riot act and it was better to leave it at that," wrote Carpizo.

That document became not just a question of national security but of the very survival of the state, riddled as it was with drug trafficking. Maybe that's why Sedena and the PGR wiped it off the map.

Today, the drug dealer's first confession simply doesn't exist, in the records of either institution. Who did the document's disappearance suit most? On August 28, 2009, using the Freedom of Information law, a request was made to the Secretariat of Defense for a copy of the document. On October 21, the answer came back that the document did not exist. The PGR likewise replied that the document was not to be found in its archives, neither as part of the initial investigation into Joaquín Guzmán, nor anywhere else.[5]

Impunity

"What happened to that information [in Guzmán's first statement]? Was it investigated? Was it true?" I put these questions to Carrillo Olea.

"I don't know. The stuff about Federico Ponce . . . Well. Those are very big, very direct accusations. Were they true or not? Why weren't they investigated? Who knows."

"Wasn't it your job to investigate them?"

Carrillo had been in charge of the fight against drug trafficking, after all, and he was the boss of the head of the Federal Judicial Police, which was the investigative police force serving the PGR.

"No. That was the job of the deputy attorney for Initial Investigations. There was clearly a loophole there, because El Chapo was arrested and charged. I try not to get involved in these things. I am not given to morbid curiosity."

"Surely, rather than morbid curiosity, it's a question of national security to know if there are any policemen or government officials, or former officials, involved in drug trafficking."

"But it wasn't up to me to do anything. It would have to be a judge or an independent public prosecutor who opened an investigation that could take in El Chino [Rodolfo León Aragón, head of the PFJ], and Lord knows who else, to look into their actions. I didn't have the scope to do that. Not unless there were an accusation based on real evidence."

"In any case, the public prosecution office ought to have instructed the Judicial Police to investigate the matter. Didn't the Judicial Police ever receive an order to investigate Rodolfo León, Federico Ponce, or Claudio Ruffo Appel?"[6]

"No, they didn't," answered Carrillo Olea emphatically.

"So even though they had the statement, they issued no instruction?"

"No."

Ponce remains to this day as a senior executive in Banamex, a bank under majority control of Citigroup.

"What role did Joaquín Guzmán play in the structure of the drugs trade at that time? How important was he? Very? Middling?"

"There weren't any outstanding leaders. There were names. Like García Ábrego [of the Gulf Cartel]. But more because of their age, because they were well known, like Don Corleone, rather than for their real strength," answered Carrillo Olea, with the clarity and perspective that comes with time.

"But I was asking how important El Chapo was . . ."

"I think this has been lost in the mists of time. What you are asking me is El Chapo's story, going right back, how he emerged . . . I don't think anyone really knows," he said evasively.

El Chapo's testimony on board the Boeing 727 was ultimately borne out by the facts. Maybe that is why the file was removed by the Secretariat of Defense and the PGR.

The scapegoat

A police officer who held a senior position in the PJF told this investigation that it was the federal government that had Cardinal Posadas killed, and that the person who coordinated the operation was thought to be the then head of the PJF, Rodolfo León Aragón.

This allegation is not new. It is the same as that made by Cardinal Juan Sandoval Íñiguez, the current archbishop of Guadalajara, who has often declared that the murder of Cardinal Posadas was a state crime, that is, one organized from within the federal administration.

"The Arellano Félix brothers would never have killed the cardinal, even by mistake. They knew him well from his time in Tijuana, he even baptized one of Ramón Arellano Félix's daughters," comments the source, who prefers to remain anonymous. "Their mother was a fervent devotee of the cardinal."

"Why would the government want to kill the cardinal? There are so many theories . . ."

"He had a lot of information about drug trafficking from the Arellanos. He knew too much," answered the former PJF officer.

Several years after the event, a one-time defense secretary told some trusted associates about the meeting where the operation to kill Posadas was planned. It seems that present at the meeting were Salinas's chief of staff, José María Córdoba; the governor of Sonora, Manlio Fabio Beltrones, social security director Emilio Gamboa, and Jorge Carrillo Olea.

On June 10, 1993, the Salinas government pulled out all the stops to present to the public a relatively minor drug trafficker converted overnight into the cream of crime bosses: Joaquín El Chapo Guzmán. The scapegoat for the cardinal's murder.

Dozens of photographers turned up at the maximum security prison in the State of Mexico for the show. El Chapo, head shaved, posed for them in khaki regulation pants and a thick nylon bomber jacket. There was a grin on his face. What did the rookie drug baron have to laugh about, with so many years in jail ahead of him?

Years before, some much more senior drug traffickers had been accused of another shocking murder, though they weren't in fact to blame.

CHAPTER THREE

A Perverse Pact

As agreed, on the morning of February 8, 1985, Ernesto Fonseca Carrillo, known as Don Neto, came to the home of his friend Rafael Caro Quintero. The house was on Mariano Otero Avenue in Guadalajara, where his criminal gang had an operations center known as the "Camp."

"Right, my friend, let's have a little chat with Mr. Camarena," said Don Neto to Caro Quintero.

The two leaders of the organization known as the Guadalajara Cartel were meeting to interrogate Special Agent Enrique Camarena, the DEA man they had kidnapped the day before as he left the US consulate in Guadalajara.

"There's no point anymore, he can't answer," Caro Quintero drawled.

At twenty-nine years old, he looked around fifteen. Apart from being ambitious, full of big dreams and big boasts, Rafael Caro Quintero was audacious to the point of brilliance, at least on other occasions. In 1982, at the age of twenty-four and with only one year of elementary behind him, he was a nobody in the drug world; but in just three years he acquired both power and fame, after managing to buy and sell drug shipments of twenty tons, which was a very large quantity at the time. In 1984, Caro Quintero devised a way of industrializing marijuana cultivation: he was supposed to be the brains behind the massive growing operation at El Búfalo ranch, outside Ciudad Juárez, in Chihuahua state. But it was surely too big an operation for a man with his limitations. El Búfalo in fact functioned with the support of the Federal Security Directorate (DFS), headed by

José Antonio Zorrilla, who reported to the secretary of the interior, Manuel Bartlett Díaz. It was a real marijuana factory farm, employing 10,000 campesinos from the area and even some from other states.

With his wavy hair, Colgate smile and goatee beard, he fancied himself a lady-killer; perhaps that's why he became known as El Príncipe, the prince. Expensive gifts and mariachi music had won him the favours of the eligible Sara Cosío, as we've seen. But this would not shield him from the approaching storm.

"What do you mean, he can't answer? Did you let him go?" demanded Don Neto irritably. He was very fond of this youngster, whom he'd first met in Badiraguato, Sinaloa, when he was just fifteen—so much so that when he had to choose between him and his nephew, Amado Carrillo Fuentes, he chose the former, and sent Amado up to Chihuahua to work with Pablo Acosta.

"No, it's just they beat him up and he's dying," answered El Príncipe.

"Fuck you! You animal! You killed him tied up!" roared Don Neto, whose anger quickly turned into sobs.

They were narco tears. Don Neto never cried, but that day he couldn't contain his fury and despair. He knew that if Camarena was doomed, so was he. He swore like a trooper. In those days everyone knew that you frightened policemen or you bribed them, but you didn't kill them. Especially not if they were gringos. Today the rules have changed in Mexico. Everyone's fair game, even US Government employees.

"It wasn't me! Miguel Ángel's people got there first," was Caro Quintero's excuse, referring to Miguel Ángel Félix Gallardo, the most powerful of the three of them.

Félix Gallardo, the Boss of Bosses, hadn't been part of the plan to kidnap Camarena, but he'd learned about it because he managed the house in Mariano Otero Avenue. They also used this building, located opposite a children's playground, as a brothel; the woman in charge was known as Paty, and she worked for Félix Gallardo. The place was usually busy, but it had been evacuated for Caro Quintero to bring Camarena.

"Can't you see the problems you've caused? With the government and internationally?" Fonseca was so angry that he was on the point of raining blows on his junior; he took a quick turn in the patio of the Camp to calm down. He couldn't believe this was happening—all the more because he had given Caro express instructions not to hurt Camarena.

"It's your shit, you clean it up!" snapped Fonseca, into Caro's face. "This is not my responsibility!"

"Don't you believe it, we're in this together," retorted Caro.

The argument got more and more heated, until both Don Neto and the Prince drew their guns. Caro Quintero was at home, surrounded by twenty bodyguards, while Don Neto had only his second-in-command, Samuel Ramírez, and one other person with him. It didn't take much to see who would come off worse, so Don Neto left the house and sped off in his blue Mustang, wishing the earth would swallow him up.[1]

The kidnapping of Camarena

A few days before, on February 5, after a heavy binge to celebrate the birthday of Gabriel González—head of the murder squad for Jalisco federal police—Don Neto had met with the unpredictable Caro Quintero to discuss Enrique Camarena, who was giving both of them sleepless nights. They resolved to give the DEA agent a fright, a tactic that had worked with other officers who had then fled Jalisco state. Félix Gallardo wasn't present at that meeting, and it seems they never informed him of the operation.

Guadalajara was a narco paradise. There was room and protection for everyone: Fonseca, Caro Quintero, Félix Gallardo, Salcido, the Arellano Félix brothers, Palma, Carrillo Fuentes, Guzmán, and all the members of the Guadalajara organization that dominated the trafficking along Mexico's Pacific coast. Don Neto had pockets deep enough to accommodate the head of the murder squad, Gabriel González, the commander of checkpoints, Benjamín Locheo, and the dozen or so state judicial police officers who had been assigned to him as personal bodyguards. Jalisco governor Álvarez del Castillo himself was an ally of the criminal organization, while the central government under President Miguel de la Madrid displayed an easy-going tolerance of the drug trade. Everything was going smoothly until El Kiki Camarena began busting their plantations and homesteads.

For Don Neto, it wasn't just that one of his Jalisco plantations had recently been destroyed; he objected even more to finding himself identified as the "brain behind the organized drug trafficking groups." For his part, Caro Quintero was spitting mad. In November 1984, his El Búfalo ranch and two other operations nearby in Chihuahua had been trashed. The raids, organized by the PJF in coordination with the DEA, had cost the traffickers an estimated $8 billion.

Fonseca and Caro Quintero needed to find out who was the source of the information used by Camarena to target them. As they planned the kidnapping of the US agent, El Príncipe summoned José Luis Gallardo, one of his right-hand men. Gallardo was a tall youth with fair, straight hair, who they called El Güero, or Blondie. He was said to be a nephew of Miguel Ángel Félix Gallardo.

"I have a friend at the consulate who helps us with visas, and he can tell me which one is Camarena," El Güero suggested when Caro Quintero asked him to take part in the operation. El Güero always went around with a guy known as El Chelín. Although the latter had curly hair, they looked alike and people said they were brothers.

On February 7, 1985, Don Neto and Caro Quintero met at midday at the Camp to finalize details of the kidnapping, due to take place at 2 p.m., just as the US consulate was closing. But first, El Güero had to identify the agent. He went in, and came back rapidly. The consulate was very close to the the Camp.

"Ready," El Güero told Caro Quintero.

It was as easy as that. Various US government employees working at the Guadalajara consulate revealed the identity of DEA agent Camarena, delivering his head on a platter. But it remains unclear how El Güero had these contacts in the visa section, and why they told him who Camarena was.

Immediately, two of Don Neto's men, guided by El Güero, went off after Camarena. To kill time, Don Neto invited Caro Quintero to a restaurant of his called El Isao. Caro declined, so the older man lunched there with two of his gunmen. When he returned to the Camp, he found a crowd of Félix Gallardo's hired guns and Caro Quintero's bodyguards. In one of the bedrooms was the kidnapped agent. They'd thrown him on a bed with his hands bound and his eyes blindfolded. As if it were a bad omen, Don Neto began to feel ill. He was cold all over, then feverishly hot, so he went to lie down in an adjoining bedroom. From there he could hear the voice of Félix Gallardo, who seemed to have his own concerns about the DEA investigations. After a while Ernesto asked his aide, Samuel Ramírez, to put some questions to the agent: "Find out why he's been going for me so much, what's the reason for that?" Samuel went to the room where the agent was, accompanied by Javier Barba and two of Félix Gallardo's men. At that point Camarena was still in good physical condition, and aware of what was going on. After questioning him, Ramírez reported back to Fonseca:

"He says his investigation is mainly focussed on Félix Gallardo, because they've just seized a big cocaine shipment of his in New Mexico and Texas. He says the second most important person in his investigation is Rafael, and you're the third."

With Don Neto by this time were Caro Quintero and a slim figure, six feet tall with a pale complexion, prominent cheekbones, and dark hair combed back with a parting: Miguel Ángel Félix Gallardo himself, the Boss of Bosses. If Don Neto was reassured by this news, it upset Félix Gallardo, who promptly left the room to question Camarena himself.

"I don't feel well, I'm going to La Pasadita to get something for it," said Don Neto to Caro Quintero, getting up off the bed. "I leave you in charge. Make sure nothing happens to him, put people you can trust to look after him and to get him whatever he needs."

"Ok," nodded El Príncipe.

Don Neto left Caro Quintero's house along with Ramírez, and went to rest. The following morning he returned to speak to Camarena. That would undoubtedly be one of the worst days of his life.

Don Neto's confession

On the afternoon of April 9, 1985, Don Neto found himself at No. 9, Lázaro Cárdenas, in the ornate seventh-floor office of Florentino Ventura, the implacable commander of the PJF and head of Interpol in Mexico.

There was no messing with Ventura, and the drug trafficker was reluctant to experience first-hand the kinds of torture this police-man used to obtain a confession. So his first formal statement was fluid and full of detail. Fifty-five years old, with thirteen of them spent trafficking, helpless and washed-up, Don Neto confessed that he and Caro Quintero had made the decision to kidnap Camarena; he gave a blow-by-blow account of the day the Prince had told him that the DEA agent was past talking.

After Camarena's death and his quarrel with Caro Quintero, Don Neto spent two days shut up at home, partly because of rage, but also out of caution. The press and the radio were hammering out the news of Camarena's kidnapping. Feeling the strain, Don Neto then sought refuge in Puerto Vallarta, in an elegant villa lent to him by Paty, the woman who ran the house in Guadalajara, an up-market prostitute who he often paid for her services. Not long afterwards, on April 7, Don Neto was arrested at the Bugambilias condominium in the resort city, along with Ramírez and nineteen other gunmen.

In those days, of course, people like Fonseca, Caro Quintero, or Félix Gallardo never acted as if they were on the run—and nor do the major-ity of their colleagues in Mexico today, unless the government announces a specific manhunt. In fact, such drug barons made a show of their impunity—attending high-society parties, throwing extravagant orgies with the best mariachi bands to celebrate the birthday of a police chief, or buying fleets of luxury imported vehicles to shower on senior figures in the Jalisco state government and the local and federal police.

Rafael Caro Quintero felt so far above the law in Guadalajara that he regularly shot up other people's cars, without the least fear of consequences. This was something that profoundly galled Don Neto, who told him off on more than one occasion: "Look here, compadre, don't be a jerk, if you keep messing up you'll set the whole city against you." Rafael, of course, ignored his advice.

According to the explanation Don Neto gave to Interpol's Ventura, his arrest in Puerto Vallarta was the result of carelessness. That day, one of his men, Ramiro, had gone out drinking with a group of gunmen known as Los Gallos, who worked for Félix Gallardo. Emboldened by alcohol, they beat up someone who immediately called the municipal police. The officers shadowed Ramiro, and happened on the house where Don Neto was hiding. After an exchange of fire, the occupants were all arrested.

Don Neto vehemently denied to Ventura any responsibility for the murder: he'd been sick at the time, he couldn't have been present when they tortured Camarena. He'd intended to talk to the American agent on February 8, but didn't, because by then Camarena was a goner. On April 11, Don Neto amplified his statement and said that it was Félix Gallardo and his people who had stayed behind to guard and question Camarena.

The day he was kidnapped, Camarena's wife reported him missing to the DEA office in Guadalajara, which immediately set wheels in motion to find him. Edward Heath, the DEA chief in Mexico, informed the United States ambassador, John Gavin, who asked Mexico's attorney general, Sergio García Ramírez, to help locate his agent. In the end, it was the DEA and not the Mexican government which discovered that Camarena had been taken by members of what was by then known as the Guadalajara Cartel.[2]

Ernesto Fonseca Carrillo, Don Neto, is languishing in La Palma maximum security prison in the State of Mexico to this day, convicted of Camarena's murder (though he never admitted to it) and of offenses against public health. Caro Quintero and Félix Gallardo were also arrested for their responsibility in the death of Kiki Camarena. Nonetheless, the DEA continued its investigation for another five years. In its Los Angeles office, a tenacious special agent by the name of Héctor Berrellez, the son of Mexican immigrants, was appointed to pursue the inquiry. What were they looking for? Who else did they think was guilty, if those who had ordered and carried out his murder were already behind bars? This was the beginning of Operation Leyenda. The investigation into Camarena's death led to one of the most perverse episodes in Mexican–US relations over drugs.

DEA versus CIA

The story was "ridiculous." The CIA hadn't trained Guatemalan guerrillas on Caro Quintero's ranch "or anywhere else," declared the veteran CIA spokesman, Mark Mansfield, on Wednesday, July 4,

1990. The CIA was not involved in drug trafficking, he told the *Los AngEles Times*.[3]

At the time, extracts had just come to light from a classified DEA document dealing with the trial, then underway, of three of those accused of killing Camarena: Rubén Zuno Arce, a businessman and brother-in-law of former president Luis Echeverría; the Honduran businessman and drug trafficker, Juan Ramón Matta Ballesteros, a partner in the Medellín Cartel and of Félix Gallardo; and one of Don Neto's bodyguards, Juan José Bernabé. In all, the Los Angeles district court indicted twenty-two people for the murder of the DEA agent.

Those were the first years of the George H. W. Bush administration, and Republicans thought the earthquake of the Iran-Contra scandal had already done all the damage it could. They were wrong. The US government was to be shaken by a fresh scandal within its own intelligence agencies, whose repercussions it was impossible to measure. At the epicenter were Mexico and the Guadalajara organization—now the Sinaloa Cartel—to which El Chapo Guzmán belonged. At the same time, various officials in the government of President Carlos Salinas had been shown to be in collusion with the drug trade. The "report of investigation," classified as "secret" and signed on February 13, 1990, by Los Angeles-based special agents Wayne Schmidt and Héctor Berrellez, was so fantastic it seemed made up.[4] Paragraph after paragraph, the seven-page report had all the ingredients of a thriller: a murdered journalist, the brother-in-law of a former president who's actually a drug trafficker, corrupt politicians and policemen, drug barons, guerrillas, and the CIA as the icing on the cake.

The DEA document tells what happened in Mexico at the beginning of the 1980s, events which coincided with the launch of the Iran-Contra plan by President Ronald Reagan and his vice president, George H. W. Bush. For almost a decade (1981–89), the CIA backed the armed movement of the Nicaraguan "Contras" who were trying to overthrow the government of the Sandinista National Liberation Front (FSLN). During the Cold War, Washington saw the FSLN as a major threat to the region because of its Marxist-Leninist leanings, and worried about a new Cuba developing in Central America.

In December 1982, Congress passed a constitutional amendment put forward by the Democrat Edward Patrick Boland, which prohibited the CIA from spending any more money on trying to overthrow the Nicaraguan government. Nonetheless, in 1984 the Reagan administration got a budget allocation of $24 million to support the Contras—less than the amount they'd hoped for. At the beginning of that same year, National Security Adviser Robert McFarlane suggested encouraging other countries to contribute something to the cause. The person responsible for this operation was Lieutenant Oliver North.

With the Reagan administration insisting on continuing to fund the Contras, in 1985 Congress placed tighter restrictions on the CIA, the Department of Defense, and any other US government agency, preventing them from lending direct or indirect support, through military or paramilitary operations, to any group or country. The ban forced the CIA to pull many of its personnel out of Central America: "Their departure left a void that North was to fill."[5]

When the Iran-Contra scandal broke in 1986, Reagan's team admitted that "some of the funds obtained from the sale of US arms to Iran were destined for the Contra." Many regard this as the most serious case of corruption in US history, involving key agencies like the CIA and the DEA. A number of CIA employees not only ignored the ban imposed by Congress, but colluded with drug traffickers in Latin America to obtain funds for the Nicaraguan Contras. The main countries involved in these operations were Panama, Mexico, Honduras, Nicaragua, El Salvador, Colombia and Guatemala.

In 1986, three special commissions were set up in the United States to investigate the matter: the Tower Commission, the Walsh Commission and the Kerry Commission. The results took months, but the conclusions were clear: various Latin American drug barons had been helped to export narcotics into the United States, provided they also donated money to the Contra movement. The traffickers involved included members of the Pacific organization, like Félix Gallardo, Caro Quintero, and Fonseca Carrillo, as well as members of the powerful Medellín Cartel. The planes that took off from the

United States with "humanitarian aid" for the Contras—meaning medicines and weapons—returned laden with drugs that came mainly from Colombia.

The Tower Commission, set up by Reagan at the end of 1986, was chaired by the former secretary of state under Jimmy Carter, Edmund Muskie, and had the task of cleaning up the president's image. Its investigations, which lasted just four months, came to the conclusion that while the Contras were indeed financed with money from the drug trade, Reagan had no detailed knowledge of it. On the instructions of US Attorney General Edwin Meese, the FBI also opened an investigation into the affair. In December 1986, Judge Lawrence Walsh was appointed to preside over an independent commission of inquiry. Finally, the commission headed by the Democratic senator, John Kerry, began its investigations in January 1987 and published its report on April 13, 1989: it found that the State Department gave support to the Contras and was involved in drug trafficking.

The Kerry report recognized that the drug traffickers provided assistance to the Contras including "cash, weapons, planes, pilots, air supply services, and other materials." It also recorded that the US State Department, as part of a program to fly in "non-lethal aid," had contracted the services of various drug barons. In some cases, such payments were made even "after the traffickers had been indicted by federal law enforcement agencies on drug charges, in others while traffickers were under active investigation by these same agencies." The most damning of Kerry's revelations was, wrote the journalist Robert Parry, that "US government agencies knew about the Contra–drug connection, but turned a blind eye to the evidence in order to avoid undermining a top Reagan-Bush foreign policy initiative."[6]

The CIA and Mexican drug traffickers

Lawrence Victor Harrison, better known as Torre Blanca (White Tower, probably because he was well over six feet tall), originally from the United States, was a technician who worked for years for Ernesto Fonseca, Rafael Caro Quintero, and Miguel Ángel Félix

Gallardo, setting them up with short-wave radio systems for commu-
nicating with one another and with their clients.

On February 9, 1990, Berrellez and Schmidt contacted Harrison
as part of Operation Leyenda. In their search for the truth about the
death of their colleague, the special agents discovered the background to one of the darkest episodes in Mexican journalism: the
murder of the influential *Excélsior* columnist, Manuel Buendía.[7]

The DEA report says:

Manuel Buendía-Tellesgiron [*sic*] supported candidate Delmaso
[Alfredo del Mazo], PRI party member who aspired to be the President of Mexico.[8] Buendía conducted an investigation into the
collusion that existed between Manuel Bartlett-Diaz, former secretary of the interior, Miguel Aldana-Ibarra, former head of the
Mexican anti-drug program [of the PJF], and Manuel Ibarra-Herrera,
former head of the Directorate of Federal Security (DFS), who were
acting in consort with narcotic traffickers.

Between 1981 and 1984, Buendía received information from
another reporter, Velasco, in Vera Cruz, that Guatemalan Guerrillas
were training at a ranch owned by Rafael Caro-Quintero in Vera Cruz
state. The operations/training at the camp were conducted by the
American CIA, using the FS as a cover, in the event any questions
were raised . . .

Harrison told Schmidt and Berrellez that DFS representatives oversaw the training camp and allowed traffickers to move drugs through
Mexico to the United States. However, it seems the DFS didn't know
that while its agents were acting in consort with the CIA and the traffickers, the PJF was doing its own investigation into drug trafficking
at Caro Quintero's Veracruz ranch. Members of the Federal Judicial
Police arrived at the ranch, and were attacked by the guerrillas (he
didn't say which group). The upshot was nineteen PJF fatalities.
Many of the bodies showed signs of torture.

It seems the journalist Buendía had also managed to gather information about the CIA's arms smuggling and its relations with
well-known drug traffickers in Veracruz. Buendía contacted Zorrilla,
head of the DFS, and told him all he knew. He asked for advice on

how to proceed. Zorrilla told Buendía that the question of drug trafficking linked to the CIA was very delicate, and it would be better
not to discuss it. He sent a group of agents supposedly to protect the
columnist and his family. Nonetheless, forty-one days later, Manuel
Buendía was killed by members of the DFS. Just one hour after that,
"Velasco"—Buendía's main source for the CIA story—was also killed,
in Veracruz.[9]

The DEA's secret report notes that:

> The DFS allegedly excluded the [PJF] from the investigation and
> removed all Buendía's files concerning the information on CIA arms
> smuggling and the connection the CIA had to narcotic traffickers.
> Shortly thereafter Eden Pastor [sic],[10] aka Comandante Zero, another
> individual who had given Buendía information about CIA arms
> smuggling, allegedly suffered a CIA sponsored bomb attack while
> traveling in Costa Rica.

Lawrence Harrison, or Torre Blanca, also told the Operation Leyenda
investigators that a German identified as Gerhard Mertins—who
lived in Mexico City from 1981 to 1985—had a company in
Guadalajara called Merex: "I knew that Mertins had links with the
CIA in relation to arms trafficking," he told them. This was entirely
verifiable, since Mertins was known to the DEA. A former member
of the SS, after the Second World War he became the German Federal
Republic's biggest arms exporter.

Buendía had published information about Mertins and the CIA in
his column in *ExcElsior*, after which the German is thought to have
left Mexico. According to the DEA report, Mertins was working for
a powerful Guadalajara family. Harrison told the investigators: "I
have heard that the Leaño family controls large marijuana plantations in Jalisco, the same area of Mexico where Mertins used to sell
large quantities of weaponry."

Apparently, some colleagues of Buendía's obtained information
to the effect that high-ranking PRI politicians were assisting the
CIA with arms smuggling, and were also informed about the
Agency's links with drug lords. By 1990 it was common knowledge that several narcotic traffickers had financed the Contra,

while poisoning US society with their wares—both activities with Washington's approval.

According to Torre Blanca, before Velasco, the reporter from Veracruz, was murdered, he had been working on a story about how the CIA, using the DFS as cover, was responsible for setting up and operating clandestine landing strips used for refueling the planes carrying arms to Honduras and Nicaragua. The pilots, said Harrison, then loaded up with cocaine in Barranquilla, Colombia and flew it to Miami. Mexico was again the refueling point. Thus the DEA report confirms that it was the CIA that really operated the drug smuggling and the secret landing strips that were used.

Torre Blanca went on to talk about the bribes allegedly taken by Major General Vinicio Santoyo Feria, the then commander of the Fifth Military Region, and about Santoyo's relations with the lawyer Everardo Rojas Contreras, who worked for Don Neto and Caro Quintero. The report affirms that for the last three years Rojas had been acting as General Santoyo's assistant in the purchase and management of real estate, involving large sums whose provenance could not be explained. For example, Santoyo bought a ranch in Puerto Vallarta for $600,000. This sum, the report claims, was actually part of the money Santoyo received for "extorting" Félix Gallardo and Salcido El Cochiloco, when they were arrested in Guadalajara in November 1988 by troops under Santoyo's orders.

Harrison renewed contact with Félix Gallardo three years after Camarena's murder: he visited him in 1988 in one of his Guadalajara residences. Despite the arrests of Don Neto and Caro Quintero, Félix Gallardo continued his narcotics operations in peace until April 8, 1989, when he was arrested by a corrupt ex-associate of his, the PGF chief Guillermo González Calderoni.

In July 1990, extracts from the secret DEA report were published in the main US newspapers. Their content was predictably dismissed by the CIA and the Mexican government. Nonetheless, the outpourings of the witnesses at the Kerry Commission on the Iran-Contra affair and the conclusions of that commission suggest that the information given by Torre Blanca, the DEA's informer, was pretty credible.

*   *   *

The Prince

"Los *gringos te hacen y* Los *gringos te deshacen*": the gringos build you up and the gringos knock you down, would be one translation of this frequent saying among drug traffickers.[11]

On April 15, 1985, Rafael Caro Quintero, El Príncipe, was arrested in Costa Rica in the company of his girlfriend, Sara Cosío. In his statement to judicial police, he said: "Miguel Ángel Félix Gallardo is a large-scale drug trafficker, mainly of cocaine which he gets from South America and takes into the United States."[12] Félix Gallardo worked with the Medellín Cartel led by Pablo Escobar, Gonzalo Rodríguez alias El Mexicano, and Jorge Luis Ochoa.

Caro Quintero told the PJF that the day they went for Camarena, while Don Neto was eating at El Isao, he had gone downtown to buy some seeds before going home to Mariano Otero, where he found fifteen of Félix Gallardo's armed men. A few minutes later José Luis Gallardo, El Güero, arrived, together with Samuel Ramírez, and one other. El Príncipe received them barefooted. "Here's the person you told us to bring," said El Güero, pointing to Enrique Camarena, whose face was covered by a jacket. Caro Quintero took him into one of the bedrooms and tied his hands behind his back.

"What's new, compadre, have they brought him in yet?" asked Don Neto, when he came back from lunch. Caro Quintero took him straight to the room where Camarena was, pushed the door ajar so he could see him, then shut it again.

White Tower

On July 6, 1990, Lawrence Harrison (who had entered a witness protection program the previous year) gave the following testimony to the Camarena hearings, before an empty courtroom in the Los Angeles federal court: "Miguel Ángel Félix Gallardo told me he thought his trafficking operations were safe, because he was giving arms to the Nicaragua Contras." Harrison was not some character out of a spy novel, he was the real thing. Long before the court hearing in California, Don Neto had confessed to Florentino Ventura that the gringo had helped get them radio communications. Harrison now admitted that he'd also installed radio equipment for the Mexican police and justice agencies in league with the crime gangs . . .

The lawyers for the three defendants (Rubén Zuno Arce, Juan Ramón Matta Ballesteros, and Juan José Bernabé, the first two well-connected businessmen, the last, one of Fonseca's bodyguards) had presented Harrison as a defense witness. They were hoping to show that Camarena's death had been planned and organized by a power higher than either the former president's brother-in-law (Zuno Arce) or the drug traffickers themselves: the CIA.

"I spoke face to face with [Félix Gallardo], and he told me that he'd managed to get others to contribute funds to the Contra movement, which was supported by the United States," Harrison told the court. He then described a number of conversations he'd had with other Mexican drug barons about their agreements with the North Americans, although only Félix Gallardo said he had protection because of his contributions to the Contras. What the others did say clearly, including Don Neto and Caro Quintero, was that "they had a kind of relationship with the United States government."

The DEA's star witness stated that in 1983, at Don Neto's house, he had met two men who told him they were US secret agents, although they never showed him any ID; they also told him they'd been involved in the Contra affair. Could these have been El Güero and El Chelín, the duo with gringo looks who worked with Félix Gallardo and had been briefly mentioned in the statements given by Don Neto and Caro Quintero? The same "brothers" who, thanks to the US consulate in Guadalajara, had delivered Camarena to the traffickers? Harrison also said that he'd once met another man, called Theodore Cash, who had flown arms shipments for Don Neto. In 1988, at a trial in Los Angeles, Cash would reveal that he had flown planes for the CIA for ten years.

"Based on my own investigations, I believe that at [Caro Quintero's] ranch there was a Contra training camp. My impression is that it was set up there on the orders of the US government," Harrison testified. He insisted he had never said the group training on the ranch in Veracruz were Guatemalan guerrillas; rather that they were Nicaraguan Contras.

It is important to emphasize that this, Harrison's first court appearance in Los Angeles, was in June 1990, in the fourth week of the Camarena murder trial. His very presence there, under the auspices of the DEA, threatened to trigger all-out war between the drug enforcement agency and the CIA. In court on June 7, 1990, Harrison recalled some conversations he'd had with Don Neto: "I once said to Ernesto Fonseca that he might be hunted down by the law." "Are you crazy? There's no danger of that," Don Neto had replied. He was sure he was untouchable.

"Did Fonseca say this, that he was sure he was safe, for political reasons?" Harrison was asked on the stand.

"Yes," he answered, without hesitation.

Defense lawyer Mary Kelly questioned Harrison about his links with an agent of the Federal Security Directorate (DFS), Sergio Espino Verdín, who the DEA said was responsible for interrogating Camarena at Caro Quintero's house. According to the report by Berrellez, who was in charge of Operation Leyenda, the DFS was the Mexican government agency that worked "in consort" with the narcotic traffickers and the CIA. Harrison answered: "I worked for Espino, who was close to Ernesto Fonseca. Espino reported to Miguel Nazar Haro. Nazar was my ultimate boss and was implicated in drug trafficking." Miguel Nazar Haro was head of the DFS from 1977 to 1982—the year the Iran-Contra operation began—and was forced to resign when it was discovered he was involved in vehicle smuggling.

When Mary Kelly asked Harrison if he knew of the links between the main Mexican drug traffickers and the CIA, Judge Rafeedie forbade him to answer. Harrison was only allowed to confirm that there was a close working relationship between the traffickers and senior Mexican officials.[13]

The conviction of Zuno Arce and the lost tapes

On July 31, 1990, Rubén Zuno Arce, brother-in-law of former Mexican president Luis Echeverría, was found guilty by the Los Angeles jury of taking part in the conspiracy to murder Camarena.

In the trial, the prosecution alleged that Zuno "acted as a link between the highest levels of the Mexican government and the multimillionaire cartel based in Guadalajara." By that time two other defendants had already been found guilty: Matta Ballesteros, the Honduran drug trafficker, and Bernabé, Don Neto Fonseca's bodyguard.

According to the DEA's investigation and forensic experts, Camarena was not tortured at the house in Mariano Otero, where Don Neto saw him for the last time, but at 881 Lope de Vega, also in Guadalajara.

The charge against Zuno related to the fact that he was the previous owner of the house where Camarena was killed, which he had sold to Caro Quintero before the murder. The main witness against Zuno was the policeman Héctor Cervantes, one of the bodyguards assigned to Don Neto, who, under a witness protection program, revealed that as far back as September 1984, after the raid on the El Búfalo marijuana farm, Zuno had ordered the kidnapping of El Kiki Camarena. Cervantes claimed that Zuno had said they needed to find out what Camarena knew about "my general," referring to Juan Arévalo Gardoqui, the then secretary of defense in the government of President Miguel de la Madrid, thus implicating the highest levels of the Mexican government.[14]

The DEA discovered that Camarena's interrogation at the hands of the drug traffickers and police had been taped. The Mexican authorities at first denied the existence of any such recordings, but in the end the attorney general, Sergio García Ramírez, surrendered copies of some of the tapes to the DEA. Other items of physical evidence relating to Camarena's torture and death were destroyed by the Mexican authorities.[15]

In 1988, during the trial of the first nine defendants in the Camarena case, some of the sound recordings of his interrogation were played back to the Los Angeles court. Those who heard them say they were excruciating. These same recordings were heard again in 1990 in the trial of Zuno, Matta, and Bernabé. In one part of the tapes played by the DEA, Camarena is asked about "Arévalo Gardoqui." Presumably this referred to the secretary of defense, but this aspect was not followed up in the trial or anywhere else. One more untouchable Mexican general.

Today, Zuno Arce is serving a life sentence at a facility in Houston, Texas. And the photo of the erstwhile DFS officer, Sergio Espino, still appears on the DEA Los Angeles division's list of fugitives.

Nine years later, in 1999, Héctor Berrellez, the head of Operation Leyenda, who obtained some of the cassettes of the interrogation in which Camarena died, gave an interview to *USA Today*: "On the tapes, the drug dealers repeatedly ask Camarena, 'What do you know about the CIA? What do you know about the CIA's involvement with the plantation?'" Berrellez said one of his informers told him that Caro Quintero got weapons through his connection with the CIA, and that while he was in Mexico investigating his colleague's case, he obtained information about strange fortified bases in Sinaloa, Veracruz, Durango, and other states, which were not military bases. Supposedly, US military aircraft landed at these bases and, according to his sources, the planes were loaded with drugs. When Berrellez alerted his superiors at the DEA and US embassy staff in Mexico City, they simply told him: "Stay away from those bases. They are training camps, special operations." Berrellez concluded, from all the information he had compiled, that the CIA was unquestionably involved in the drug trade.[16]

The return of Torre Blanca

On December 4, 1992, Lawrence Harrison took the stand again in the Los Angeles district court, this time as prosecution witness in a new trial of Zuno Arce and a gynecologist, Humberto Álvarez Machaín. The latter had been kidnapped in an undercover DEA operation in Mexico in April 1990, and was accused of participating in Camarena's torture.

Torre Blanca's return to the witness box was crucial to the trial of Álvarez Machaín. Next day, the newspapers described how for more than two hours he held the jury "spellbound" with his bizarre stories of life in the circle of drug traffickers around El Príncipe Caro Quintero. For example, on one occasion Harrison and several other men spent four or five weeks counting out $400 million that were to be paid as a bribe to a senior figure in the Mexican government. He also described one of the many parties held by Caro Quintero in Don Neto's houses. "Caro was sitting on a dancing horse, smoking cocaine like an animal," he recalled.

Luis Echeverría worked for the United States

In 2006, the journalist Jefferson Morley revealed some information that appears even more relevant in the light of this story, linking both the Mexican and US governments to the narcotics trade. Thanks to declassified CIA documents, Morley was able to reconstruct the history of the Agency in Mexico between 1956 and 1968, as well as that of its station chief, Winston Scott. Scott was a "charming" American with considerable influence over the Mexican government, having recruited to the CIA's payroll senior figures in the federal administration.

Scott set up a network called LITEMPO, through which Mexican officials could work on behalf of US government interests. Naturally, this labor did not come free. "How much Scott paid his LITEMPO informants is not disclosed in the records, but at least two CIA officials thought it was excessive. In a review of the LITEMPO program in 1963, the chief of the clandestine service's Mexico desk griped that 'the agents are paid too much and their activities are not adequately reported,'" wrote Morley. In one declassified document the program was said to be "a productive and effective relationship between CIA and select top officials in Mexico."

Among the public figures included on the CIA' s payroll were the future presidents Gustavo Díaz Ordaz (LITEMPO-2) and Luis Echeverría (LITEMPO-8), as well as the head of the secret police or DFS, Fernando Gutiérrez Barrios (LITEMPO-4). The main aim of LITEMPO was for these officials and the CIA to cooperate in detecting "subversive" and "communist" groups.[17] And there's no doubt that later, the United States identified the Sandinista government as a communist threat to the region. In this context, the help given during the 1980s by various Mexican officials and the Guadalajara Cartel to the Nicaraguan Contras could be seen as a natural continuation of these links between the CIA and the Mexican government.

*   *   *

Where drug traffickers are made

While in Mexico the CIA was making pacts with the Félix Gallardo clan, Don Neto, and Caro Quintero, further south a certain substitute member of the Colombian senate was beginning to emerge as a dark legend: Pablo Escobar. In the small world of drug trafficking, sooner or later Félix Gallardo and Escobar, the two big barons, would meet, facilitated by the United States.

Behind an innocuous pen-pusher's face, with pallid skin, thinning hair and huge glasses, hid the chief accountant of the powerful and feared Medellín Cartel. The Cuban-American Ramón Milián Rodríguez, responsible for laundering $11 billion worth of profits, was one of the main witnesses at the Subcommittee on Terrorism, Narcotics, and International Operations, set up by the US Senate in 1987 to investigate the links between drug trafficking and the CIA. Milián was said to be the link between Escobar and the leaders of the Cuban-American drug dealers, and the person who delivered $10 million to the Nicaraguan Contras from Escobar.

Milián's criminal talents were unbounded, and he was happy to acknowledge them on Capitol Hill before Senator John Kerry's investigating commission. While he laundered money for the Medellín Cartel and for businesses linked to the drug trafficking of Panamanian president Manuel Noriega, Milián also cleaned up assets for the CIA itself, helping the Agency to conceal some of its payments made abroad, at least until 1982.

"From what we have learned these past months, our declaration of the war on drugs seems to have produced a war of words and not action. Our borders are inundated with more narcotics than at any time ever before," Kerry declared to PBS in 1988, as his committee's investigations proceeded. They would conclude a year later. Nothing could have been more unpopular at the time than exposing President Reagan and Vice President Bush's sham war on drugs. Reagan could hardly talk of a "war" when he was willingly sleeping with the enemy—something that was proven time and again by testimony given before the special commissions investigating the Iran-Contra affair.

In 1991, the co-founder of the Medellín Cartel, Carlos Lehder Rivas, confirmed that his organization had delivered $10 million to the Contras.[18] Clearly, like the good businessman he was, Escobar's contribution to the anti-Sandinista movement was not a gift but an investment. Thanks to the ever-obliging CIA, Escobar's generous donation opened up for him the door to the United States—in particular, through the airport of Mena, in Arkansas.

CHAPTER FOUR

Raising Crows

The Informer

"I'm going to tell you the real truth," he said, through a thick cloud of smoke blown out through nose and mouth at once. This was someone who had watched, from within the Mexican government, all the changing phases of the drug trade over the last thirty-five years. The Informer, as we'll call him, was impeccably dressed in a suit, tall and thin, holding the precious pack of Montana cigarettes that he smoked as swiftly as he talked. The conversation with the The Informer for this book took place in 2010. At my insistence, he finally broke the silence he had kept for years. He told his story in the kind of detail you can only pick up from a front-row seat.

North of the Rio Bravo it is the Iran-Contra affair that is key to understanding the growth of drug trafficking in the 1980s; to the south, The Informer's account completes the mafia's family tree.

His face is hidden behind cigarette smoke and his name must remain a secret; his life depends on it. For thirty-five years, his story was interwoven with that of the drug traffickers he dealt with face to face on dozens of occasions. First, The Informer points out,

In 1970 the term "cartel" didn't exist. There were just "cliques," which grew and transported across the border marijuana and "gum" [*goma*, heroin]. Almost no state in Mexico was free from this activity in some form or another. . . . Drugs were grown in Guerrero, Michoacán, Sinaloa, Durango, Chihuahua, Veracruz, and Oaxaca. It was the time of the Vietnam War, and the US government permitted the drug trade to ensure access to stimulants for its soldiers in the field and for those returning home who were already addicted.

As The Informer went on, the ashtray filled up with butts. Once he'd started, he couldn't stop; it was as if he were exorcizing his own ghosts.

It was at the beginning of the presidency of Luis Echeverría (1970–76). Mexico's Attorney General was Pedro Ojeda Paullada, who was also a personal friend of the president's. The secretaries of defense and the interior were, respectively, Hermenegildo Cuenca Ríos and Mario Moya Palencia. The head of the Federal Judicial Police (PJF) was Manuel Suárez. Luis de Barreda was officially in charge of the Federal Security Directorate (DFS), but Fernando Gutiérrez Barrios had been its real chief since the times of President Gustavo Díaz Ordaz. In those days it was more dangerous to be a guerrilla, or a political dissident, than a drug trafficker. The state agencies that mercilessly hunted down the former were the same bodies that kept the latter in check and periodically charged them millions of dollars out of the profits of this fledgling but already highly lucrative business.

There were 600 federal police officers for the whole country, each with fifteen to twenty assistants. These were the so-called madrinas, "godmothers," who never appeared on the official payroll of the federal Attorney General's Office (PGR), but whose illegal and uncontrolled activity was essential to its operations. In the hierarchy of the PGR there was the attorney general, Pedro Ojeda Paullada at the time, two general coordinators, and a senior officer called Alejandro Gertz Manero, who some thirty years later would become the first secretary of public security. At that time Gertz had a bodyguard called Rodolfo León Aragón, who would go on to write his own dark legend of corruption.

The Judicial Police received no budget for expenses, equipment, or even office space. Each regional coordinator supplied his own people with cars, weapons, radios, and offices. The only thing they didn't supply was the badges. They raised money from cock fights, horse racing, and drug trafficking. That's how things were. I'm not saying it was good or bad, just that that's how it worked.

In those days the government had almost complete control over drug cultivation and transport. Hardly a consignment got through without the permission and supervision of the Mexican army, the Federal Security Directorate and the Federal Judicial Police. Control meant it was "arranged" with the army, the DFS, and the PJF. To plant fifty or sixty hectares you needed permission from the head of the military zone or region.[1]

Once the fields had been sown, they stuck little colored flags on them, according to the arrangement. This meant that when the helicopters flew over, instead of fumigating them they would water them. Every three months, when the harvest was ready, the growers asked for a permit to take the drugs to a warehouse. Then the transporters had to get another permit to convey the drugs to a border crossing; for example, from Oaxaca to Miguel Alemán in Tamaulipas. To stop the goods from being stolen, the trucks had federal police protection. There were clear instructions that not one kilogram could stay in the country. There was no retail trade inside Mexico. When we caught anyone with drugs for sale locally, the full weight of the law would come down on them and they'd be locked up, whoever they were.

The Informer insists that the secretary of the interior and the secretary of defense, the attorney general, and even the president of the Republic, were all fully aware of these operations. In addition, the authorities in the United States knew from the beginning of the 1970s that the DFS was involved in drug trafficking, yet they continued to support and protect the agency.[2]

The suitcase ritual

In the upper echelons of the state, everyone had a job to do and everyone was handsomely rewarded for doing it "well":

The Mexican army kept watch over the plantations; the PJF was in charge of transporting the merchandise; while the DFS was in direct contact with the traffickers and controlled them. The drug traffickers paid a kind of "tax" to the federal government—sixty dollars per kilo. Twenty dollars were for the local army commander, twenty for the

PJF, and another twenty for the DFS. Inside the federal police, each regional coordinator took a cut of this money to pay for weapons, offices, equipment, and the wages of the assistants ["godmothers"]. These weren't bribes, they were a tax authorized at the highest level—explained The Informer in self-defense—. In particular, of the money charged by the PJF to the traffickers, half remained to cover the police's own expenses, while the other half went to the attorney general's office.

Religiously every month, a suitcase made the long journey around the whole of Mexico. Its final destination was the PGR headquarters, then located in Mexico City's historic center. Simultaneously, other suitcases made their way to the Secretariats of the Interior and National Defense.

At regular intervals the suitcase made this trip, starting at the bottom, with those who directly collected the money, until reaching the attorney general's desk. It was a long trip, but nobody would have dared to take any money out. There were wads and wads of bills, greenbacks. You can close your eyes and imagine even the smell of those bills every time the suitcase was opened. What happened to the suitcase later nobody knew. It was lost from sight as it passed from hand to hand towards the presidential palace of Los Pinos.

The taxes paid by the drug traffickers made fortunes overnight for government figures and businessmen in Mexico. Another part of the proceeds, as happened in the US, was spent on the struggle against subversive movements. These were considerable sums. At the time there was no National Human Rights Commission in Mexico, and no Public Oversight Office; government officials were exempt from scrutiny. All this was seen as a way of protecting national security. Drug trafficking was a matter of state. All that was asked of the traffickers was that they not carry weapons in public or draw attention to themselves, in order to protect the police and the army, but above all to protect the civilian population.

The Informer sketched the typical profile of early traffickers as follows: "They are violent people by nature, or, if you prefer, by the nature of their business. They got involved in this because they have no education or prospects." The immense majority of those involved in narcotics production at that time were men and women of humble, rural origins, who never got beyond fourth grade at elementary school.

In the years when the business was controlled, those who paid their tax to the authorities included Salcido, Eduardo Lalo Fernández, the Cuban Alberto Sicilia, Pedro Avilés, Pedro Díaz, Don Neto, the legendary Quintero Payáns, Félix Gallardo, Acosta, Esparragoza and Zambada.

It was in 1973 that a thirty-two-year-old Ernesto Fonseca, the future Don Neto, planted his first two hectares of marijuana at El Dorado in Sinaloa. He harvested three tons and took them to Tijuana, where he sold them to "the González brothers," according to his later sworn statement. In those days Pedro Avilés used to receive everybody's harvest and stored it in a warehouse in San Luis Río Colorado.

"The drug traffickers paid even to get a hearing from the authorities," continued The Informer.

Just to listen, the regional police coordinators or the local police commander could charge a million dollars. Just to *listen*! When the trafficker and the official were face to face, the former would discreetly slide a suitcase full of money under the table in exchange for the right to an audience. Once they'd listened to him, they'd ask for instructions from the capital. Nothing was done behind the backs of the supremos at the PGR, the Secretariat of the Interior and Sedena.

The suitcase ritual continued during the presidency of José López Portillo (1976–82). It was during his term that, in 1978, Miguel Nazar Haro took charge of the DFS. Nazar, a favorite of the CIA, was to play a leading part in the story of US government tolerance of and aid to the international drug trade.[3]

In 1976, an eradication campaign in collaboration with the US, known as Operation Condor, was launched under the command of General José Hernández Toledo. Yet "in those days the drug traffickers operated by different rules. They would never attack the civilian population or a public official, however lowly his position. There was respect for authority and a clear division between the sides. It wasn't like today, when drug traffickers are public servants, there's no separation, and you can't see where the line is."

In his fourth annual state of the nation report, President López Portillo referred for the first time to the "war" on drugs, in emulation of President Reagan.

> It was the first time, as far as I can remember, that a president spoke of it in public. Javier García Paniagua [the head of the DFS before Nazar] began to involve the DFS in drug trafficking, no longer to control it, but to join in; what earlier wasn't seen as corruption now began to be corruption. The phase known as the "years of control" lasted from Echeverría until 1982, with the difference that by López Portillo's time the volume of produce was considerable. During de la Madrid's presidency, everything began to change.

Moral renewal

Miguel de la Madrid began his six-year term in office in 1982 with the slogan of "moral renewal." However, many leading figures from the previous administrations of Echeverría and López Portillo took positions in the new government, and they had no intention of behaving "morally."

Ronald Reagan was beginning his second year as president, while Vice President George H. W. Bush was the next most powerful man in the US administration. In Mexico, the secretary of defense was General Juan Arévalo Gardoqui, one-time commander of the Fifth Military Zone, in Chihuahua. A controversial figure from Jalisco, Sergio García Ramírez, was attorney general, and the secretary of the interior was Manuel Bartlett. From that time on, the US government would never lose sight of any of them. As under secretary of the interior there appeared a military man, Jorge Carrillo Olea—someone who over the years would become key to understanding the current situation of insecurity and impunity in the country. Chief of the DFS was José Antonio Zorrilla, while Manuel Ibarra headed the PJF. Fernando Gutiérrez Barrios, the legendary leader of the DFS, was officially made director general of roads and bridges, but continued to pull the strings in the intelligence agency at the Secretariat of the Interior.

"Sergio García sent the commanders most trusted by the new government team to head the regional offices of the PGR and federal police located along the main trafficking routes," recalled The Informer. That was how the fine line between drug traffickers and public officials began to blur.

> The taxes paid by the drug traffickers began to turn into direct payments to politicians and state officials. Fortunes were made and political projects got financed, but the levers of control over the traffickers began to be lost. García sent in people he could trust, not to control the traffickers but to take their place. The regional coordinators of the PJF ceased to be policemen and became drug traffickers, who used the professional traffickers for their own ends.

One of García's trusted acolytes was Guillermo González Calderoni, whom he had released from jail, and now sent to Tamaulipas. "On the one hand, these policemen created drug traffickers of their own to do their dirty work and the actual trafficking for them. On the other, they gave support and protection to some of the most important drug barons, in exchange for money which no longer went into government coffers or to buy equipment, but into the pockets of politicians." The Informer went on:

> That's how the organization of the Arellano Félix brothers was born. It was Commander Salvador Peralta who taught the Arellano Félixes how to work when they were still just third-rate car thieves and smugglers. He gave them equipment to intercept communications so they could find out where the goods were heading, steal them, and then share the proceeds with Peralta.
>
> When González Calderoni arrived in Tamaulipas he became good friends with [Gulf Cartel lynchpin] Juan García Ábrego. Very soon, González turned a local band of people smugglers into important drug traffickers. It was he who provided protection for Miguel Ángel Félix Gallardo and Amado Carrillo Fuentes.

In 1987, González Calderoni was head of the PJF in Guadalajara, where he met Félix Gallardo, according to letters sent to journalists by the drug baron from the Almoloya de Juárez maximum security prison.[4]

Explaining that "the nub of cocaine trafficking was in the state of Oaxaca," The Informer described his experience of the transportation arrangements:

> The Cessnas flew down to the Isthmus of Tehuantepec—in Oaxaca state—from Tijuana, Juárez, and Matamoros, picked up the cocaine and returned to their home base, where the storage centers were. Sometimes the US government came for the merchandise in person. Its planes might equally be carrying Colombian pelo rojo [red marijuana] or cocaine. I saw it with my own eyes. In the early 1980s, when I was in Puerto Escondido, I had to look after a US Air Force plane that arrived with a load of pelo rojo from Colombia. The only difference between Mexican and Colombian marijuana is the color: the red kind is extra prized, even today. This plane landed at Puerto Escondido to refuel, and went on to the United States.
>
> Any contacts between the Mexican drug lords and their Colombian colleagues had to be through the goverment. Anybody who wanted to buy cocaine, Félix Gallardo, El Chapo Guzmán, El Azul, anybody, they had to do it through the government.

The figures, dates, and events narrated by The Informer coincide in time with the CIA's Iran-Contra plan, which encompassed an area from Colombia to Mexico. Obsessed with its anti-communist mission in Latin America, denied resources by Congress, the unscrupulous CIA fell into the arms of the narcotic traffickers.

From Medellín to Guadalajara

Juan Ramón Matta Ballesteros, known as El Negro, is remembered as the man who offered to pay off the national debt of his country, Honduras. They say he made the proposal directly to the then president, José Azcona Hoyo, but was turned down.

In Matta Ballesteros, everything is dark: the colour of his hair, his skin, and his shifty eyes, his violent character and his history as a trafficker. In the hearings of the Kerry subcommittee on the Iran-Contra affair, his name came up repeatedly, as did that of his company, Setco. Setco was an airline hired by the CIA to carry "humanitarian aid" to the Contras, in spite of all the evidence the agency had that Matta was a drug trafficker—or perhaps precisely because of that.

In 1977, El Negro Matta had forged the link between the Medellín and Guadalajara cartels, when he introduced the Colombian, José Gonzalo Rodríguez Gacha—one of the founders of the Medellín Cartel—to Miguel Ángel Félix Gallardo. The two drug barons soon struck up a close understanding.

Rodríguez Gacha was born to a peasant family. He began his rise in the midst of a violent conflict in the emerald-producing region of Colombia. He was only just twenty-nine when he joined the organization being set up by Pablo Escobar Gaviria, along with Carlos Lehder and the Ochoa brothers Fabio, Juan David, and Jorge Luis. When he met Félix Gallardo, he was thirty. At that time, the Guadalajara Cartel was simply a well-organized operation ferrying marijuana and heroin into the United States. Rodríguez opened Félix Gallardo's eyes to a more appealing business: cocaine. For much smaller volumes, the profits were vastly higher.

Rodríguez Gacha felt so at home with the "Mexican model" that his taste for mariachi culture soon earned him the nickname of El Mexicano. He developed the eccentric habit of naming his Colombian ranches after Mexican states and cities, like Cuernavaca, Chihuahua, Sonora, or Mazatlán. The fake "war on drugs" begun by Reagan did not mean the Medellín Cartel distanced itself from US territory; on the contrary, it helped it get closer.

The biggest narco of them all was CIA

In 1981, a curious character entered the story of the Medellín and Guadalajara cartels, and of the Matta Ballesteros group: the multi-faceted Adler Berriman Seal, better known as Barry Seal. Seal became the perfect combination. "The biggest drug smuggler in American history was a CIA agent," wrote Daniel Hopsicker in the *Washington*

Weekly in August 1997. In fact, Seal, with his sparkling eyes and knowing expression, had a triple personality: in addition to flying planes for the Medellín Cartel, he was an undercover agent for the CIA and later for the DEA.[5]

Like El Negro Matta, Barry Seal worked for the CIA supporting the Nicaraguan Contras.[6] The connection between these two, and between both of them and the Medellín and Guadalajara cartels, was by no means fortuitous.

Seal's wife, Deborah, stated that he had begun to do occasional jobs for the CIA in the 1950s.[7] In 1972 he was arrested in New Orleans in a DC4, accused of trying to fly explosives to anti-Castro Cubans operating in Mexico. Thirteen years later, this same plane was the link between Seal and El Negro. The aircraft was used by a company called Hondu Carib to carry aid for the Contras to Honduras, before being loaded up with drugs destined for the United States. The owner of the company was one Frank Moss. Previously, Moss had worked as a pilot for El Negro's airline, Setco, which like Hondu Carib received funds from the CIA.

Moss flew from Florida with the weapons for the Contras; on the way back from Honduras with the drugs, he would make a stopover in Mérida and load some frozen fish to distract the US customs.

Barry Seal began to work officially as a pilot for the Medellín Cartel in 1981. He soon moved on from flying light aircraft with 100 kgs of cocaine to flying a plane that could carry a ton. It is said this miracle was achieved by the CIA, spurred by its impatience to get more resources to the Contras. Being so productive, Seal became very important to Pablo Escobar and his organization. And they paid him well for his services: $1.5 million per round journey, according to his own account.

Barry Seal began to land his main drug flights for the Medellín Cartel at Mena airport, in Arkansas—whose Democratic Party governor was then Bill Clinton, before he became the country's forty-second president in 1993. From 1981 to 1985, Mena was a foremost center for international smuggling. According to estimates by the Internal Revenue Service and the DEA, as well as to sworn testimonies, the volume of cocaine and heroin being trafficked at that time was several thousand kilograms, and the profits reached hundreds of millions of dollars.

In exchange for an open door for its drug shipments, the Medellín Cartel gave cash to the Contras. In essence it was the same agreement as with the Guadalajara Cartel in Mexico. Since the Medellín and Guadalajara cartels had been partners since 1979, due to the cordial relations between El Mexicano and Félix Gallardo, today we can conclude that the two agreements were one and the same, and that this is one reason why the two cartels grew so much stronger in the region during the 1980s.

In 1983, Barry Seal was arrested while transporting cocaine from Colombia to Florida. The CIA were not about to endanger their entire operation to defend Seal, and so the pilot turned to the DEA, offering information about the Medellín Cartel in exchange for immunity. For the first time ever, the US anti-drug agency saw a precious opportunity to learn about the inner workings of this nefarious Colombian cartel and to destroy it from within. Agent Ernest Jacobsen, of the DEA's Florida office, became Seal's handler.

Consolidating the alliance between Colombia and Mexico

The Medellín Cartel's favorite pilot told Jacobsen that between 1984 and 1986 the organization had a roughly sixteen-hectare ranch on the Yucatán peninsula in south-east Mexico, where there was a storage facility for cocaine being shipped on to the United States in small aircraft.[8] The story is quite plausible. A recently declassified CIA report from 1998[9] states that throughout the 1980s and 90s, South American traffickers used the Central American isthmus as an important route for transporting cocaine and marijuana; as well as for importing drugs that would be refined using chemicals, and for laundering the proceeds of their illicit operations.

It is impossible not to draw a connection between this operating base in Yucatán and Torre Blanca's testimony in the California district court about the ranch belonging to Rafael Caro Quintero in Veracruz being used for the Nicaraguan Contra, in collaboration with the CIA and the DFS. Nor can we forget what The Informer told us for this book about United States Air Force planes in Oaxaca.

Jacobsen indicated that Seal, already acting as a DEA informer, asked him for a larger plane because the Medellín Cartel wanted him to fly eighteen-ton loads of coca paste once a week from Peru to three processing laboratories in Nicaragua, and from there on to the ranch in Yucatán.[10] The DEA helped Seal get a Fairchild C-123K, called *Fat Lady*, in order to secure his relationship with the Medellín Cartel. But before Barry Seal began to use the plane for this big operation with the Colombian traffickers, the CIA installed cameras and a satellite tracking device. The Reagan administration wanted to use the photographs to discredit the Sandinista government, so that Congress would release funds for the Contras. So, while the CIA was pushing to leak the photos to the press, the DEA was refusing, because this might jeopardize the operation to capture Escobar and his band.

In an interview given to the British journalist Ambrose Evans-Pritchard, Ernest Jacobsen said that Barry Seal had told him the Colombians wanted to show the CIA their operating base in Yucatán, and their cocaine warehouses in Georgia and Florida.

In December 1985, Seal was put on six months' probation by federal judge Frank Polozola for two drug felonies. One condition of his probation was that Seal had to be at the Salvation Army halfway house in Baton Rouge, Louisiana, from 6 p.m. to 6 a.m. every night. Another was that he was barred from carrying weapons or hiring armed guards. The probation sentence was thus turned into a death sentence. The DEA could do nothing to protect its witness, just as he was about to testify in open court against the leaders of the Medellín Cartel. The Colombians were patient. On February 19, 1986, Seal returned to the Salvation Army hostel at 6 p.m. As he was parking his white Cadillac, a man with a MAC-10 machine gun shot him dead. The official account identified Jorge Luis Ochoa as the person responsible for having him killed.

A year earlier, in February 1985, the Guadalajara Cartel murdered DEA agent Enrique Camarena. Ernesto Fonseca Carrillo and Rafael Caro Quintero were jailed for the crime. But their partner, Miguel Ángel Félix Gallardo, the friend of Matta Ballesteros and the link between the Guadalajara and Medellín cartels, remained free to go about his business for many years to come. Was it just by chance that Don Neto and Caro Quintero were put away, but not the connection to the Medellín Cartel?

During the 1980s, the Medellín Cartel reached the peak of its power. It was the principal exporter of cocaine to the United States. According to the DEA's own figures, in 1985 the number of US citizens who admitted to regularly taking cocaine went up from 4.2 million to 5.8 million.[11]

In the second half of the 1980s, Mexican traffickers became increasingly important. Mexico became a strategic location, halfway between producers and consumers.

The DEA files

In August 1985 at its offices on 8–61 Calle 38, in the heart of the Colombian capital, Bogotá, the DEA wrote a graphic report on the growth of drug trafficking in Mexico during the presidency of Miguel de la Madrid, from 1982 to 1988.

It's a small file of yellowing pages that looks as if it will fall apart if you so much as look at it. On the outside is written in block capitals: "STRICTLY CONFIDENTIAL," then "Brief report, updated to August 1985, on links between Latin American narco-terrorists."

Latin America was ablaze with drug scandals. The pages of the DEA report reek with blood, corruption and impunity. The list of names of prominent Mexican politicians, past and present, is invaluable for understanding the long history of impunity.

In the beautiful Peruvian city of Lima, the Villa Coca scandal had just erupted.[12] The clues left by the trade attaché at the Mexican embassy in Peru, Ricardo Sedano, pointed to three top-level Mexican officials who were then protecting drug traffickers. The DEA found in the debris at Villa Coca the remains of a private telephone line from Sedano's home to the laboratory that blew up. The report moves from establishing Sedano's links with the Peruvian trafficker Reynaldo Rodríguez, to qualifying the narco-terrorist connections in Mexico: since the elimination of guerrilla leaders such as Lucio Cabañas, an accord between Mexico and Cuba prevented more local outbreaks. Instead, "terrorists" from other Latin American countries who had obtained political asylum enjoyed protection from state security forces. Among the police chiefs, politicians, and traffickers in league with the Peruvian Reynaldo Rodríguez, the report singled out three important political figures at the heart of the networks traced by the DEA: Sergio García Ramírez, Victoria Adato Green, and Fernando Gutiérrez Barrios.

The anti-drug agency was keeping a close watch on Mexico's attorney general, Sergio García Ramírez. The DEA document also makes detailed observations on Victoria Adato. She began her career as a deputy public prosecutor in Mexico City, and ended up as a full member of the Mexican Supreme Court (SCJN). She was especially tainted by her family connections. Her brother-in-law, Manuel Ibarra Herrera El Chato, as head of the PJF had promoted Armando Pavón Reyes, who got 60 million pesos from Rafael Caro Quintero El Príncipe "to let him escape to Guadalajara airport." Her other brother-in-law, Arturo Ibarra, was said by the DEA to run a money laundering operation in Tijuana, involving ghost companies and currency exchange outlets.

As for Fernando Gutiérrez Barrios, the report alluded to a 1984 Interpol dossier showing that President López Portillo, Attorney General Agustín Alanís, and Under Secretary of the Interior Gutiérrez Barrios all were thoroughly cognizant of the facts behind the 1981 Tula River massacre, in which thirteen Colombians were killed "for belonging to a different narcotics gang," the report said. It also noted that Gutiérrez Barrios had brought off a massive electoral fraud in the mid-term elections of 1985.

The era of Escobar and Félix Gallardo comes to an end

In 1989 the DEA estimated that 60 percent of the cocaine consumed in the United States came from Colombia via Mexico.[13] In January of the same year, the Republican George H. W. Bush became president of the United States. His strategy for continuing Reagan's supposed war on drugs was to concentrate on an extradition treaty with Colombia to lock up traffickers who took drugs into the United States. The Iran-Contra operation had already done its work. The counter-revolutionary movement, combined with the Sandinistas' own mistakes, forced Nicaraguan President Daniel Ortega and the FSLN, under pressure from the Organization of American States, to open a national dialogue that year.

On April 8, 1989, in Guadalajara, Félix Gallardo, Escobar's Mexican partner, was arrested by his own good friend González Calderoni. In August the Managua accords were signed, which included holding "democratic" elections and demobilizing the Contras. Now that the CIA had no more use for Escobar and Félix Gallardo, drug barons began to be captured or killed. It all happened quite naturally. There seemed to be no connection.

At the beginning of August 1989, a list of the twelve drug traffickers most wanted by the United States was made public. At the top were Escobar, Lehder, and the Ochoa brothers, all of them partners of the CIA in supporting the Contras. Escobar's reaction was immediate. On August 18, on his orders, the candidate for the Liberal Party's presidential nomination, Luis Carlos Galán, was assassinated. He was in favor of extraditing drug traffickers to the United States.

Before that fateful year of 1989 was up, Gonzalo Rodríguez Gacha, El Mexicano, was executed in a high-profile aerial operation organized by the Colombian intelligence service, the DAS (Department of Administrative Security). With a bullet in the head, the drug baron's body lay splayed on the marshes by his El Tesoro ranch on the paradise beaches of Coveñas and Tolú, on Colombia's Caribbean coast. Press reports said Rodríguez Gacha was unrecognizable, and could only be identified by his fingerprints.[14]

In 2006 the Colombian magazine *Cambio* published an article that gives a further twist to the story of CIA links to the Medellín Cartel. It revealed that, during a search of Rodríguez Gacha's properties, the Colombian authorities found a copy of a covenant for $60 million supposedly paid to the US Government by his relatives, in exchange for his not being implicated in criminal activity and being allowed to keep the rest of his ill-gotten gains. The obvious question is whether El Mexicano is really dead, or whether he bowed out, with a reward for services rendered: money in exchange for silence and impunity.

Escobar, on the other hand, became an uncontrollable liability for both the Colombian and US Governments. Escobar wasn't like the Ochoa brothers. He wasn't about to give up the power he'd acquired. Of all the crows that had been raised in the CIA nest, he was the most dangerous. He was quite prepared to set Colombia ablaze, and he proved it. Three minutes after taking off from Bogotá airport en route to Cali, on November 17, 1989, Avianca Flight 203 exploded in thousands of pieces. There were 107 fatalities as a consequence of the drug baron's fury.

On April 25, 1990, Ortega was defeated in the Nicaraguan presidential elections by Violeta Barrios de Chamorro.

In January 1991, Jorge Luis and Juan David Ochoa gave themselves up to the Colombian authorities, on condition they would not be extradited to the United States. They were sentenced to just eight years in prison, and are currently free. Of the three brothers, only Fabio was extradited, in 2001. He was charged with trafficking drugs into the United States, and with the murder of the US government informer Barry Seal. In 2003 Fabio Ochoa was condemned to life imprisonment.

Weakened and stripped of North American support, Escobar gave himself up in June 1991, expecting the same treatment as the Ochoa brothers. When he found out they were going to extradite him, he escaped, the following year, from his luxury prison known as "The Cathedral." A day after his forty-fourth birthday, on December 2, 1993, Escobar was shot dead by police on the roof of a house in the busy La América neighborhood of Medellín. The operation was carried out by a fifteen-man police commando unit known as the Search Block, including, by some accounts, US government personnel.

Twenty-five thousand people turned out for Pablo Escobar's funeral. Over the years the legend surrounding him had swelled out of all proportion. He was reputed to be "intelligent," "audacious," and "cruel," as well as vastly rich. In reality the Medellín drug boss was not extraordinary in any sense. Who wouldn't have been successful trafficking tons of cocaine into the United States with the help of the US Government itself? When Pablo died, his successor was already warmed up and waiting, in Mexico. It was his one-time partner, Amado Carrillo Fuentes. Along with a new cohort of traffickers led by El Chapo Guzmán, the Beltrán Leyva brothers, and El Güero Palma, he was poised to take over the baton and create his own legend as El Señor de los Cielos, The Lord of the Skies.

During the 1980s the United States authorities raised a murder of crows that today are pecking their eyes out. Two clans of drug traffickers, separated by geography and history, were brought together by the CIA in an alliance that has endured to this day. The most complete expression of that alliance is the Sinaloa Cartel and El Chapo Guzmán, the currently unchallenged leader of the most powerful drug gang in the world.

CHAPTER FIVE

El Chapo's Protectors

From Compostela to Forbes

In 1993, Joaquín Guzmán smiled for the cameras as it rained in the yard of Federal Social Rehabilitation Center No. 1, in the State of Mexico. The pictures taken by dozens of press photographers are misleading. At thirty-six, this harmless-looking man, a junior in the world of organized crime, already possessed all the traits of a professional criminal. Behind his unexceptional physique—just over 5' 5" tall, regular build, square face, brown eyes, fair skin, thick eyebrows, wavy, chestnut hair, average forehead, and straight nose—was hidden a complex personality.

When El Chapo was admitted to the penitentiary, the PGR carried out a thorough analysis of his criminal profile. Guzmán was found to be "egocentric, narcissistic, shrewd, persistent, tenacious, meticulous, discriminating, and secretive," with a "high level of criminal capacity," and a "medium to high level of social adaptability" which had enabled him to develop networks of loyalty and complicity. Of all his character features, three single him out from the run-of-the-mill drug trafficker: he is ingenious, manipulative, and charming. Those who know him admit to falling prey to one or more of these. Who could forget his resourcefulness in sending cocaine to the United States in cans of jalapeño peppers at the beginning of the 1990s? Furthermore, Guzmán differs from his predecessors by being a master in the art of seduction.

Yet behind this amiable exterior, and the supposedly charitable works undertaken in the communities where he lives or does business, lies a ruthless egotist. His generosity is a mask. According to the prison's analysis, Guzmán is driven entirely by self-interest, with no concern for how this affects others. His personal relationships are superficial and "exploitative." He is capable of inflicting physical harm casually, without a thought, because other people's needs and feelings have no real meaning for him. "Only his own desires are important and absolute."

In 1993, El Chapo was a man who had difficulty controlling his sexual and aggressive impulses, and could not deal with frustration. During his eight years in various prisons, the drug baron from La Tuna committed countless excesses, all as a result of his limitless power to corrupt. And like any self-respecting mafia boss, he was big-hearted: at the time of his arrest, he had relationships with four women.

In 1977 El Chapo contracted his one legal matrimony, with María Alejandrina Guadalupe Salazar, the mother of his five acknowledged children. There is a saying among drug barons' partners: "Once you marry a drug trafficker, you stay married to him, even when you don't want to be." These women can go for months without seeing their husbands, and have to put up with them having one or twenty lovers in the meantime, from those they pay for to those they fall for. Alejandrina could never have had another partner herself, but their marriage was no obstacle to El Chapo pursuing other women.

One girlfriend was Griselda Guadalupe López, alias Silvia Escoto, with whom he had another four children: Joaquín or Quiquín, Edgar, Ovidio or Ovi (a tribute to one of his brothers who died in a car crash in 1991), and Grisel Guadalupe. In 1993 they were seven, six, five and three years old; but in his statement to prosecutors, El Chapo denied knowing either Griselda or Ovidio.

In May 2010, just before President Felipe Calderón began a trip to Washington where there was expected to be criticism of his failure to arrest El Chapo, the Mexican government tried to give the impression it was out to get Guzmán with a high-profile operation involving agents from the Federal Public Prosecutor's office supported by the Federal Police, the army, and the navy. They carried out seven searches of properties linked to Guzmán in Culiacán. Many of these locations had been known to the security services since 2007. In the course of the operation they arrested Griselda López.

The DEA had been waiting for the drug baron's ex-partner to be arrested to investigate her for suspected money laundering. The agreement with the Calderón government was that she would be kept in custody. Griselda arrived handcuffed and hooded at the Attorney General's Office (PGR) in Mexico City, but then unexpectedly walked out again, free as air. When the DEA discovered that she'd been released on orders from the Mexican government, it leaked the information to the *New York Times*: "[Felipe Calderón] played a role last week in the quick release of the wife of one of Mexico's top traffickers because of concern that her detention would prompt a round of reprisal attacks, said officials briefed on the matter," wrote Marc Lacey for the New York broadsheet.[1]

In 1993 Joaquín El Chapo Guzmán was also seeing a woman called Estela López. And when he was arrested in Guatemala, he was accompanied by María del Rocío del Villar Becerra, from Aguamilpa in Nayarit, where he has an operations center.

And yet, Guzmán is a solitary man. People in his profession get few opportunities to spend time with their families. Perhaps once or twice a year they manage to meet up at a hotel or a ranch. A few minutes, a few words, and *adiós*. That is why, over the course of their criminal careers, drug traffickers tend to acquire a lover in every town. Some such relationships are purely physical, but when they involve children, these are never forgotten. Fatherhood is another symbol of power.

When El Chapo was arrested, many thought his criminal career was over. However, drug trafficking is a business where you make money quickly and by the fistful; and Guzmán was a businessman whose potential was far from exhausted. At the time, even though he was only a secondary player, he already owned eleven properties, three private planes, twenty-seven bank accounts, four companies in different Mexican states, and hundreds of millions of dollars.

He had gone to live in Guadalajara in 1988, to work alongside other Sinaloa colleagues like Héctor Palma under the orders of Miguel Ángel Félix Gallardo, Rafael Aguilar Guajardo, and Amado Carrillo Fuentes. He left the city in 1992, after his car was sprayed with bullets by the Arellano Félix brothers, and moved back to Sinaloa with Alejandrina and the children, where he continued to prosper.

Between 1985 and 1990 Guzmán Loera shifted scores of tons of cocaine for Amado Carrillo Fuentes, linked with the Medellín Cartel, from a base in El Tonino, near Compostela in Nayarit state. This tiny village of no more than 100 souls lies on the Pacific coast, not far from the lush resorts of Guayabitos, Paraíso Escondido, and Playa Hermosa. Here El Chapo used a clandestine airstrip and the beach itself to receive the merchandise arriving from Colombia by plane or by boat, and ensured that it proceeded safely towards the buoyant US market.

Here he could also rely on the help of a local politician, Julián Venegas Guzmán, in tasks such as bribing members of Nayarit's armed forces to work with him. The partnership between El Chapo and the strongman of Compostela was sealed when Julián made them compadres by inviting him to be godfather to his daughter Brenda; in Narcoland, this "co-parent" relationship is the equivalent of a blood covenant. At El Tonino, Venegas and Lieutenant Adrián Pérez welcomed numerous planeloads of cocaine guarded by Mexican soldiers, according to the testimony given in late 2001 by Marcelo Peña García, brother of one of El Chapo's girlfriends, speaking under the pseudonym Julio as a protected witness for the PGR.

According to Julio's expert testimony, El Chapo knew that the Mexican government was after him and was provident enough to prepare two bundles of dollars that would ensure the operation could continue functioning. He gave one to his compadre Julián and the other, consisting of $200 million, was entrusted to a cousin, Ignacio Burgos Araujo.

Although in 1993 Guzmán acknowledged his connection with Burgos, and gave his interrogators many details of the latter's activities, including arms trafficking, the authorities made no move to capture either him or Venegas. They only got around to it after the scandal of Guzmán's jailbreak in January 2001, in order to look as if they were cracking down on El Chapo. On September 21 of that year, Venegas was apprehended at his well-known residence in Compostela, Nayarit, and charged with felonies against public health and belonging to an organized crime group.

Straight after El Chapo escaped from the Puente Grande prison, he was hidden by Venegas on one of his properties. Had the authorities arrested Venegas before, El Chapo could never have found refuge in Nayarit, since the other members of his gang preferred to keep their distance until things calmed down.

Most of the Compostela team has now been dispersed, killed, or arrested—some, like the renegade Lieutenant Antonio Mendoza Cruz, were arrested as late as 2009, when the *Forbes* list placing Guzmán among the world's richest men shamed Calderón's government into a performance of pursuit. The municipality of Compostela is still frequently visited by the invisible man (invisible to the forces of law and order, at least): Guzmán owns at least eight properties in the area. They are registered in the name of Socorro García Ocegueda, Julio's mother.

In 1993, the PGR had recorded only two high-profile crimes involving El Chapo Guzmán: the first was the homicide of nine members of Félix Gallardo's family, whose bodies were found on September 3, 1992, in Iguala, Guerrero, with signs of having been tortured; the second was the failed attempt to kill the Arellano Félix brothers a few months later at the Christine Discotheque in Puerto Vallarta, an incident in which eight others did die.

Of these two events, it is the first that yields most clues as to who are El Chapo's protectors. In 1993, on that flight from Tapachula to Toluca, he had revealed the protection he received from Deputy Attorney General Federico Ponce, as well as from commanders José Luis Larrazolo and Guillermo Salazar. Still more disturbing, however, were the names he left out. The tentacles of organized crime reached everywhere.

Kidnapping in Las Lomas

It was 19:39 on the evening of September 4, 1992, when an anonymous call interrupted the peaceful routine at the duty office of the Judicial Police in Mexico City, whose boss was the corrupt Rodolfo León Aragón. The caller warned that in the exclusive district of Bosques de las Lomas, a cherry-colored Suburban van was driving around with no plates and carrying several armed men. The phone call rang alarm bells. The duty office already had reports that people in a similar vehicle, posing as Federal Judicial Police, had kidnapped two bodyguards of Miguel Ángel Félix Gallardo.

The attorney general at the time was Ignacio Morales Lechuga. One of his responsibilities was the so-called Special Affairs Prosecution Service.

Immediately after the call reporting the mysterious Suburban, the Special Affairs team launched an operation led by public prosecution officers Óscar Lozano and Ignacio Sandoval, assisted by four commanders and three investigating officers. At 22:00 the SUV was detected traveling at high speed in Ahuehuetes Street in the same neighborhood. When the PJF officers ordered the driver to stop, he accelerated and tried to escape; the other occupants poked their guns out the rear windows and started shooting at the police, with wild inaccuracy.

The dark night and heavy rain made ideal conditions for an escape. The chase lasted several minutes. When they got as far as Limones, the Suburban made a turn and headed for Almendros, where it stopped at number 42. Luckily for the police, the electric gate was too slow and they managed to catch up with the car. Its five passengers leaped out and scattered, firing as they went at the police officers, who were unable to follow. The suspects left their vehicle with the engine running and the doors open on both sides. Lozano and Sandoval got out of the patrol car and went to look. They found an M2 .30-caliber rifle with no magazine, and a cream-colored valise containing the deeds to a number of properties in the name of Félix Gallardo and other members of his family.[2]

The day before, on September 3, the sister of the head of the Guadalajara Cartel, Gloria Félix Gallardo, had reported to public prosecutors that a group of armed men had forced their way into their mother's home at number 142, Cerrada de la Colina, in the Pedregal de San Ángel neighborhood. They had stolen an identical valise and kidnapped her son, her nephew, her brother, two lawyers who worked for the drug baron, and two others. It seemed obvious to the officers that the passengers in the Suburban were connected with the kidnapping of members of the family of the Boss of Bosses.

The police also found in the van a light brown leather jacket fitted with a bulletproof vest, various items of radio equipment, and another case containing rifle magazines—two for an AR-15, an empty thirty-round magazine and a forty-round one with thirty-two cartridges left. In the rear of the vehicle they found two tickets for the toll road between Cuernavaca and Puente de Ixtla, three credit cards belonging to those kidnapped the day before, the remains of some marijuana, a rope, blindfolds, and a bloodied pocket tissue. The key exhibits found in the Suburban that night were two enormous oil paintings. They were separate portraits of two men: one, in a white shirt and light grey pants, was Martín Moreno, a friend and associate of Joaquín Guzmán; the other, with his unmistakable mustache and baby-face, was El Chapo himself.

Nobody moved from the place. The police officers decided to wait for the suspects to make the next move. At eight o'clock the next morning, twenty-one-year-old Cristina Sánchez arrived at the house. She was one of the domestic staff working there. The officers immediately got out of their car and intercepted her.

The cherry Suburban had indeed been used to kidnap the nine people connected to Miguel Ángel Félix Gallardo, who was then in prison at the Reclusorio Sur, from where he continued to run his empire. Two days before the police chase in Bosques de las Lomas, a group of men had kidnapped Marco Antonio Solórzano Félix—a half-brother of the Boss of Bosses—from a house in Coyoacán, in the south of Mexico City; the gunmen also stole some valuables. Around noon they had carried out a similar operation at the home of Félix Gallardo's mother, as his sister had reported. The kidnappers burst into the house in Pedregal de San Ángel claiming to be federal agents; in the end it turns out they were, only they were acting on behalf of drug traffickers rather than the law. The group was led by Ramón Laija, El Coloche, from the General Anti-Narcotics Directorate, who would later become the brother-in-law of El Güero Palma. They snatched seven people from the house in Pedregal: Alberto Félix, Alfredo Carrillo, Ángel Gil, Federico Livas, Teodoro Ramírez, and two others. Livas and Ramírez were the lawyers who were seeking a writ of habeas corpus for José Luis Félix López, another relative of the Boss of Bosses who had been picked up twenty-four hours earlier in Guadalajara, also by supposed federal agents.

According to the investigation reports, the kidnappings had been ordered by Amado Carrillo Fuentes, Rafael El Sha Aguilar, El Chapo, and El Güero Palma; they had been carried out by members of the Federal Judicial Police under the command of Rodolfo León Aragón.

The bodies of the nine victims were found south of the capital, on the Cuernavaca-Puente de Ixtla road, close to Iguala in Guerrero state. It was like a scene out of Dante's *Inferno*. The men had their hands tied behind their backs with electrical cable, handcuffs, pieces of cord, and ties. They had clearly been tortured. The motive for the "Iguala massacre" was to find out by the most brutal methods what information they had given to the DEA—supposedly on instructions from Félix Gallardo—about the group led by Carrillo Fuentes and Aguilar Guajardo.

The PJF commander, Jorge Núñez, who had persuaded León Aragón to carry out this operation in Iguala, gave him $10 million to blame everything on El Güero Palma and get rid of any evidence that might point to the other traffickers.

El Chapo's accountant

When the investigating officers stopped Cristina Sánchez, the maid who was going into the house in Almendros Street, she explained that she had been hired a year and seven months earlier by a certain accountant, Miguel Ángel Segoviano Berbera, and before that she had worked for the previous owner, Abraham Cohen Bisu. Segoviano paid her wages, but didn't live there.

> At first I worked for various people, five to eight of them, who used to stay here. They had Sinaloa accents. My job was to keep the house clean, do the laundry, and cook for them. That was the first six months. Then nobody came for five months until February or March this year, 1992, when Mrs. Ana Salazar arrived, with her little boy, Arturo, the nanny Josefina Hernández, and a friend of the madam's called Claudia Meneses.
>
> Señora Ana had a holiday home in Cuernavaca, at number 1, Magnolia Street. I never went in, I always waited outside, but I noticed

several people coming and going with guns. One of them was Jerón-imo Gámez. Mr. Gámez was always armed, and he also visited the house in Bosques de las Lomas. Another one who sometimes came was El Chapo's friend, Martín Moreno, and his personal bodyguard Antonio Mendoza. That gentleman was sometimes accompanied by a pale, blond-haired man with light eyes who they all called Mr. Palma.[3]

After her detailed statement, Cristina was taken to the PJF offices at 4, López Street. Rodolfo León Aragón assigned her statement to the PGR's preliminary inquiries department, where two inquiries were opened, labeled AP4971/D/92 and AP4992/D/92.

As the days passed, the PJF officers were able to piece together the jigsaw puzzle. On September 21, public prosecutors issued a warrant to find and detain the accountant, Miguel Ángel Segoviano, who worked for Carrillo Fuentes, Guzmán, and Palma. The search for Segoviano led them to a Mexico City-registered company called Galce Constructora, in which Segoviano was a partner. The police officers went to the premises, but nobody there had seen Segoviano for days.

In his statement of June 9, 1993, El Chapo would deny knowing Segoviano. Luckily, when he amplified his testimony on September 7, 1995, at least some of his memory had come back: "Carlos is the brother of Miguel Ángel Segoviano. I met them at a disco in the Zona Rosa in Mexico City, though I don't recall which," Guzmán said, when the public prosecutors showed him a photo of Carlos Segoviano.

It seems that Miguel Ángel Segoviano's own memory was in better shape when, in California in 1996, he testified at the trial of Enrique Ávalos Barriga, one of El Chapo's men who had been caught building a 350-meter tunnel intended to ferry drugs, undocumented workers, and weapons across the border between Tijuana and San Diego. "Guzmán had an assembly line packing the coke in tins of jalapeños. The drugs were exported to the United States by rail. In exchange for the drugs, Guzmán took millions of dollars back to Mexico in suit-cases that were flown to Mexico City airport. They bribed federal agents to make sure there were no inspections," declared Segoviano, El Chapo's accountant who since 1993 had been a protected witness for the DEA.[4]

Without specifying names, El Chapo's accountant insisted that they had handed a lot of money to people working in the PGR.[5] This coincided with Guzmán's first statement on the plane from Tapachula to Toluca, the one that disappeared from the archives.

Segoviano said he had met El Chapo through his father, who owned a warehouse and a trucking company. He recounted in detail the criminal exploits of El Chapo and El Güero Palma, as well as their daily lives: parties, christenings, cock fights, even English classes. He also revealed how Galce Constructora had been contracted to refurbish properties occupied by the drug traffickers in the Desierto de los Leones district of Mexico City, as well as in Cuernavaca and Acapulco.

He evoked a house in Acapulco, in the luxury quarter of Punta Diamante, where SUVs with Jalisco and Sinaloa license plates regularly turned up. The passengers were men bedecked in gold chains, wearing denims and cowboy boots. The parties went on for days at a time. From the mansion, El Chapo Guzmán could see the two yachts named after his sons anchored in front of the exclusive Pichilingue beach in Puerto Marqués.[6]

Luis Echeverría's awkward neighbor

Continuing their enquiries, the federal police agents visited the home of Segoviano's mother—only to find that someone else had been living there for five years. They eventually tracked down the address of the accountant himself: 205 Santiago, in San Jerónimo in the south of Mexico City. To their surprise, the house where Segoviano lived was not only next door to the home of Mexico's ex-president, Luis Echeverría: it actually belonged to him. The person responsible for letting it had been his son, Luis Eduardo Echeverría Zuno.[7]

The federal police officers were getting worried about the dimensions this investigation was taking on, and about just how far the drug traffickers' web of complicity went. The trail was leading to the very highest levels of state power in Mexico. And of course they knew that searching the home of a former president could have serious consequences for their own careers.

When they asked Echeverría about the situation, he told them his son had employed a real-estate agent to rent the house out, and that they knew nothing about the tenant or his activities. This was difficult to believe, because the ex-president's house had a squad of soldiers in civilian clothes assigned to it from the Presidential Guard; they would hardly be indifferent to what was going on next door, the kind of people who came in and out, and, in this case, their blatant display of weapons. This was the second time that the Echeverría family had appeared to be linked to members of the Guadalajara Cartel: the first was when the former president's brother-in-law, Rubén Zuno Arce, had been acquitted of involvement in the murder of DEA Special Agent Enrique Camarena.

The Mexican police didn't find anyone in the house rented by the accountant. It seemed they had arrived too late. Neighbors said they hadn't seen the family for several days, although there had been no sign of them moving.

Attorney General Ignacio Morales gave the green light for the agents to proceed. A judge issued the appropriate warrant. The historic search of the house belonging to the former Mexican president took place on October 1, 1992.

Just as the investigators were about to begin their work, a couple of men arrived identifying themselves as Vicente Calero and Salvador Castro, employees of the accountant's. They had orders to load everything in the house into two trucks belonging to Arce Removals. Segoviano's wife, Rebeca Cañas, had paid them $10,000 for the job. They were due to meet her at 7 p.m., outside the cinemas in Plaza Universidad. Calero, intimidated by the policemen's questions, confessed that not long ago he had also hidden a car for Segoviano. The trap was set. When Cañas arrived at the mall, the PJF officers were waiting. They stopped and questioned her. "My husband doesn't live with me, because he has problems with the police. He's on the run because he works for various drug traffickers. He lends them his name so they can put their properties in his name, and he launders money for them. They pay him very well for these services," Segoviano's wife told them.

In one of the vehicles they searched at Segoviano's house the police found the payroll for El Chapo and his highly placed clients. It contained lists of expenses, wages, loans, and the names of people who had been paid various sums in pesos and dollars. "The accountant looked after all of El Chapo's financial dealings. He was very meticulous. He kept lists with the name of the official, the amount in dollars that he was paid, the equivalent in pesos, and what the money was for. Not all the money was paid in cash; some was in kind, for example a bottle of cognac, cars, houses, and suchlike," one of those involved in the operation told us for this book.

The inquiry revealed, among other things, that Rodolfo León Aragón, the head of the PJF, was involved with the cartel El Chapo belonged to, as was Commander Luis Solís, Director General of the Federal Highway Police—in whose house at number 5600 J, Avenida Desierto de los Leones, El Chapo Guzmán even lived for a while.[8] The narco-payroll also indicated the apparent complicity of Jorge Carrillo Olea, the country's anti-narcotics coordinator, of Jorge Núñez, operations director of the PJF, as well as other agents of the Federal Judicial Police and the public prosecutions service.

The Salinas project

The administration of Miguel de la Madrid (1982–88) saw the emergence of a tightly-knit team that would come to the fore in the following presidential term. It included Carlos Salinas de Gortari, the planning and budget secretary; Manuel Camacho Solís, first the under secretary for the same department, and then head of urban development and ecology; and Emilio Lozoya Thalmann, the under secretary of social security in the Secretariat of Labor. The group also included José Francisco Ruiz Massieu, Salinas's brother-in-law; General Juan Arévalo Gardoqui, the secretary of defense; Emilio Gamboa Patrón, the president's private secretary, and General Jorge Carrillo Olea. They were collectively known as Los Toficos, after a popular—and sticky—brand of toffee.

"The politicians wanted the drug money: they wanted it for themselves, for their private businesses, and for their political campaigns," remarked The Informer in relation to drug trafficking operations during Salinas's six-year term as president.

Executions of the "old guard" of drug traffickers began before the end of the de la Madrid government, opening the way to a new generation with a more modern mentality. No more "paying taxes": now you had to offer hefty bribes, enough to make the fortunes of politicians and businessmen overnight. At the same time there was a move to dismantle Mexico's intelligence agencies, which had never been very effective and were riddled with corruption, but which at least made it possible to see who was in bed with who.

The first notable execution of an older drug trafficker was that of Pablo Acosta, murdered in 1987 by Guillermo González Calderoni in Ojinaga, on the US border in Chihuahua state. His removal strengthened Carrillo Fuentes and allowed him to take control of the Chihuahua region and the jewel in the whole crown, Ciudad Juárez.

"There was no longer any idea of keeping the drug trade separate from politics. And drug trafficking was now carried out, not just by the drug barons, but by politicians and public officials as well," said *The Informant*. It was in this climate that the controversial Salinas administration got underway, cementing a new relationship with the recently revamped security and intelligence services.

As we've seen, Salinas's first attorney general was Enrique Álvarez del Castillo (1988–91), followed by Ignacio Morales Lechuga (1991–93), and Jorge Carpizo McGregor (1993–94). The post went to Diego Valadés Ríos in 1994, and finally to Humberto Benítez Treviño. Antonio Riviello Bazán was chief of defense, and Fernando Gutiér-rez Barrios, secretary of the interior. Carrillo Olea set up and headed the Investigation and Security Department (Disen, later Cisen). His number two here was Jorge Enrique Tello Peón, who spearheaded the recruitment of young college graduates to the new-look Mexican intelligence frameworks.

One of these new boys was an engineer named Genaro García Luna, whose stammer earned him the nickname Metralleta (Machine Gun). The most recent post of his long career was as secretary of public security under Felipe Calderón, until 2012. García Luna's dream of joining the PJF was shattered when he flunked the entrance exam. Instead he joined Cisen, becoming an expert wire-tapper—his great, but only, talent, according to his workmates. The duo of Guzmán Loera and García Luna encapsulates, perhaps, the most reprehensible overlap of the evils of the old system with those of the new, as each rose to prominence in their chosen branch of organized crime.

Concurrent reshuffles in the narco leadership were equally significant. Some bosses vanished and others arrived, more prepared to play by the new rules. Once Acosta was out of the picture, for example, he was replaced by Aguilar Guajardo, who shared power in Juárez with Carrillo Fuentes. However, on April 12, 1993, Aguilar met his end in sunny Cancún, enabling Carrillo Fuentes, El Señor de los Cielos, to tighten his grip as lord and master of the drugs business. Several others formed alliances with him, including El Azul Esparragoza; El Mayo Zambada; Arturo, Alfredo, and Héctor Beltrán Leyva, known as Los Tres Caballeros (the Three Knights), and the Valencia Cornelio brothers.

The death of Pablo Escobar a few months later, in December 1993, would strengthen Amado even more, because now he could strike a deal with the Cali Cartel, headed by the Rodríguez Orejuela brothers. Once he was linked to both the main Colombian cartels, El Señor de los Cielos began to move forty times more cocaine into the United States than Félix Gallardo had ever managed. The DEA now ranked Carrillo Fuentes as the most powerful Mexican drug trafficker.[9]

The murky dealings of the Vásquez brothers

On the trail of El Chapo's accountant, Miguel Ángel Segoviano, the investigators of the Special Affairs unit discovered that Segoviano not only had links with Galce Constructora: he was also on the board of Aero Abastos, a freight company whose two planes occupied a hangar at Mexico City's international airport, very close to the presidential hangar. On October 5, 1992, they showed up at the hangar with a warrant and were surprised to find the building leased to two notoriously shady brothers of Spanish origin, Mario and Olegario Vázquez Raña. They were still more surprised when a flight log on the premises revealed the registration there of other users, namely Amado Carrillo Fuentes, Joaquín El Chapo Guzmán, and Héctor El Güero Palma.[10]

The log book found in 1992 named one of Aero Abastos's regular pilots, Captain Carlos Enrique Messner, who in turn identified three regular passengers: a couple of PJF commanders, and an individual these referred to as "Mr. Guzmán." The Transport Secretariat officially confirmed, when asked by this investigation, that Messner was a pilot, although his license had expired by 2010. However, none of his documentation could be located.

The planes' cargos consisted of drugs, and copious quantities of cash. Those were the days when El Chapo, El Güero, and Amado were working with the Reynoso brothers, Jalisco men who had moved to the US where they ran a successful canning outfit under the trade names of Reynoso Brothers, Tía Anita, Grocery Depot, and Cotija Cheese. They were the receivers of the apparent cans of chilli peppers. According to a later report in El *Norte* newspaper (January 27, 1997), it was in their Learjets, based at the Vázquez Rañas hangar, that El Chapo took drugs to the Mexican border and brought money from the US.

The attorney general at the time, Ignacio Morales, told this investigation that after the discoveries in the hangar, Olegario Vázquez Raña himself assured him he had no idea who the other planes belonged to. Avoiding our query as to whether he believed this, Morales merely mentioned that the preliminary inquiry remained open until he himself left the PGR, in 1992. But any record of these inquiries, relating to the Iguala massacre and involving the Vázquez Raña hangar, has vanished as completely as El Chapo's first confession. Their original file numbers (AP 4971/D/92 and 4992/D/92) are now, thanks to the collusion of the PGR, ascribed to a street brawl and a homicide. Thus the case of the Vazquez Raña brothers and the narco-hangar was closed. As for the overzealous Special Affairs agents, their unit was dissolved shortly afterward, and its members were banished to minor duties in far-flung states.

Despite the persistent whiff of corruption surrounding the business empires of the Vázquez Raña brothers, and the allegations linking them to drug-money laundering, nothing has hindered their progress; any investigation of their financial and fiscal maneuvers, as in 1995–96, was soon shelved. Olegario Vázquez Raña has acquired airports, hotel chains, private hospitals, and media companies, and founded a bank. Both brothers are said, by sources close to Carrillo Fuentes's gang interviewed for this book, to have been involved with laundering money for El Señor de los Cielos, and to currently do the same for El Chapo Guzmán. They were protected by successive presidents; Olegario was especially friendly with Vicente Fox and his wife (sexennial 2000–06).

Raúl Salinas and the Juárez Cartel

Attorney General Ignacio Morales Lechuga had always had a rocky relationship with President Carlos Salinas.[11] It broke down completely when Morales agreed to receive the father of Roberto Hernández Nájar El Chiquilín, a middle-ranking member of the Juárez Cartel, well below Aguilar Guajardo or Carrillo Fuentes. In December 1990 El Chiquilín was in Juárez, at his house in the comfortable, cobble-stoned neighborhood of Rincones de San Marcos. The telephone rang and, in a moment of carelessness, he answered it himself. Fifteen minutes later, fifty rounds had been pumped into his body.

Two years after that execution, El Chiquilín's father stepped into Morales Lechuga's office. He wasn't asking for his son's assassins to be brought to justice. What he wanted was help in retrieving the $50 million his son had given to "the president's brother" to invest in an airline, which he was now refusing to give back to the family. Fifty million greenbacks were not so easily written off.

"One of the president's brothers? Which one?" Morales Lechuga asked.

"Raúl . . . Raúl Salinas de Gortari," came the nonchalant reply. The surprise on the attorney general's face was obvious.

Staff at the PGR quickly drew up a report of the accusations leveled by the drug trafficker's father against the president's brother. The attorney general then personally informed the president of the details of his meeting. Salinas glared at him, tugging his mustache. It was something he did when he was annoyed. That was when Morales knew he would shortly be out of a job. In January 1993 he was relieved of his duties.

For many years it has been widely thought that the Salinas family's connection with organized crime was exclusively with García Ábrego and the Gulf Cartel. This was based on the close relationship between Don Raúl Salinas Sr. and Juan Nepomuceno, the godfather who created García Abrego, or rather who pulled his strings. The frequent visits made by the president's father to Don Juan, and the chummy photographs of the two of them that hung on the walls of his restaurant, Piedras Negras, showed just how close they were.

In those days there was no open warfare between the drug cartels. By and large a civilized coexistence reigned, and everyone enjoyed official protection. This was especially true of the Gulf and Juárez cartels, which even collaborated on making shipments to the United States, according to The Informer. In fact, the ties of the Salinas family were not only with the Gulf Cartel; they also had links with Carrillo Fuentes, who had brought together the drug traffickers of both Sinaloa and Juárez.

The case of Guillermo González Calderoni, revisited

The Salinas family's PR man with the Gulf and Juárez cartels was the controversial commander of the Federal Judicial Police, Guillermo González Calderoni. He knew Carrillo Fuentes from his time serving in Chihuahua. The PJF chief protected both El Señor de los Cielos and García Ábrego.

Jorge Carrillo Olea remembers González Calderoni as "a likable guy, respectful, like all policemen. He seemed very young, he must have been about forty-two, but he looked younger. He was always very polite and easy to talk to, so he inspired confidence." Nonetheless, General Carrillo recalls, in 1990 Calderoni had been frozen out; there was simply "no place for him" in the PJF. That same year, Attorney General Morales Lechuga told Carrillo Olea that they had to open an office in Quintana Roo state, in south-east Mexico, and wondered whether they should approach González Calderoni for the job. Carrillo told him he thought that would be a "crass mistake," because everyone knew what Calderoni was like and this would be giving him "a virgin territory where the Gulf Cartel didn't exist."

When Tello Peón, the future Cisen recruiter, then director of planning, learned of Morales Lechuga's plans, he also opposed sending González Calderoni. They told the attorney general about the police commander's links with organized crime in Tamaulipas, about his relationship with García Ábrego, and also about the properties he had mysteriously acquired in McAllen and Monterrey. Carrillo Olea says that even León Aragón was afraid of trespassing on Calderoni's territory: "El Chino wouldn't go near it, if I mentioned it to him he'd just play deaf."

Three years later, after Calderoni had indeed gone to Cancún in Quintana Roo, and the anticipated trouble had begun, Jorge Carpizo (who had just replaced Morales as attorney general) said to Carrillo Olea: "My dear Jorge, only you will know my secret. We are going to arrest Calderoni. You go to Washington, speak to the director of the DEA and tell them not to get involved, otherwise it will be a dreadful sign of how they're protecting him."

"We knew perfectly well how the DEA worked," recalled Carrillo. "They hooked up with the drug traffickers to obtain information. What the Mexican state has never understood is that information is a commodity; those who possess it have power." So the general went to Washington and met the then director of the DEA and current Director of Immigration and Customs Enforcement (ICE), John T. Morton. Carrillo was taken aback to learn that González Calderoni had not only received US protection, he had even been given a green card.

In the US, Calderoni had told numerous stories about Raúl Salinas and his supposed links with Juan García Ábrego. In General Carrillo's opinion, "these were tricks. For the Americans, it was like gold dust; even though they knew it wasn't true, they could exploit it." Nonetheless, in an interview he gave to the newspaper *Reforma* on January 29, 1996, when he was no longer attorney general, Morales Lechuga said that he had obtained information linking Raúl Salinas to the Juárez Cartel, but as Carrillo Olea controlled the Judicial Police, he could do nothing about it.

During the first year of Ernesto Zedillo's presidency, in March 1995, Raúl Salinas was arrested on murder and corruption charges.

González Calderoni's secrets

Towards the end of the ten years he spent in exile in Texas, González Calderoni repeatedly threatened to return to Mexico and tell "everything" he knew.

In December 1996, in an interview with the *New York Times*, he well and truly destroyed the reputation of the former president's brother. The article was signed by Sam Dillon, who had won a Pulitzer Prize for other pieces on drug trafficking in Mexico. Dillon writes:

> In two days of interviews in McAllen, Tex., Mr. González said a major Mexican drug trafficker had told him of making large cash payments to Raúl Salinas de Gortari during the presidency of Mr. Salinas's brother, Carlos. Mr. González said he relayed these allegations to President Salinas in 1992 and to American officials a year later.[12]

In 1992, Carlos Salinas had already heard from Morales the accusations made against his brother by El Chiquilín's father. In his interview, Calderoni also claimed he had told various US officials of the drug trafficking corruption at the highest levels in Mexico.

But in spite of all the reports that Washington received about Raúl Salinas's alleged complicity with drug trafficking, "the Clinton Administration never expressed concern to the Mexican government about the reported activities of the president's brother; nor was an investigation requested," US officials told Dillon. The most anyone in the Clinton administration ever said was a brief insinuation during a meeting between President Salinas and US ambassador James Jones, after Mexico had asked for Calderoni's extradition. "González Calderoni has so much bad stuff on your administration that it could bring down your government," Jones warned the Mexican president, who "did not flinch," according to one US official who talked anonymously to Dillon. In fact, the US government did nothing. It was not the first time that Washington put its foreign policy interests ahead of combating the drug trade.

In October 2000, just after the National Action Party (PAN) led by Vicente Fox had for the first time won the presidential election, Guillermo González Calderoni continued to level accusations against Raúl Salinas from the United States. The Sinaloa Cartel was set to prevail during Fox's government, and Calderoni got a second chance.

Once the new administration had taken office, he made himself useful to the ambitious sons from an earlier marriage of first lady

Marta Sahagún, who were desperate for good business opportunities. Manuel Bribiesca Sahagún helped the former police commander to obtain, indirectly and using a front name, a major contract with Pemex to buy a much sought-after petroleum solvent, used for dry cleaning but also to adulterate gasoline and produce synthetic drugs.

González Calderoni received protection and began to collaborate with the DEA through his contact with Special Agent Héctor Berrellez, who years earlier had headed Operation Leyenda. In an interview with *Frontline*, Berrellez said Calderoni had asked for help:

> He wanted our assistance in hiding in the United States, as his life was in serious jeopardy. We had heard that there were plainclothes Mexican military officials in the L.A. area looking to assassinate him. And at that time, he reported to us that a major drug lord had actually been given the contract to assassinate two political opponents of Carlos Salinas de Gortari.
>
> He told me he was disgusted and frustrated because it not only involved just the drugs, it also involved other crimes, such as murder, and that shocked González Calderoni.[13]

Commander González Calderoni, the man who knew the sewers of the Mexican police system, also claimed that Amado Carrillo Fuentes was alive and well in the United States, even though he was supposed to have died in July 1997 as a result of botched cosmetic surgery.

On February 5, 2003, at 12:45 p.m., González Calderoni, now fifty-four years old, had his own appointment with death. As he left his lawyer's office at 6521 North 10th Street in the border city of McAllen, he was killed with a single shot. His troublesome stories would be heard no more.

CHAPTER SIX

The Lord of Puente Grande

Joaquín Guzmán Loera began to take off the brown uniform with the number 516 printed on the back of each garment. He removed his pants, his shirt, and his jacket, and threw them carelessly on the top bunk bed in cell 307 of Block 3 at Puente Grande—the penitentiary where he had spent the last five years and seven months. Usually El Chapo liked to keep his quarters neat and tidy, because at any time he might have a female visitor: Zulema Yulia, a co-detainee; Yves Eréndira, the prison cook who he had fallen in love with, or one of the prostitutes he liked so much.

On January 19, 2001, the drug baron's prison routine came to an end. Guzmán changed into black clothes. No one could see him in his cell. Behind the sheets he'd tied to the bars he had built his own private space, out of sight of the prison guards—who were always attentive to his wishes—or his fellow prisoners El Güero Palma and Arturo Martínez Herrera, El Texas. His stay hadn't been too bad after all, thanks to his pals, and his disdain for the rules.

El Chapo raised a plastic cup and took a swig of rum and cola. His final toast in Puente Grande was to himself, and drunk in the solitude that was his true nature. Everything was planned and ready well in advance. Each piece was in place. Nothing could go wrong.

Two months earlier, on the evening of November 21, 2000, the first warden of Almoloya prison and former head of the PJF, Juan Pablo de Tavira, had been shot four times in a university dining hall in Hidalgo. Two weeks after that, on December 3, in a manner reminiscent of the murder of de Tavira, a man entered a modest house in the Haciendas del Valle projects of Zapopan, in Jalisco state. Once in the living room he opened fire. Fifty-one-year-old Juan Castillo Alonso was mown down in front of his wife, son, and grandchildren. As in the earlier killing of the ex-warden of Almoloya, the gunman vanished without trace. Juan Castillo had been assistant warden of the maximum security prisons of Almoloya and Puente Grande, and was close to de Tavira.[1] In March 1999, when he left his job at Puente Grande, he was replaced by Dámaso López Núñez, who arrived with a whole team from Sinaloa.

The two crimes had to be connected. The corpses of the two men were trying to speak, but the authorities couldn't decipher the message. Both officials knew the high security prisons inside out. They knew exactly what could happen and what could not. That was the key to their deaths.

Before he was executed, de Tavira had confided to friends his concerns about levels of corruption at Puente Grande. He complained that the reforms he'd introduced had been thrown out overnight: "the filthy drug dealers run the prison." The rumors circulating in the corridors of the Secretariat of the Interior and the Human Rights Commission were bound to reach his ears, sooner or later. The event heralded by Castillo and de Tavira's deaths finally took place on January 19, 2001 at Puente Grande, hours after El Chapo Guzmán tossed his prison uniform onto the top bunk.

Hotel Puente Grande

From Corridor 1A in Block 3 you could see the cell number, 307, painted in blue on a white background. But the view into the cell was blocked by three beige sheets hung like curtains.[2] Curtains in a maximum security prison? Epifanio Salazar, the director general of forensic services, must have asked himself as he stood in the doorway to El Chapo's accommodation and examined the way the bars were covered. This was the height of impunity, as he saw further when he drew back the sheets to reveal a space measuring ten feet by thirteen, as snug and cozy as an egg—indeed, the walls were painted bright yellow. There was a pair of built-in concrete bunk beds, a concrete table with a bench, and another bed that didn't seem to belong. The floor was of polished cement, splashed in places with the same yellow paint used on the walls.

Outside the so-called high security prison, located at kilometer 17.5 of the Zapotlanejo freeway, the media were desperate for a story, for any kind of a lead. How could the drug baron have escaped from a prison that had been specifically designed to prevent this from happening?

The alarm had been raised a little more than twenty-four hours earlier, when the drug trafficker hadn't been found in his cell. The signs of El Chapo's last minutes there were still fresh. The first thing that Salazar examined was the bunks. On the bottom bed there was a peach-colored pillow with a white pillowcase waiting to be put on, a brown blanket with coffee-colored edging, two white sheets and a duvet. On the top bed El Chapo had left his shirt, pants, jacket, and some unbranded fawn shorts. There was also a large white towel hooked on the bunk's ladder, and that unforgettable khaki baseball cap with no logo that features so clearly in the prison photos of Guzmán that have been published hundreds of times in recent years.

On the bed there was also a fawn sweatshirt, on the lower part of which the number 516 had been scrawled in black marker pen; three pairs of white socks, two Hugo Boss t-shirts, size M, and three underpants of the same make and color. Beside the bunks were three shelves for the prisoner to keep his personal effects. They looked like the shelves in a grocery store. On the top shelf were packets of Ruffles potato chips, Lara cookies, and Canapinas crackers, Ricolino chocolate almonds, a bag of assorted sweets, some chocolate cereal, and two pieces of amaranth-seed candy wrapped in cellophane. Of course all these items would be forbidden under the prison rules, let alone by any nutritionist in their right mind. But Joaquín Guzmán's appetite was insatiable.

On the middle shelf stood some pink Hinds skin cream, a razor, and a packet of paper handkerchiefs. On the bottom shelf El Chapo had left an open bottle of Snoopy baby oil, a small blue jar of Nivea cream, a blue plastic tub of Gillette shaving cream, a Pro toothbrush, some white Hinds hand cream, a tube of Colgate toothpaste, and a bottle of Folicure shampoo, against premature hair loss. On one of the shelves stood a plastic cup containing the dregs of his last drink.

To the right of the small room was a washstand with a round basin where Guzmán had left two eroded bars of green soap. In the corner was a white toilet. On the table lay twelve school books, a dictionary, and the small Bible he frequently read. The only thing El Chapo had taken with him were his books on Mexican history and geography. The drug baron's sneaker collection was no longer in the cell, but the hundreds of statements made by prison employees say he had as many as twenty pairs of Reeboks and Nikes—a fortune in sports shoes.

El Güero and El Chapo, together again

El Chapo started his sentence with three years in the Almoloya de Juárez prison in the State of Mexico. Little is known of his daily life there. Juan Pablo de Tavira came to know him well. As warden, he had the job of admitting him on June 9, 1993. The following year, de Tavira left to become head of the PJF. On one occasion someone asked him which of the drug lords he'd had in the prison was the most dangerous. "El Chapo," he answered without hesitation, before adding: "Guzmán is a quiet, disciplined man who obeys all the rules without complaint. But when he looks at you, you can see the hatred in his eyes; he is a dangerous man."

On November 21, 1995, Guzmán succeeded in getting transferred to the Puente Grande facility, then under the direction of Leonardo Beltrán Santana. That day an official letter, reference number 12879/95, arrived at Almoloya from the General Directorate of Prevention and Rehabilitation—part of the Secretariat of the Interior—whose head was Luis Rivera de Montes de Oca. It requested the drug trafficker to be moved to another prison, according to the documents seen by the author. After a swift review of Guzmán's administrative file (0451/AJ/93), no reason was found not to transfer the dangerous inmate.

El Chapo was facing a string of lawsuits: for bribery, for felonies against public health—in the form of possession of cocaine and diazepam—for trafficking marijuana and cocaine, for unlawful assembly, and for homicide. By 1995 he had only been sentenced on one count, to seven years and nine months in prison, but there were four other cases pending. Such circumstances were no barrier to his being transferred in under twenty-four hours to Jalisco. On

November 22, 1995, at 1:55 a.m., Guzmán was handed over to prison staff from Puente Grande by officials from the PGR. El Chapo had taken an important step towards freedom.

At Puente Grande, Guzmán met up again with his old partner, El Güero Palma, who had been held there since June 27 of that year. Palma had won fame and power working for Amado Carrillo Fuentes since 1993, when the two of them had delivered up El Chapo. However, his luck had suddenly changed. On June 12, 1995, El Güero boarded a Learjet 36 in the company of two bodyguards, flying from Ciudad Obregón to Guadalajara. El Güero's plane crashed, but he survived. Everything seemed to be back under control until, on June 23, the military police burst into the house where El Güero was recovering. Someone must have betrayed him, revealing his whereabouts and the delicate state of his health. There was nowhere to run. Not even his pistol, with its butt encrusted with diamonds and emeralds in the shape of a palm tree—his symbol—was enough to bribe the soldiers. Far from us to suggest that they were incorruptible. But orders were orders: the implacable Amado Carrillo Fuentes had leaked the information about El Güero to his henchmen in the Mexican army.

The re-encounter between El Chapo and El Güero strengthened both of them. It's not known whether Palma ever had the guts to confess to El Chapo that he and Carrillo Fuentes had betrayed him by telling Fatty Coello that he was in Guatemala. But soon after, from behind the bars at Puente Grande, the two of them watched their boss, Amado, fall.

Gutiérrez Rebollo and Amado Carrillo's green army

Amado Carrillo Fuentes's reign began to come to an end on February 5, 1997, with the arrest of General Jesús Gutiérrez Rebollo, head of the National Anti-Drugs Institute (INCD) attached to the PGR, when Jorge Madrazo was attorney general. The general had been appointed to that post by President Ernesto Zedillo in 1996. The president was looking for someone with a broad knowledge of the drug cartels and tough enough to fight them. Gutiérrez came from a rural background in Morelos state, and his CV suggested he was the best man for the job. (He also came with a recommendation from the then defense secretary, Enrique Cervantes Aguirre.) Those who know him describe him as brusque, ignorant, and coarse.

In 1989, when Miguel Ángel Félix Gallardo's star was on the wane, Gutiérrez worked at the third regional command which included Sinaloa. Later, from 1989 to 1996, he was in charge of the Fifth Military Region in Jalisco, where he scored some hits: for example, the capture of El Güero Palma and the arrest of the Lupercio brothers, who were important members of the Arellano Félix cartel. Gutiérrez was effective because he was getting his information from Carrillo Fuentes and his gang.

Enrique González Rosas, from Jalisco, had three sons: Eduardo, Enrique, and René. In public they posed as growers and cattle ranchers. In fact, they were members of the Pacific organization based in Guadalajara. The family started out in the drug business in the 1980s, working for Félix Gallardo; when that kingpin fell, they went to work with Amado Carrillo Fuentes. In the 1990s, Eduardo González Quirarte was identified by the DEA as a key player in Carrillo Fuentes's organization, with links to the Army and various elements of the Mexican judicial system. El Flaco, as he was known, was responsible for sending cocaine shipments to the United States and seeing that the profits came back to Mexico.[3]

When General Gutiérrez was head of the Fifth Military Region, El Flaco González got in touch and asked if he could rent some land on the Zapopan military airbase. The family began by growing maize on Secretariat of Defense land, and ended up leaking information about drug shipments, or the whereabouts of Amado Carrillo's rivals.

González gradually tightened the net around Gutiérrez Rebollo. Several people acted as liaison: Sub Lieutenant Juan Galván Lara, the general's chauffeur; the teacher Gerardo López, son of Luis Octavio López, who was involved with El Chapo Guzmán, and Sub-Lieutenant Pedro Haro, another of Gutiérrez's drivers, who subsequently became El Flaco's bodyguard.

After Gutiérrez Rebollo was made anti-drug czar, he asked González, through Galván, for an apartment to house one of his lovers, Lilia. Galván arranged to meet González himself in Mexico

City, at number 1000, Calle de Tamarindo, in Bosques de las Lomas, to see if the accommodation was suitable. When he arrived at the door, he got a shock.

"Let me introduce you to Amado Carrillo Fuentes, the Lord of the Skies," El Flaco said to the general's chauffeur. "You should be proud to meet him. There are a lot of people who want to."

"How do you do? I'm Juan Galván," responded the shaken sub-lieutenant, as he held out his hand.

Amado looked nothing like the bearded hippie in the press photos of the time. He had a long face with an aquiline nose, green eyes, no facial hair, and no scars. He was almost as tall as El Flaco, but more sturdily built. What most stood out was the nervous tic in his left eye whenever he fixed his gaze on something.

"Amado Carrillo, pleased to meet you," he said, giving him a big embrace as if they were old friends. "Eduardo has told me all about you."

"My compadre knows about the general's request," explained Eduardo. "If you don't mind waiting, the keys will be here in a moment so you can see the apartment and then show it to the lady."

That day they showed the general's chauffeur a profusion of houses and apartments to choose from. Within weeks the general's lover was installed in an apartment belonging to Carrillo Fuentes in the residential district of Tecamachalco, State of Mexico. The head of the anti-drug institute himself lived there at the end of 1996, something that came up as the first piece of evidence against him, and the main justification for his arrest.

Once General Gutiérrez Rebollo was put on trial, his driver Galván turned protected witness for the PGR, and his account of the general's relations with El Flaco and El Señor de los Cielos was taken as absolute truth. In self-defense, Gutiérrez insisted the secretary of defense had full knowledge of all his movements, and the only reason he himself had been in contact with Eduardo González was to get information about the drug cartels. As proof, he said that on at least three occasions, at the end of 1996 and the beginning of 1997, González had attended meetings with Defense Secretary Enrique Cervantes Aguirre and a group of generals in the Sedena offices.[4]

Someone once said that in Mexico, politicians and public officials "are not punished for their felonies, but for their mistakes." It seems that General Gutiérrez's big mistake was to tell Secretary Cervantes that he possessed photos and recordings linking President Zedillo's family to the González Quirarte brothers. One of the president's cousins, León Zedillo, had worked for years in Zapopan at a food processing plant they owned, called Camichinez. The families were so close that when the president's first cousin got married in 1997, the wedding party was held at that same factory. The celebration was presided over by Rodolfo Zedillo, Ernesto Zedillo's father.[5] It was Don Rodolfo who made the speech congratulating the couple, in which he also paid tribute to the González brothers as "exemplary young entrepreneurs."

Gutiérrez Rebollo produced various pieces of evidence: a video of the wedding, and photographs of the party which showed President Zedillo's father and cousin with the González brothers. But when he told this story in the dock, it was ignored. Every time he started to talk about the links between other public officials and the Carrillo Fuentes cartel, the prosecutor shut him up, telling him he could only testify if it was to confess his own guilt.

Gutiérrez was accused by military prosecutors and the PGR of abuse of authority, corruption, offenses against public health, infringement of the Federal Law against Organized Crime, and illegal arms stockpiling. He was sentenced to more than seventy years in prison, and now resides in the Altiplano federal penitentiary. For three years we have used the federal freedom of information legislation to try to obtain from the PGR a copy of the initial investigation against General Gutiérrez. They refused. On the grounds of res judicata, in 2007 the Federal Freedom of Information Institute (IFAI) ordered the investigation to be produced; but the PGR appealed.

The Gutiérrez Rebollo case is one of the most important for understanding the degree of connivance between the Mexican authorities and the drug traffickers. Why are they so reluctant to make it public? In spite of everything, it has been possible to obtain some of the statements taken in the course of the general's trial. They contain names of state officials and military brass who have never been tried, or even investigated, for their apparent collusion with Carrillo Fuentes's organization. The list is a long one, and some on it were still in public service under Felipe Calderón.[6]

- Justo Ceja, former private secretary to Carlos Salinas de Gortari.
- Brigadier General Enrique Cervantes Aguirre, secretary of defense in the administration of Ernesto Zedillo.
- General Vinicio Santoyo, former commander of the Fifth Military Region—before Gutiérrez Rebollo—deceased in 1998.
- General Francisco Javier Velarde Quintero, regional coordinator in Colima of the organization of retired military officers, Alianza Nacional Revolucionaria, in 2006.
- General Luis Mucel Luna, Calderón's director of the Investigative and Preventive Police Training Center, in Chiapas.
- General Augusto Moisés García Ochoa, Calderón's administrative director at Sedena.

Rest in peace

On July 5, 1997, the Mexican media reported that at the age of forty-two, Amado Carrillo Fuentes, the all-powerful Señor de los Cielos, had died in the elite Santa Mónica clinic in Mexico City, after plastic surgery that went horribly wrong. El Chapo and El Güero had color TV in their respective cells, so no doubt they followed every detail of the news. The death happened on the night of July 4; next day, Carrillo Fuentes's body was taken to the García López funeral parlor in Colonia Juárez, before being conveyed to the San Martín funeral chapel in Culiacán, where it was confiscated by the PGR. All that starts comes to an end. No drug baron can hold sway forever, and The Lord of the Skies knew it all too well. After almost a decade at the top, Amado Carrillo had left the drug business.

It was a matter of "national pride" that Carrillo Fuentes stayed on the FBI's Fifteen Most Wanted list from October 1995 until June 2002. The Mexican trafficker was regarded as so important that the US agency devoted more hours and more staff to investigating him than they did to Osama bin Laden. The FBI saw Carrillo Fuentes's criminal gang as the main drug trafficking operation in Mexico.[7]

In the United States, the DEA confirmed the gangster's death two days after it was announced, without saying how they had reached this conclusion. In Mexico, the PGR still wasn't prepared to assert that the deceased really was the feared drug baron.[8] From the start there had been speculation over whether the corpse at the Santa Mónica hospital was that of Amado Carrillo Fuentes. Suspicions grew when the authorities were unable to confirm anything for five days.[9] We know that after it was confiscated, the body in question was taken to the Military Hospital. One senior officer involved in intelligence at the time has told us that he is convinced the body was not Amado's.[10]

Several of the drug trafficker's employees, who knew him well, were contacted in the course of the enquiries, said this source. Apparently, Amado had two unmistakable identifying marks: a dark, hairy mole on his back, and a prominent scar on one buttock. The corpse in the Santa Mónica didn't have either, according to our informant. After his "death," one of Carrillo Fuentes's girlfriends, La Quemada, disappeared off the face of the earth. And the employee who saw most of him, Jaime Olvera, who was apparently the one who said the body wasn't his, was executed in 1998 when he was a protected witness for the PGR—he'd talked too much. Carrillo Fuentes's people reckon that Amado pulled the trigger himself.

Mexican government sources say that after faking his death, El Señor de los Cielos moved to Cuba; and that when Fidel Castro distanced himself from Carlos Salinas, he asked Salinas to remove two people from the island: Justo Ceja, his former personal secretary, and Amado Carrillo Fuentes. In 1997, the *Washington Post* revealed a little-known fact about Carrillo's life that lends credibility to this version: the drug baron had a second family in Cuba. Very few people are in a position to know for sure whether Carrillo is alive or dead. What is certain is that he retired from organized crime. The leadership of his organization was taken over by his younger brother, Vicente Carrillo Fuentes, known as El Viceroy.

Those who know him say that Vicente Carrillo lacked his brother's talent for leadership. Although El Mayo Zambada and El Azul respected him for who he was, they doubted his ability to hold the Pacific organization together. Arturo Beltrán Leyva was loyal to him, and that bolstered his strength. But his sometimes quick-tempered and violent character made him less than the ideal candidate to replace El Señor de los Cielos. The only other possible successor was Juan José Álvarez, El Compadre, regarded as the financial brains behind the Juárez Cartel. But friends say he never sought the top job, because he respected Amado too much to challenge his brother. The throne remained vacant.

After Amado's death, the Pacific organization was formally split in two: the Sinaloa Cartel, led by El Mayo Zambada, and the Juárez Cartel, under the command of El Viceroy Carrillo. Although the two groups continued to work together in some areas of the business, their overall might had diminished.

Bankers to the Pacific organization

While exporting historic quantities of hard and soft drugs to the United States, Amado Carrillo Fuentes forged close links with the Mexican political, military, and business class, who gladly laundered the millions of dollars he gave them. Carrillo not only had connections with Raúl Salinas; his organization was also tied to bankers like Roberto Hernández, the erstwhile proprietor of Banamex. In 1997, the Yucatán newspaper *Por Esto!* published an article based on photographs allegedly taken on the beaches of Punta Pájaros, Hernández's private island off Felipe Carrillo Puerto, in Quintana Roo state. The article said this was where shipments of cocaine were stored, after arriving from Colombia on speedboats guarded by armed men.

In 1998, Banamex, along with other Mexican banks, was involved in the Operation Casablanca scandal. This was a secret, three-year investigation by the US Treasury Department, which discovered that a number of banks were laundering money for the Carrillo Fuentes organization and for the Cali Cartel. The Mexican government learnt of the findings just minutes before they were made public. Among the other banks involved in the laundering of more than $100 million were Bancomer and Banca Confía. Some lesser employees were sent to prison, but never the big fish, the board members.

The links between Mexican banks and the drug traffic were nothing new. Ever since the 1980s, the DEA had identified the head of the

Mexican Association of Bankers, Arcadio Valenzuela, as "the patriarch of money laundering," who carried out white-collar work for Félix Gallardo and Caro Quintero. The Mexican government never took any notice of the DEA's accusations. For his part, our Informer alleged that Banamex had also received money from Juan García Ábrego, and when the latter was arrested, Roberto Hernández kept his entire fortune for himself. "García Abrego's wife, who was very beautiful as it happens, even went to a Banamex board meeting to demand the money, but they never gave it back."

Between 1999 and 2001, Banamex faced fresh allegations of money laundering, which this time also involved the organization which Amado Carrillo had led. The DEA accused Banamex of carrying out financial operations with money from the drug trafficking proceeds of Mario Villanueva, the former governor of Quintana Roo (who was finally extradited to the US in May 2010). According to the US government, between 1993 and 1999 the former governor "provided federal and state support" to Amado Carrillo's cartel.[11] Thanks to the investigative work of the DEA office in Quintana Roo, in May 2001 the newly installed government of Vicente Fox had the narco-governor arrested.

In 2009, Vicente Carrillo Leyva, Amado's son, described his father's links not only with the Army and the police, but also with prominent businessmen. The thirty-two-year-old junior trafficker, nicknamed El Ingeniero, the Engineer, had been arrested on April 1 while jogging in a park near his home in Bosque de las Lomas.[12] The PGR accused him of playing a leading role in the cartel, and of concealing the proceeds of drug trafficking when the organization was taken over by his uncle, Vicente Carrillo Fuentes, El Viceroy.[13] When he made his statement in the cold cells of the Organized Crime Special Investigations Unit (SIEDO), Vicente Carrillo Leyva said that after his father's death in 1997, he, his mother, and his brothers went through his father's hidden safes in search of money, but they couldn't find more than $7 million. El Señor de los Cielos was so modern that the secret coves where the old Mexican and Colombian drug barons used to bury their money seemed old-fashioned and impractical to him.

Vicente Carrillo Leyva went cap in hand to his uncle, El Vice-roy, and to his father's other partners, to demand the family's share of the assets. But they laughed in his face. The new head of the cartel, his uncle, assured him that Amado didn't have any assets: all he had had been embargoed, or sold to pay off "debts," so there was nothing left.[14]

The cheated son continued doing the rounds. In 1998 he met with Juan Alberto Zepeda Méndez, his father's alleged front-man and private secretary to the businessman Jaime Camil Garza, a friend of President Zedillo. Vicente knew his father had bought $30 million worth of shares in the Grupo Financiero Anáhuac through Zepeda, and he wanted the money back.

Directly or indirectly, the Anuáhauc group represented the conflu-ence of the interests of two "presidential" families, the de la Madrids and the Zedillos. When Carrillo Leyva asked Zepeda to return his father's investment, he received the excuse that the National Banking Commission had the Anáhuac under surveillance, so unfortunately he couldn't oblige.[15]

Amado Carrillo had purchased his shares in the bank through the good offices of Jorge Bastida Gallardo (a business partner of Zedillo's brother Rodolfo), as well as those of Zepeda; a prominent PAN poli-tician, Diego Fernández de Cevallos, was also paid to help in the deal. Fernández never hid his connections with Bastida, nor the latter's with Carrillo Fuentes, but the shady coincidences don't stop there: the PAN politican was also the legal representative of both the clinic and the funeral parlor associated with Amado Carrillo's demise.

After his capture, Vicente Carrillo Leyva vengefully declared to the PGR that Zepeda was dealing in ephedrine with the Sinaloa Cartel. But no action was ever taken, even though the SIEDA had arrested narcotic traffickers and public servants on the other side—i.e., enemies of El Chapo Guzmán—for far less than that, over the last four years.

Military intelligence sources maintain that Jaime Camil Garza (Zepeda's former employer) often hung out with El Chapo in Acapulco. In a photograph of the pair on Guzmán's yacht, you can also spot an attractive young woman with a nose job: Maru Hernán-dez, at the time a close aide to President Fox's wife, Marta Sahagún, and known to reminisce anxiously about "suitcases" she collected from Acapulco. Camil himself cultivated successive presidents, first Zedillo, then Fox. Before the 2012 election, he became very friendly with Enrique Peña Nieto, the current head of state.

Helpful neighbors

In April 1999, El Chapo Guzmán and El Güero Palma got some news that would be to their advantage: Commander Dámaso López Nuñez was taking over as assistant warden of Puente Grande, while Leonardo Beltrán Santana was coming back as warden. And these changes were not fortuitous: it seems El Chapo had just the right contacts to make sure certain things happened. At the beginning of 1999, the secretary of the interior, Francisco Labastida Ochoa, a former governor of Sinaloa state and PRI candidate for the Mexican presidency in 2000, made a number of appointments within the Secretariat that were to transform the situation inside Puente Grande. Especially for El Chapo.

In February 1999, Enrique Pérez Rodríguez was appointed subdirector of prevention and rehabilitation at the Secretariat of the Interior; days later, his old friend Miguel Ángel Yunes Linares became the director; in May, Labastida made Jorge Enrique Tello Peón (Jorge Carrillo Olea's intelligence man under Salinas) their boss, as under secretary of the interior.

It was while Tello, Yunes, and Pérez were in charge of the country's federal jails that El Chapo Guzmán took control of the Puente Grande prison. All of them knew what was going on, but none of them did a thing to stop it.

The new assistant warden, Dámaso López Nuñez, had once been head of car theft investigations, but in reality he worked for the Sinaloa Cartel, more particularly for the group led by Ismael El Mayo Zambada. He had been sent by El Chapo's friends. He brought with him a close-knit staff who became known as Los Sinaloas: Commanders Carlos Ochoa, Jesús Vizcaíno, and Fidel García; corrections officers including José de Jesús Cortes, El Pollo, and José Barajas, El Veneno. All were corrupt from head to toe. From the moment of their arrival, prison discipline went out the window.

The appointments were made in a hurry. Labastida was due to resign at the end of May, so that he could compete in the internal selection process of the PRI's presidential candidate for July 2000. His successor as interior minister, Diódoro Carrasco, respected his choices. Indeed, in April 2000, Yunes was made Carrasco's chief adviser, while his friend Pérez was promoted to replace him as head of prevention and rehabilitation. Under Secretary Tello stayed on as Pérez's boss until one month after El Chapo's escape.

From 1987 to 1992, Francisco Labastida Ochoa had been governor of Sinaloa, the cradle of Mexico's foremost drug barons. At the end of his term, Labastida fled the country, allegedly because of threats from the traffickers; he became the Mexican ambassador to Portugal. Over time, Mexicans have learnt that the threats or attacks made against public officials by the narcos are not always because of their efforts to combat the drugs trade; they may also be because they have betrayed it.

Labastida's tenure as governor in Sinaloa, like that of almost all the state's governors, was tainted with suspicion.[16] In February 1998, the *Washington Times*'s fortnightly magazine, *Insight*, published an article based on a "CIA report" which claimed that Labastida had links with drug traffickers in his state when he was governor. According to the report, Labastida had denied taking bribes, but privately admitted to reaching "unspecified" agreements with the drug traffickers to overlook some of their activities. Labastida denied these accusations.

It is not often that information comes to light about how, when, and through whom, drug traffickers make contact with government figures. It is mentioned so often, but without hard evidence, that it almost seems a fantasy. The only convincing testimony relies upon some Deep Throat emerging from within one of the criminal gangs. As far as we know, nobody had made direct accusations against Labastida. Nobody, that is, until Pablo Tostado Félix appeared. He was reputed to be a close aide to another leader of the Sinaloa clan, Juan José Esparragoza, El Azul. In 2005 Tostado was behind bars in Irapuato, Guanajuato state, accused of kidnapping. Over fifty years old, of medium build, he was dark and bald, with a country accent. Two things were as important to him as the air he breathed, and he was never without them: his baseball cap and his black bullet-proof vest. In March and April, Tostado was visited by José Antonio Ortega Sánchez, a lawyer for the Guadalajara archdiocese.

They'd heard at the archdiocese that Pablo Tostado had valuable information about the Sinaloa Cartel, and Cardinal Sandoval wanted to know what it was as he sought to clarify the murder of his predecessor, Cardinal Posadas. They understood the prisoner's days were numbered, and they had to make the most of what time they had. Ortega had already tried to speak to El Chapo: he had been to see him in 1995, when he was still in Almoloya de Juárez. The lawyer had waited for hours, but when Guzmán eventually appeared in the small air-conditioned office, fresh from the shower, he refused to answer questions.

On April 13, 2004, there had been an attempt on Tostado as he was being transferred between jails. Eight members of the Sinaloa Cartel, wearing uniforms of the Federal Investigation Agency (AFI)—headed at the time by Genaro García Luna—tried to snatch him. At first the PGR thought it was a rescue attempt. But later one of the eight, Miguel Ángel Beltrán, admitted that the plan was to kill him, as the revenge of Juan José Esparragoza for having targeted Esparragoza's family.

Questioned by the cardinal's men, Tostado revealed a wealth of new information about the Pacific organization. It was a treasure chest of facts—one which the government had no interest in opening. In spite of the allegations Tostado had made as part of his defense during his trial, none of the authorities had ever come to press him on the names and whereabouts of important drug barons linked to El Chapo Guzmán.

Pablo Tostado told how he had started out in the drug trade as a driver for El Azul Esparragoza. Low-level employees in his position often worked for more than one boss at a time, and Tostado had also worked for El Chapo: "We all know each other. I've known El Chapo Guzmán since he was just plain 'Chapo' [Shorty]. He's a traitor; he'd double-cross his own mom if he could." He also said he'd known El Mayo Zambada ever since he was a "poor bastard and broke." Tostado's criminal career had been on the rise until he had the bad idea of kidnapping some of El Azul's relatives. That signed his death warrant.

Tostado explained that "drug trafficking without government protection and government without the support of the drug traffickers wouldn't be able to do anything, they couldn't work. Both have to work together. It was Raúl Salinas de Gortari who was in charge of drug trafficking during his brother's presidency; we all paid Raúl for the right to work a territory, and the go-between was El Chapo Guzmán. Nothing moved in Mexico until it was authorized by [Raúl]."

Every word he said confirmed the unremitting presence of the drugs trade in the very fabric of government: "The traffickers pay for the campaigns, and then get protection when their guys are elected." Labastida's presidential campaign in 2000, he asserted, was paid for by Manuel Beltrán Arredondo, Labastida's compadre and a well-known mining entrepreneur. But behind that public image, Beltrán was also a member of the Sinaloa Cartel, and one of El Chapo's closest friends and assistants. "When Juan S. Millán was governor [of Sinaloa, 1999–2004], Manuel Beltrán had a bunch of federal judicial policemen as his bodyguards," recalled Tostado. "So when El Chapo [from inside Puente Grande] wanted to get hold of him and couldn't, he'd get on the radio to the head of the Federal Judicial Police who in turn would contact Beltrán though his police bodyguards."

Pablo Tostado stated bluntly:

> Manuel Beltrán Arredondo is one of the leaders of the Sinaloa Cartel, even though you may not be too familiar with his name, because the United States hasn't put a price on his head yet. Because, as you know, in Mexico drug traffickers lose their protection as soon as the US puts a price on them.

On November 2, 2007, Beltrán Arredondo was gunned down in a Culiacán mall. But it was not until 2009 that the PGR officially recognized his involvement with the drug traffic.[17] It was Beltrán Arredondo, the friend of Secretary of the Interior Francisco Labastida, who sent Dámaso López as assistant warden to Puente Grande.

Pablo Tostado knew he would have to pay for his indiscretions. On April 22, 2009, he was acquitted in Irapuato, and transferred to Social Rehabilitation Center No. 1 in Durango, to face other outstanding charges—where, as it turned out, it was not the criminal justice system that caught up with him, but the drug traffickers he had betrayed. He only lasted thirteen days. On May 5, he was found hanged in his cell with a bullet in the heart.

Labastida achieved his goal of becoming the PRI's presidential candidate, running against Cuauhtémoc Cardenas of the left-wing PRD, and Vicente Fox of the right-wing PAN. But on July 2, 2000, for the first time in Mexico's history, an opposition party won the presidency. Fox won by a clear margin, and Labastida went to lick his wounds in Spain, in a fine house owned by Olegario Vázquez Raña, one of his biggest supporters.

Many people believed that the victory of the PAN under a businessman like Fox spelt the death of the old, corrupt regime, and the beginnings of a transition in Mexico. They thought this might shake the grip of the illegal organizations. Curiously, however, Labastida's defeat had no consequences in Puente Grande. El Chapo's power in the prison was not diminished; in fact it increased.

During the tenure of Felipe Calderón (2006–12), Labastida served as senator for the state of Sinaloa. He went about Mexico City without visible bodyguards, seemingly oblivious of the threats that made him scuttle off to Portugal some twenty years ago.

Lord and master

El Chapo Guzmán formed a common front with El Güero Palma and Arturo Martínez Herrera, El Texas—a member of the Gulf Cartel, and one of the monsters created by Guillermo González Calderoni. The staff at Puente Grande dubbed them Los Tres, the Three. With Commander Dámaso and Los Sinaloas behind them, they were invincible.

To secure their privileges, The Three set up an elaborate payroll. Monthly stipends were allocated according to the recipients' status and tasks: the guards and ordinary employees got 2,000 pesos (about $200 in 1999); the commanders usually got 3,000 ($300); a head of section was paid 10,000 pesos ($1,000). Commanders Ochoa and Vizcaíno, as members of Los Sinaloas, received 15,000 ($1,500) each, and the prison warden pocketed between 40,000 and 50,000 pesos

($4,000 to 5,000). A number of inmates were also allowed to work as servants and bodyguards.

Numerous prison employees became part of El Chapo Guzmán's retinue. For example, workers in the prison laundry washed not only the prisoners' clothes, but also those of Guzmán's relatives when they came to visit. None of this would have been news to the officials Labastida had appointed. Jorge Tello, Miguel Ángel Yunes, and Enrique Pérez not only received complaints from prison staff who objected to the corruption; they also witnessed it for themselves.

In January 2000, the retired Major Antonio Aguilar Garzón, with a long and notably honorable trajectory at Sedena, was sent to work under Yunes as supervisor of security and transfers. It wasn't as if he'd won the lottery—Aguilar would be responsible for overseeing the proper running of Mexico's federal prisons, and the transfer of low-risk inmates. After a few phone calls and interviews with former colleagues and honest officials in different penitentiaries, he soon became aware of the irregularities in the prison system.[18]

In Puente Grande, the situation looked especially dire. Under the management of Beltrán and López, it was chaos—anything was allowed in, cell phones, prostitutes, liquor, cocaine, and restaurant food, mostly for El Chapo, El Güero, and El Texas. According to the reports Aguilar was getting, things had gone askew after May 1999, when Tello, Yunes, and Pérez had been put in charge of the country's high security prisons.

"I verbally informed my boss, Mario Balderas Álvarez, about all these irregularities. He told me he'd already informed Enrique Pérez," Aguilar declared to public prosecutors on February 9, 2001. A few days after his conversation with Balderas, Aguilar decided to make quite sure that Pérez knew about the anomalies at Almoloya and Puente Grande:

> I mentioned it to Enrique Pérez, who responded that Miguel Yunes's administration had done more than any other to bring prison staff to account for irregularities. He said I should put my comments in writing, stating who had given me the information, which I didn't do, because I knew that nobody had been brought to account.

Antonio Aguilar wanted to make it clear that he had done everything he could, and that those who could have done more chose not to.

When Enrique Pérez was promoted to director general of prevention and rehabilitation in May 2000, replacing his friend Yunes, he decided to put Aguilar to the test. Maybe he wanted to prove to himself that everybody was just as rotten as he was. At the end of August, he asked Aguilar to investigate the irregularities at Puente Grande first-hand. Before traveling to Jalisco, Aguilar called some former colleagues who now worked at the prison. On arrival, his first action was to meet with them in Guadalajara; they confirmed that the prison was controlled by El Chapo, El Güero, and El Texas. Aguilar sent a report to Pérez the next day, with a precise enumeration of the irregularities detected in the prison.

On September 15, Pérez called Aguilar to tell him he'd received the report, and that they should make the inspection together. Pérez assured him that not a word of this plan would go beyond his office. That night, a team set off towards Puente Grande: Antonio Aguilar, a driver, and three more assistants, to be joined by Enrique Pérez who was flying in.

The "surprise operation" kicked off at 2 a.m. on September 16. Aguilar quickly got the impression something was not quite right. Everything seemed strangely tidy. His suspicions were confirmed by a prison employee, who told him they'd been expecting his visit since the day before. Aguilar kept hearing Pérez's voice: "Not a word goes beyond this office."

But you can't hide an elephant behind a tree for long. At 8 a.m., Miguel Ángel Cambrón, commander of the Third Custody and Security Company, arrived with the usual suitcase. López asked him to hand it over, at the request of Aguilar, who proceeded to open it. Inside was an assortment of vitamins, plus cash. Aguilar informed Pérez of the find, and he had Cambrón taken to the warden's meeting room. There the officials questioned him about the objects in his case. Cambrón replied quite naturally that the money was to pay off a debt of his brother's, which he was planning to do after leaving work.

Aguilar had him empty out his pockets. There were US dollar bills of different denominations, a coded list of prison "services" with an accompanying list of cash values, and a series of addresses in Guadalajara where the Puente Grande employees would go to receive their pay. Then they searched Cambrón's locker, where they found a veritable pharmacy: masculine and feminine Viagra, vaginal lubricants, pessaries, contraceptive pills and injections, remedies for vaginal infections, and more than forty tablets of synthetic drugs. When Cambrón had no alternative but to confess, more than one of those present had reason to hold their breath. The commander said he brought all these things into the prison at the request of inmate Jaime Valencia Fontes, El Chapo's main henchman, and that he, Cambrón, was the only person involved.

But there was to be no sanction for Cambrón.

Even so, on the drive back from the village of El Salto to Guadalajara airport, Aguilar summoned up the courage to say to Pérez:

"Surely we should transfer Joaquín Guzmán, Héctor Palma, and Arturo Martínez to different federal prisons, as a matter of urgency. What happened today confirms everything I was told about the irregularities in Puente Grande."

"I'll think it over," was the only answer he got.

No doubt about it. At Puente Grande there was only one lord and master, and that wasn't any of the officials there, it was El Chapo. If only Aguilar had understood this sooner.

The plumbers

Each of The Three had a private secretary, as though they were governors or legislators. El Chapo Guzmán's secretary was Jaime Valencia Fontes, whose cell was strategically located five doors down from the boss. Fontes managed El Chapo's diary, which was always full with people wanting to speak to him. He made sure the drug baron had everything he wanted: live music, food, alcohol, women, Christmas decorations for his cell. Fontes was also responsible for the performance and remuneration of the co-opted staff at Puente Grande.

Fontes would use three words to sum up his boss's character: "Solitary, serious, and calculating." For enforcement he relied on a group of miscreants inside and outside the jail that the guards came to know as Los Fontaneros, the Plumbers. "If you don't behave, Los

Fontaneros will sort you out," Valencia Fontes would say cheerily to anyone that refused to work for El Chapo.[19] Any correctional officer unwilling to allow intimate visits at all hours, or to let in drugs, sexual stimulants, or special food, would get beaten up by the Plumbers.

Assaults often occurred in their homes or when out with their families, not just inside the prison. One example of intimidation was the experience of Manuel García Sandoval, who on the night of October 15, 2000, was on dormitory duty in Module 3 when El Chapo summoned him to his cell.

"I want to go for a walk," the prisoner announced in peremptory tones.

"It's late, I'm on duty and I can't allow that outside of hours," replied the law-abiding guard.

"Fine, no problem," Guzmán said, with mock humility. "It's good to know there are guys like you in here. I appreciate the way you do your job."

Days later, García was brutally assaulted by three thugs. As Juan Pablo de Tavira used to say, "El Chapo never forgives or forgets."

Joaquín Guzmán was not stupid. At least he didn't act that way. Violence was not his preferred method for controlling the prison staff. That would provoke collective hostility, and nothing could be worse than having the guards united against him. His first step towards corruption was always seduction. He won the trust of the guards by making them think he was their friend.

In December 1999, Miguel Ángel Leal began to work as a guard in the prison. A colleague, Pedro Rubira, soon took him to see El Chapo.[20]

"Thank you so much for coming. We're not going to put any pressure on you here," El Chapo said to him in a friendly tone, as if he were welcoming him into a club. "Where are you from?"

"From Culiacán," answered Leal, disconcerted by the drug baron's attitude.

"What's your surname? What are your parents' names?"

Leal nervously muttered a few names.

"I think we must be related," El Chapo said with a genial smile, as if to put any fears to rest.

Leal continued with his work in peace. He thought the fact he hadn't asked for money might go down well with El Chapo Guzmán.

It was the beginning of a strange relationship. The guard once told him he was going on holiday, and Guzmán gave him a thousand pesos. On another occasion, Leal said his wife was very ill with a brain tumor, and El Chapo kindly offered to help him with expenses.

In February 2000, Leal was promoted to supervisor, with two or three other guards under his command. The more power he had, the more useful he could be to El Chapo. Then, at the end of that year, he took several weeks off work, only coming back in January 2001. On January 7, El Chapo sent for him. The guard went along with some trepidation; he'd heard that the drug baron didn't like his people in the prison to miss work, because he needed them on the spot.

"What's up? Where have you been?" Guzmán gently reproached him. Then he gave him a big New Year hug, completely throwing Leal because that was the last thing he had expected. "Come on in, have something to eat!"

"No, thanks, I already ate. I was off looking after my son. He's sick with a heart problem, and he's not getting the treatment he needs through the Social Security. I only came back to hand in my resignation. My sister-in-law has a mini-market in Culiacán, and she's asked me to run the business for her. She wants to go and live in Tijuana with her youngest daughter."

El Chapo listened as if Leal were telling him the most important thing in the world.

"In the store I'll earn twelve thousand a month."

"You don't need to quit," Guzmán told him, breaking his silence. "I'll help you with the expenses for your son. How much do you need in the meantime?"

"About fifteen hundred pesos."

"If your boy needs an operation, I'll pay for it," said the trafficker magnanimously, as if it were up to him to decide matters of life and death for everyone else. "They're going to let me out me soon and I need people like you, to provide security—legally, of course!"

Leal was tongue-tied. Whatever he said now, there'd be no backing down.

"I hope everything turns out well. Go see Fontes," said El Chapo, by way of dismissal.

Leal went to see the "private secretary."

"Mr. Guzmán sent me about some money," he said to Valencia Fontes, who went to consult his boss and came back with 2,000 pesos.

Tests showed that Leal's son suffered from an atrioventricular canal defect, plus dextrocardia. If he wasn't operated on within six months, the ventricle would not be able to develop normally. On January 13, 2001, with El Chapo aware of this diagnosis, Leal was summoned along with Valencia Fontes and another officer at 10 p.m.

"Soon I shall be free, I'm clean," Guzmán informed them. "My lawyers have been looking into it and I have no more charges in Mexico, the only case still pending is with the gringos . . ." El Chapo paused, as if saying to himself that this small inconvenience might not be so easy to overcome.

"When I get out I want to set up a security company that can work legally, so that when I travel they can watch out for me and carry weapons without any problems."

The drug baron was inviting them to be part of this new firm.

El Chapo's women

During his detention in Puente Grande, Joaquín Guzmán killed time with sex, alcohol, drugs, volleyball, and push-ups. Like El Güero Palma and El Texas Martínez, he was well supplied with Viagra and other prowess-enhancing products. Given their age, it seems unlikely they would have been prescribed Viagra, unless of course they suffered from some dysfunction. Witnesses among the prison commanders and warders say the obsession with sex was so great that The Three held competitions to see which of them could keep going the longest.[21]

Prostitutes came and went from Puente Grande unimpeded; prison managers referred to them pejoratively as "las sin rostro," the faceless females. They would be brought in official cars, wearing blonde wigs. Prisoners received them in the Psychological Care section, in the conjugal visits rooms, or in their own cells. If ever there was a shortage, they would get their hands on female staff or inmates, with the connivance of Warden Beltrán. These women didn't have much choice. Any who dared to resist the sexual demands of the drug barons had a rough time.

Of all the women El Chapo had at Puente Grande, three stood out: Zulema Yulia, Yves Eréndira, and Diana Patricia. Each learned what a hell it is to be the current favorite of a gangster. Their desperate stories blow apart the myth of the "love-struck drug baron."

On February 3, 2000, Zulema Yulia Hernández, a young woman just twenty-three years old, was incarcerated in Puente Grande for robbing a security van. Even if she deserved to go to jail, the maximum security facility seemed an excessive punishment. There was no separate wing for women. They were kept in the Observation and Classification Center, where they had neither the appropriate medical services, nor adequate physical protection in the midst of an overwhelmingly male population.

Guzmán's family visits coincided with those of Zulema. She quickly caught El Chapo's eye. The drug trafficker's obsessive nature and the young woman's vulnerable situation were to shape their dark tale.

Through one of the members of The Sinaloas, known as El Pollo, Guzmán sent "love" letters to Hernández. The almost illiterate drug trafficker dictated these letters to an unidentified scribe, who embellished them with a dose of drama. Of course, writing to a female inmate was one of the thousands of forbidden things that he was allowed to do quite freely. Very soon, Guzmán began to have intimate relations with the young delinquent barely more than half his age. Their meetings took place in the communications area, aided and abetted by female guards and by the prison management.

Hernández got pregnant, and all the indications are that the baby was El Chapo's.[22] She was not allowed conjugal visits, so there was no justification there. The authorities wanted to prevent a scandal over the abuse of women in this male prison. In September 2000, she was forced to have an abortion inside the jail, which was carried out by prison doctor Alfredo Valdés. Afterwards, she tried to commit suicide.[23] This level of degeneration, covered up by the Secretariat of the Interior, ruined Zulema's life. After a few months as El Chapo's favorite, the vulnerable young woman ended up as a piece of merchandise to be used at will by prison managers and inmates alike. On one occasion she was even sent to El Güero Palma's cell.[24] In May

2001, after Guzmán's escape, Hernández had another abortion, requiring a blood transfusion. She was seventeen weeks pregnant, so that baby too could have been El Chapo's.

Several guards recall that, by the end of her time in Puente Grande, Hernández had lost the last shreds of dignity. Through the bars of her cell she would open her legs and display herself. It was perhaps a last act of revolt. They had reduced her to this: a piece of meat available to the highest bidder. When Zulema Hernández finally left prison, her life became a ceaseless search for death. On December 17, 2008, her body was found in the trunk of an abandoned car in the municipality of Ecatepec, State of Mexico. The press reported that the woman's body had the letter Z inscribed with sharp objects and black paint on the buttocks, back, both breasts, and abdomen.

Diana Patricia was twenty-seven when she was transferred to the maximum security prison in Jalisco on July 10, 1999, accused of murder. There she discovered a whole new meaning for the word purgatory. When she got to Puente Grande, she was the only woman there. The place was already completely controlled by The Three. She was put in a narrow cell, outside which she could move in a radius of eight yards. Nothing could save her. Within a few months, Diana Patricia had begun to waste away of hunger and depression in the prison hospital. She lost fifty-five pounds in six months, and tried to hang herself.

At the end of 1999, Diana Patricia got some female company: Érika Zamora and Virginia Montes arrived at the prison, accused of belonging to an armed movement, the Revolutionary Popular Army (EPR).[25] In February 2000, Zulema Hernández arrived.

Diana Patricia was sexually abused by El Chapo and other inmates. A female warder made notes about the gang rape, listing the names of those who took part,[26] but nobody took any notice. Nobody, that is, except Guadalupe Morfín, president of the Jalisco Human Rights Commission, who in a private conversation described Joaquín Guzmán as an "animal." She also tried to speak out but was ignored. The Lord of Puente Grande was untouchable. The day before El Chapo's escape, Diana Patricia tried to commit suicide again.[27]

*   *   *

The story of Yves Eréndira Moreno, the cook at Puente Grande, is quite different. A thirty-eight-year-old single mother, she had worked at the prison since 1996 and had just been assigned to Block 3. She was older than Zulema Yulia and Diana Patricia, and not as pretty, but there was something about her that made El Chapo treat her like a person and not an object. While he was sleeping with Zulema, he began to woo Yves Eréndira. He saw her for the first time in May 2000, when she had had to bring him one of his special dishes. He'd liked her immediately, asked her name, and began to inquire about her and her family. In June 2000, Guzmán went over to the grille separating the kitchen from the dining room and tried to strike up a conversation.

"Hasn't your boss told you about me?"

"No," answered Moreno, as she collected the last dirty plates from the prisoners' meal. She felt alarmed by the drug baron's approach: the rot at Puente Grande had already reached the kitchen. Prisoners with money demanded sexual favors from the kitchen workers, who were made available to them with the agreement of the prison management.

"Oh dear!" exclaimed El Chapo at this curt response. "On the next shift we're going to have a little get-together, the other girls and us, and you're invited. What do you drink, whisky or tequila? I'd really like it if you could come. We'll pick you up here."

Moreno already knew from Silvestre de la Cruz, the kitchen manager, what the drug trafficker's intentions were. When the time for the party came, feeling under pressure from her boss and her colleagues, Moreno went back to the kitchenette in Block 3. El Chapo was waiting for her.

"Are you ready to come up?"

"I'm not coming up. I have kids, I live alone and I don't want gossip. Even if I come up just for a chat, people will say I've been with you."

"That's okay, in any case I offer you my friendship," he replied pleasantly.

The next day, when she arrived back at her modest home in Guadalajara, Moreno found a bunch of roses with no card. In the evening, El Chapo called her on her mobile—of course she'd never given him the number: "Did you like the roses I sent?" Yves couldn't mistake El Chapo's voice, with its strong Sinaloa accent. Thanks to the good offices of Francisco Camberos, El Chito (who also liaised between Guzmán and his wife Alejandrina), the bouquets continued to arrive.

By the end of July 2000, the conversations between the gangster and the cook were so easy and frequent that "the fortress fell," as traffickers say. Yves Eréndira agreed to have sexual relations with El Chapo in the same cubicle that the psychologists, doctors, and priests used to attend to the prisoners.

The drug trafficker liked to give a special touch to each of their encounters. He got his employees to fix the place up, perfuming the pillows and sheets, and converting the blankets into rugs. When the session ended, the drug baron would write amorous notes that Moreno would tear up and throw away, for fear that the guards would find them as she was searched on her way out of the prison.

On September 19, 2000, Moreno gave in her notice. But El Chapo wasn't going to let her go that easily. He offered to buy her a house and a car, and set her up with a business. She refused. Nonetheless, she couldn't resist his advances for long. On October 19 she went back to Puente Grande, to begin "conjugal" visits to Guzmán. Sometimes she was paid for it. On occasions she'd run into the warden, Leonardo Beltrán, who would greet her as if nothing had happened. She was never searched, or registered as a visitor. One day she said to El Chapo:

"I feel embarrassed about the warden. Today he saw me."

"Don't worry," said Guzmán, "Mr. Beltrán knows about everything. I give him forty or fifty thousand pesos a month, or sometimes I pay him in dollars. It's all right, I've got everything under control."

After sex, El Chapo could become very talkative. He told Moreno about the houses he owned in Las Lomas de Chapultepec, one of the most expensive parts of Mexico City. He went into some detail about his properties in luxury neighborhoods of Guadalajara. He said he had a fleet of aircraft and an island in the Caribbean, like an international jet setter. "When I get out, I'll take you for rides in my planes,

I've already got them ready," the drug trafficker promised. He told her that her enchiladas, which she'd send via El Chito, were just like those his mother made.

As time went by, El Chapo Guzmán came to trust Moreno. He told his lover how he had built a house and a chapel for his mother in his hometown of La Tuna. At the beginning of December 2000, he mentioned that El Güero Palma was his partner, and that he'd had problems with the Arellano Félix brothers for defending him: "They've already sent me a message here in the prison," said the drug baron. He didn't say how it had come or what it contained, but it obviously wasn't a message of peace and love. That same day El Chapo told her that all the prison guards "were already with him," which was hardly news to the cook. Later he calmly announced: "I'm very nearly out of here, it'll go just fine."

After a while, Yves Eréndira refused to go back to see him or to talk on the phone. On the morning of January 20, she learned that her lover had escaped from Puente Grande.

An escape foretold

On January 4, 2000, Guadalupe Morfín heard first-hand about the control exerted in Puente Grande by El Chapo. The information came from a prison official called Felipe Leaños, who came to her offices at the Jalisco Human Rights Commission to complain of harassment at work, after refusing to bow to pressures to go along with the corruption. She passed it on to the national human rights commissioner, José Luis Soberanes, and to the person ultimately responsible for the prison, Jorge Tello Peón.[28]

Antonio Aguilar, for his part, had not given up, even though his inspection had come to nothing. He continued to inform Enrique Pérez Rodríguez of the corruption in the prison. In mid 2000, Commander Dámaso López, the leader of The Sinaloas, resigned as assistant warden of Puente Grande; after all, it would be easier for him to control the prison staff from outside the jail. As director general of the prison service, Pérez came up with a perverse plan. He proposed the post to Aguilar, and Aguilar accepted the challenge.[29]

"I need a team to work with me. I'll also need your department's full support, because I know very well the irregularities at the prison and we have to put a stop to them," said Aguilar enthusiastically.

"Make your proposals and we'll consider them, but in the meantime, go there on your own," Pérez instructed him.

When Aguilar started at Puente Grande, his first step was to appoint Felipe Leaños, a man of proven honesty, as head of a company of prison guards, to give himself more control. Over the next three days, the new assistant warden brought the staff together in the prison auditorium to explain how he intended to work: "I know many colleagues in this room have things to hide. I invite them to leave the institution immediately. If irregularities continue, I will act strictly in accordance with the law," stated the commander. Aguilar made it clear that he was ready to do battle to take back the power the The Three exercised over the prison.

At the beginning of October, Commander Aguilar put his words into practice and began to apply sanctions to El Chapo Guzmán and El Güero Palma, if they were caught in infraction. One day he took away from Palma his television and his phone privileges—something unthinkable for drug traffickers who are used to having everything their own way.

After ordering the punishment, Aguilar called Beltrán to put him in the picture. "I see," was the warden's reserved reaction. Next Aguilar called Pérez, and left a voice mail recommending the dispersal of Joaquín Guzmán Loera, Héctor Palma Salazar, and Arturo Martínez Herrera to different high-security jails, without delay.

"How did Mr. Palma react?" asked Beltrán, when Aguilar phoned again to update him.

"He's pretty upset that we took his TV and suspended his phone calls."

"It's not a good idea to punish these people. It could create problems in the prison," cautioned Beltrán.

"We're just following the rules," said Aguilar.

"Well, I advise you to lift the punishment," insisted the warden.

"If you like, we can talk about it tomorrow, in your office."

Next day, Beltrán again asked Aguilar to rescind the penalty against El Chapo's partner.

"Tell me why I should do that," said the assistant warden angrily.

"Look, to avoid trouble in here, it would have been better not even to make a report," replied Beltrán flatly.

Thirty-six hours after ordering the sanctions against El Güero Palma, which were supposed to last five days, Antonio Aguilar revoked them. The following day, Warden Beltrán informed him, without further explanation, that they had to go to Mexico City for a meeting with Pérez.

In his office, the director general of prevention and rehabilitation, cynic that he was, congratulated the new assistant warden. Pérez told him to keep up the good work, but that for the time being they weren't going to make any changes to the staff. It was a contradictory message. How was Aguilar to keep up the good work, if the majority of the prison staff were in league with The Three and their group of drug traffickers? He reminded Pérez that several of the guards were the main organizers of the corruption, and he listed them by name. They were all members of The Sinaloas.

"Sir, Commanders Carlos Ochoa, Jesús Vizcaíno, Pablo Rodríguez, Francisco Herrera, and Héctor Guerra must urgently be dismissed."

"The federal police are already onto them. Any moment now they'll be arrested, don't worry about that," said Pérez.

"I have a list of another twenty-five prison staff who are also involved in irregularities," persisted Aguilar.

"We'll see about that later," answered Pérez, whose evasions revealed his complicity. "Ernesto Zedillo's government is coming to an end, and until it does we should keep things calm and problem-free at the prison. We'll make the changes after the new government comes in."

Antonio Aguilar was out of arguments. It was becoming obvious what role the head of the prison service was playing. Commander Aguilar decided to request a vacation, which was gladly granted.

When Aguilar went back to work, Warden Beltrán told him he could take some more days off if he wanted. He said that wouldn't be necessary. The following day, the warden told him that Enrique Pérez had received anonymous calls to his cell phone warning him to "back off or all hell will break loose," because people "are getting very edgy in Puente Grande."

"I'm getting similar calls myself," added Beltrán, with feigned concern. "I suggest you ease up a bit on the security measures. There's a lot of tension among the inmates."

"What kind of easing up are you suggesting?" asked Aguilar.

"The prisoners need to be able to communicate, to get better food and some sexual relief, and other little things like that which don't affect prison security."

"They already have a dietician working to improve the food. What's more, they have regularly scheduled phone calls and conjugal visits," answered Aguilar, who was nobody's fool.

"I'm not talking about those kinds of amenities," replied Beltrán testily.

"What *are* you talking about, then?"

"They need to communicate more than that," explained the warden, candidly now. "They need to make frequent calls, so we should allow them to have cell phones."

"That would be difficult, because the intelligence people at Cisen track all the calls," said the deputy governor, not realizing that for the last year the use of cell phones had been the norm at Puente Grande— with or without Cisen, and possibly thanks to them.

"The inmates can be given phones that Cisen cannot detect," said Beltrán with growing irritation, as he failed to get Aguilar to play along.

"And how might their meals be improved?" asked the assistant warden, continuing to challenge his boss.

"They can have restaurant food brought in," answered Beltrán, falling into the trap.

Antonio Aguilar went on asking questions until the warden gave himself away completely.

"What kind of sexual support do the inmates need?"

"Just the opportunity for a brief romp, that's all."

"What sort of a romp?"

"There are people in administration who see to all that."

"How else can we support them?"

"Well, we could give them a bit more freedom to move around outside their cells."

"Don't count on me," protested Aguilar. "I'm not putting my hand in the fire for you. If I'm in your way, get the Secretariat to transfer me and I'll clear out today."

"Commander, there is no point in sacrificing yourself for the institution. We are only here temporarily. If we don't do it, someone else will."

"My moral principles and values make it impossible for me to share your point of view," declared Aguilar, as he made to leave the warden's office.

"I only ask that this conversation remain between the two of us," said Beltrán.

"I promise."

In the corridor, Aguilar bumped into Carlos Arias, an intelligence officer from Cisen attached to the Puente Grande prison. The assistant warden couldn't resist telling him that Beltrán had just tried to co-opt him. Arias made a note and said he'd inform Mexico City. That night, the intelligence officer told him he'd filed his report.

The head of Cisen at the time was Alejandro Alegre Rabiela. A lawyer trained at the University of Anáhuac, he was a loyal follower of Jorge Carrillo Olea and Jorge Tello. He'd worked for them since 1986, when he was just twenty-two. Since then his career had progressed meteorically. In May 1999, Alegre was made director general of Cisen. However, it was Tello, who was then responsible for federal prisons, who really controlled the intelligence agency. Alegre stayed in the job until December 2000, and although El Chapo's escape was already widely anticipated in the prison he was responsible for watching, he never reported this. He now oversees the government's monetary affairs as a top official in the Bank of Mexico (as chief cashier, his signature appears on all new banknotes).

From at least 1999, Cisen maintained a permanent presence in Puente Grande. Arias had a team of sixteen officers. Several guards have said that the intelligence operatives were based near the legal affairs area on Level B, and were well aware of the irregularities.[30] Their presence in the prison was crucial: the Cisen staff were responsible for the information coming out of the control center. They would analyze the phone calls made by both inmates and staff; they would record conversations in the family and intimate visiting areas, and in other parts of the prison where they put microphones.[31] Genaro García Luna, later to be President Calderón's secretary of public security, was then general co-ordinator of Cisen and part of Tello's trusted inner circle. His tasks had to do with national security,[32] so the reports of what The Three were up to in Puente Grande must have gone through his office.

For Alejandro Alegre, these stories of corruption organized by El Chapo were hardly a novelty. He was familiar with the drug trafficker's capacity to corrupt; in fact he'd heard it from the horse's mouth. For he had been one of the passengers on the Boeing 727 that flew from Tapachula to Toluca on June 9, 1993, and he had heard the drug baron name all the serving and former PGR officials whom he had paid for protection.[33]

On the evening of October 10, 2000, Warden Leonardo Beltrán had a meeting with El Chapo, El Güero, and El Texas, on orders from Enrique Pérez. The purpose was to negotiate an end to the growing tensions. He who pays the piper, calls the tune. In the course of the meeting, Pérez tried urgently to call Beltrán. Commander Antonio Aguilar had no choice but to interrupt the meeting—to which he had not been invited—to tell his boss he was wanted on the phone. A few minutes later, Beltrán told him once again that they would be flying to Mexico City the next day.

On October 11, Aguilar walked into Pérez's office and immediately saw he was angry.

"What is the meaning of this note?" the director general shouted at Aguilar, who took the note and read it. "Why are you giving information to my enemies?"

The note contained the report that Cisen agent Carlos Arias had sent to his superiors. But how had it come into Perez's hands? It could only be through one of three people: García Luna, Alegre Rabiela, or Under Secretary Tello himself.

"Who are your bosses?" demanded Pérez reproachfully.

"I take orders from you. I don't have any other bosses."

"So why are you giving them information?"

"My breach of discipline was because Leonardo Beltrán handled the situation in a way that implied that you were aware of everything he was saying to me. That's why I asked the Cisen officer to intervene. I understand that you are upset and angry, and for what it's worth, I apologize," said Aguilar, trying to tread carefully. By this stage he had realized he was risking his life.

"I'll kill you!" growled Pérez.

"We'll kill each other!" Aguilar threw back.

Pérez ushered him into the meeting room where Beltrán was waiting, and showed the warden the Cisen note.

"Commander, this is an act of disloyalty," said Beltrán angrily.

"You have no right to call me disloyal," responded Aguilar. "You made a written pledge to uphold the Constitution and the laws deriving from it, and that commitment you have broken."

"This situation will force me to resign, which is just as well because I was already thinking of doing just that," said Pérez, rather puzzlingly, as he ended the meeting. Because of course he was not the one about to change jobs.

On October 13, Antonio Aguilar was given his marching orders. "You are to report for work by the 16th of this month to federal penitentiary number 1 at Almoloya." He didn't even have time to collect his belongings from Puente Grande. It was so important that he never set foot there again, they were sent by parcel service to Toluca for him. He was replaced by Luis Fernández, who had been working in maximum security prisons since October 1999, at the express invitation of Miguel Ángel Yunes.[34]

News of Aguilar's departure spread like wildfire through Puente Grande. The guards soon found out he had been sacked on El Chapo's express orders to Enrique Pérez.[35] When Aguilar travelled from Guadalajara to Mexico City for the last time, The Three remarked jokingly to the guards: "That one's not coming back."[36] And he didn't.

CHAPTER SEVEN

The Great Escape

Just before seven in the morning on January 20, 2001, when it was still not completely light, a heavily armed special commando unit of the Federal Preventive Police (PFP), wearing dark uniforms, hoods and helmets, along with sixty elite officers from the Federal Judicial Police (PJF) commanded by their new director, Genaro García Luna, took control of the Puente Grande maximum security prison and its immediate environs. They arrived six hours after the prison warden, Leonardo Beltrán Santana, had told his superiors that Joaquín Guzmán had disappeared. Mexico's first right-wing government, under President Vicente Fox, had only recently taken office.

The PFP seized all the entrances and exits, as well as the Control Center. Then they spread out through all areas of the prison, including the staff dormitories. Meanwhile, García Luna and his people began to search the perimeter for some trace of the missing drug baron.[1]

At 11 o'clock the night before, Warden Beltrán had been given the bad news by a shocked-looking Commander Jesús Vizcaíno: prisoner 516 was not in his cell, and couldn't be found anywhere.

At about 10:30 p.m., Vizcaíno and two other commanders had gone to the dormitory with orders finally to move Joaquín Guzmán to the Observation and Classification Center.[2] They went straight to Unit 3 and up to level 1-A. Stopping at the cell of Guzmán's "private secretary," Jaime Valencia Fontes, they asked for "Mr. Guzmán." There were torn photographs and other papers on the floor of the cell. Looking dejected and smelling of alcohol, Fontes smiled wryly and mumbled something that only one of the commanders, Juan José Pérez, understood. To judge by his expression, it wasn't good news.

They rushed to El Chapo's cell, whose bars were covered by a beige sheet. "Mr. Guzmán, get dressed and pack your things," said Pérez as he drew back the makeshift curtain. Nobody answered. He pulled back the blankets on the bed and realized that El Chapo wasn't there: instead he saw two pillows arranged to look like the outline of a body. As he ran down the corridor, distraught, the commander could only yell "He's busted out!"[3]

A government for change

President Fox's administration began on December 1, 2000. It rapidly transferred all of the Interior Secretariat's police powers to a newly created Secretariat of Public Security, with the exception of those of the intelligence service, Cisen. Although one of Fox's campaign promises had been to rid government institutions of the PRI—the party which had run Mexico for the last seventy years—he strangely left in post many of the officials responsible for public security and the prison service.

Fox made Santiago Creel, from his own party the PAN, Secretary of the Interior, while he appointed as head of Cisen someone with absolutely no experience in intelligence or investigations, Eduardo Medina Mora—whose only known merits were that he had been on the board of the leading private TV company, Televisa, and that his brother was a top executive at Banamex.[4]

Alejandro Gertz Manero was named secretary of public security. He had been in charge of public security for the Mexico City federal district during the PRD administration of Cuauhtémoc Cárdenas. Jorge Tello Peón stayed on in the new role of under secretary for public security, with the same responsibilities he had had when security was a department of the Interior. These included the management, operation and oversight of federal prisons. Enrique Pérez Rodríguez continued in his post as director general of prevention and rehabilitation, that is, as the immediate head of the prison service. And, of course, Leonardo Beltrán and Luis

Fernández kept their jobs as warden and assistant warden of Puente Grande.

"Intelligence" tasks inside the prison were the remit of the Federal Police. They were in charge of the surveillance cameras, microphones, and other means of monitoring what went on inside the jail.

When the new government came in, some staff at the prison thought things would change. One of them was the head of the prison's Control Center, Guillermo Paredes, in charge of the security cameras. For two years he had witnessed, through the lenses of those same cameras, all the anomalies taking place in the prison. At last, at the beginning of December 2000, he thought he saw an opportunity to stop the rot. Some of the Federal Police who came to replace the intelligence officers from Cisen, among them Armando Ruiz, asked him about the irregularities.[5] Paredes told them that El Chapo, El Güero and El Texas had complete control of the prison, and he also warned them that the situation was very delicate.

A few days later, Ruiz told Paredes that he'd already spoken to his boss, Humberto Martínez, director general of technical services at the PFP, about the corruption. What neither Ruiz nor Paredes knew was that Martínez was one of Tello's men. Without a doubt, the fact that many such officials continued to run the prison system allowed El Chapo Guzmán to enjoy that year's Christmas festivities in peace.

Instead of taking up the matter himself, Martínez sent word that if anyone wanted to make a complaint, they should raise it directly with him. Paredes was no fool. He decided to keep quiet.

The last Christmas in Puente Grande

It was after 10 p.m. on Christmas Eve. The silence hanging over the broad freeway between Guadalajara and Zapotlanejo was broken by the roar of a convoy of SUVs, speeding towards the prison. At the junction outside the gates, there was a temporary checkpoint where perimeter guard José Luis de la Cruz stood watch with a colleague. He'd had specific orders from the deputy director for perimeter security not to let anybody in; he'd even been told to park a pick-up truck transversally across the road, to block access to the jail.

When de la Cruz saw the vehicles approaching without switching off their lights, he nervously swiveled his weapon and chambered a round, thinking it could be an attack. The driver of the lead vehicle suddenly slammed on the brakes, opened the door and jumped out.[6] The guard's fears vanished when he recognized the smiling face of prison commander Juan Raúl Sarmiento. "It's us," he shouted jovially, like someone arriving at a party. De la Cruz moved his truck to let the line of vehicles pass. Joaquín Guzmán's relatives were traveling in some of them; Héctor Palma's in others. There was also a big group of mariachis and 500 liters of alcohol for the Xmas party.[7] The sumptuous feast arrived a few minutes later. It had been prepared at the last moment, but the menu was first-class: lobster bisque, filet mignon, roast potatoes, prawns, green salad, and trays of nibbles, with canned sauces to spice up the dishes after reheating.

El Chapo and El Güero had been planning the celebration for weeks. They sent for a brighter yellow paint than that usually used in the prison; the prison guards themselves worked overtime painting the walls. The corridors and cells of Units 3 and 4 were hung with Christmas lights and decorations. Guzman's outside gofer, El Chito, had been entrusted with organizing the banquet and buying the family gifts, as well as getting special food and drink for the ordinary prison inmates.

Corruption had been rife in Puente Grande for the last two years, but this cynical display of power was unprecedented. The party went on for three days. El Chapo and El Güero's relatives stayed until December 26, taking advantage of the authorities' extreme laxity. Although it had looked as if the change of government might mean the drug barons would lose their privileges, they were acting with extraordinary confidence. In fact, one of the guests at the party was the prison warden himself; Leonardo Beltrán never let go of the briefcase full of wads the traffickers had given him for Christmas.[8]

With the supposed democratic transition in Mexico, something had certainly shifted, deep down in the creaky structures of the old system; but they had not been weakened, quite the contrary. Now that the presidential office was occupied by Vicente Fox, a very special place in the pantheon of drug traffickers was being prepared for Joaquín Guzmán. The story of a second-rate gangster trussed like a pig in the back of an old pick-up truck was about to change profoundly, thanks to the Fox government.

January 2001

Once the festive season was over, El Chapo stepped up his recruitment drive—but now he wanted people to work for him not on the inside, but on the outside, as if he knew for certain that he would soon be free. Although there were a number of charges still pending against him, the only one he lost any sleep over was the request for extradition to the United States. Many drug traffickers hardly fear going to jail, because they know that in Mexico their power to corrupt means they can continue to do business from inside, via their relatives or associates. But in the US it's a different story; extradition is a sentence to living death.

Prison guard José Salvador Hernández Quiroz testified to several disturbing approaches made to him in those January days.[9] One evening a prison commander, Miguel Ángel Godínez, came up and said:

"Mr. Guzmán told me he was to be freed shortly, which means he's looking for men to work for him outside. I thought of you as a good candidate."

"No way," said Hernández tersely.

"Think about it," said El Chapo's ad hoc head hunter. "You'd get between twelve and fifteen thousand pesos a month. The work might be in Jalisco, Colima, Nayarit, or Sinaloa."

Days later, Jaime Flores Sánchez told him he'd also been invited, directly by Guzmán, and he was going to accept.

"Don't rush into anything," advised Hernández. "Your family's peace of mind is on the line when you get mixed up with such people. Godínez asked me, but I said no." He warned off another guard two days afterward; but he was beginning to feel cornered. Before long Miguel Ángel Leal confessed to him that he'd accepted, too, largely because El Chapo had again offered to pay all his son's medical expenses. Other people were bribed with cash up front.

Puente Grande was abuzz. In the corridors, restrooms, meeting rooms, and visiting areas—places where Cisen had powerful microphones planted—all the talk was of El Chapo's imminent escape. Yes, but how? And when? And who would be helping him?

Farewell

If the Jalisco human rights commissioner, Guadalupe Morfín, still had any doubts about the complicity of senior government figures in the corruption at Puente Grande, these were finally dispelled on January 19, 2001.

The resounding defeat suffered by Antonio Aguilar had left his right-hand man and Morfín's original informant, Felipe Leaños, perilously exposed. On November 7, 2000, he visited Morfín again, this time accompanied by a guard named Claudio Ríos, to denounce the beating of two colleagues by prison staff who were still on the "payroll." Leaños had reason to fear for his life.

On January 16, 2001, Lupita Morfín—as her friends call her—tried to get hold of the national human rights commissioner, José Luis Soberanes, to complain about his decision to shelve the complaint Leaños had made a year before. The only action taken had been for Enrique Pérez and Leonardo Beltrán to move Leaños to work in another part of the prison, where he was soon the target of renewed harassment. Soberanes wasn't in his office; Morfín left a message; the ombudsman never returned her call.

The next day, prison officers Claudio Ríos and Salvador Moreno requested an urgent meeting with Morfín. When she received them they were almost in tears. They couldn't take any more. On top of the pressure from The Three, The Plumbers, and The Sinaloas, now it seemed members of the human rights commission had become another co-opted group. The guards related how, on January 15, two representatives of the National Human Rights Commission (CNDH) had arrived in Guadalajara. They had called Claudio Ríos and asked him to come to their hotel with the other guards who had complained about the harassment and corruption in Puente Grande. "At last!" Ríos must have thought. But in fact the visitors had no intention of investigating the matter: they just wanted the guards to drop their complaint. The collusion between these representatives of Sober-anes's commission and the corrupt prison officials was clear. As a result, only three correctional officers maintained their complaint to the CNDH: Felipe Leaños, Claudio Ríos, and Salvador Moreno.

The following evening, January 16, all three were summoned to Warden Beltrán's office. One by one, they were called in by the CNDH representatives to confront the prison authorities they had denounced. The aim was obviously to intimidate them, and get them to retract their accusations about who really controlled the prison. The ever cynical director general of the prison service, Enrique Pérez, was also present at this illegal confrontation.

On the morning of January 17, in Morfín's office, what most worried Ríos and Moreno was that since then their fellow guard Leaños hadn't answered his phone. By now, they told her, the whole prison knew about their complaints, because the CHDH representatives had shown no discretion at all. Morfín immediately called the secretary of public security, Alejandro Gertz. He wasn't there, so she left a message: they needed to take immediate action to ensure the whistle-blowers' safety. She also phoned Soberanes again, to no avail. She left another message.

Given the seriousness of the situation, on January 18 Morfín called the secretary of the Interior, Santiago Creel. She couldn't get through to him, either. Later she did manage to speak to the special ambassador for human rights and democracy at the Secretariat for Foreign Affairs, Marieclaire Acosta, who suggested she talk to the president's national security adviser, Adolfo Aguilar Zínser—the only one who responded at all.

On the morning of January 19, under secretary Jorge Tello phoned Morfín, to say that he was in Guadalajara to investigate the irregularities at the federal jail. Two years after he was first fully apprised of the abuse and corruption, Tello had developed a plan, and he would use Lupita Morfín's complaint to help him carry it out.

"I'm now number two at public security, and Secretary Gertz has sent me to investigate what you told him [on voice mail]. Can we get together?"

"Yes," she answered immediately.

"I'm on my way to the prison," said Tello.

"I think you'd better come back and speak to me first," cautioned Morfín.

"I'm already at El Salto."

"Never mind, just turn around."

Morfín then heard Tello ask someone about directions.

"Excuse me?" said Morfín, thinking he was talking to her.

"No, I'm asking the prison warden, who's right here with me."

"You mean you're coming here with Leonardo Beltrán?" asked Morfín, surprised and outraged.

"Yes, but relax, he won't come in, he'll wait outside."

"You are putting my safety at risk, I have nothing to tell you, and I won't see you!" shouted Morfín, and hung up.

Guadalupe Morfín couldn't understand what was happening. She found it hard to credit that everything Leonardo Beltrán had done over the past two years at Puente Grande had been with the clear knowledge and approval, not only of Enrique Pérez, but also of Jorge Tello, the overall boss of both of them. She tried to contact the secretary, Alejandro Gertz, to express her surprise at the way his team were behaving. It seemed obvious to her that Tello should not go to her office with Beltrán. It would immediately give her away as a source of information, and further endanger the guards who had placed their trust in her.

That day was unfolding strangely at Puente Grande. From very early, the staff who monitored the video cameras were diverted from their duties and given cleaning chores outside the Control Center.[10] The door to the corridor that led to El Chapo's cell was covered with a sheet of plywood, at the top of which were small openings so you could see out. It was the first time in five years that the drug baron had taken such a liberty.[11] The plywood was removed at 11 a.m. by one of Guzmán's goons, and put back an hour later, remaining there until the evening.

El Chapo had a busy day ahead of him. First he played a game of volleyball, his favourite sport. After that he began to receive visits in his cell, almost non-stop, one after another, well into the afternoon. The first audience was at 11:15 with El Güero Palma and El Texas. It lasted twenty minutes. At midday, El Chapo spent fifteen minutes with Commander Pérez Díaz, who he saw twice again in the course of the day. He also had two brief meetings with Commander Navarro, of the perimeter guard. Other visitors included commanders Vizcaíno and Ochoa, and even the prison doctor, Alfredo Valdez, the same one who had carried out a forced abortion on Zulema Hernández. There were so many people who wanted to say goodbye that at 2 p.m. Guzmán didn't go to the canteen for lunch: the food on tray number 516 remained untouched.[12]

Jorge Tello arrived at Puente Grande after midday, on a lightning visit to the maximum security prison which he was ultimately responsible for. With him were the head of the prison service, Enrique Pérez, and two top Federal Police officials, Humberto Martínez and Nicolás Suárez. As soon as Tello arrived, Valencia Fontes—as if reminding his boss of an appointment—handed El Chapo a card with the names of all the visitors written on it.[13] El Chapo was breathing calmly; he seemed quite unruffled.

During his visit, Tello dropped into the Control Center, where everything that went on in the prison was supposedly filmed. As he left that room packed with TV monitors, the under secretary was overheard to murmur something strange: "Today they are not leaving the prison."[14]

Ostensibly, Tello had come to investigate the accusations of corruption made by the guards. However, the under secretary didn't even bother to meet them in the total of forty-one minutes he spent at the prison.[15] The only thing he did was order that El Chapo, El Güero and El Texas should be moved to the prison's Observation Center. Before he left, Tello had a brief meeting with Pérez, Suárez, Martínez, and the prison warden, Beltrán. In spite of the allegations of corruption in the prison, they agreed to put off until the following week an examination of technical issues at the Control Center and possible changes in personnel. This gave Joaquín Guzmán a window for leaving the prison in the following hours.

No, Tello had not come to look into irregularities, but to coordinate a quite different plan. In 1993, from his office in the Secretariat of Defense, he had helped to lock up El Chapo Guzmán. Now, eight years later, he was going to unlock the door. Immediately after he left, fifteen people from internal security were seen inside the staff dormitory—wearing not their regulation blue uniforms, but the black ones used by external, perimeter security; while those who really were from external security were also deployed inside the prison, still in their black kit.[16] The same color as the clothes that El Chapo put on before leaving the prison. At 4 p.m., four Federal Police personnel were seen on the roof of the prison clinic and communications area.[17] Something was afoot.

Meanwhile, El Chito Camberos was engaged in his last outside job for El Chapo. He called his friends José de Jesús Briseño and Ramón Muñoz, asking them to drive him to Plaza del Sol, a Guadalajara mall, in the gray Golf he'd recently bought on Guzmán's orders.[18] El Chito, clutching a small valise, seemed unusually nervous and taciturn; all he said was he had to collect some air tickets to the capital, plus a car from El Chapo's son César, a business administration student. At around 4 p.m. they arrived at the mall and parked outside a pizza house. Before long they saw a grey Cutlass approach.

"There's César, in the armored car. Keep your phone turned on, and if you don't hear from me, leave the Golf in my mom's garage or in yours," said El Chito to Briseño, as he got out and went over to talk to his boss's eldest, a stocky young man with streaked hair and dark glasses. Then El Chito drove off, reaching Puente Grande around 7 p.m.—the time when Guzmán went to bid farewell to his old accomplice and compadre, Héctor Palma, in the latter's cell. They conferred for barely five minutes, before strolling together down the corridor to the exit of Unit 4. "Take care, compadrito," Palma said.[19] They would not see each other again.

El Chapo did not escape in a laundry cart

About half an hour later, at 7:30 p.m., Guzmán was seen on Level C of Unit 3, talking to fellow inmates Valencia Fontes and Vázquez Méndez and two guards, Antonio Díaz and Victor Godoy. El Chito, was also there. A few laundry carts stood nearby. El Chapo asked his fixer to put blankets and food in one cart, and more blankets and some religious paintings done by a fellow prisoner in another. Then El Chito and Godoy began pushing them towards the kitchen area. A third cart was pushed by Valencia Fontes, El Chapo's "private secretary."[20]

At 8 o'clock, El Chito pushed one of the carts out of Unit 3 and apparently passed security checkpoints V7, V6, V4, V2, and V1 until he got to the vehicle checkpoint. The guards who saw him pass later declared to public prosecutors that the cart he was pushing must have been pretty heavy, because of the effort he was making, but they never said that he looked nervous or in a hurry.[21] At 8:15, guard Miguel Ángel Leal Amador waved El Chito out through the main gate, trundling his laundry cart covered in blankets. The checkpoints at Puente Grande have sophisticated heat and movement sensors, capable of detecting a living creature the size of a cat. If the cart had indeed been carrying Joaquín Guzmán, the alarms would necessarily have gone off.[22]

It was quite common, albeit against the rules, for The Three's "trash" to be taken out of the prison in a laundry cart whenever an inspection was due. Usually these were things they weren't allowed to have, like microwave ovens, clothes, telephones and so on. The items were then handed to intermediaries sent by the prisoners.[23]

In the staff car park, El Chito abandoned the laundry cart once he had passed the wire fencing.[24] He had taken El Chapo's household items, but not the man himself. At 8:40, the guard in charge of the prison's mail, Jesús Cortés Ortiz, was ordered to bring back the laundry cart that had been left out by the guard post. There were only a few dirty blankets inside.[25]

Joaquín El Chapo Guzmán did not leave Puente Grande with El Chito. Nor did he leave in a laundry cart. Guzmán was seen inside the prison after his fixer had driven off. This is clear from the hundreds of written witness statements contained in Case 16/2001-III, dealing with the escape.[26] In these legal proceedings, the Attorney General's Office (PGR) under the Fox government states that El Chito left the Puente Grande car park at 8:40 p.m., and that El Chapo left with him, thanks to the supposed trick with the laundry cart. However, the PGR also asserts that El Chapo escaped from the prison at 9:30.[27] Clearly, both things cannot be true.

What really happened that night is that at 9:30 p.m., El Chapo, Valencia Fontes, and Vázquez Muñoz walked down the corridor on level 1B. Vázquez was carrying a mattress folded in half, and a white sheet like those on prisoners' beds. The guard Antonio Díaz was intrigued by their behaviour, and discreetly followed them. All three entered the medical cubicle where Dr Velázquez usually saw patients; access to this area, next to the prison uniform storeroom and close to the exit, was prohibited for inmates.[28] They left the third laundry cart outside the door.

A few seconds later, Valencia and Vázquez came out again; Guzmán was not with them. Díaz slipped into the security cabin and from there observed how El Chapo's two companions stood guard outside the medical area, as if to prevent anyone from entering. When he left the cabin at the end of his shift, at 9:55 p.m., they were still there. At almost the same time, Commander Vizcaíno and his two companions were heading to dormitory A to carry out their orders to move El Chapo Guzmán to the Observation Center. He was not in his cell, and nobody thought of looking for him in the medical area.

Maximum alert

At 10:30 hours, Vizcaíno knocked on the door of Warden Beltrán's office.

"Joaquín Guzmán is not in his cell," said the commander, clearly agitated.

"Mobilize all of the staff, including those on breaks. They're to make a thorough search of all parts of Unit 3," ordered Beltrán calmly. He didn't seem surprised by the news.

Then Beltrán himself went over to the Control Center, supposedly to direct the operation and keep abreast of developments. But he never set off the jailbreak alarm.[29]

It was not until after 1 a.m. on January 20 that Beltrán called Enrique Pérez Rodríguez, the head of the prison service, to tell him the drug baron had disappeared. Pérez told him to keep searching, but they found nothing. At 2 a.m. Beltrán informed the Federal Police in Jalisco what was happening. Twenty minutes later he called the regional military command, and then the local PGR office.[30] At the same time commanders Pérez and Vizcaíno gathered all the correctional officers together inside the prison.[31]

Beltrán phoned his chief again at about 3 a.m. to tell him El Chapo still hadn't been found. It was only then that Pérez Rodríguez attempted to inform his own superior, Under Secretary Tello Peón. He dialed his cell, his office, his home, without success. Eventually he got hold of him on his wife's phone. Tello merely responded that he would inform the secretary of public security, Alejandro Gertz, and get back to him in half an hour. At this, Pérez told Beltrán also to call back in half an hour. Thirty minutes later the prison warden complied, reporting that El Chapo still hadn't appeared and that he'd informed all the relevant authorities of this fact. Precious time was passing, and nobody was doing anything.

Under Secretary Jorge Tello took no initiative; he was acting as if he didn't care, or maybe as if he was waiting for something. At 4 a.m. the head of the prison service called him again. This time Tello instructed Pérez to meet him at the PJF hangar at Mexico City airport in an hour and a half, so they could travel to Puente Grande. At the airport, Tello, Pérez, Nicolás Suárez, Humberto Martínez, Octavio Campos, and two other men from the Federal Preventive Police (PFP) whose names are not recorded, boarded a plane belonging to the PFP.

Tello arrived at the prison at 7 a.m. on January 20. The story had begun to be reported on radio and TV, and President Fox was soon informed by his spokesperson, Marta Sahagún. A few minutes later, Secretary of Public Security Alejandro Gertz filled them in further, telling the president that according to Tello, Guzmán had escaped in a laundry cart through the garbage area. However, presidential advisers familiar with the high-security prison systems told Fox that this was impossible, because of the sensors.

Gertz gave orders for the Federal Police to take over perimeter security at Puente Grande. Meanwhile Attorney General Rafael Macedo de la Concha had sent the new head of the PJF, Genaro García Luna, and the director of UEDO (the government's specialized organized crime unit), José Larrieta, to Jalisco, along with two elite detachments to begin hunting for Guzmán between Jalisco state and the northern border. In a press conference that same day, Tello Peón explained that initial investigations showed that the fugitive "must have had help from prison administrators, which represents a betrayal of the institution. This is a criminal conspiracy," he charged cynically, in spite of all that he had done himself to aid the drug baron's flight.

"There are clear indications of who may have had a hand in springing the leader of the Sinaloa Cartel," he added.[32] Obviously, he didn't include himself on the list.

That same day the warden of Puente Grande, Leonardo Beltrán, and thirty-three prison officers who were on duty at the time, were placed under provisional arrest on suspicion of abetting the drug baron's escape. Jaime Fernández López was appointed acting warden. All the tapes of Tello's visit to the jail, right up to the operation on January 20, were wiped.[33] However, in spite of the obstacles, as the sworn statements piled up, the truth began to emerge.

At 11 a.m on February 9, 2001, Commander Antonio Aguilar Garzón made a statement to the UEDO public prosecutors about what he had witnessed at Puente Grande: it was a tale of complicity, corruption, and concealment, from Under Secretary of Public Security Tello on down, since early 1999. The web of deceit involved Miguel Ángel Yunes, head of the prison service from April 1999 to April 2000, his deputy and successor Enrique Pérez, and the warden of Puente Grande, Leonardo Beltrán. Aguilar also told how he had been relieved of his post at the prison after revealing how it was controlled by El Chapo Guzmán and his friends.

Right from January 20, Guadalupe Morfín, the Jalisco human rights commissioner, had bravely offered to give testimony. "I wish to denounce acts which may constitute a crime," her statement began. Morfín related how the the national human rights commission headed by José Luis Soberanes had tried to shelve the complaints of corruption and harassment of employees at Puente Grande. She not only confirmed that Enrique Pérez and Leonardo Beltrán were aware of the irregularities; she also denounced the strange behavior of Jorge Tello when it came to investigating the abuses in the jail. On February 2, Morfín presented a series of documents proving her points. However, neither her accusations nor her documentation had any effect. The investigations were exclusively targeted at the corruption lower down, that of Warden Beltrán and the prison guards who were complicit; there was no probe into those responsible for the corruption at the top, those with the power to prevent or permit El Chapo's escape. Thus the investigations by the PGR and the PJF quickly turned into a farce. One explanation is that the new head of the PJF, Genaro García Luna, was one of Tello's most loyal subordinates, who had worked with him since 1989.

García Luna's servile nature and personal loyalty to his bosses, rather than to any institution, made him just the right man to lead the investigation into Guzmán's escape. He put one of his own most faithful subordinates in charge of the enquiries; Edgar Millán was so obliging that he never produced a report into what really happened at Puente Grande. For the best part of a month, Jorge Tello and Enrique Pérez could sleep in peace. Nobody troubled them and nobody questioned them. They were part of the group doing the investigating, not that being investigated. It was only after Antonio Aguilar appeared before public prosecutors that they were called on to testify. Still, it was only a formality; they appeared as witnesses, not as suspects.

Enrique Pérez Rodríguez made his statement on February 11, 2001. Speaking of the visit to Puente Grande on January 19, 2001, Pérez said that the prison warden "never mentioned any signs, suspicions, or rumors of a possible prisoner escape, so we had no prior knowledge of what would happen." It was a barefaced lie. He was never confronted with the five clear and decisive statements implicating him, made by Antonio Aguilar, Felipe Leaños, Claudio Ríos, Salvador Moreno, and Guadalupe Morfín.

Jorge Tello Peón took the stand on the afternoon of February 12, 2001. It was twenty-four days since the escape. If his lies had been bricks, you could have built a wall with them. The under secretary stated that in the meetings with the representatives of the human rights commission, no irregularities had been detected: "Director General Pérez Rodríguez informed us that some of the complaints made proved to be false, and that when the representatives of the CNDH interviewed the complainants in the presence of the prison authorities, nothing came up in their view that amounted to any kind of infraction." Tello further claimed that during the visit he had undertaken on orders from Secretary Gertz, all he noticed was "clear signs of disorder resulting from inadequate cleaning and maintenance." Thus he had merely ordered Guzmán, Palma, and Martínez to be relocated, because up until then he did not have any "concrete information about a possible escape." It was obvious that Tello was lying, and they were letting him lie. In the absence of questions, such testimonies became demented monologues. The enquiries carried out by the Fox administration were a joke.

Tello Peón would not be troubled again by the PGR. At the end of February 2001, he resigned as under secretary of public security, for "personal reasons." His resignation was news for a couple of days, then it was forgotten. The following month he became a top executive in Cemex, the Mexican cement company that is one of the biggest in the world.

Pérez Rodríguez also resigned, four weeks later. Neither of these two officials was held responsible for El Chapo Guzmán's escape from prison, in spite of all the testimony incriminating them. The full weight of the law fell on the prison warden, Leonardo Beltrán Santana, the assistant warden, Luis Francisco Fernández Ruiz, and sixty-one lesser members of the prison staff who had been in detention since January 20, 2001. Three of these were released almost immediately for lack of evidence, while fifty-nine of them were charged. El Güero Palma and El Texas Martínez were also indicted for bribery, organized crime, and helping a prisoner to escape. Antonio Aguilar's honesty and bravery were rewarded by sending him to the Federal Center for Psychosocial Rehabilitation, in June 2001.

The El Chito Show

On September 5, 2001, Francisco Javier Camberos, El Chito, arrived unexpectedly in a lawyer's office to say that he feared for his life, and wanted to hand himself in. El Chapo's fixer knew rather too much about the escape, and many people had an interest in his silence. The affair was getting tense, since the guards' testimonies contradicted the official version. In fact, it was Guzmán Loera who had told him to go to the law and tell the story of the laundry cart.

Obedient to his script, El Chito stammered that he alone had achieved the springing of the Sinaloa boss.[34] "Nobody helped me, I have sole responsibility for the little favor I did him," was how he confessed his guilt to a judge at the Reclusorio Oriente prison—in the presence of the fifty-nine former guards and employees of the prison, his co-defendants in this trial, as well as a score of defense attorneys. The performance lasted more than four hours.

"I, too, am a Mexican, and I don't think it's fair for the authorities in this country to do whatever they want. Mr. Guzmán said to me that even though he'd done his time, they still wanted to drag him away to the States!" Camberos conveyed the pathos of this, then added: "There was no plan, I just suddenly thought of it."

El Chito Camberos sacrificed himself, but he saved the current and former public security chiefs who were beginning to fret at the turn the case was taking. He produced a giant sketch of the Puente Grande layout, in order to illustrate how he had pushed the cart with El Chapo inside through seven security checkpoints until the exit booth, which they cleared at 7:28 p.m. By the end of his exhausting performance, El Chito hadn't lost his sense of humor:

"I've had enough, bring me a laundry cart so I can get out of here, no, wait, a trailer truck so we can all get out!" he said, to laughter in the court.

Many were relieved by his statement. Although it was a poor lie, well told, the custodians of Mexican justice took it at face value. Yet there is not a shred of evidence for it. On the contrary, there is the solid fact that El Chapo was seen inside the penitentiary after his man left with the cart.

Today, El Chito is serving out twenty-five years in the Reclusorio Oriente. Apparently Guzmán only sent him maintenance money for the first five. If he knows how El Chapo really escaped, his mind is now too drug-sodden to recall it.

Impunity

In spite of the evidence against them, in January 2002 a federal court acquitted drug traffickers El Güero Palma and El Texas Martínez of helping in the escape of Joaquín Guzmán. The court adduced "lack of evidence," and also overturned their conviction for organized crime.[35] In April that same year, the story of Guzmán's escape became the center of conversation once again when the Fourth District Judge, José Mario Machorro, called on Pérez Rodríguez and Tello Peón to testify as defense witnesses for some of the prison guards on trial. Neither attended. Pérez was fined, while the former under secretary of public security could never be located in time to notify him of the summons. Nonetheless, the judge persisted.

Tello finally showed up to testify for a second time on April 29, 2002. Once again, he lied to evade responsibility. In front of the judge, Tello declared that Cisen—the intelligence service he had directed in the two years before the escape, precisely the period in which the drug barons took control of the jail—had not monitored the Puente Grande prison.[36] This was false. There are dozens of statements by prison guards and administrators in the files on the escape, that even identify the Cisen officers by name—Carlos Arias is one of them. They say quite clearly that one of the tasks of the Cisen officers was to record the prisoners' conversations, and that their offices were located on Levels B and C of the prison.

Tello declared that only the Intelligence Coordination of the PFP—then headed by García Luna—carried out surveillance in the prison, but that it never got wind of the escape.[37] Tello knew that the same García Luna, his ever loyal subordinate, was one of those in charge of the investigation, and that there was no way he would be investigating himself.

Over the course of eighteen questions, the examination covered much of the same ground as the first time. Why had he ordered the "immediate" reassignment of the three felons' cells on January 19? Because some guards had complained of corruption, and an inspection had been conducted jointly with the CNDH, and the guards had retracted their accusations (though of course those guards had taken their concerns to the Jalisco ombudsman, Morfín). He thought that rehousing the drug traffickers would avoid trouble. Before the court, he repeated that no "concrete information" about any escape had come to light at that moment.

Pérez Rodríguez testified the same day. Judge Machorro heard an identical script: the head of the federal prison service never dreamed that El Chapo was planning to escape.

In the end, there was only one way Tello and Pérez could be linked to El Chapo's escape: the evidence of Antonio Aguilar Garzón. The retired major was called as a defense witness on behalf of the guards and other Puente Grande staff. However, he was unable to appear: in May 2002 he died in a mysterious car accident as he drove to work along the Mexico-Cuernavaca highway.

After El Chapo's escape, Felipe Leaños, the first prison officer to denounce corruption there, stayed on at Puente Grande and even became commander of his sector. However, according to a freedom of information request made for this book, his last day on the job was May 15, 2007. Although "the motive is unknown," his former colleagues say he was found dead in a sack in a Guadalajara back street. As for the other warder to present a similar complaint, Claudio Ríos, the most recent information is that in April 2009 he was still a commander at Puente Grande prison.

In January 2005, Luis Fernández, the former assistant warden of that prison, spoke for the first time from his cell in Mexico City's Federal District. He had been incarcerated for almost five years and still hadn't been sentenced.[38] Fernández repeated what he had told the public prosecutors in 2001, that it was Miguel Ángel Yunes who had invited him to work in the maximum security prisons. He also talked about El Chapo Guzmán: he described him as tidy and diffident, never overbearing or rude, and "very intelligent." He said El Chapo read a lot about the history and geography of Mexico.

Maintaining his innocence, Fernández recalled how after the escape "Federal Police took control of the prison, we were all shut into the hall, and armed personnel in balaclavas moved in." His lawyer, Eduardo Sahagún, emphasized that the PGR had always avoided conducting a reconstruction of the events. Soon after that interview, Luis Fernández was released and allowed to complete his trial proceedings outside jail.

Nine years after Guzmán's escape, in 2010, only six of the sixty-two defendants charged were still in prison. One of the most shocking cases was that of Leonardo Beltrán himself. For just over nine years the former warden of Puente Grande was lodged in the VIP wing of the Oriente prison. Tall, thin, with grey hair and tired eyes behind his spectacles, he was always very discreet. He paid his dues in silence, and never betrayed those who had really orchestrated and carried out the escape—the escape of a gangster who now has the entire country cowed by a climate of uncontrollable violence. In 2009, the Fifth Criminal Court of the Federal District sentenced Beltrán to eighteen years and nine months in prison, but the Fourth Unitary Criminal Court, in spite of the evidence against him, reduced the sentence to barely eleven and a half years.[39] In fact, soon afterwards, on June 24, 2010, Beltrán left the Oriente prison. He didn't have to escape. Why should he? He was freed by the Federal Administration for Social Rehabilitation, courtesy of the then secretary of public security, Genaro García Luna.[40]

Wanted: adviser with drug trafficking experience

In 2006, Jorge Tello Peón returned to public office during the handover from the Fox government to that of Felipe Calderón. For some reason the latter wanted him as his secretary of public security. The shadow cast by the escape of the country's main drug baron did nothing to temper the president-elect's enthusiasm for the Cemex executive. At the time it was rumored that Genaro García Luna would head the PFP; his disastrous spell in charge of the PJF, which later became the Federal Investigations Agency (AFI), did not suggest he'd get anything better. Tello was cautious. He turned the job down for "health reasons"—apparently an incurable cancer—and pushed the ever servile García Luna to take it instead. Eventually, on November 30, 2006, Calderón announced that García Luna would indeed lead the Secretariat of Public Security (SSP).

Two years later, Tello did agree to return to public office. On October 19, 2008, the president made him his adviser in the fake war on drugs. The fact is that the advice of the former under secretary of public security, whatever it may have been, did not help to win the "war." The violence only got worse.

The following year, on March 25, 2009, Tello became executive secretary of the National Public Security System, which came under García Luna's jurisdiction. The pupil had overtaken his teacher. Of course, García Luna had changed a lot since the time he had blocked any investigation of Tello for El Chapo's escape. Now he didn't need anyone. His proximity to Calderón gave him unbounded power.

When men like García suffer humiliation at the hands of their bosses in order to go up in the world, once they get to the top they want nothing more than to crush their former mentors. At first Tello tried to distance himself from García Luna. He even denied it was he who had recommended him to the president. His offspring had grown more than he'd intended. After a few months under the secretary's yoke, demoralized by García Luna's bullying behavior, Tello Peón retreated. He asked to be moved, and his request was granted.

Turf wars

At the beginning of 2009, from his confinement in the Altiplano prison in Almoloya, the one-time drug baron Miguel Ángel Félix Gallardo gave a written interview to journalist Diego Enrique Osorno. There is one basic fact in his account that puts El Chapo Guzmán's escape in proper perspective: "Senior officials came to Altiplano and offered some of the best known inmates to escape. Nobody accepted."

Some prisoners at Altiplano say one of these officials proposing "escape" was Miguel Ángel Yunes Linares. The politician from Veracruz state had, they suggest, made the offer while Ernesto Zedillo was still president, and he himself was chief adviser to Interior Secretary Diódoro Carrasco, another long-time Institutional Revolutionary Party (PRI) figure who had recently defected to the PAN.

In 2004, after Yunes resigned from the PRI, the leader of the teachers' union (SNTE), Elba Esther Gordillo, got him a good job in the sphere of national security. In spite of his poor record as director general of the prison service, on January 1, 2005, Yunes was appointed under secretary for citizen participation in the Secretariat of Public Security; in 2006, Fox made him executive secretary of the National Public Security System, giving him even more power in that area. Contrary to expectations, Yunes survived the change of presidency. Calderón must have seen him as useful in some way or other, making him director of the Public Employees' Social Security Institute (ISSSTE). Later, in June 2008, Yunes joined the PAN and clad himself in its protective blue mantle.

We should remember that at the time of El Chapo's escape, Yunes was no longer head of the prison service at federal level. That post had been taken over by Pérez Rodríguez, who had been his private secretary back when Yunes was secretary of the interior for Veracruz state. Nonetheless, it is said that Yunes was well aware of the repeated warnings of a possible escape. After Guzmán's escape, Pérez waited a prudent time before returning to public office. And when he did, alongside his friend and former boss, it was done with great discretion, almost imperceptibly. In February 2007, Yunes made him ISSSTE delegate in the Federal District. Later he sent him as the ISSSTE office in Veracruz.

At the beginning of 2010, Yunes Linares requested leave from his post as head of the ISSSTE and was nominated as the PAN's candidate for Governor of Veracruz state in the elections due on July 4 that year—his coalition partner was Elba Esther Gordillo's New Alliance party. Quite unashamedly, Yunes brought Pérez into his pre-campaign team, and then made him operational coordinator of the campaign itself. In the run-up to the poll, the press asked Yunes about his relation with Pérez and the latter's links to El Chapo's escape. He refused to answer, saying he no longer commented on security issues, only on social ones. In fact, there was a clear link between the impunity surrounding El Chapo Guzmán's escape from Puente Grande and the protection the drug baron enjoyed from the very start of the Fox administration.

The race for governor of Veracruz turned out to be rather more than an electoral contest between the PRI and the PAN. Many people insisted that at root it was a fight between drug cartels for control of the territory. Historically, Veracruz had been seen as belonging to the Gulf Cartel, now led by Ezequiel Cárdenas, brother of the much-feared Osiel. But the Sinaloa Cartel had been disputing that control for months. Yunes did not win the governorship of Veracruz.

Official protection

In May 2006, the DEA obtained valuable information about the drug trafficking networks in Mexico, after it managed to infiltrate a cell of the organization led by Ignacio Coronel Villareal, one of the Sinaloa

Cartel's main partners and a personal friend of Guzmán. According to the US anti-drug agency, in that year a number of officers were investigating the details of a story involving Vicente Fox.[41] It was said that the then president had received a bribe worth $40 million, in exchange for providing political protection for El Chapo's escape. But Fox's alleged involvement didn't stop there. The DEA had direct reports from its informants infiltrated with Nacho Coronel, which stated that the Fox presidency had provided protection to Guzmán and the Sinaloa Cartel throughout its six years in office.

Mexican military and civilian intelligence sources have told this investigation that the alleged link between the Sinaloa Cartel and Vicente Fox go back to the time when he was first seeking election as governor of Guanajuato state in 1991. At that time Guzmán was still free, and working for Amado Carrillo Fuentes. Pablo Tostado—who had been a member of the group led by El Azul Esparragoza—revealed that traffickers belonging to the Pacific organization had moved into Guanajuato back in the 1980s for logistical reasons. For example, El Azul had interests in the small neighboring state of Querétaro, but he began to use the airport in Irapuato, Guanajuato, for drug shipments because it was better equipped.

When Vicente Fox was governor of Guanajuato—and later as president of the Republic—he was close to Luis Echeverría, allegedly one of the protectors of the Pacific organization ever since his own sexennial in power, 1970–76. Members of both Fox's campaign team and his government have told how, as president, he often sought advice from Echeverría, either directly or via Marta Sahagún. Their relationship was much closer than it seemed in public.

Given the alleged links between the Fox administration and the Sinaloa Cartel, the privileged treatment given to the narco-business-man Manuel Beltrán Arredondo—El Chapo's protector—by "the government of change," as this first PAN administration liked to be known, is nothing less than outrageous. Between 2001 and 2002, the federal government granted Beltrán Arredondo exploration rights at seven mines in Tamazula, Durango state, for a period of six years. This was of course the same Beltrán who had financed much of of the presidential campaign of the PRI candidate, Francisco Labastida, in 2000. The rewards rained down until 2004, when he was given the concession for two mines, La Fortuna and La Fortuna Fracción, in Concordia, Sinaloa state. By then a scandal had already broken out after the drug trafficker and kidnapper, Pablo Tostado, in detention in Irapuato prison, had revealed Beltrán's real occupation: "I'll tell you who Manuel Beltrán Arredondo is. He is one of the main leaders of the Sinaloa Cartel, which operates in the states of Durango, Jalisco, Nayarit, Chihuahua, and Sinaloa. Joaquín El Chapo Guzmán, Julio Beltrán Quintero, Adolfo Beltrán Quintero, Ignacio Coronel, Juan José Esparragoza, El Azul, are all members of the same cartel," stated Tostado to the court. Even so, the mining concessions granted to El Chapo's sidekick were not withdrawn.

After his escape, El Chapo Guzmán told friends, and even negotiators sent by the president of the Republic, how it really happened. It was not until the morning of January 20, 2001, when Under Secretary of Public Security Jorge Tello, the head of the prison service, Enrique Pérez, and Humberto Martínez of the PFP arrived to investigate the supposed jail break, that the drug trafficker actually left Puente Grande. The deployment of police officers from the PFP and the PJF created a deliberate confusion, all the more so on a dark winter morning. Dressed in a PFP uniform, his face concealed by a regulation police helmet and mask, Joaquín Guzmán walked out of the prison surrounded by a group of PFP officers. He was then driven a few miles in an official vehicle. At some point down the road, he got out of the car and into a helicopter which flew him to Nayarit. That was where the real legend of Joaquín Guzmán began.

In 1993, when he was betrayed by Carrillo Fuentes and El Güero Palma and arrested, El Chapo was a virtual nobody. However, just eight years after his escape he had become one of the 701 richest men in the world, and *Forbes* magazine estimated his profits from drug shipments at a billion dollars.[42] It put him on a par with Emilio Azcárraga, the main shareholder in Televisa, or with Alfredo Harp Helú, the former owner of Banamex. Only one other person in the history of drug trafficking had ever won a place in *Forbes*—Pablo Escobar. The long-empty throne of Amado Carrillo Fuentes had finally found a "worthy" occupant.

Joaquín "El Chapo" Guzmán: "In 1993, when he was . . . arrested, El Chapo was a virtual nobody. However, just eight years after his escape he had become one of the 701 richest men in the world, and *Forbes* magazine estimated his profits from drug shipments at a billion dollars." (p. 160)

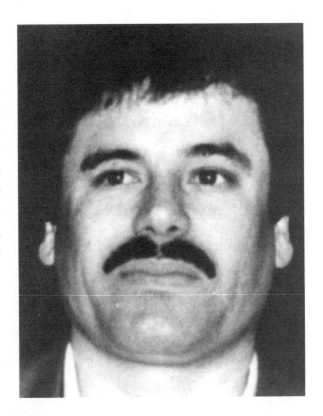

Heriberto Lazcano, a.k.a. El Verdugo (The Executioner): "Lazcano [is] one of the founders of Los Zetas, the indestructible group that for years was the armed wing of the Gulf Cartel. Today it is regarded by the United States government as an 'international threat.'" (p. 200)

Anti-Chapo graffiti on a wall in the Juárez Valley east of Ciudad Juárez, Mexico.

Vicente Fox, president of Mexico 2000–06: "The rules governing the relation between drug traffickers and government changed forever during the Fox administration: the public officials became employees of the drug traffickers, and their armed wing." (p. 195)

Felipe Calderón, president of Mexico 2006–12: "The US Drug Enforcement Administration says that during Calderón's six-year term, Guzmán became the most powerful drug trafficker in history, while his enemies were decimated. El Chapo's empire is Calderón's chief legacy." (p. 8)

A man killed execution style on the banks of a river in Culiacán, Sinaloa, the cradle of many of the drug cartels and their leaders in Mexico.

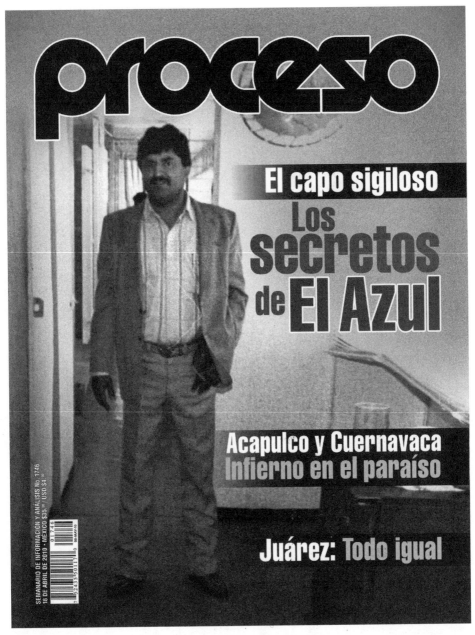

Juan José "El Azul" Esparragoza Moreno: "El Chapo, El Mayo, and El Azul are firmly in control of an empire. Between them they have achieved a virtual monopoly of narcotics trafficking in Mexico and the United States, a dominion based on blood, sweat, and tears." (p. 301)

Ismael "El Mayo" Zambada Garcia (pictured right): "Within the organization, El Mayo has been seen as the man behind El Chapo's throne ... Of all the drug barons, El Mayo is the one that provokes the most contradictory reactions. He is either loved or hated. There is nothing in between." (pp. 180, 184)

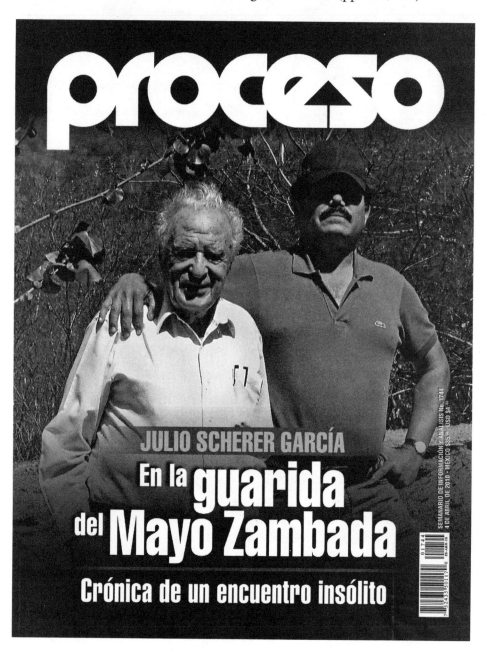

Edgar "La Barbie" Valdez Villarreal: "As the time of our meeting approached, my heart was racing. I had waited seven years for this moment. In the course of my research I had spoken to many people inside and outside of the law, but never had a drug baron or one of their employees wanted to make a direct, public confession." (p. 309)

Amado Carrillo Fuentes: "While exporting historic quantities of hard and soft drugs to the United States, Amado Carrillo Fuentes forged close links with the Mexican political, military, and business class, who gladly laundered the millions of dollars he gave them." (p. 111)

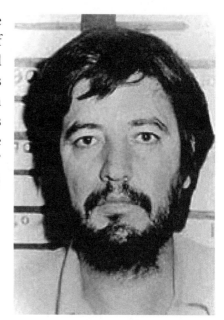

Vicente Carrillo Fuentes: "The organization created by Amado Carrillo, which was then one of the most powerful in Latin America, was eventually handed to Vicente Carrillo, El Viceroy." (p. 177)

Ignacio "Nacho" Coronel Villarreal: "Ignacio Coronel acquired most power as a pioneer in the drugs of the future, ephedrine and methamphetamine, made in clandestine labs in Jalisco. Nacho supplied the huge market for these synthetic drugs in the United States—a market that is now controlled by the Sinaloa Cartel." (p. 189)

George W. Bush at the border: "By concentrating on the Gulf Cartel and Los Zetas, US authorities allowed The Federation to grow exponentially under their very noses, on their own side of the border." (p. 231)

Barack Obama and Felipe Calderón: "The United States . . . for years has claimed to be challenging drug trafficking in Mexico, with no positive results." (p. xi)

A US Drug Enforcement Agent aims a flashlight down a 55-foot-deep drug-smuggling tunnel cut through the floor of a small industrial unit south of Yuma, Arizona, in the town of San Luis. The tunnel runs almost 240 yards under the US-Mexico border and is estimated to have cost up to a million dollars and to have taken one year to build.

A woman whose family member was killed in drug-related violence in Ciudad Juárez, Mexico.

CHAPTER EIGHT

Blood Ties

On April 24, 1999, a few yards from the Eighth Naval Zone, on the magnificent beach of the Acapulco Hyatt Regency Hotel, the Mexican fashion designer Armando Mafud—who had just held a successful exhibition of his work at the Louvre in Paris—was showing his latest collection to a large but select group of guests. The couple who lent most glamor and aristocratic cachet to the evening was Baron Enrico di Portanova—one of the most flamboyant members of the international jet set, according to the *New York Times*—and his delightful wife, Baroness Sandra di Portanova.[1] Enrico had the kind of personality that never went unnoticed. In his sunset years he resembled Don Corleone, with slicked-back hair, pencil mustache and bushy eyebrows, and obvious signs of surgery on his face revealing a vain attempt to hang on to the remains of his youth. The baron was crazy about Monte Cristo cigars, which he had sticking out of various pockets.

Little by little the guests began to arrive. The evening was graced by the presence of Saba Masri himself; the French ambassador to Mexico, Bruno Delaye, as well as the director of fashion events, Beatriz Calles, a leading figure in the industry, now the organizer of Mexico Fashion Week, and the producer of the show that night. Other Mexican society figures were there too, like actors ready to take part, perhaps unknowingly, in a show that would make history.[2]

The sponsors of the fashion parade were an unknown Mexican businessman, Alonso Rivera Muñoz, and his wife, Clara Laborín Archuleta. Ostensibly the aim was to raise money for the Mexican

Foundation to Combat AIDS, headed by Guillermo Ocaña, a personal friend of "Engineer" Rivera and his wife. In reality, Clara wanted to publicize the luxury Debanhy spa she was building in Acapulco. So keen was she on this that a few days before the parade, the couturier Mafud and she had hosted cocktails at La Gran Casona restaurant in Mexico City, to announce details of the event.[3]

Rivera was over six feet tall, slim and pale, with a thin mustache. He would do anything to please his restless wife; and besides, events like this helped him to develop his business contacts. Rivera's presence was discreet. He watched from the bar area like a hyena on the prowl. Of all the actors who turned up to the show that night, his performance was surely the most complete. Had it been publicly known that the generous "engineer," so concerned at the plight of AIDS victims, was in fact the daring and ruthless drug trafficker Héctor Beltrán Leyva, El H or El Ingeniero, from Badiraguato, Sinaloa, who along with his brother Arturo, El Barbas, controlled the Guerrero territory where Acapulco is located—the Baron di Portanova and his fellow guests might have wound up at the Attorney General's Office (PGR), or on the DEA's list of suspects. They might have thrown up their canapés if they'd known of the macabre, santería-based rituals El H is now reputed to practice on those he kills.[4]

The Beltrán Leyva clan has been one of the most reckless, innovatory, and bloodthirsty in the history of the Mexican drug trade. They have proved capable of infiltrating all areas of Mexican society: politics, law enforcement, the judiciary, high society, and the gossip columns. This is the real achievement of Mexico's drug traffickers—to work their way into every nook and cranny of the social edifice, like damp.

How El Chapo became a narco, according to his mother

In the Mexican army they say that while Joaquín Guzmán was in prison, his mother Doña Consuelo, back in the village of La Tuna, used to tell everyone how her son became a drug trafficker. Soldiers describe a video tape, apparently made by a French journalist, which for many years was used by the army in specialist training courses.

In the recording, El Chapo's mother tells how when he was born the family was so poor that they could only afford to buy him a pair of coarse cotton pants.

His father, Emilio Guzmán, like many peasants in the region, grew both grain for immediate consumption, and drugs, to provide a little better for his large family. Don Emilio was a strict, irascible father who often hit his six children—especially El Chapo, the eldest and most unruly. Soon the boy was six, old enough to accompany his father to tend the cannabis and poppies that thrive in the dry soil of the "golden triangle."

It is common for boys to be taken out of school and into the sierra for weeks during the sowing season. Months later they are again required to help with the harvest: their short stature and little hands are ideal for poppy-tapping. This means slicing with a razor blade into the bulb, not so deeply as to harm the plant, and setting small tin cans to collect the sap which dries into a rubbery gum, the basis for heroin. The cannabis branches are hung on special lines to dry. The work is strenuous, and there is little food or water. Many boys are fatally poisoned by pesticides, others die of sunstroke. The conditions make it practically impossible for any of them to finish elementary school. These kids can only aspire to being drug traffickers, hopefully with a fleet of SUVs and plenty of women.

Nothing will change until public policies are in place to offer such children different opportunities and goals. Otherwise the production of narcotics, including dope, crack, and synthetic drugs, will continue to swell; it seems that coca, too, is beginning to be planted in Guerrero and Michoacán. To date, however, the so-called war on drugs waged by the Mexican government has not included a single social program in response to the intractable cycle. Apparently it's in nobody's interest to cut the chain of delinquency.

Older children accompany their fathers to sell the crop. El Chapo and his dad would head through spectacular mountain scenery to Cosalá, in south-east Sinaloa—a miniature, colonial, cobble-stoned gem currently advertised as "magical" by the Tourism Secretariat. It was here that El Chapo's evil legend was born, as the hungry, ragged youth saw the good things that could be bought with drug money, or so his mother said. Once the produce had been sold, Don Emilio used to go on days-long binges in the cantinas and brothels. The little cash left over he spent on groceries and supplies for the family, returning home like a bread-winning hero.

El Chapo, eager to enjoy the small privileges his father earned, started his own plantations behind his family's back. A general who had served in the "golden triangle" recalled that, on one remote inspection, he was mobbed by kids of no more than thirteen years old, who begged him not to destroy their small marijuana plots. The money, they pleaded, would enable them to celebrate Christmas.

Young Joaquín was supported in his aims by his brothers, the most gifted of which turned out to be the youngest, Arturo El Pollo. He also got help from his distant cousins, the Beltrán Leyva brothers, who lived in La Palma, another small community in Badiraguato. It is said to have been Arturo Beltrán Leyva, El Barbas, who first helped Joaquín to get started.

When Guzmán was in prison, it was El Barbas who helped El Pollo smuggle his brother's shipments. They even made joint deliveries. As a favour, Arturo Beltrán sent Guzmán his share of the profits, to make life easier for him in Puente Grande. The money was delivered in briefcases by the businessman José Bargueño, and by Marcelo Peña, brother of one of El Chapo's girlfriends. Both would later become protected witnesses for the PGR, using the pseudonyms César and Julio.[5]

In mid 2000, El Chapo needed to pay his retinue in the jail, so he asked Peña to find Cousin Arturo in Acapulco, the territory he and his brothers had controlled for some time. Peña located El Barbas and met him at a McDonald's on the coast. They didn't exchange many words—just a slap on the back and a case full of money. After he got out of the prison, in just nine years El Chapo Guzmán and the Beltrán Leyva clan would forever change the shape of organized crime in Mexico, the United States, Central America, South America and, quite simply, the entire world. But their fraternal relations would not endure.

The Three Knights

Carlos Beltrán and Ramona Leyva had been neighbors in the community of La Palma, in Badiraguato. They were as poor as most campesino households in the region. Their fathers and grandfathers had grown drugs in the Sierra Madre Occidental, as had Rafael Caro Quintero and his brothers, Ernesto Fonseca Carrillo, Juan José Esparragoza, and Joaquín Guzmán. Their children, the Beltrán Leyva brothers, had it in their blood; the mountains gave them the opportunity, and time did the rest.

Four of the six brothers decided to continue the family "tradition"; they developed from drug-growing peasants into powerful traffickers. The best known and most active were Arturo, Héctor, and Alfredo, who became known as the Los Tres Caballeros, The Three Knights. There are intelligence reports that a sister, Gloria, is also involved in running the family business. The youngest of the Beltrán Leyva children, she is married to Juan José Esparragoza Monzón, son of El Azul, one of the most respected traffickers of the older generation.[6] The religious ceremony tying together these families—the Beltráns, Esparragozas, and Guzmáns—took place in 1995 in a church in Querétaro.[7] The FBI's theory is that these blood ties were promoted to forestall betrayal and to encourage loyalty. Big mistake.

El Barbas

Marcos Arturo, the eldest of the Beltrán Leyva brothers and the most seasoned in the dark arts of trafficking, was born in 1958. He was tall and rangy, with fair skin and a permanent beard. Always well dressed, he could easily have passed for a businessman if his overbearing manner hadn't given him away. In the course of his criminal career he used many nicknames, principally El Barbas (The Beard), and the final one that stayed with him until the end: El Jefe de Jefes, The Boss of Bosses. That was how he signed off on the grotesque murders committed on his orders across Mexico. Some who have met him speak of a vibrant, cheerful, ostentatious man, who was also extremely violent and vindictive. In spite of everything, he respected people who looked him in the eye and spoke to him straight. Arturo was a creation of Carrillo Fuentes. He began working with him at about the same time as Joaquín Guzmán, his distant cousin, and Héctor Palma, his brother-in-law.

When Guzmán was arrested in Guatemala in 1993, El Barbas was below him in the criminal hierarchy. Nonetheless, he didn't take long to become one of El Señor de los Cielos's leading deputies. He specialized in laundering money and the logistics of drug shipments, which included buying off public officials who could provide protection. El Barbas began operating in Querétaro, a state where many drug traffickers were domiciled. He bought up property and companies, and extended his business to Monterrey in Nuevo León and the towns around it.

Because he was efficient, Carrillo Fuentes entrusted El Barbas with jobs around the country. Arturo Beltrán helped to build Carrillo Fuentes's empire, and his legend too. In the 1990s, working with a team of assistants, businessmen, and public officials, he sent big shipments of cocaine to the United States. They used a fleet of aircraft that included Boeing 727s as well as smaller planes like the King Air, Learjet, and Velocity that were almost impossible to pick up on radar and posed a real headache for the DEA. They also used launches and bigger craft to unload drugs from Colombia on the coasts of Yucatán, Quintana Roo, and Veracruz, as well as along the vast Pacific seaboard. Sometimes the airliners carried up to 10,000 kilograms of cocaine, as well as millions of dollars in profits.

At the same time as Arturo Beltrán Leyva was supporting Amado Carrillo Fuentes, with the latter's permission he was also supporting El Azul—his sister's father-in-law—his cousin El Chapo, and Ismael El Mayo Zambada, thereby strengthening his position in the criminal organization. The figure of El Barbas took on mythical proportions. In 2009, several State Department reports blamed him for the growing violence in Mexico. They said his organization was responsible for "kidnapping, torture, murder, and other crimes against men, women, and children in Mexico."[8] This inherently violent man reaped the fruits of his own dark legend. The armed gangs under El Barbas were considered the most ruthless and brutal of them all. They have been blamed for the killing of numerous public officials in recent years.[9] In the United States they never forgave him for threatening to kill officers of the US Immigration and Customs Enforcement (ICE) in 2008. Those who have had dealings with him say that for him the word "loyalty" is written in blood, and any infringement must be paid in the same currency.

El H

Héctor Beltrán Leyva, El H, El Ingeniero (the Engineer), or El Elegante, was born in 1966. He is married to Clara Elena Laborín. He was his elder brother's right-hand man. They did not use names or aliases with each other, it was always "carnal," or "bro." Héctor handled PR: Arturo gave him the task of developing links with senior public officials in both the police and civil administration. It was a task he was very good at.

His smooth appearance, polished manners, and good taste in clothes allowed him to pose easily as a businessman. In this guise he organized events like that at the Hyatt Regency Hotel in Acapulco in 1999. Héctor Beltrán was always attentive to any politicians doing well in electoral campaigns in the states where his brother operated. His job was to get close to them and fund their campaigning activities, so that when they won, the gang would benefit.[10]

Héctor would often arrive at the Hotel Aristos in the Zona Rosa tourist area of Mexico City, discreetly flanked by his entourage. He could also count on his wife, Clara Laborín, for cover. She was the pretty face of El H. She'd been a contestant in the Miss Sonora beauty contest in 1993–94, the kind of event that often seemed like a marriage bureau for young beauties and drug traffickers.

Laborín was fascinated with the world of show business, and at the beauty contest she'd met Guillermo Ocaña, the well-known artistes' agent.[11] Come what may, she was determined to break into that world. So with her husband she set up a company called Rotceh[12] Noticias y Espectáculos, and invited Ocaña to work with them. He accepted. It's not clear exactly when the partnership began. Ocaña told public prosecutors it was in 1997.[13] What is certain is that by 1999, Laborín, Beltrán, and Ocaña had been the object of complaints made by company employees to the Federal District Arbitration and

Conciliation Board.[14] It seems things were not going well at the company. At the same time, the services Ocaña supplied for the drug baron were multiplying.

Better known as Ocañita, he had the ability to combine his interests in the world of organized crime with those in show business, the media, and Mexico's most select social circles. He was a real *insider*. In the 1990s he represented many of the most popular artists of the day, from Juan Gabriel to Tania Libertad and Gloria Trevi. On March 16, 2003, he coordinated a mass gathering in Mexico City's Zócalo square for Salma Hayek, who had just been nominated for an Oscar as Best Actress. Her film, *Frida*, was projected for free to 5,000 people.

In spite of his drug trafficking activities, he never let up on his intense social life, because the one depended on the other. He rubbed shoulders at social events with politicians like the then governor of the State of Mexico (now president of the Republic), Enrique Peña Nieto, or even the PRD politician Dolores Padierna. Ocaña's contribution to the drug trade was not limited to satisfying the whims of Mrs. Héctor Beltrán Leyva; he would also be accused of laundering assets for the Pacific organization.

Eventually, the showman got careless. He relied too much on the protection the Fox administration had been providing to the criminal organization led by Joaquín Guzmán ever since they'd got him out of Puente Grande. On March 6, 2005, police arrested two men at the airport in Barcelona, Spain—José Arturo Ponce and his brother, Héctor Gerardo. They were about to board a jet to Los Angeles. Nothing unusual about that; except they were also trying to take with them $5.5 million belonging to the Beltrán Leyvas and the Colombian Valle del Norte Cartel, with which the Sinaloans had been working for over a decade.

On April 5, 2005, the Spanish Interior Ministry issued a statement saying that Ocaña was the leader of the ring the Ponce brothers belonged to, and "responsible for the illegal transfer of money from Spain to Mexican territory." José Arturo Ponce and his brother had fled back to Mexico; Ocaña didn't bat an eyelid. In December that year, the PGR mounted a raid in the Tecamachalco area of the State of Mexico, acting on a tip-off from the DEA about a group of Colombians, aided by Mexicans, involved in transporting cocaine and money laundering. Eight suspected traffickers were arrested. One was the illustrious Ocañita, who was admitted to the Oriente prison in the Federal District in January 2006. The charges were not trivial: organized crime, handling illegally obtained resources, and felonies against public health.[15]

As long as the Beltrán Leyva brothers were part of Guzmán's organization, Ocaña could not be disturbed, whatever the evidence against him. He was soon released from prison, even though the Spanish authorities had blacklisted his name through Interpol. The Mexican office of Interpol came under Genaro García Luna, the head of the Federal Investigations Agency (AFI, formerly called the Federal Judicial Police, PJF). So Guillermo Ocaña continued to live his life of King Midas. One party—for which he earned the description "host of the decade"—was inspired by the *Thousand and One Nights*. He hired a camel and an elephant to greet the guests, and the only drink available was champagne.

In June 2009, Ocaña's accomplice, José Arturo Ponce, was extradited to Spain. Guillermo Ocaña's good fortune was about to run out. In April 2010, in the midst of the federal government's war against the Beltrán Leyva clan, the authorities decided to arrest him. Strangely, the accusations against him were exactly the same as they had been the first time he was arrested. Mrs. Héctor Beltrán was deprived of her best contact for living in a soap opera, but her political connections held firm, and her own siblings did extremely well.

Héctor was regarded as the second-in-command of the family's criminal business, responsible for planning and running the trafficking and financial operations in Mexico City. Now he is top dog.

Since 2004 he has been accused in the District of Columbia Federal Court and the New York Eastern District Court of smuggling tons of cocaine and marijuana into the United States.[16]

El Mochomo

Alfredo Beltrán Leyva, El Mochomo, is the youngest of the brothers.[17] He is married to Patricia Guzmán, with whom he has two children: Karmina and Alfredo. Patricia is a cousin of El Chapo, her father Ernesto being half-brother to El Chapo's father, Emilio.[18]

El Mochomo had an iron grip on several units of armed followers, and is the only one of the Beltrán Leyva brothers to have developed a relationship with the younger generation of traffickers, in particular with Vicente Zambada, El Mayo's favorite son. By the age of twenty-five his brothers were already giving him important tasks, like taking charge of relations with the Colombian drug baron, El Profe. Alfredo looked after the shipments of cocaine to Monterrey, from where he organized passage over the border into the United States. El Mochomo had at least three accounts at Banamex, the bank that had been implicated in cases of trafficking and money laundering for Amado Carrillo Fuentes and his group, to which the Beltrán Leyva brothers had of course belonged. He was arrested on January 21, 2008, in Culiacán.

The Beltrán Leyvas's workforce

Arturo Beltrán Leyva, El Barbas, had an efficient team working with him for Carrillo Fuentes. It included Alcides Magaña, El Metro, Albino Quintero; Sergio Fierro Chávez, José Javier Bargueño Urías, and others amounting to a "dream team" of Narcoland. In the name of El Señor de los Cielos, Arturo had set up a broad protection network, both within the federal government and among the local authorities from Baja California to Veracruz. The chain of corruption and bribery stretched from members of the Judicial Police to the top echelons of Sedena.[19]

Since 1997 El Barbas had some of the Mexico City airport police in his pocket, a group called Los Pachangos, useful for shepherding cocaine through the terminal. Any luggage they were warned contained drugs from Colombia was put on a separate conveyor by co-opted baggage handlers and taken to the airport branch of the PGR, where the Pachangos collected it for delivery to El Barbas's men outside. Each operation was paid something between $150,000 and $220,000.

As for Magaña, El Metro, around 1993 he was holding down two theoretically incompatible jobs: head of the anti-narcotic squad at the PJF, and chief bodyguard for Carrillo Fuentes. El Metro grabbed headlines when he was detained in November 1993, after defending

Carrillo Fuentes, quietly dining in the capital with his wife, from hit men sent by the Arrellano Félix gang.[20] However, the judge quickly let him go "for lack of evidence," and though he lost his police badge, he continued to serve Carrillo Fuentes.

Albino Quintero, El Beto, was a compadre of Arturo Beltrán Leyva, and very effective along the Atlantic coast. Other valuable operators were Humberto and Jesús Loya Pérez. Humberto was adept at buying up police commanders. Through a civilian named Fernando Brigas, Humberto also made the arrangements with military authorities involved in protecting the cartel. The brothers recruited excellent men for El Barbas, such as Bargueño Urías and his boss Sergio Fierro Chávez; the latter was a well-connected cocaine smuggler with a base in Colombia. It was a delicate negotiation, since Fierro had long ago fallen out badly with El Chapo Guzmán, no one knew why. The Loya brothers spoke to Guzmán in jail, and got him to pardon the offense. Thus Fierro was cleared to work with the Beltrán Leyvas, recalled Bargueño in declarations made in 2000 and 2005. It was a fruitful relationship all round.

The governor and the secret airstrip

At the beginning of 1995, Fierro Chávez was informed by his PGR contact that he could no longer conduct business in that state, because the territory now belonged to the Arellano Félix family. Fierro decided not to plunge the region into a blood bath. Instead he ordered an airstrip to be built in Guaymas, Sonora, where he got protection from the Federal Judicial Police chief, Rodolfo García Gaxiola, known as El Chipilón.[21]

The "secret" airstrip, if you can call it that, was to be a massive one and a half miles long by seventy-six yards wide. The runway had just been finished when Commander García Gaxiola announced that the Mexican army had "discovered" the immense construction and destroyed it, supposedly because it lay on an existing flight path. The project was abandoned. It is curious that it was the army and not the Sonora state authorities that destroyed the landing strip. Could that be because Commander García had a direct relationship with the then state governor, now an illustrious senator for the PRI,

Manlio Fabio Beltrones, who had hoped to win his party's nomination for the 2012 presidential elections?

García Gaxiola was regarded as very close to Governor Beltrones and to his brother Alcides, who was director of Tijuana airport.[22] Just how close was seen when they took charge of the initial enquiries into the murder of Luis Donaldo Colosio in 1994.[23] García Gaxiola was the Federal Police commander in Tijuana when Beltrones suggested to President Salinas that he, Beltrones, travel to the border city to oversee the investigation into the assassination of their presidential candidate.[24] Federal prosecutors would later say that "this phase of the Federal Police investigation, in particular, was marred by the falsification of evidence, the manipulation of witness statements, and other irregularities." One such irregularity was when Commander García and Governor Beltrones took the main suspect, Mario Aburto, to a house near the PJF offices and questioned him on their own account for hours. It has often been suggested that this was when the true story of the assassination got twisted. Soon after that, García was removed from Tijuana and sent to Sonora state as head of the PJF there, and as deputy representative of the PGR.

Manlio Beltrones has been accused of ties to drug trafficking more than once. Even former president Vicente Fox has said that the DEA had a file on Beltrones's involvement with drug smuggling. Beltrones denied it, as he always has, and Fox himself was hardly in a position to point the finger. Soon after he was posted to Sonora, General Sergio Aponte identified Rodolfo García Gaxiola as one of the PJF commanders who protected the traffickers of the Pacific organization.[25]

Either way, Sergio Fierro found a new base for his operations in Sonora, in the port city of Guaymas, where he enjoyed the best possible facilities without any interference from the Army.

Both God and the Devil

Arturo Beltrán Leyva became a top drug baron in his leadership of the Juárez Cartel. In Colombia he developed links with the dangerous drug boss José Vicente Castaño Gil, El Profe. Along with his brother Carlos, El Profe has been identified as a founding leader of the now-dissolved, far-right paramilitary group, Autodefensas Unidas de Colombia (United Self-Defense Forces of Colombia, AUC), notorious for drug trafficking, extortion, robbery, kidnapping, and terrorism. This sinister partner of El Barbas is even accused of murdering his own brother in order to keep control of the AUC.

So close was the oldest of the Beltrán Leyva brothers to El Profe that in 1997 he did him the favor of ordering the killing of another trafficker, Raúl Ibarra, who operated in upper Sinaloa state and owed the Colombian $7 million. El Profe may now be leading a third generation of paramilitary groups in Colombia, known as the Águilas Negras (Black Eagles), although some believe he was killed in March 2007.[26]

Mexican drug traffickers played an important role for the then all-powerful Colombians. It wasn't just that they controlled the porous US border. They were also building an extensive and essential distribution and retail network inside the United States. At present the Mexican drug cartels, especially the Sinaloa Cartel, are the only ones able to operate in every part of the US and are seen by the Justice Department as the "single greatest drug trafficking threat."[27] This predominance of Mexican organized crime inside the US is largely the work of El Barbas—and it greatly increased his standing and power within the Pacific organization.

El Barbas suffers casualties

A number of those who worked most closely for El Barbas in the 1990s have been arrested; others were executed. All those who fell were rapidly replaced. There is no shortage of would-be kingpins among the rank and file of organized crime. Some end up rotting in jail, after being used as cannon fodder. Others, if they're lucky, get a narco-corrido[28] written about them and become legends, even if they are later extradited. Only a select few acquire immortality; some magically disappear from the most-wanted list and become unrecognizable corpses to be interred in a splendid mausoleum, while in reality they are enjoying their retirement or still operating, without unwelcome attention from the media or the courts. Others again are simply untouchable.

In spite of the official protection given to the Sinaloa Cartel during the presidency of Vicente Fox, one of El Barbas's deputies, Albino Quintero, was arrested on May 26, 2002 in Veracruz, as he tried to flee from the Mexican army across the roofs around the safe-house where he and his bodyguard had been holed up. In his statement, Quintero said he had enjoyed the protection of the former governor of Quintana Roo state, Mario Villanueva. When he was arrested, one of his guards was Óscar Barrón, a serving member of the judicial police force rebranded as the Federal Investigation Agency (AFI), then under the command of Genaro García Luna. But of course Albino was arrested not as a result of official diligence, but because he was betrayed by his bosses. They'd found out that their efficient deputy had also been working for the Gulf Cartel, an unforgivable treachery.

Federal police commander Rodolfo García Gaxiola, El Chipilón, was executed in May 1998 in Sonora. He too was riding two horses at once. The Carrillo Fuentes organization discovered he was also working for the Arellano Félix brothers. Drug barons don't like public officials who work for two cartels at the same time, especially if the others are the enemy. No servant can serve two masters well. In exchange for the large sums of money they pay, they expect loyalty and efficiency. On his death, El Chipilón left almost $10 million to his widow.[29] Later, the PGR admitted that one line of investigation into the murder of presidential candidate Luis Donaldo Colosio had pointed towards García Gaxiola.[30]

In 1997, Rodolfo's brother and accomplice Filemón García Gaxiola, who also worked for the PGR in Guaymas, was arraigned on charges of helping to transport cocaine from Tapachula in Chiapas to Mexico City, on board a PGR plane. He soon walked free.[31] In 1999 another arrest warrant for him was issued, but apparently never used.[32] In spite of the direct accusations against him, and although the Calderón government knew exactly where he was, it made no move to arrest him. Indeed, in 2008 and 2009, Filemón received substantial funds from the public purse through the program for Agricultural Marketing Services and Support (ASERCA), run by the Secretariat of Agriculture. It is not clear if the former police commander still protects drug traffickers, or continues to combine lawful and unlawful activities as before.

Joel Malacón, a crony of El Barbas's tame PJF commander Julio Moraila, had the brilliant idea of setting up shrimp and fish farming businesses which, naturally, would be located on the Pacific coast. In Nayarit state he used a prawn culture laboratory as a warehouse for his bosses' cocaine. Currently, Malacón, who witnesses have accused of extensive participation in shipping drugs for the Pacific Cartel, is the owner of a pisciculture company called Granja Acuícola La Vecina, based in Navolato, Sinaloa.

Malacón is not only free; he receives financial support from the government for his business. One of the drug trade's most important tasks is moving "dirty money" into clean businesses, which in turn become operational centers. In recent years one way the drug traffickers have sought to place their businesses above board is to receive public funds from central government, mainly through the agriculture and economy secretariats. Malacón is on the executive committee of the Sinaloa State Committee for Aquaculture and Public Health, as a representative for the North Navolato region.

While he continues to go about his business unmolested, Malacón's family have been the victim of executions. In March 2008, his sister Patricia was shot in Navolato, but survived; her son, Arsenio, was shot dead in October that year in the same area. On September 28, 2009, a hit man shot his brother Jorge, aged fifty-three, in a supermarket car park. The Culiacán papers described him as the "owner of a trucking company." He was badly wounded. In a second attempt, two days later, they didn't fail again. Armed men burst into the clinic where he was being treated and shot him dead.

Humberto and Jesús Loya Pérez are also continuing with impunity along their criminal path. They have acquired considerable power in recent years. Allied to El Chapo Guzmán within a cell that includes the boss's brother, Ernesto Guzmán, they are based in Sinaloa with influence in Sonora, Tamaulipas, Nuevo León, Michoacán, and Jalisco.

Sergio Fierro Chávez is also at large. In 1999 the front man of his aviation company Aerotonalá, the pilot Jaime Madrid Sánchez, had a close shave after flying a Learjet 24D 1974, with Mexican registration number XA-RMF, from Brownsville to Lexington. In Lexington the DEA, which had been tipped off, found traces of marijuana and a secret compartment. After a tussle in the district court, Madrid could not prevent the aircraft being embargoed, but he himself got off scot-free.

In 2002 Jaime Madrid was arrested for the execution of nine people, including a woman, in the hamlet of Los Mendoza, in Michoacán state. The media was shocked by this atrocity. The Attorney's Office of Michoacán discovered that Los Mendoza was one place where locals in the pay of the Sinaloa Cartel would pick up packets of merchandise tossed out of a helicopter. The employees were killed for having tried to keep some for themselves. It was a foretaste of the violence that in years to come would overtake the whole country.

The Federation

Bolstered by Guzmán's escape from prison, the Sinaloa Cartel soon began to show its strength. This came not only from the government protection it enjoyed, but also from the fact that El Chapo was not alone. He became the chief of an ambitious criminal alliance, known as The Federation, which brought together the main members of Amado Carrillo Fuentes's old organization.

In October 2001, a historic gathering was held in the city of Cuernavaca and in the capital, which changed forever the rules governing the drug business both inside and outside the cartels. With it, the history of Mexico also changed forever. The choice of Cuernavaca was significant; it had been one of Carrillo Fuentes's favourite operational locations, as well as his home. And Mexico City, despite the presence there of all the federal authorities, is more popular as a narco rendezvous than one would think.

The idea for the meeting was Guzmán's, with the support of El Mayo Zambada. Otherwise it wouldn't have been possible. It was nine months since El Chapo had left Puente Grande. Just recently, his fixer while in prison, El Chito, had given himself up and taken the blame for the escape, but things were still tense. Calling the meeting had been a titanic effort. Many must have thought it was a trap. What's more, a climate of suspicion and unspoken discontent prevailed among the group: Vicente Carrillo Fuentes, El Viceroy, who formally had taken over the position of his brother Amado, was not living up to expectations.

More than twenty-five top drug traffickers traveled from all over Mexico to the meeting, in response to the invitation from El Mayo Zambada. If he was the convener, that was because he deserved to be. Among those who came were Vicente Carrillo Fuentes, Vicente Zambada, El Mayo's son, Ignacio Coronel Villareal, Arturo Beltrán Leyva, and his brother Alfredo, in lieu of El Azul Esparragoza. Armando Valencia Cornelio was also there, along with a representative of the Amezcua organization. They all turned up armed to the teeth. At first the atmosphere was very tense. It seemed like the clock was ticking on a time bomb.

After the death, or disappearance, of Amado Carrillo Fuentes in July 1997, it's said there was much jostling over who would take over the leadership of his flourishing organization. Vicente Carrillo Leyva, his son, was still too young. Some members thought that Juan José Álvarez Tostado, El Compadre, would make a bid. A discreet money-laundering specialist with the air of a businessman, he was one of Amado's closest collaborators.

It is also said that in the middle of the succession process, El Mayo and El Compadre clashed over the former's ambition to lead. El Compadre apparently stopped him short, saying firmly, "You traffic drugs because I let you." To avoid a bloodbath, Juan José Esparragoza proposed forming a council to run the organization created by Amado Carrillo, which was then one of the most powerful in Latin America. Eventually, command was handed to Vicente Carrillo, El Viceroy.[33] Everyone accepted the choice, albeit through gritted teeth. El Mayo withdrew to Sinaloa and asserted his control over the state; Amado's son, Vicente Carrillo Leyva, distanced himself from his uncle, while Arturo Beltrán Leyva asserted his loyalty. The result was that the various cells of the Carrillo Fuentes organization became dispersed and weakened, although they continued to conduct their dirty business very actively.

When El Chapo Guzmán left Puente Grande, his partners were skeptical. Of course, nobody believed the tale about the laundry cart. They were more inclined to think he'd been freed so that the authorities could use him to track and capture the organization's leaders. El Chapo, from his first hideouts in Nayarit and Quintana Roo, sought out two people: his cousin Arturo Beltrán Leyva, and El Mayo

Zambada.[34] At first, Arturo kept his distance. El Mayo, on the other hand, saw an opportunity finally to take control of the cartel, and was the only one to support Guzmán, including financially.

The main item on the agenda of the historic meeting called by El Chapo and El Mayo in Cuernavaca and the Federal District was the consolidation of the different strands of the Pacific Cartel into one national organization, pooling their separate efforts. Once the drug barons at the meeting agreed to join together, each brought a territory and a payroll of employees, within their organizations and within the government, to put at the service of the new association. The only one who brought nobody was El Chapo. But he brought something better: the support of the federal government. This was the capital he offered the new criminal body.

El Chapo introduced the first point in The Federation's agreement. He proposed that they eliminate the Arellano Félix brothers, with whom Guzmán had begun a war in the 1990s which he still hadn't forgotten. In previous epochs, none of the cartels would have dared to declare war on another, nor would any government have allowed it. But the promise of protection for El Chapo and the rich pickings offered by the Tijuana Cartel's territory led them to tear up the rules and support the war, which would be waged on two fronts: The Federation's own fight, hand to hand, bullet for bullet, against the Arellano Félixes, and the one the Fox government would fight, using the country's security forces. During the Fox administration, El Chapo sought the death of his enemies and the fall of their empire with the help of the Mexican government, and the information he had leaked to US agencies while he was in prison.

Rapid results

In the spring of 2002, the Arellano Félix organization began to collapse under the blows to its heart and nervous system. First came the murder of Ramón Arellano Félix, and the arrest of Benjamín Arellano Félix. The former was a matter of destiny, the latter was down to the Fox government's support for the Sinaloa Cartel. In a short space of time, almost 1,000 employees of the Tijuana Cartel had been arrested, on both sides of the border. The US administration applauded the Mexican government's decision to fight the drug gangs, but its reading of events was mistaken. The authorities weren't fighting the drug trade—just the enemies of The Federation. There are many who think the brilliant idea of creating a drug traffickers' union came from the DEA, whose agents visited Guzmán in jail to get information from him about the Arellano Félix brothers.

In Mexican intelligence circles, some say it was easier for the US authorities to deal with just one organization when it came to controlling the flow of drugs on their territory. But others say this was precisely the argument used by sectors of the Mexican army and by the secretary of public security, García Luna, who had been protecting El Chapo Guzmán ever since his escape.

Guzmán's scheme broke with all previous practice. Most of the drug barons at the meeting had their own gang, and still controlled the routes they had worked for Amado Carrillo Fuentes. On occasions they'd help each other out, taking a delivery of cocaine,[35] or providing assistance in exchange for payment in cash or in kind. However, the drug traffickers did not cooperate systematically, and this is exactly what El Chapo was proposing. This was the only strategy that could ensure growth, with an advantage over the Colombian and Asian gangs inside the United States. Though there must have been misgivings, by the end of the meeting The Federation had been established. It was set up on the basis of strict hierarchy and discipline. To maintain internal order, it's said The Federation imposed a verbal code that all members were obliged to follow.[36] Everyone would share the routes that different leaders had secured over the years, as well as their respective armed groups, and even their money-laundering men. Thus were unified the operations in sixteen Mexican states, representing more than half the country: Sinaloa, Sonora, Chihuahua, Coahuila, Durango, Colima, Jalisco, Nayarit, Morelos, the Federal District, the State of Mexico, Yucatán, Quintana Roo, Guanajuato, Aguascalientes, and Querétaro. At the top of the pyramid sat Joaquín Guzmán as the coordinator, with a vertical chain of command below him. Why him? Not just because it was his idea, but because he was the one who had the arrangement with the government, indeed with the Presidential Office of Vicente Fox—who was himself investigated by the DEA during his sexennial.[37]

In this way The Federation began to function as a council, with representatives from the main leaders of drug trafficking organizations. "Through a network of corrupt police and political contacts, it directed a large-scale narcotics transportation network involving the use of land, air, and sea transportation assets, shipping multiton quantities of cocaine from South America, through Central American and Mexico, and finally into the United States."[38] If at times there were "rifts and in-fighting among the leaders of the Federation," they managed to keep these to a minimum, to ensure their "common political and judicial protection."[39] Public officials and politicians who had provided protection to one member of the group would henceforth extend it to all. The Federation became virtually immune.

Apart from El Chapo and his cousins, the Beltrán Leyvas, the main leaders of The Federation were Ismael El Mayo Zambada, Ignacio Nacho Coronel, Juan José Esparragoza, El Azul, Vicente Carrillo Fuentes, El Viceroy, and Armando Valencia.

El Mayo Zambada

Within the organization, El Mayo has been seen as the man behind El Chapo's throne. Ismael Zambada García is from a village known as El Álamo, in the district of Costa Rica, Culiacán, Sinaloa. It's a tiny community that has gradually been swallowed up by the urban sprawl. El Mayo is from a very poor background, a campesino who began planting marijuana and poppies. Tall, swarthy, and stout, now aged around sixty, he is married to Rosario Niebla Cardoza, with whom he had at least six children. His favorite is the youngest, Vicente, his right-hand man in the business (his left-hand man is his brother, Reynaldo Zambada García). He boasts of having at least five other sets of wives and children, otherwise he could hardly call himself a narco.

El Mayo was introduced to the drugs trade by José Inés Calderón, one of the main traffickers in Sinaloa and in Mexico in the 1970s and 1980s.[40] People still remember him paying his "drug taxes" in the PJF offices in 1978, during the so-called years of control. He also experienced first-hand the period when drug trafficking became a political weapon for the CIA, and observed how its fat profits made it a tempting business proposition for the Mexican establishment.

Ismael Zambada is certainly the most experienced of all the drug barons today. His name features in all of Mexico's big drug cases—for example in the "Maxitrial," which put the former governor of Quintana Roo, Mario Villanueva, behind bars in the United States. El Mayo was also involved in the case of the Anáhuac Financial Group, which revealed links between prominent Mexican politicians, of both the PRI and the PAN, and money-laundering schemes.

The United States government has been after him since 2002, putting a reward on his head of $5 million—a snip compared with what El Mayo can pay for his protection. He is known to own many properties in Jalisco, the Federal District, and Sinaloa, where he is said to be the proprietor of the Hotel El Mayo, in downtown Culiacán.

On June 20, 2000, the Mexican army carried out a raid on a ranch of El Mayo's called Puerto Rico, near Culiacán. The 650-hectare property was producing milk for his company, Industrias de Ganaderos de Culiacán. The soldiers found 5,700 head of cattle, more than 100 farm workers, a stable of thoroughbreds, and thirty-seven vehicles.[41]

After the raid, El Mayo's wife Rosario went to the PGR with an irate representative of the local businessmen's association, Coparmex, in tow and divorce papers in hand, to demand her property back. She claimed she had nothing to do with the drug baron, and that the jobs of 1,500 families were at stake.[42] But the wives of drug barons are wives for life, and their husbands' rule endures. Nobody in the drugs world would believe for a moment that the properties in Doña Rosario's name were independent of her ex.

El Mayo's compadre: drug dealer and politician

It was precisely at the Puerto Rico ranch, more than twenty years ago, that El Mayo had a meeting with the businessman and cattle rancher Jesús Vizcarra, a former mayor of Culiacán for the PRI and a candidate for the governorship of Sinaloa in the elections of July 2010. Six months before those elections, the national paper *Reforma* published a front-page photo apparently showing Vizcarra with various drug traffickers, including El Mayo.

According to the article, the gathering at the Puerto Rico ranch had been to celebrate the Day of the Virgin of Guadalupe. However, Jesús Vizcarra stated publicly that the photo had been taken at a cattle trade event, and that he couldn't remember where it had been. Either way, by the time the photo was published, stories of Vizcarra's alleged links to drug trafficking were nothing new. It was said that El Mayo was a compadre of his, something he never dared deny, for the simple reason that it was true.

When the photograph was published, Jesús Vizcarra explained to his campaign team that he did know El Mayo. Some years before, he told them, one of his sons was kidnapped, and the only person who helped rescue him was the drug baron. But he insisted that was their only connection. Soon his loyalty to El Mayo Zambada would cost him the governorship of Sinaloa. A few weeks before the election, in the last debate between the candidates, Mario López Valdez, nicknamed Malova (an old PRI hand recently converted to the PAN), asked him the question that killed his aspirations dead: "Are you or are you not a compadre of El Mayo Zambada?" asked Malova on live TV. Nobody in Sinaloa could forget the sight of Vizcarra struck dumb. Eventually he managed to mumble something incoherent about how "I have never done anything illegal," and other such phrases. If he had denied it, El Mayo might have understood it, but he wouldn't have forgiven it. On the other hand, admitting it would have meant the end not only of his candidacy, but probably also of his multimillion-dollar interests in meat and allied businesses.

López Valdez concluded triumphantly, "Silence is as good as assent." But the topic of drug trafficking clearly makes Malova nervous. He clasps and unclasps his hands, sweating.[43]

López Valdez won the governorship of Sinaloa. But contrary to appearances, El Mayo did not lose out thereby. People close to him say that López was also his candidate. Indeed, the drug baron could not forgive Vizcarra for his ingratitude, and the fact that he didn't even have the grace to greet his wife when they met in some public event. It seems Vizcarra went to see El Mayo to tell him he wanted to be governor of Sinaloa. The message was clear, he wanted his support. El Mayo simply wished him well in his new venture. A few days later, they say, he decided to back López Valdez, to teach his old friend a lesson.

In 2010, the former PAN politician Manuel Clouthier, referring to the elections in Sinaloa, denounced the mafioso clique led by the outgoing governor for the PRI, Jesús Aguilar Padilla. He accused him, and his predecessor Juan Millán, of working for the Sinaloa Cartel. Clouthier insisted that Vizcarra represented the clear intention to keep the Sinaloa Cartel in charge of the state administration. The big question is whether López Valdez, Malova, represented anything different.

During his campaign, this *priísta* opportunistically disguised as a *panista* publicly recognized that, apart from his own biological father, he had a debt to two other men: Leonardo Gutiérrez, El Nalo, who had been a father to him in his business career, and Millán, his father in politics. El Nalo has also been linked to El Mayo Zambada. He was identified by a journalist in 2006 as the owner of six planes allegedly used to transport drugs, and of car dealerships acquired with drug money.[44]

In earlier times, the two governors, Aguilar and Millán, were part of the same group and were fed by the same hand. The split between them led to a political dispute in the state, with each supporting his own candidate: Vizcarra and López respectively, both originally from the PRI, in other words from the same "political mafia."

There was indeed a change of political party in Sinaloa, which led many to jump to the conclusion that more than eighty years of PRI hegemony had come to an end. But underneath it seems there was no change in the ruling clique, nor, in all probability, in their underlying interests.

Mario López Valdez became governor on December 31, 2010. Within months, doubts gathered over him. On May 30 people awoke to the sight of eight banners draped around the state capital, Culiacán. They read, "Malova, when you went to Mexico City you told the president you'd met El Chapo Guzmán on September 6, 2010, at the Kila ranch—don't deny he [El Chapo] told you to clean out northern Sinaloa to make way for him and to supply him with information."

On July 2, 2011, the warnings were signed in blood. Two decapitated bodies were left in front of two newspapers in Mazatlán, *El*

Debate and *Noroeste*, accusing the governor and the mayor of protecting El Chapo and the Sinaloa Cartel. "If this continues, there will be reprisals."

Public enemy

Of all the drug barons, El Mayo is the one that provokes the most contradictory reactions. He is either loved or hated. There is nothing in between. Some describe him as a generous, easy-going man. As one of the old generation of drug traffickers, they say he's the kind that lavishes money on the rural communities where he carries on his illegal business. They tell of people queuing up when he comes to their village. He has never tried to look refined like others of his colleagues. He regards himself as a simple rancher, and behaves like one. He was one of the biggest growers of marijuana and poppy before getting into the world of cocaine. But this was the future, so he adapted. He had the staff, the routes, and the contacts in the United States; he just had to sell a different product. They say that when he started out in the white powder business, he used his dairy companies to move it in milk cartons.

But while some speak of him so highly, others describe him as manipulative and treacherous. Even members of his own organization accuse him of delivering up one of his most trusted lieutenants, Javier Torres. El JT had managed to get out of prison three times, and was the sole survivor of a massacre carried out by the Arellano Félix brothers in El Limoncito, Sinaloa, where one of his brothers and eleven other people died. But he didn't survive the maneuvers of El Mayo. Torres was arrested by the Mexican army in January 2004 without a shot being fired. They caught him unawares, usually a sign of betrayal.

Like other drug barons, El Mayo is no angel. He is criticized because supposedly he is El Chapo's real boss, but prefers the latter to take the limelight. However, if this is the strategy it hasn't worked that well. For thirty-five years, El Mayo's criminal activities went almost unnoticed in the United States. Thanks to The Federation, on May 31, 2002, the Bush administration classified him as a Grade I drug trafficker, a true public enemy.

During Vicente Fox's presidency, El Mayo Zambada began seriously to exasperate the US Treasury Department, in view of the freedom with which the drug baron was able to operate in both Mexico and the United States. Zambada ran an extensive network of companies that he used to traffic drugs and launder assets, with either the tolerance or the ignorance of both governments. In May 2007 the Treasury identified six companies and twelve individuals as part of El Mayo's financial network. It froze any assets they might have in the US, and blocked any US financial or commercial dealings with them.

Among El Mayo's companies is a nursery called Estancia Infantil del Niño Feliz. It has all the necessary permits from the Mexican Institute of Social Security, which even gives it a subsidy for every child that has attended since November 22, 2001[45]—one of the benefits introduced by the Fox government. However, it seems nobody bothered to check when Zambada's gang gave the nursery's Culiacán address as that of another of his companies, the Santa Mónica stables, also cited by the Treasury Department as a money-laundering operation.

Other companies listed include the Gasolinera Rosario—a gas station with the same address as the nursery—Multiservicios Jeviz, Jamaro Constructores, another stables called Establos Puerto Rico, and the dairy outfit Nueva Industria de Ganaderos de Culiacán. If there were any doubt these companies belong to the drug baron, in July 2008, two decapitated bodies were left in bags outside the gate of Nueva Industria, where El Mayo produces the popular Santa Mónica brand of milk. They had messages with them saying "THE GOVERNMENT PROTECTS YOU TOO MUCH," and "DON'T SEND THE FEDS."[46]

After the Treasury's move in May 2007, Adam Szubin, Director of the Office of Foreign Assets Control, said the action exposed even further "the network of front companies and financial partners that Zambada used to conceal and launder the money from drugs that he then takes out of the United States' financial system."[47] If there's one thing that upsets the US authorities, it's when the drug barons remove money from the US.

The reaction of Felipe Calderón's government was a disappointment. The secretary of finance said that the Mexican businesses and accounts of those identified by the Treasury Department would not be touched until the Mexican authorities could determine their guilt, given that the US investigation had presented "only indications."[48] As a result, the government's support for those same companies continued through programs for small and medium-sized businesses (SMBs) as well as the Secretariat of Agriculture and even the National Water Board (Conagua). The Puerto Rico Stables is a case in point. Between 2001 and 2008 it received more than 5 million pesos (about $450,000 in 2005) from the government through the Agricultural Marketing Services and Support (Aserca) facility. This was a nice windfall for Vicente Zambada, El Mayo's eldest son, who owns the Stables.

In 2001, Conagua gave a concession in Costa Rica district of 127,000 m² of state-owned land, to be used for the extraction of resources or for agriculture, pisciculture, or forestry. And in 2002, the Board gave a new concession for the use of a further 383,000 m² of state land. At the time, the head of Conagua was someone very close to the president, Cristóbal Jáquez: a former executive of Coca Cola and of the Grupo Industrial Lala. President Vicente Fox not only failed to combat El Mayo's money-laundering activities, he actually lent him public resources to help him carry them out. The concessions remain in place to this day.[49]

El Mayo was astute enough to enroll the Puerto Rico Stables in an experimental program of the UNFCC (United Nations Framework Convention on Climate Change), carried out in Mexico between 2005 and 2006, to improve the disposal of dairy cattle waste so as to reduce emissions of methane and nitrous oxide in an economically sustainable way. It's an example of the drug traffickers' skill at infiltrating many other domains. Of course, a certificate of participation in UN activities is an excellent way of legitimizing illegal businesses.

At the beginning of 2010, El Mayo Zambada did something unprecedented: he agreed to meet a journalist, Julio Scherer, the respected editor of *Proceso*—a weekly news magazine seen by the government as one of its great foes, apparently just because it is critical.

Strictly speaking, the interview yielded no new information. It seems the drug baron was more interested in sending some coded messages to those who were in a position to understand them. One of the addressees was President Felipe Calderón: "If they catch me or kill me, nothing will change." "So far, no one has betrayed me," El Mayo also said, almost menacingly, this time perhaps to those partners who might be beginning to feel uneasy about him. What his laconic remarks show most clearly is the nature of fear among Mexico's big drug bosses. They don't worry that the government, the police, or the courts can or will take decisive action; they fear betrayal from within.

"Your friendship with El Chapo Guzmán is well known, so it's not surprising that you were waiting for him outside Puente Grande on the day of his escape. Can you tell me how you felt that day?" asked Scherer.

"El Chapo and I are good friends. We often talk on the phone. But that story's not true. It's one more lie they tell about me. Like the idea that I planned an attack on the President of the Republic. I wouldn't dream of such a thing," asserted El Mayo. It sounded more like a confirmation than a denial.[50]

Ismael Zambada had a score to settle with Felipe Calderón. They both knew it; it was just a question of when. Each had struck at the other's heart, and neither was likely to forget.

The King of Crystal

He always was independent, even when he belonged to Guzmán's organization. Like many others, he was a policeman before he became a drug trafficker. He went by the pseudonym of César Arturo Barrios Romero, although on his government file he was mistakenly given another alias, Dagoberto Rodríguez Jiménez. This mistake would later become the basis for one of the Calderón government's biggest deceptions.

Ignacio Nacho Coronel has many nicknames: Cachas de Diamante (Diamond Hunk), El Licenciado, El Rey del Cristal—the last because he had led the field as a seller of crystal meth. However, his own people always call him Nacho Coronel. And now he has acquired the aura of immortality. His FBI and Mexican intelligence files concur that he was born on February 1, 1954, but it's not clear if that was in

Veracruz or in Canelas, Durango. The trafficker Pablo Tostado Félix, in an interview before he was killed in Durango prison in 2010, insisted that he and Nacho Coronel were about the same age, fifty-two, and that both were brought up in Canelas He is married to Teresa Galindo, with whom he has one son; he keeps another partner and son elsewhere. He is said to be a distant relative of El Mayo Zambada.

Nachito Coronel—to those closest to him—was a "madrina"[51] to the PJF commander, José Luis Fuentes, in Baja California. Fuentes was the husband of Sandra Ávila Beltrán, the so-called Queen of the Pacific, a cartel leader in her own right. It's said that after Fuentes's death in 1992 Nacho became romantically attached to her, and that they remained lovers for a long time.[52]

Coronel's complete immersion in the drug trade occurred in the shadow of Amado Carrillo Fuentes at the end of the 1980s, when he worked alongside Héctor El Güero Palma, Joaquín Guzmán, Ismael El Mayo Zambada, the Beltrán Leyva brothers, and Juan José Esparragoza. In June 1993, a few days after the murder of Cardinal Posadas, Nacho's elder brother Raymundo was killed by intelligence officers from the Fifth Military Region under General Gutiérrez Rebollo. The operation was part of the investigations into the cardinal's death. Two aspects were noteworthy. The first was the attitude of Raymundo Coronel himself: he confronted the security forces with a machine gun in each hand, firing furiously. The second was that in the trunk of one of his cars they found a notebook with the names of police chiefs, army officers, and politicians who were being paid by South American mafias for protection in Mexico. After Gutiérrez Rebollo handed over this evidence to attorney general Jorge Carpizo, Carpizo made sure it did not appear in the Posadas case files.

According to Tostado Félix, Nacho's rise in the organization came in the wake of his brother's death. In June 1995, he had a further stroke of luck: the arrest of El Güero Palma strengthened his growing influence in the Guadalajara area. Later, in 1997, the disappearance of another close collaborator of Carrillo Fuentes, Eduardo González, consolidated his leadership in Guadalajara still further.

Ignacio Coronel was able to develop his own networks. His file says he had a connection with Alejandro Patrón Laviada, known as

La Vaca (The Cow), the brother of Patricio Patrón, a former PAN governor of Yucatán state and until recently head of the Federal Environmental Protection Agency (Profepa). Apparently he also had links with General Guillermo Álvarez Nahara, who was head of the Military Judicial Police during Carlos Salinas' presidency,[53] then of the PJF at the end of Ernesto Zedillo's term.[54] To date, neither La Vaca nor General Álvarez have been investigated.

Ignacio Coronel acquired most power as a pioneer in the drugs of the future, ephedrine and methamphetamine, made in clandestine labs in Jalisco. Nacho supplied the huge market for these synthetic drugs in the United States—a market that is now controlled by the Sinaloa Cartel. That is why the US government christened him The King of Crystal. He is said to operate throughout Mexico, as well as in the United States, Central and South America, and even in some European countries, with the help of his trusted army of associates. He became indispensable to El Chapo and El Mayo.

Los Güeritos and El Tirso

Ignacio Coronel had two brothers under his command, Luis and Esteban Rodríguez Olivera, better known as Los Güeros or its diminutive, Los Güeritos (Blondies). They were under investigation by the DEA throughout the presidency of Vicente Fox, suspected of being one of the links between the president's family and The Federation. The Rodríguez brothers were based in Guanajuato,[55] and have been linked in particular to Manuel Bribiesca Sahagún, the son of Marta Sahagún, President Fox's spokeswoman and then his second wife. Thanks to this connection, it is said, they got support for transporting drugs by sea. The brothers are currently wanted, along with Nacho Coronel, El Mayo, and El Chapo, by a federal court in Brooklyn, and are officially classified as fugitives from justice. It is striking that the warrant issued by this court names the two brothers along with a third person whose name is, unusually, redacted on several pages of the court papers. All three are accused of drug trafficking and money laundering.

In 2008, the Rodríguez brothers made themselves felt in Michoacán, beyond their usual base, in the form of macabre messages to the new and threatening players on the cartel scene, Los Zetas: corpses with signs of torture and their throats cut, accompanied by the notice, "THIS IS A GREETING FROM LOS GÜERITOS, JOSÉ LUIS RODRÍGUEZ OLIVERA AND ESTEBAN RODRÍGUEZ OLIVERA AND LA CALABAZA, TO EDUARDO COSTILLA AND HERIBERTO LAZCANO AND EFRAÍN TEODORO, AZ 14."

They are also connected to Tirso Martínez Sánchez.[56] In his mid-forties, a native of Guadalajara, Tirso runs his own outfit, with direct links to Colombia, while performing importation and distribution services for The Federation and others. He uses a string of cocaine warehouses purchased or rented via front companies.[57] There is a $5 million reward in the US for any information as to his whereabouts.

El Azul

If there is one drug baron in Mexico who understands the importance of blood ties, it is Juan José Esparragoza, one of the veteran Godfathers of the trade. He was born in 1949 in Huixiopa, Badiraguato, Sinaloa. Tall and brown-skinned, with dark hair and mustache, regular mouth, aquiline nose, rounded chin, and average build, he weighs around 200 lbs. His most striking features are the bushy eyebrows and bulging eyes. His FBI file speculates that he may have had plastic surgery, but he could hardly change those peculiar eyes, hence no doubt his fondness for dark glasses. His false identities include José Luis Esparragosa, Juan José Esparragoza-Italino, Juan José Esparraguza-Valino, Raúl González and Juan Robles;[58] but in the criminal underworld they know him as El Azul.

The US authorities call him The Peace Maker. Although he doesn't always succeed in making peace between the groups, he invariably comes out on good terms with everyone. For each he has a tender word or some wise advice. He is the consigliere. In exchange, the others let him traffic on his own routes and participate in joint deals. Those who know him say he is the most skillful of them all; he gets what he wants without risking too much.

In the 1970s, Esparragoza was one of the agents of the Federal Security Directorate (DFS), the Mexican intelligence agency, whose commanders were friends with Miguel Ángel Félix Gallardo, Rafael Caro Quintero, and Ernesto Fonseca Carrillo. El Azul was one of Carrillo Fuentes's most trusted men, not as his subordinate but as his negotiator, in both Mexico and Colombia. In the 80s he established a base in the towns of Querétaro and Cuernavaca. Lacking the incendiary temperament of Arturo Beltrán Leyva, the brother of his son's wife, he is not as ambitious as El Mayo Zambada, his compadre, and not as boisterous as another compadre, the jailed Rafael Caro Quintero, whose sister is married to El Azul's nephew.

In the name of his official wife María Guadalupe Gastélum he owns a mall in Culiacán, the Plaza Comercial Residencial del Lago, which has reaped state funding worth more than 3 million pesos (around $270,000 in 2004) through the Law of Investment Promotion for the Economic Development of Sinaloa.

In 1992, El Azul completed a sentence in the prison of Puente Grande. His connections in government were nonetheless so good that in 1993 he was able to obtain a passport like any ordinary citizen.[59] That same year, thanks to his good offices, a bloody showdown was avoided between the Gulf Cartel and Carrillo Fuentes's Juárez organization. A pact was made, which became known as "The Northern Peace."[60] Ten years later, however, Esparragoza himself would be one of the instigators of the most brutal war for the spoils of the drug trade that Mexico has ever seen. El Azul is an astute man, one of the quiet ones, who softly climb up rung by rung.

The government of Felipe Calderón identified at least thirty-two properties belonging to Esparragoza, in at least seven states, although there is no indication that it has raided any of them. Since 1998 there have been three arrest warrants out for him, for drug trafficking and organized crime, but nobody seems to be keen on using them. One of these is for extradition to the United States. The gringos have put the usual price of $5 million on his head. Some people think El Azul could be the big winner from the war between drug traffickers, and that his best moment may be yet to come.

The Viceroy

Vicente, the second son of Don Vicente Carrillo and Aurora Fuentes, was used to being overshadowed; he'd never been a natural leader, like his brother Amado. He was born in 1962 in Guamuchilito, Sinaloa. His parents had moved there from Chihuahua. Don Vicente was taken on by La Primavera sugar mill, never imagining his children would wind up selling a different kind of white product. The couple had seven children, four boys and three girls.[61] Their favorites were the eldest, Amado, and the youngest, Rodolfo, who was known as El Niño de Oro, the Golden Boy.

Vicente was sandwiched in between. He wasn't as good-looking as Amado, nor did he have the charm that meant things always came so easily to his brother. He was always second-best, always just the kid brother of El Señor de los Cielos. His character was weak. Of all the partners in The Federation, he is the only one the DEA records as being addicted to drugs. They also believe he may have undergone plastic surgery.

After Amado disappeared from the scene, and thanks to El Azul's always timely intervention, Vicente, El Viceroy, took over as head of the powerful Juárez Cartel. The Beltrán Leyva brothers accepted his leadership, and continued to collaborate. But El Viceroy's reign was unsatisfactory. The empire built by his brother drained away through his fingers like water. Nonetheless, El Viceroy managed to hang on to one of the most important drug territories in Mexico, on the invaluable border with the United States. Thanks to the Beltrán Leyvas, he also kept the vital contacts in Colombia who supplied him with cocaine, and so he could ensure that his patch remained highly productive.

At least until July 2009, the Juárez–El Paso corridor was one of the three main trafficking routes across the northern frontier. Many tons of cocaine made their way there from the Norte del Valle Cartel, which had taken over what was left of the Medellín Cartel and the United Self-Defense Forces of Colombia (AUC). El Viceroy also began charging other cartels for the right to use "his" border crossing.[62] In a case filed in the New York District Court, it is estimated that between July 2, 2000, and December 1, 2005, Vicente Carrillo

Fuentes obtained more than $10 million in annual gross receipts for the "manufacture, importation, and distribution of cocaine." On July 24, 2009, the court announced that, in connection with the charges against him, it would seek to confiscate $2 billion from Vicente Carrillo, which gives some idea of the size of his fortune.

The murder of Rodolfo Carrillo Fuentes

In late 2004, Doña Aurora begged her son Vicente to break off relations with El Chapo Guzmán. And there's not much you can refuse your mother. On September 11 of that year, her Golden Boy Rodolfo and his wife, Giovana Quevedo Gastélum, along with their two children, were leaving a cinema in Culiacán. On the way to their car, they were attacked by a group of gunmen. The shooting went on for fifteen minutes—an eternity. The little ones survived. Now they are in the care of their Aunt Celia, Giovana's sister, who married Vicente Carrillo Leyva, Amado's son—as if to keep the tragic family saga going.

The execution was blamed on El Chapo, at least by Vicente. Nonetheless, Sinaloa Cartel insiders say the order came from El Mayo. It seems Rodolfo wasn't sticking to The Federation's ground rules, and a line had to be drawn. The murder would have repercussions that can still be measured in the number of bullets fired in the name of El Niño de Oro.

"A Funeral Fit for a Prince," is how they described it in the headlines the next day. In a double coffin with gold fittings, beneath a picture of the bleeding Christ, Rodolfo and his wife were buried in the grounds of the Santa Aurora ranch in Guamuchilito. While the funeral cortège paid its last respects to the drug baron, the Sinaloa band Los Plebes de Navolato played a new corrido, El Niño de Oro. The bodies were buried in a marble mausoleum where Don Vicente senior and the supposed remains of El Señor de los Cielos were already interred.

For Doña Aurora there would be no forgetting and no forgiving her son's murderers. Yet, despite his mother's request, Vicente continued doing business with El Chapo and El Mayo. They brought him the government protection that might one day enable him to match his elder brother's legend. If he had followed his mother's advice straight away, his disappointment would surely have been less. When he did follow it, in January 2008, it was too late. Doña Aurora now lives alone, praying for her remaining sons; she has heard nothing from Vicente for years.[63]

"The Mexican government, the police, the military: they are the cartel"

Guillermo Ramírez Peyro, alias Lalo, is a peculiar man. Perhaps that's because of the dozen executions he has on his conscience, in which he also decreed the means of finishing off the victims: bullets, or a plastic bag over the head. All of them were drug trafficking rivals of his boss, Vicente Carrillo Fuentes. What El Viceroy didn't know was that Lalo was a US government informer, under cover for ICE (US Immigration and Customs Enforcement), with the code name SA-913-EP.

Lalo's case has been highly controversial in the United States. It's been on the front pages of the main papers and on National Public Radio. Ramírez belonged to the Federal Highway Police in Guerrero state. In 1995 he joined Amado Carrillo Fuentes's organization. And in 2000 he decided to sign up on another equally or more dangerous payroll, that of ICE informers.[64] He provided information for the next four years (the first four of the Fox administration).

Ramírez was a prolific stool pigeon. It is said he contributed to the arrest of more than fifty people, including Heriberto Santillán, one of the most senior aides in the Juárez Cartel, and a number of bent US immigration officers who took bribes from traffickers. Lalo was also very productive as a criminal. Presumably with the knowledge of ICE, this thirty-six-year-old smuggled drugs for Carrillo Fuentes and witnessed the killing of at least twelve people in Ciudad Juárez. Apart from giving him carte blanche to commit crimes, the United States government paid him for his information: $220,000 over the period of his employment.[65]

After the murders, Lalo revealed the location of the so-called "house of death." That was the end of his American dream. A scandal erupted in the United States when it became clear that ICE had known about the executions, even as they were happening, and done nothing to stop them. After wringing all the information they could out of him, the US authorities began proceedings to deport Lalo back to Mexico. However, in March 2010, the US Board of Immigration Appeals gave protection to the now ex-informer, on the grounds that if he returned to Mexico he would immediately be tortured and killed by the cartel he had betrayed.

Ramírez Peyro was thoroughly familiar with the organization of Vicente Carrillo Fuentes, both before and during the era of The Federation. Indeed he had been the right-hand man of Heriberto Santillán, the boss he betrayed to the US. His account of what happened during Fox's presidency is essential to understanding Calderón's. He claimed to have worked with federal and local authorities in Chihuahua, and with the Mexican army, in drug-related activities, including transporting the goods in Navy boats and PGR patrol cars.[66]

In a sworn statement filed in federal court in Bloomington, Minnesota, Ramírez said that he had been told that the office of the Mexican president had an arrangement with the Juárez Cartel. Santillán explained to me that President Fox had decided to coordinate and consult with the Juárez Cartel. He [Fox] would attack the opposing cartels like those of Tijuana and the Gult; then the Juárez Cartel could work without the government being on top of them."'[67] And that is what happened.

Ramírez Peyro's testimony corroborates what a DEA official in Mexico said in May 2006: that the Fox government was giving protection to Joaquín Guzmán and his partners.[68] "The Mexican government, the police, the military: they are the cartel," said Ramírez, with unquestionable exactitude.[69] At the same time, the rules governing the relation between drug traffickers and government changed forever during the Fox administration: the public officials became employees of the drug traffickers, and their armed wing.

The Juárez Cartel's sanguinary hit squad, La Línea, which in the last two years has defended that coveted border crossing with blistering violence, is made up mainly of local and federal police and members of the Mexican army, according to Ramírez Peyro. They are the narcos' hired assassins, using the guns, uniforms, and badges that are paid for by us, the same Mexican taxpayers who are assaulted by death from every side. This is the true nightmare: that the enemy, the mafioso, who is tearing society apart, goes unnoticed in public office. Many officials are capable of doing anything to protect their positions, the coveted posts they actually hold at the behest of the drug barons. Because even government ministers, as far as the drug traffickers are concerned, are nothing more than their employees, their servants, part of the staff.

The judge dealing with the immigration status of the ICE's witness noted that "the police and security forces" in Mexico have been implicated in "unlawful killings," and that "there were numerous reports of executions carried out by rival drug cartels, whose members allegedly included both active and former federal, state, and municipal security forces."[70] Lalo had put names and faces to this collusion ever since 2005. In one of his statements to the US court, he alleged that at all levels of the Mexican police there are unlawful ties to drug trafficking. But of all these police forces, he only specifically mentioned one: the AFI—then led by Genaro García Luna—which he accused of passing on to drug gangs the names of protected witnesses so they could be eliminated. "In light of the serious documentation submitted," the judge found Lalo's testimony "to be credible."[71]

The names of President Calderón's secretary of public security and his team, along with the initials of the different police forces that García Luna has led over the last decade, little by little have begun to appear more frequently in drug cases connected with Guzmán and his associates. Not, of course, as investigating authorities, but as accomplices.

In the savage gang wars that kicked off in 2001, the battles have not been equal. The armies available to either side are asymmetrical. That of El Chapo Guzmán and his camp is composed primarily of senior government officials. This is no isolated or fortuitous occurrence, but such a constant feature that it looks like government policy. And that is what inflames the belligerence of El Chapo's enemies.

Two years after creating The Federation, with the support of central government, in 2003 Joaquín Guzmán and his partners decided to start a new war. This time the artillery would no longer be aimed at the Tijuana Cartel, but at the Gulf Cartel. The violence, death, and brutality redoubled. Mexico has been plunged into a dark and seemingly bottomless pit, because federal government institutions decided to protect the Sinaloa Cartel and use the state apparatus to combat its rivals.

CHAPTER NINE

Narco Wars

I belong to The Zetas and we look after the boss.
We are twenty bodyguards, loyal and brave.
Ready to give our lives to serve the Man.
Since I was small, I wanted to be what I am.
My father he told me, there's nothing like honor.
The man who believes that is naturally brave.
We are twenty Zetas, united like a family.
We twenty are the mighty, with suicide diplomas,
We know that in every mission we could die.
How fine is my Tamaulipas, where no one is afraid.
To go up to the mountains, I'll stay here in Victoria,
to serve my boss, from Tampico to Laredo.
I'm from Matamoros, Tamaulipas is my land,
Victoria is my capital, at the foot of the mountains.
Greetings to XR, who's made of the same stuff.
We are twenty Zetas, united like a family.
We twenty are the mighty, with suicide diplomas,
We know that in every mission we could die.

These are the lyrics of "Escolta Suicida" (Suicide Bodyguard), a "narco-corrido" dedicated to the armed group known as Los Zetas. It was playing on many radio stations in the states of Tamaulipas and Nuevo León back in 2008. The chorus blared out over and over again at full volume from the pick-up trucks doing their rounds in the city of Monterrey. "We twenty are the mighty, with suicide diplomas, we know that in every mission we could die . . ." rang out gaily, in an atmosphere of tense calm. It was some time before the city understood that this was the beginning of the end to a period of economic prosperity and peace.

Many think the narco-corridos are popular hits with no value beyond their unusual and amusing lyrics. But the Mexican army takes a different view. At the Army and Air Force Studies Center, part of the Defense Secretariat, there is a module in the Military Intelligence course entitled "Content Analysis of Narco-corridos." In the class, officers deconstruct the songs to learn more about the enemy. They know that most narco-corridos have been authorized by the individuals they extol, and that at least some of the words tend to be true. The singers, in their cowboy boots and Texan hats, are the modern minstrels of war and destruction.

If there's anything to be learned from "Suicide Bodyguard", it is two of the features that set the Zetas apart from other armed drug gangs: its members are kamikazes, and they have built up around the organization a sense of brotherhood that is almost religious. They are bound by a cult of death.

The Executioner

Heriberto Lazcano was always getting into trouble, ever since he was a boy. The military strictness imposed by his father led him to take it out on his classmates at a boys' primary school in Mexico City. Yet nobody would have imagined that this kid would become the most bloody, feared, and wanted man in Mexico. He is the perfect assassin. Now in his mid-thirties, he is dark-skinned with almond eyes, and of athletic build. People know him as El Lazcal or Z3, but the nickname that suits him best is El Verdugo, The Executioner. It's a title he's earned by the merciless way he puts traitors and enemies to death.

In war, the difference between victory and defeat can hang upon a single man. This is the case with Lazcano, one of the founders of Los Zetas, the indestructible group that for years was the armed wing of the Gulf Cartel. Today it is regarded by the United States government as an "international threat." In the deals made by the armed forces and police of the Fox government with the Sinaloa Cartel, they never reckoned with the strength of El Verdugo and his armed group:

violent men turned into veritable killing machines. When Lazcano is asked why his paramilitary group adopted the name Los Zetas, he answers chillingly: "Because nothing comes after 'Z.'"[72]

Originally Los Zetas were mostly comprised of highly-trained former soldiers in the Mexican army. Some of them had belonged to the Special Forces Airmobile Group (GAFE), set up at the end of the 1990s to combat the drugs trade. Later they recruited members of the Guatemalan army's elite unit, the Kaibiles. Now it's said that any bandit, for less than 5,000 pesos ($400), can join the paramilitary group and kill who they want.

Heriberto Lazcano Lazcano was born in 1974, in Pachuca, Hidalgo. His father, Gregorio, was in the Mexican army and his mother, Amelia, was a housewife.[1] Following in his father's footsteps, Heriberto joined the army in 1991, when he was just seventeen. Some say he attended the Heroic Military College, graduating as a lieutenant. However, Sedena insists there is no record of him ever attending this institution.[2]

He is a violent and profoundly mistrustful man, but insists he has never hurt women or children. He places his own idea of "honor" above even the interests of the drug business. And where honor is at stake, no amount of killing will suffice to compensate for the offense. What happened with his accountant provides a graphic illustration. At the end of 2008, the Mexican army arrested her in Acapulco. Now she is behind bars in the Topo Chico prison in Monterrey. At the time of her arrest, she was brutally raped by soldiers taking part in the operation, as she herself has recounted in her sworn statement.[3] When Lazcano learned what had happened, he was incandescent, and ordered the soldiers who raped her to be hunted down.

On December 21, 2008, residents in Chilpancingo, Guerrero, were treated to a scene out of Dante's *Inferno* that rocked the whole country. The severed heads of eight soldiers attached to the 35th Military Region were left in a shopping mall. Their bodies, bearing signs of unspeakable torture, were dumped on different stretches of the highway that leads to the state capital.

In the middle of the turf wars between drug traffickers, Lazcano is like Nero: he'd rather see the country go up in flames than lose the war to El Chapo Guzmán, or the government that defends him. El

Verdugo belongs to a generation of drug traffickers who fear neither death nor chaos. Between them all, they have turned Mexico into a graveyard.

The official, Sedena version of Lazcano's career is that he joined the army as a private in the infantry. His number was B-9223601. As a result of good performance, in July 1993 he was promoted to the rank of corporal.[4] In this capacity he learnt to use special weapons and to command squads of men. The Secretariat will never admit it, but El Verdugo did indeed belong to the GAFE.[5] As such he was trained to carry out special and covert operations. He took the best courses in intelligence, counter-intelligence, and combat that the Mexican army had to offer. In fact, the United States armed forces gave part of the training at Fort Benning in Georgia.[6] However, according to US government archives, no Zeta has been trained by them.

On May 15, 1997, Lazcano was seconded to the Attorney General's Office (PGR)[7] when the secretary of defense, Enrique Cervantes Aguirre, assigned hundreds of soldiers to reinforce the work of the Federal Judicial Police (PJF), headed by General Guillermo Álvarez Nahara. President Ernesto Zedillo had been persuaded that the soldiers would bring to the PGR order, discipline, and improved results in the fight against organized crime. The soldiers-turned-policemen were sent mainly to the border area of Nuevo León and Tamaulipas. General Álvarez gave strict instructions that only the soldiers seconded to the PJF should enter this region. If any civil judicial police officer were found patrolling or carrying out operations in the area, they were immediately sanctioned and sent to Mexico City.[8]

On September 30, 1997, the PGR dismissed Lazcano, although we do not know why. The Secretariat of Defense only became suspicious of him on February 18, 1998, when he was arrested in Reynosa along with several others; all were released.[9] Contrary to what many think, Lazcano was not a deserter, which is a capital offense in most armies. Before fully joining the Gulf Cartel, he requested his discharge from the Mexican army, and this was granted on March 27, 1998.

His right-hand man, among the handful of blood brothers who have been at his side for a decade of mayhem, is Miguel Ángel

Treviño, alias El Muerto, or Z40. Though he does not come from a military background, he seems to have been born with a machine gun in each hand.

With the fortune amassed through his criminal activities, Lazcano appears to have acquired numerous properties. A house in Plaza San Marcos, in Garza García, Nuevo León, is apparently used by Kaibiles as well as by Lazcano himself.[10] There are four properties in Pachuca, Hidalgo, and it is said that one of these, close to the military zone, is where he resides most of the time, next door to his parents and a sister. Another home has been identified in Coatzacoalcos, Veracruz.[11] His main operating base is in the little municipality of Valle Hermoso, a few miles from Matamoros.[12]

At the turn of the twenty-first century, the corrupting power of Osiel Cárdenas Guillén, the leader of the Gulf Cartel, was immeasurable. He had the idea of recruiting former soldiers to be his personal bodyguards. The first soldier to get caught up in the web was Arturo Guzmán Decena, Z1, a young lieutenant from Puebla who had been trained in the GAFE. Lazcano and others soon followed. It's not known exactly how many men Guzmán initially commanded, but reports range from thirty-one to sixty-seven former members of the GAFE.[13] In time, the paramilitaries were given responsibility for guarding drug shipments from Mexico to the United States. With the attacks from El Chapo and the government, the Zetas's role changed substantially: from being the boss's bodyguards, they became the armed wing of the Gulf Cartel. Now the Zetas conduct their own drug trafficking operations, with contacts in Guatemala, Belize, Colombia, Peru, and Venezuela; they operate in alliance with criminal gangs like the Ndrangheta of Calabria, Italy, one of the most powerful in Europe, and they also have a presence in the United States.

In order to replace their casualties, and deal with the attacks from The Federation, the Zetas set up training camps to recruit civilians and drill them in military skills and discipline. Among the instructors were Kaibiles—veterans of the ugly battle against Guatemalan left-wing guerrillas, who brought to Mexico the fashion for beheading and dismembering their victims as an example to anyone who dared defy them. One of these training camps was on a ranch between the communities of Villa Hermosa and Río Bravo, Tamaulipas.[14]

The existence of Los Zetas went unnoticed by the authorities for several years. The US government didn't identify them until March 2002, when there was a spectacular firefight in which the drug traffickers used weapons and tactics never seen before. In the process, they managed to prevent the capture of Jorge Eduardo Costilla, El Coss, Cárdenas's second-in-command.[15] In 2005, FBI reports suggested there were between 300 and 350 Zetas, including old and new members.[16] Today there may be thousands, including what the FBI calls Zetitas (baby Zetas), or "Zetas wannabes," criminal bands that borrow the name and the methods to spread terror through kidnapping and extortion. In 2005, an intelligence center in McAllen, Texas, had identified around 270 such groups. Some of these were set up by Joaquin Guzmán himself, to gather intelligence on his enemies, and to "discredit" them by means of acts the Zetas would not normally commit.[17]

The paramilitary group created by Cárdenas spread like poison ivy. It soon made an alliance with a faction of the Hermanos Pistoleros Latinos gang, based in Laredo, Texas; part of that organization had previously worked for El Chapo Guzmán.[18] Los Zetas also linked up with members of the so-called Mexican Mafia in California, who they have contracted as hit men.[19] Los Zetas became an indestructible military force, and the organizations that imitate them have turned into a national curse more difficult to eradicate than the drug traffickers themselves. Their membership soars, because they will accept anyone who's prepared to pull a trigger for no reason. The droves of Mexican youth without a future are fertile ground for them and other criminal organizations—mere boys and girls, robbed of all chance for a meaningful life.

Currently, the government and some NGOs accuse the Zetas of organizing mass captures of Central American migrants who pass through Mexico just hoping to make it alive to the States. Many don't. Between 2010 and 2011, more than five mass graves were found full of brutalized bodies, many of them beaten to death; undocumented, anonymous workers whose families will never know their fate.

The horrors told by some survivors are beyond comprehension. They even tell of migrants forced to eat the flesh of their dead companions, to prove the loyalty they have promised in exchange for their lives.[20] Are these real Zetas? Copycats? It hardly matters. It is the impunity enjoyed by some that makes such hell possible.

The Federation started the war

In 2002, when the strength of the Arellano Félix brothers was in dramatic decline, The Federation's consigliere had a brainwave. Juan José Esparragoza, El Azul, suggested opening a new battle front, this time against the Gulf Cartel.[21] He proposed to liquidate the Zetas, who all now saw as their main enemy (and they weren't wrong). To implement the plan, they would have to invade the Nuevo Laredo territory. This delicate operation was decided at a meeting of The Federation's leaders in Monterrey.[22]

It was The Federation's clear intention to make itself the leading force in drug trafficking in Mexico. To do that it had to control the main border crossings into the United States. In those days, if the organization wanted to move drugs across the porous frontier in Tamaulipas state, it had to ask for permission and pay a fee, which was getting more and more expensive. Osiel Cárdenas knew exactly how much every inch of his territory was worth.

No cartel had ever thought of eliminating the Gulf Cartel before. If Amado Carrillo Fuentes had lived, he surely wouldn't have authorized such a move. But El Azul was very persuasive when he reminded his partners that since 2001 they'd had support from the government officials at the highest level, especially from the AFI—led by Genaro García Luna—and the PGR, particularly in the person of Deputy Attorney General Gilberto Higuera, who supposedly took money for appointing the people they wanted as state representatives of the PGR. What's more, they were protected by Los Pinos, the presidential palace itself.

The first step towards war was taken by a man born for warfare, Arturo Beltrán Leyva, El Barbas. He contacted someone he trusted, Dionicio García, El Chacho, with whom he'd organized many drug shipments in the past. In 2002 El Chacho was operating in Nuevo

Laredo with permission from Osiel Cárdenas, who had sent the Zetas to look after the territory. When he was already working with The Federation, El Chacho kidnapped and murdered a member of Los Zetas, unleashing a wave of killings in the border town. To put an end to the bloodshed and win the trust of Los Zetas, El Barbas went to see their leader, Guzmán Decena, and told him he didn't want any problems with his men. He offered to give them access to El Chacho to do what they liked with him, and in exchange he asked for a fresh chance to work that territory. Guzmán Decena accepted, on condition that no member of The Federation would come armed to the area, and that they would always advise them of every drug shipment.

In May 2002 Los Zetas executed El Chacho, along with his deputy. Having fulfilled his promise, El Barbas asked a further favor of Osiel Cárdenas: that a young man by the name of Edgar Valdez Villareal should be allowed to operate in Nuevo Laredo, in place of El Chacho. Contrary to expectations, Cárdenas accepted. Los Zetas were not too happy with their boss's arrangement. They smelled a rat. But military discipline won the day: "Orders are to be obeyed, not questioned or altered," say the Zetas.[23]

The paramilitaries had a good sense of smell. The odor of betrayal was perceptible in advance, like that of rain before it falls. In November 2002, Z1 was shot dead in a restaurant in Matamoros. Every year his friends and family leave flowers outside the place where he was killed, to show that there is no forgetting. After Guzmán Decena's death, Heriberto Lazcano, The Executioner, was anointed head of Los Zetas. As the Gulf Cartel was regrouping, its enemies seized their chance. On March 15, 2003, Osiel Cárdenas was captured by Mexican army forces and the PGR in Matamoros, after a birthday party for one of his daughters.[24] A fortnight later, in the name of The Federation, Edgar Valdez, or La Barbie as he became known, sent a friendly warning to El Verdugo: "You have one week to vacate the territory from Reynosa to Nuevo Laredo." The narco war had been declared. And the Mexican government has been a part of it ever since. Not as an independent authority or even arbiter, but as an active combatant on one of the sides—that of El Chapo.

La Barbie

They say that for the peg to fit it must be carved from the same wood. Arturo Beltrán took the measure of the enemy facing him, and for that reason sent his secret weapon to Tamaulipas. The secret weapon was Edgar Valdez Villareal, La Barbie or La Muñeca (The Doll). Valdez was born in Laredo, Texas, in 1973, a year before El Verdugo. He looks harmless but is just as violent and bloodthirsty as the Zetas leader. Both belong to a new generation of traffickers, with different codes and a different approach to the business.

If his mother hadn't made his childhood so unhappy, the story of his life might have been different. He has told friends how painful he finds it to remember her alcoholism. For a time she abandoned him completely. He began to cause problems at home as a pre-teen, when he got involved in Laredo's youth gangs. To avoid prison he went to Mexico. There he was taken in by a couple in Zapopan, Jalisco. They are the only family he recognizes.

In 2001, Valdez was recruited by El Barbas. He earned his place in the drug hierarchy through a brawl in a bar. It is said he had a violent fight with one of the cartel's hired killers—whose identity he didn't know at the time—over a woman. He gave the hit man such a beating that the latter's boss, instead of killing him, went after him and offered him a job. First it was as a bouncer, then as a gunman. La Barbie developed a close friendship with El Barbas, who by 2002 had sent him to Nuevo León and Tamaulipas as a Federation rep. He was a born killer, and became the organization's chief assassin. Valdez commanded three armed detachments founded specifically to fight the Gulf Cartel and its Zetas armed wing: Los Negros, Los Chachos, and the Mexican Mafia.[25] In the absence of Guatemalan Kaibiles, in 2004 La Barbie recruited gang members from the Mara Salvatrucha, with its origins in El Salvador. This was discovered because in some of the executions carried out by Los Zetas against The Federation there began to appear corpses with tattoos similar to those used by the Maras.

Since 1998, Valdez has been wanted in the United States on charges brought in the southern district of Texas. However, although he traveled frequently to the US, he was never arrested. This may be why many people thought that he might have been a DEA plant.

La Barbie is a man with a caustic sense of humor. He speaks little and tends to mumble, because of a problem with his jaw. To avoid capture when leaving his hideout, he used many disguises, some of them reputedly bordering on the comical. He is rebellious by nature and although he worked for Arturo Beltrán Leyva, he never felt he was anyone's property.

He is also fascinated by the world of show business, and often frequented the glitzy bars and discos of Mexico City, Acapulco, and Cuernavaca in the company of stars. His ego is so big that his lawyer—who later became a protected witness for the Mexican state under the codename Jennifer[26]—told how the hit man ordered a film to be made of his life with the actor Sergio Mayer, son-in-law of businessman Jaime Camil, who has also been linked to drug trafficking.

The alleged biopic was complacently titled Brazo Armado (Armed Wing). In spite of this information, the PGR never issued an arrest warrant for the powerful businessman's son-in-law—even though much lesser allegations by Jennifer have put several public officials behind bars.

La Barbie was a useful, as well as lethal, weapon.

Sergio Villarreal, El Grande

In the new circle of people closest to Arturo Beltrán Leyva there was another man who was key for the war against the Gulf Cartel: Sergio Villareal, also known as El Grande (The Great). His height and breadth justified the name, and so did his cruelty. He was born in Coahuila state on September 21, 1969. His sister-in-law's family is closely connected to President Calderón, something that has never been properly explained.

Unlike his bosses, El Grande got as far as the second year of a law degree. Like many policemen in Mexico, he ended up hiring himself out to the drug lords. He was in the Judicial Police in his home state, then in the Federal Police and finally was recruited by the Juárez Cartel and the Carrillo Fuentes family. In the year 2000 he began to work directly under Arturo Beltrán Leyva. To begin with he organized drug trafficking in Coahuila and Durango. The results were so good for The Federation that his jurisdiction was soon expanded to include the states of Morelos, Guerrero, Puebla, Quintana Roo, and the Federal District. In the last of these he took charge of the organization's operations at the International Airport of Mexico City. He managed units of enforcers and drug distributors like "Los M." He was known for the severity with which he imposed discipline, and for the methods he used to collect debts.

However, despite the skills of La Barbie and El Grande, and the weakening of the Gulf Cartel after the capture of Osiel Cárdenas, in 2003 the members of The Federation realized they needed a more specialized body to confront their rivals. They had men in arms who were ready to waste anything that moved, but these could never match the levels of training, discipline, and technical skills of Los Zetas, much less their *esprit de corps*. Guzmán's organization couldn't wage war on the Gulf Cartel on its own. To have a good chance of victory, it needed extra help. Help from someone who enjoyed total freedom of movement and complete impunity.

El Chapo's army

Just when he most needed it, Guzmán got the chance to meet the heads of the Federal Investigation Agency (AFI), whose director was Genaro García Luna. It happened in 2003, when supposedly four senior AFI commanders arrested El Chapo Guzmán in the state of Nayarit, where he had his base. They were Luis Cárdenas Palomino, director general of police investigations, Javier Garza, director of special operations, Igor Labastida, director of federal investigations, and Domingo González, director of the Control Center. It seems these close aides to García Luna let El Chapo go, in exchange for a few millions of dollars.[27] Contact had been made: the relationship just needed time to develop.

In the 1980s and 90s, this group of AFI commanders had worked together as something of a brotherhood in the Federal District Attorney's Office (PGDF). Other senior figures in the AFI were also part of this set, and they too had been "Judases," as the judicial policemen are popularly known in Mexico. They more than justified the nickname. All had a long trail of ill-repute, which followed them to the PJF when García Luna invited them to join him.

At the end of 2001, García Luna succeeded in changing the name of the Federal Judicial Police (PJF) to the Federal Investigation Agency (AFI). But he never managed to change its poor reputation, largely because of the rogue group of police chiefs who made up his inner circle.

Once at the AFI, the group led by Luis Cárdenas Palomino was joined by other officers recruited by García Luna, with whom they had much in common. Some came from the intelligence service, Cisen, or the Federal Preventive Police (PFP). Others were recommended directly. Some were already in the force, and got promoted when García Luna took over. That is how Facundo Rosas and Víctor Gerardo Garay, among others, joined the unholy band.

In some government offices, this group became known as The Mega Cartel. The police chiefs could count on the complicity of many of their subordinates, creating a chain of corruption that prevails to this day. All of these senior officials have been investigated for alleged involvement in a variety of crimes including murder, kidnap, rape, misuse of public funds, receiving illegal payments and, above all, providing protection to drug traffickers. They were the perfect fit for the private army El Chapo was looking for.

Such was the complicity between the AFI and El Chapo, that the latter is said to have been often seen in 2003 in Xicotepec de Juárez, Puebla state, dressed in AFI uniform. The drug lord wore this outfit in order to pass unnoticed, along with his bodyguards—many of whom really were federal agents.

From 2005, there is documentary evidence that the AFI began to operate fully as El Chapo's army. They were his official armed wing, his group of hired kidnappers and killers. The agency not only arrested El Chapo's enemies to order, while he was protected; they also formed death squads to capture, torture, and execute The Federation's adversaries. In exchange, The Federation—via the Beltrán Leyva brothers, who administered the narco-payroll—delivered briefcases and egg boxes stuffed with dollars, making fortunes for the AFI chiefs overnight. The most patent and inexplicable wealth is that of García Luna himself.

All wars have a first great battle. For the narco war, it took place in Guerrero.

War in paradise

Early in 2005, the state of Guerrero was a powder keg. It only needed some crazies to light the match. And sadly, there's always someone ready to make sure the party gets going. Fed up with his rivals' incursions into Gulf Cartel territory, Heriberto Lazcano decided on an invasion of his own, into Guerrero state, which for decades had belonged to members of The Federation. He began with Acapulco and Ixtapa-Zihuatanejo. Lazcano the Executioner was at that time under the orders of Ezequiel Cárdenas—brother of Osiel—and Eduardo Costilla, El Coss. From his operational center in Valle Hermoso, Lazcano organized a posse of twenty armed men to go after La Barbie, the Beltrán Leyva brothers, and one of the armed groups protecting them, known as Los Pelones. His order was to kill them all.[28] It seemed like a suicide mission. This would not be easy, even for Los Zetas. First, they had to locate the enemy. Then they would have to watch their movements, identify the places they most visited and the vehicles they used. To smoke them out of their lairs, they had orders to kill policemen, toss grenades, and blow up the sales outlets, storehouses, and dives run by The Federation, which in Guerrero was represented by the Beltrán Leyvas.

Part of the commando unit went to Acapulco, the other to Ixtapa. The party was scheduled to start in Ixtapa on the night of May 14, 2005, and the fireworks would be for real. El Pollo, one of the leaders of Lazcano's men, called his comrade, José Lara, La Parca, to tell him to bring some grenades to a discotheque. La Parca went along with another member of the group, El Cascanueces. When he called El Pollo to tell him he was there, the voice that answered sounded strange.

"Where are you?" demanded El Pollo.

"Right outside."

"Wait there, I'll be right out," said El Pollo.

A few seconds later, he called back.

"What are you wearing? I can't see you."

La Parca got a bad feeling. He told El Cascanueces that they needed to get out of there fast. As they walked along the coast road, they were spotted by some men in pickup trucks, who began talking into their radios. The two Zetas took a taxi to the house where they were staying. They'd only been there a few minutes when several AFI and other vehicles surrounded the place, reinforced by officers of the Municipal Police. The Beltrán Leyvas didn't have to lift a finger. That's what they paid the commanders of the AFI for: to do the dirty work.

La Parca and El Cascanueces escaped onto the roof, jumped down, tripped, scrambled up again, and kept running. As they fled they broke into a house where a man was sleeping. They saw his phone and grabbed it to call two other comrades, Tachavo and El Karin. Only the latter answered, distraught: they were screwed, he shouted, the AFI had already captured El Pollo, El Moto, and two more. He told them to lay low and the next day take the bus to Acapulco, where they would regroup. Just then, the sleeper woke up and saw them. Whether because of their guns, or out of simple charity, he hid them, and in the morning he drove them to the bus station himself.

Throughout the night, AFI agents had been raiding hotels and houses in Ixtapa and Acapulco where the Zetas had been staying. Since they'd already captured El Pollo and El Moto, they'd been able to use very persuasive means to find out where their colleagues were.

That Sunday, May 15, a beach in Acapulco served as the meeting point for what was left of the group of Zetas. There were only six of them: La Parca, El Cascanueces, Pompín, Karin, Tachavo and Cuije. As well as El Pollo and El Moto, the AFI had captured Peterete, El Cascarrabias, and El Ojos. As an extra, they'd seized Juan Manuel Vizcarra, El Pizcacha, who had nothing to do with the operation. He just happened to be in Acapulco on holiday with his wife, Norma, and their two year-old daughter, who were also captured by the federal agents. It was a very delicate situation. It's one thing for groups of hit men to tear each other apart, but quite another to hurt innocent family members. In those days, for Los Zetas, the family was still regarded as sacred.

The same day, Miguel Treviño, El Z40, called from Valle Hermoso to the cell phone of one of the kidnapped Zetas. Of course, the person who answered was from the other side. Treviño demanded to speak to La Barbie.

"Let go of El Pizcacha's wife and daughter, they have nothing to do with this," said El Z40, fearful of what could happen to them.

"I'll only let the girl go," answered La Barbie, raising the tension further.

What the wife could expect in the hands of such ruthless men was worse than death. That would come later, as a release.

"Leave the family out of it, we haven't touched yours. If you start that, then we'll go after your family and kill them too," threatened Treviño.

El Z40 must have made his point, because La Barbie agreed to release the woman and the girl. He even gave them 1,000 pesos to leave the state immediately. As soon as she was freed, Norma went to the Guerrero state prosecutor's office to report the kidnapping of her husband. For months she knew nothing of his whereabouts.

That Sunday, an unexpected call was made to the PGR. There was nobody there so the caller left a voice message. It was a man who said he belonged to the Gulf Cartel and was ringing to complain that the day before agents attached to the AFI in Acapulco and Ixtapa had detained six Zetas, but instead of delivering them to the Public Prosecutors, they had handed them over to the Beltrán Leyva organization. "AFI agents have no business playing at being narco-cops," complained the caller, and hung up.[29]

Along with the call arrived a fax addressed to the then attorney general, Daniel Cabeza de Vaca, and the assistant attorney general for Special Investigations on Organized Crime (SIEDO), José Luis Santiago Vasconcelos. It directly accused García Luna of being responsible for what happened in Guerrero: "We already know that the director of the AFI [García Luna] is working with Arturo Beltrán Leyva's organization, and has received large sums of money from the [AFI's] former director of special operations, Domingo González." The authors asked the attorney general to turn their comrades over to the public prosecutors. They denounced the fact that along with the Zetas, three women and three children related to the hit men had been taken (including El Pizcacha's wife and daughter). The warning was clear. If those kidnapped didn't appear within five days:

We will come down on these narco-policemen with all our rigor and anger. We will release all this information to the media, and two days later they will receive a personal message from us. . . . We know how to lose fairly to such an institution, but in this case they have acted in a base and cowardly way by failing to respect our families. We have always respected the institution you command, but if you do not respond we will be forced to use violence.[30]

When the PGR still kept quiet about the scandal of corruption in its ranks, Los Zetas carried out their threat. In the early hours of August 2, 2005, the deputy director of the Guerrero public prosecutor's investigative police (PIM), Julio Carlos López, was executed in a tourist area of Acapulco as he left an upmarket steak house. The local press reported it as an attack on the Guerrero prosecution office, but in reality it was revenge against the AFI. While López was serving as deputy director of the PIM, he was also a commander in the AFI, under Edgar Millán.

México Seguro, Fox's war

The AFI's activity in favour of The Federation was formalized on June 11, 2005, with the México Seguro program (Safe Mexico). That day a press release from the Presidential Office announced that Vicente Fox was launching a military operation, backed by civil institutions, "with the aim of combating organized crime and ensuring the safety of communities that have been victims of the violence resulting from disputes between criminal gangs."[31] The program was designed and managed by members of the security cabinet: Interior Secretary Santiago Creel, Public Security Secretary Ramón Herta, Defense Secretary José Clemente Vega, Navy Secretary Marco Antonio Peyrot, Finance Secretary Francisco Gil, Attorney General Rafael Macedo, and the director of the AFI, Genaro García Luna.[32]

The program was applied in several Mexican states. The first, of course, was Tamaulipas, in the city of Nuevo Laredo.

By then, The Federation had already established permanent contact with Los Pinos through Héctor Beltrán Leyva. At the end of 2004, the DEA discovered that the director of the Department of Presidential Tours, Nahúm Acosta, a member of the governing PAN, was holding telephone conversations with Héctor Beltrán Leyva, El H. The DEA passed the information on to the man they were closest to, the SIEDO deputy attorney general, José Luis Santiago Vasconcelos.

For Santiago, it was a decidedly delicate situation. He must often have wondered whether the contacts between Acosta and El H were unknown to the presidential couple, or took place with their consent. In the hierarchy of Los Pinos during the Fox administration, there were only three levels above Nahúm Acosta: Enrique Ruiz, the coordinator of presidential tours, Emilio Goicoechea, the president's private secretary, and Fox himself. If there was one person that symbolized the improvisation and rampant ambition in the Fox government, it was this fair-haired cowboy, Nahúm Acosta. From a modest family background in Coahuila, he had grown up envying everyone. Impulsive and careless, now he loved to show off his position. He suffered from delusions of grandeur.

Héctor, the most sophisticated of the Beltrán Leyvas, had moved to the exclusive Herradura neighborhood of Huixquilucan, State of Mexico. Compared with the other mansions, this one, with its black gate and pink stonework, hardly stood out. In fact it looked rather less opulent. Nonetheless it had six levels, an enormous garden, and a discotheque where the occupant often held parties. His stylish ways and the flair of his wife, Clara Laborín, helped the couple to sneak into the Acapulco jet set, after which they set their sights on Mexico City. Their millions—the main criterion in such circles—helped them to be accepted as "decent people." They could also count on the contacts of the showbiz PR man, Guillermo Ocañita Ocaña.[33] But El H's low profile was imperiled when his elder brother, Arturo El Barbas, began to visit with his band of bodyguards in cowboy gear, flashing their weapons. Their looks and demeanor were a giveaway.

On January 25, 2005, a call was made to the PGR number for anonymous citizen complaints. Somebody claiming to live in Herradura reported that the people living at 17, Cerrada de la Loma, were acting aggressive with the neighbors. If anyone happened to glance at them they'd say, "What the hell you looking at, asshole? Mind your own business or I'll lay you out," and other abusive threats.

When El Barbas arrived, one of the thugs at the gate would shout, "Señor Arturo Beltrán has arrived, clear the way!" At once another bodyguard at the house door would shout inside, "El Barbas has arrived. Tell El H!"

The DEA report and the anonymous phone call gave Santiago Vasconcelos the green light to act. The first thing he did was to ask the AFI for information about the house. To his surprise, the agency came back to tell him that the telephone number of that address, in the name of Clara Elena Laborín, had been given as a reference a year earlier by a member of El Mayo Zambada's organization. Inexplicably, the AFI had done nothing to follow up. Next, Santiago ordered federal agents to go stake out the house. For three days they also spied on every movement of Héctor Beltrán Leyva and his wife. El H would usually go out alone at night. He frequented the swankiest spots in Mexico City and the State of Mexico, like the Hacienda and Lomas Country golf clubs. The elegant Clara Elena, with whom Héctor now had two children, was also very active, carrying briefcases to various addresses. When she couldn't go, someone else took them, in a white Camry. The same man also went two or three times a day to an apartment at number 18, Avenida Club de Golf, near the La Vista golf club. Each time he arrived or left, cases would be put into or taken out of the trunk.

Here was a chance for the AFI to catch Héctor Beltrán Leyva and his men red-handed. But they let him get away. At that time the Beltrán Leyva clan was an integral part of The Federation, and enjoyed complete impunity. The agency waited until the beginning of February before it searched the seven homes used by Héctor, his wife, and his employees, but no one was arrested. What they found at the house in La Herradura were a series of cassettes on which El H had recorded conversations with Nahúm Acosta; the topics seemed trivial. There were also recordings of conversations with his subordinates, specifying the quantities of money to be delivered to Acosta. Witnesses stated they had seen Acosta's wife visit number 17, Cerrada de la Loma. The Beltrán Leyva brothers, ever cautious, made a habit of recording, on video or in audio, all the public officials they bribed. It was a way of protecting themselves from future misunderstandings or betrayals.

Santiago and his boss, Attorney General Macedo, accused Acosta of leaking confidential information about President Fox's activities to the criminal organization led by El Chapo Guzmán. Acosta was arrested on February 3. He was sent to the maximum security jail of La Palma, where he was held for all of fifty-three days. On April 9 he was freed "for lack of evidence," and the PGR declined to appeal against his release. "It shows with what impartiality cases are examined and reviewed, and then decisions are taken," declared the Presidential Office, in a brief, unruffled communiqué. Nobody mentioned the subject again. To the end of his days, Santiago Vasconcelos maintained in private that there had been enough evidence to charge the official who organized the president's tours, and whose contacts with the Pacific Cartel had begun in 2001, when El Chapo was sprung from Puente Grande. But the problem wasn't what the deputy attorney general thought; it was what Los Pinos wanted.

After the scandal had died down, and four months before the end of the Fox administration, Nahúm Acosta landed a new job, as head of one of the departments in the state energy company, Pemex Gas.

The protection provided by the Mexican Presidency to The Federation became "official," as it were, on June 13, 2005, during the first public event for the México Seguro program. The streets of Nuevo Laredo reverberated with the sound of marching boots, as 600 members of the AFI and the PFP, as well as special forces of the Mexican army's GAFE, paraded to mark what they called the "first phase." It's worth mentioning that days before this official ceremony the local municipal director of public security, Alejandro Domínguez, was executed. He'd been in the job just seven hours.

In this first phase, the federal government relieved the municipal police of their duty to patrol the streets, on the pretext of purging and retraining them. In their place, federal forces, mainly the AFI, took over, generating an atmosphere of tension and violence. The war against the drug trade was as false then as it is now. Central government used the federal security forces to help consolidate The Federation and remove the Gulf Cartel from this prized territory. The maneuver turned out not to be such an easy one. After more than five years of of open warfare, they still haven't succeeded. These have been years of blood and terror for a population caught in the middle of a battle between cartels, and where the government has been not on their side, but on the side of one of the cartels.

It soon became obvious that the México Seguro program was producing very contradictory results. The federal government forces, that were meant to bring security, left a trail of death and destruction behind them. They were in fact the cause of the violence. On August 3, 2005, a few weeks after the launch of President Fox's program, two bodies appeared in Nuevo Laredo. The killers had left a written message on the corpses, the first time such a thing had been seen in Mexico: "DAMN YOU BARBIE AND ARTURO BELTRÁN, YOU WON'T GET IN HERE NOT EVEN WITH THE SUPPORT OF THE SPECIAL FORCES OR BY KILLING INNOCENT PEOPLE." Since then, tortured bodies, dismembered or decapitated, have become the ghoulish messengers between the drug gangs. After the launch of México Seguro, the violence concentrated in the border zone of Tamaulipas spread to the rest of the state, and then to almost all of the states of Mexico.

The most brutal image of this first phase of the drugs war came courtesy of the *Dallas Morning News* at the beginning of December 2005, when it released a blood-curdling video. That day, Norma Olguín learnt for certain what had happened to her husband, Juan Manuel Vizcarra, El Pizcacha. The video showed four of the Zetas seized by the AFI on May 14 and 15 in Ixtapa and Acapulco. The men had been handed over to The Federation and looked beaten and frightened as they sat beside each other on the floor. Behind them a black plastic sheet concealed any details of the location. The Zetas were questioned about their activities in the group. Neither the questions nor the answers made much sense, except to those directly involved. Suddenly a voice asks the fourth Zeta sitting on the far right of the picture, "What's up with you?" Then there's a single deafening shot to his head. It was El Pizcacha. The language of blood is more direct and effective than any other, all its grammar contained in a single drop. Of the two other women and their children who were seized in May 2005 in Guerrero, according to the letter sent by Los Zetas to the PGR, nothing more has been heard. Los Zetas say they were savagely abused and killed, and that this too was filmed.[34]

The part played by the AFI enraged the Gulf Cartel to a point beyond return. At the same time, the brutal images in the *Dallas Morning News* created such a public commotion that the PGR was forced to break its silence. In a stormy press conference, Santiago Vasconcelos admitted that AFI agents in Guerrero were involved in the illegal detention of the Zetas. He also admitted that the authorities had known about the video since September 12, when somebody had left a copy in a manila envelope outside the PGR offices. Santiago announced that eight AFI officers had been arrested, accused of involvement in organized crime, felonies against public health, kidnapping, and possession of ammunition reserved for the exclusive use of the armed forces. Five of these, including José Luis Sánchez, the head of the AFI agency in Guerrero, belonged to the department led by Edgar Millán. Santiago affirmed that all of these agents were being held at the Oriente prison in Mexico City. The charges against them would have been enough to keep them behind bars for many years, even while the facts were still being investigated. At the same time an initial investigation was opened into the the AFI chief, Genaro García Luna.[35]

However, the apparent punishment dealt out to the AFI was a charade. A joke, as in the case of Nahúm Acosta. One day after Santiago's press conference, the Federal District Prison Service informed that of the eight AFI officers supposedly in prison, only three were in fact still there. Citing a "lack of grounds for prosecution," the Fifth District Tribunal ordered the immediate release of the five, including Sánchez who were Millán's men. Legal proceedings continued against the other three.[36] But ironically, because these were supplementary police attached to the Public Prosecution service, it was the AFI itself that had to carry out the investigation and present the evidence. Santiago Vasconcelos was looking ridiculous.

In spite of the direct accusations against him, Sánchez went straight from prison to work in the AFI head office in Mexico City, under Millán. He stayed for two more years, resigning of his own accord on April 30, 2007—a month after Millán had left to follow García Luna to the Secretariat of Public Security, where he would coordinate many new operations. The other four released with Sánchez continued to work in the AFI.[37]

As part of its phoney war on drugs, the federal government proposed to Congress to change the name of the AFI to the Federal Ministerial Police (PFM). From May 29, 2009, the disgraceful police force created by Genaro García Luna changed its title yet again, as if that might erase its appalling record.

The Public Prosecution service was convinced the AFI was acting as the armed wing of The Federation, with the direct involvement of José Luis Sánchez. So much so that the story of the hunt for the Zetas ordered by La Barbie and the Beltrán Leyvas, and carried out by federal agents, was used as evidence against the Beltrán Leyvas in 2008. But despite the finger pointing directly at them, the AFI officers working with the drug traffickers seemed untouchable. Deputy Attorney General Santiago Vasconcelos was getting frustrated. Ever since García Luna had created the agency, with the support of the president and Attorney General Macedo, it had become almost a parallel prosecutor's office. The stuttering García Luna gave himself airs, and the arrogant Santiago couldn't stand it anymore.

Throughout the presidency of Vicente Fox, Santiago Vasconcelos saw how García Luna and his team continued to act with impunity. The head of the AFI had moreover acquired a fairy godmother, Marta Sahagún, the president's ex-spokeswoman and now wife. He visited her frequently at Los Pinos, and it's said he took her very nice gifts, contained in briefcases. Not collections of jewels, like those she had got from businessman Olegario Vázquez Raña,[38] but cash from the drug trade.

The sudden fortune acquired by Sahagún and Fox remains one of the great black holes in the universe. Nobody knows its size or how it was created. We only know that they arrived in December 2000 almost bankrupt, and were filthy rich by the time they left.

Narco-cops

It is said that like attracts like. In the case of the team that has surrounded García Luna for the last twenty years, it seems to be a golden rule. Throughout his shady career in the police, as full of lies and myths as that of El Chapo himself, García has done everything possible to keep the corruption in his team under wraps. In the PGR there is a pile of case files sleeping the sleep of the just, which contain direct accusations against him and his team of links with organized crime. They are considered a state secret, and the authorities refuse to hand them over.[39]

From the outset, García Luna and his team have been part of the problem, not the solution. Every city and municipality they have entered has ended up worse off than before in terms of chaos and corruption. "They're not cops, they're robbers," say those who have good reason to know, especially after having worked with them.[40] The story behind the whole group is a dark one.

The district of Iztapalapa, the roughest and most densely populated in Mexico City, is sadly notorious as a nest of kidnappers, drug peddlers, car thieves, and other crooks. It was here that the nucleus of the García clan came into being.

At the end of the 1990s, Luis Cárdenas Palomino, known as El Pollo, Javier Garza Palacios, alias El Frutilupis, Igor Labastida, José Ayala Aguirre, and Edgar Millán,[41] the renegade quintet, were sent to Iztapalapa by the Attorney's Office of the Federal District (PGJDF). Their average age was less than thirty. They already had form: Garza Palacios, for example, had previously been deputy director of the PGJDF in Álvaro Obregón district, where helped by Labastida, his second, he fleeced small drug dealers and car thieves in exchange for letting them carry on.

It was in Iztapalapa that the five first experimented with kidnapping. They unlawfully arrested a trader in the Iztapalapa Central Market, one of the largest in Mexico City, and demanded a ransom of a million pesos (almost $100,000 at the time) from the man's family. They got away with it thanks to the intervention of lawyer Marcos Castillejos, Cárdenas Palomino's father-in-law,[42] who was himself executed on July 9, 2008. Feeling confident they branched out into another lucrative area: car theft. On one occasion, Garza and Cárdenas were caught red-handed, but the officers who arrested them didn't know they were policemen. When they identified themselves, their colleagues, who had already informed their superiors of the arrest, let them go but demanded a scapegoat in exchange: someone had to be blamed for the theft.[43]

Their lawless activities expanded. It was in Iztapalapa that their contacts with gangs of kidnappers and drug dealers began. They reputedly charged 35 percent of the ransom money for turning a blind eye. Sometimes they even got their patrols to block the roads, to let the kidnappers get away.[44] Iztapalapa became a haven for some of the most merciless kidnap gangs Mexico has ever seen, including, for example, that of Humberto Ortiz, better known as El Apá.

The fifteen men of García Luna's inner circle at the PGJDF included the likes of Armando Espinosa de Benito, who first became friendly with delinquents when he worked as a prison guard. After his enlistment in the PGJDF, he was accused of robbery and rape, but remained unpunished; García Luna saw no impediment to naming him head of the Organized Crime unit at the AFI. Then there was Rafael Avilés, who during the 1990s had created a Mexico City group of police from different forces, called La Hermandad, The Brotherhood. They specialized in high-profile kidnappings and hold-ups, and extorted criminal gangs in exchange for allowing them to operate. Yet in 1996 Avilés spent a few weeks as interim secretary of public security.

Rubén Hernández Esparza, who from being in the PGJDF joined the PJF in 1994, was rapidly promoted when García Luna arrived. In 2005 he was investigated, but let off, for alleged links to The Federation; indeed, he was so intimate with the Beltrán Leyva brothers that there is talk of his appearance with them in one of the incriminating photos they used to take to guarantee the loyalty of their tame policemen.[45]

Luis Jafet Jasso Rodríguez, with an allegiance to Cárdenas Palomino ever since his PGJDF days, entered the AFI as soon as it was inaugurated in November 2001. Besides his expertise in bribe collection, and alleged involvement in torture and homicide, Jasso was involved in the impudent attempt to hold up the presidential payroll van at the beginning of Fox's sexennial. The PGJDF intervened to stop the robbery, accompanied by Jasso from the AFI; when the robbers saw him, they demanded he call the other policemen off. Despite his complicity in the attempted heist, Jasso was spared the consequences when his bosses put in a good word for him. He temporarily left the AFI in 2002.

These were the kind of men who joined the PJF/AFI under Genaro García Luna, in order to apply the recipes so successfully trialed in Mexico City to the country as a whole. They got on famously with colleagues who were already in the force, such as Francisco Javier Gómez Mesa, who after thirty years as a PGR pen-pusher found a new, exciting career open to him in the AFI. Others came over from the Federal Police, such as Aristeo Gómez, Facundo Rosas, and Gerardo Garay, who had been close buddies with García Luna in Cisen.

Still other members of the team arrived highly recommended, from non-police backgrounds: one such was Mario Arturo Velarde, the spokesman of Zedillo's last foreign secretary; he acted as private secretary to García Luna from 2001 to 2006. At the other end of the scale, men were recommended with nothing more than an IT degree or experience of working in a department store.

Luis Cárdenas Palomino, El Pollo, the AFI director general of police investigations, was born on April 25, 1969. Of all García Luna's inner circle, he is the one to whom the secretary is most indebted, as the latter tacitly admits by his tolerance of everything Cárdenas gets up to. It was Cárdenas who got him promoted, from an insignificant official in the Federal Preventive Police during the Zedillo government, to director general of the AFI under Vicente Fox. Cárdenas had an excellent line to Rafael Macedo de la Concha, tipped to be the new Attorney General responsible for approving García's appointment: Cárdenas's wife is Minerva Castillejos, daughter of one of Macedo's closest friends, the (since executed) lawyer Marcos Castillejos.

El Pollo Cárdenas wanted a top job for himself, too, but his criminal record was an obstacle. To the outside world, he is decent-looking and presentable—the acceptable face of García Luna's team. But colleagues who have worked with him complain of arrogance, bullying, and corruption. Beneath that handsome face is a man capable of killing in cold blood.

When he was eighteen he was accused of taking part in a murderous spree in Lindavista, a smart neighborhood of Mexico City. His chilling, signed confession is in a file in the Federal District Attorney's Office.

On August 12, 1987, Luis Cárdenas, along with one René Álvarez, did nothing to intervene when their friend Octavio Navarro blew the brains out of a taxi driver who had just given them a ride. They didn't have the money to pay him; a bullet that left the windscreen covered in blood was his solution.

"It's your unlucky day," said Octavio menacingly, when the driver demanded his fare. After a brief argument, he shot him and laughed. Later, Cárdenas went on with his friend to drink champagne and look for some hookers.

Two more people were to die that evening. After a lot of champagne in the Sugar Bar, for which he had no intention of paying, Octavio started an argument with the bar staff, and Luis ran away. But he didn't go to the police to report what had happened. In the early hours of August 13, after negotiating with the owners of the bar, Navarro shot them. In his statement, Cárdenas swore that he had not been present at these two other killings, but Octavio's wife Rosana assured the public prosecutors he'd been there.

Cárdenas Palomino got off thanks to the influence of his father, but he knew that the episode would dog him forever. That's why he decided to push forward his good friend Genaro García Luna, for director of the PJF. Cárdenas had the run of the PGR, thanks to his father-in-law's friendship with Macedo and the fact that his brother-in-law was the new attorney general's chief adviser. To begin with, García Luna's relationship with Attorney General Macedo was very good, and the latter was cooperative with the name change of the PJF to the AFI.

The policemen who saw them arrive at the PJF still recall how García Luna, accompanied by Cárdenas Palomino and others, requested an intensive course in torture. Of course the training was given as a practical, hands-on course, and García and Cárdenas were fast learners.

One of the most repugnant moments of that training involved a young man falsely accused of kidnapping. Guillermo Vélez, Memo as he was known, worked in a gym whose owner, Maciel Islas, had been kidnapped days earlier. On March 29, 2002, the manager asked Vélez to go with him to meet a client who was interested in buying the gym. Memo agreed, thinking the money would be used to pay the ransom. It was all a trick. The following day his father found what was left of him in the morgue. What they did to Guillermo Vélez was indescribable.

The cruel anonymous letter sent to his family mocked how Memo had cried while he was tortured. His father fought for justice like David against Goliath, because he knew his son was innocent. On November 26, 2009, for the first time ever, the PGR had to admit publicly that it had made a mistake: Memo was not a kidnapper. The PGR publicly apologized to the family, and paid substantial damages. With García Luna's arrival at the AFI, and later at the Secretariat of Public Security (SSP), torture once again became common practice, especially against the innocent. With the guilty, you could usually reach a deal.

Cárdenas carefully cultivated Enrique Peña Nieto, the current Mexican President, when he was a governor, in hopes of being named secretary of public security if Peña Nieto won. However, the Secretariat has been dissolved and its functions moved to the Interior. In December 2012, Cárdenas Palomino announced his resignation from the force and intention to move into the private sector.[46]

Edgar Millán was born in 1966. He was two years older than García Luna, who he had known since 1989, longer than any other member of the team. First they were together in the intelligence agency, Cisen, where they worked for four years. Then their careers parted for a while, coming back together in the PJF. It was Millán who carried out the police investigation into El Chapo's "escape" from Puente Grande, taking care in the process to watch the back of García Luna as well as that of his mentor, Jorge Tello Peón. He was soon rewarded by being made director general of regional deployments at the AFI. Millán, who had only completed high school, was thus in charge of appointing the agency's regional chiefs throughout the country, making him one of the most powerful figures in the AFI. They say he charged the drug traffickers, especially members of The Federation, between $200,000 and $1 million for appointing a particular boss to a given region, as well as a monthly fee of $50,000 to $100,000 for the AFI director general of the moment.[47] In time, Millán became a time bomb waiting to go off in García Luna's face.

Francisco Javier Garza Palacios, El Frutilupis, was born in 1965. He has amassed a fortune since going into police work, and is reputed to own luxury apartments and bars, as well as three Cessna 206 aircraft which he keeps in the AtizApán de Zaragoza airport, in the State of Mexico, a popular airport among drug traffickers. As AFI's director of special operations, he was implicated in the affair of the execution of the Zetas members in Acapulco.[48] With Cárdenas Palomino's blessing, Garza allowed members of The Federation to actively supervise the police actions ordered by the Beltrán Leyvas against their adversaries.

Another notoriously corrupt member of the team was Igor Labastida. He arrived at the AFI as deputy director of crime investigation under Cárdenas Palomino, and was promoted to area director. Labastida used to complain that García Luna and Cárdenas left all the dirty work to him, and that whereas García and others had taken money from all the cartels, they had only remained on good terms with that of El Chapo Guzmán.[49] He feared for his life because of all the foul deeds he'd committed, and with good reason.

There was no way García Luna's boys could hide their real nature. They looked like ducks, they swam like ducks, and they quacked like ducks: they were ducks.

The unforgivable ones

Kidnapping is one of the the most reprehensible of crimes. Its perpetrators rob the other not only of their money but of their dignity. It is based on a display of power in which victims can be raped, tortured, mutilated, put into unimaginable situations; pain is pitilessly inflicted in order to force families to pay up. Among the different kinds of kidnapping gangs operating in Mexico, a particular network of interrelated groups has flourished over the last twelve years, all linked to drug trafficking, and whose brand of terror shares one key feature: the involvement of senior police officers, the unforgivable ones.

During the Fox presidency, the AFI's anti-kidnapping squad led by Luis Cárdenas Palomino became one of its most active. The government was only recently installed when a number of murky episodes came to light. Some kidnappings were brought to a satisfactory conclusion, with the arrest of those responsible. But other cases, the more newsworthy or violent ones, often ran into difficulties, with the family finally paying millions of pesos or dollars after receiving fingers or ears, and videos showing the abuse.

On many occasions, when police officers were getting close to solving a case, Cárdenas and Millán would put the brakes on; sometimes they even threatened them if they persisted with their investigations. This was especially the case when the gang under investigation was working in Iztapalapa or the State of Mexico. Some AFI staff were surprised to notice that Cárdenas and Millán would send unarmed officers to accompany relatives when they went to pay a ransom. In fact, they only went along to make sure that payment was made, and for the correct amount. The suspicion that these commanders were in league with the gangs became a certainty when five of the best officers that the AFI had trained to negotiate with kidnappers, resigned: they had discovered that top police officials, their bosses, had been involved in several kidnappings, presumably with the approval of the top boss of all, García Luna.[50] Not of course that the AFI chiefs were to be distracted from their main business, which was to serve the barons of the Pacific organization: many of the kidnapping gangs they were protecting were sub-cells of the cartel itself, or linked to one or other of its members.

Kidnapper Marcos Tinoco, nicknamed El Coronel, believed to be responsible for at least eleven high-profile kidnappings between 1999 and 2000, confessed in 2002 that one of the cells of his organization was led by Cynthia Romero, the sister-in-law of El Güero Palma, and a close friend of El Chapo Guzmán.[51] Tinoco directly accused García Luna of covering up for the kidnap gangs, but nothing was done about it. A scoundrel like that was not to be believed.

Kidnapping has been a spin-off from drug trafficking for more than a decade. It is not a recent result of the supposed war on drugs, as President Calderón and his inseparable secretary of public security, García Luna, tried to make us believe.

The largest and most vicious kidnap gang of recent times, blamed for some of the most shocking instances, was nurtured and protected by Genaro García Luna and his inner circle; the documentary evidence is decisive. Authorities in the Federal District have baptised it La Flor (The Flower). Its different cells are believed to have been responsible for over 200 kidnappings, and in some cases murders, provoking an outcry from society.

In 2001, the Mexico City government began to note a series of kidnappings characterized by the particular savagery with which the targets were treated, especially women. However, these victims took their cases not to the capital's District Attorney but to the PGR, which in turn put the investigations in the hands of the AFI.[52]

By 2003, the AFI had got precise information, including addresses and phone numbers, on members of a gang led by a true predator: former cop Sergio Ortiz Juárez, El Apá or El Patrón. The gang boasted to their associates that they got support from the SIEDO (the specialized organized crime investigations unit) and were protected in the capital by members of the AFI, the PFP, and the Secretariat of Public Security. This was confirmed by the initial investigations opened— paradoxically as ever—by the SIEDO itself into El Apá's gang in 2003. For three years the AFI headed up the investigation, but it never got anywhere.

In June 2005, during a routine investigation into petty dealing in the Polanco neighborhood of Mexico City, officers from the Federal District Attorney's Office detained a man by the name of George Khouri Layón. El Koki, as he was called, was a genial, well-known figure of Mexico City nightlife, the owner of two discotheques, who liked to hang out with soap stars and other celebrities. He was also known to The Federation, as he had links to the Beltrán Leyvas and worked for La Barbie. They caught him red-handed with two guns, one .35 and one .22 caliber, and a whole store of psychotropic pills.

The yuppie businessman resisted arrest and demanded they call his friend Igor Labastida, the AFI commander and one of García Luna's men, to have him set free. El Koki became increasingly defiant, warning he was on good terms with a gang called La Cancha and "you don't want to mess with them." It's not known if anyone did call Labastida, but the fact is the narco-businessman was soon released.[53] The only person to suffer any consequences was a federal agent who lost his job.

Before working for the drug traffickers, El Koki had collaborated with a gang of kidnappers led by Luis López, El Vale, thought to be responsible for some forty kidnappings and to have amassed a fortune of over $100 million from ransoms. Ortiz, El Apá, was also a member of this gang,[54] before he joined another, and finally went on to lead his own outfit, La Flor. This was made up of at least eight cells, a hydra-headed monster in which El Apá apparently had the help of his sons, both in carrying out the kidnaps and in processing the receipts.

El Apá continued collaborating with El Vale and El Koki; anything goes in the ugly world of kidnapping. Sometimes El Vale would sell his victims on to El Apá when he got tired of waiting for the family to pay. He handed them over in a very bad state. El Apá would then push the family to the verge of madness. Any money made he made over and above the sum paid to El Vale was pure profit. The organization charged with investigating El Apá's gang was the AFI. Its lack of results was no accident. Years later, the reason would become clear.

Another cell of El Apá's gang was led by Abel Silva. His group was known as Los Tiras (The Cops) because it included policemen. They are believed to have been responsible for the kidnapping of the singer Thalía's sisters. After the women were let go in September 2002, their testimony suggested that the AFI were involved, either directly or as accomplices.[55] Today we know that Los Tiras were indeed an extension of Ortiz's gang and the AFI, and that AFI agents were indeed involved. Silva was apprehended in 2006, and tried as sole perpetrator of the ambitious snatch; his place at the head of Los Tiras was taken by Luis Ignacio Torres, still under the umbrella of Sergio Ortiz, El Apá.

The way they worked was this. Ortiz carried out the kidnapping and collected the ransom, with the help of the AFI. Los Tiras or another cell were responsible for guarding the victims. El Apá always dropped by, to torment them.[56] When Calderón moved into Los Pinos, and García Luna took over at the Public Security Secretariat, El Apá's protection remained intact. Except that now his protectors were more powerful. It's estimated that El Apá amassed a fortune of more than $35 million from kidnapping—not including the 35 percent of receipts earmarked for García Luna and his team, just like in the old days in Iztapalapa. The Federal District SSP says El Apá owns hotels in Cancún, as well as houses in Xochimilco, Jardines en la Montaña, San Jerónimo, and Santo Domingo.

As his impunity grew, mainly thanks to the AFI, so El Apá became more brutal. The hallmark of his organization was cruelty. Often, whether or not the ransom was paid, they would execute their victims just for the fun of it. To begin with, many of their prey were small businesspeople: a builder, a gas supplier, a florist. This last case, of a woman with a flower company in Xochimilco, may be why prosecutors in the capital called the gang La Flor.

There's no doubt that Joaquín Guzmán had got hold of the perfect men for his war on the Gulf Cartel, and the other wars to come. Deep down, they were no different from Los Zetas: drug traffickers, kidnappers, and evil through and through.

The continued pressure from Santiago Vasconcelos bothered García Luna, who didn't conceal his own dislike. Luckily for him, during the Fox presidency García found a number of natural allies in the PGR, all the more necessary given his falling-out with the attorney general himself, Rafael Macedo de la Concha, and this dispute with Deputy Attorney Santiago. The most powerful of these allies was Gilberto Higuera, who was directly in charge of appointing the PGR's delegates in states across the country. Higuera has been accused of making these appointments in accordance with the interests of The Federation. This supposedly happened in the State of Mexico, Durango, Campeche, Veracruz, Sonora, Yucatán, Sinaloa, Chihuahua, and Guerrero.

In February 2005, the protected witness Julio (who was El Chapo's brother-in-law), in a statement made in the Mexican embassy in Washington, said that El Chapo Guzmán, with whom he'd worked for years, had told him that Higuera was keeping him up to date about the cases against him and the request for his extradition to the United States. The PGR dismissed this evidence against Higuera. In a brief press release it said the declarations were based on hearsay, and were therefore legally invalid. Later a judge had Julio's testimony struck out.[57] Yet there are public officials currently behind bars on far less evidence than this, once they're defined as inconvenient. In 2010, Higuera openly backed Juan Vizcarra for governor of Sinaloa—the same candidate who couldn't bring himself to deny his friendship with El Mayo Zambada. After that he worked with García Luna in the Secretariat of Public Security.

Rafael Macedo left the PGR in April 2005, and was replaced by Daniel Cabeza de Vaca. Gilberto Higuera stayed on, supposedly to show the new attorney general the ropes. Macedo's resignation came just months before his name appeared in an FBI report. This quoted the McAllen Intelligence Center' conclusion, that the Zetas were working that part of the frontier with the "blessing" of the attorney general.[58]

See no evil

By the end of the Fox presidency in 2006, the balance of the crusade against drugs was disastrous. The group of traffickers that came together in The Federation, under the leadership of El Chapo Guzmán, had become very powerful. Joaquín Guzmán, Ismael Zambada, the Beltrán Leyva brothers, Juan José Esparragoza, Ignacio Coronel, and Vicente Carrillo, all were completely impregnable. Their interests remained undisturbed by so much as the brush of a feather.

Even before Fox left Los Pinos, the DEA had begun investigating him and his family. The Tijuana Cartel had almost ceased to exist after 2002, what with the killing of Ramón Arellano Félix and the arrest of more than 2,000 members of the organization in the course of that year, including Benjamín Arellano Félix. At the same time the Gulf Cartel had been decapitated in February 2002 with the arrest of Osiel Cárdenas. In contrast, no leader of The Federation had been captured.

The United States government also had its share of responsibility for what happened. Panic and a mistaken diagnosis—whether deliberate or accidental—meant they focussed their attention on the Gulf Cartel and their fearsome Zetas. Between May 2004 and May 2005, thirty-five US citizens were kidnapped in Nuevo Laredo, apparently by the Zetas. Twenty-three were freed, nine remain unaccounted for, and two were killed. In the same period, twenty-six people were seized in San Antonio, Texas, presumably by the same organization.[59] By concentrating on the Gulf Cartel and Los Zetas, US authorities allowed The Federation to grow exponentially under their very noses, on their own side of the border. The war for control of the US market became a lot more ferocious and lethal.

In just a few years, the map of drug distribution across the States was radically redrawn. The National Drug Intelligence Center

(NDIC) in Johnstown, Pennsylvania, divided the United States into seven regions:[60] Pacific, Midwest, South West, North West, Great Lakes, North East, and South East. In 2004, the zones were divided roughly evenly between drug traffickers from Mexico, Colombia, Jamaica, and the Dominican Republic. The Colombians were dominant in New York and also Miami, the two most important markets for cocaine; the Mexican cartels held sway in cities like Atlanta and Houston, while in Chicago and Los Angeles the market was fairly evenly divided. The distribution of methamphetamine was heavily dominated by Mexicans, even though most of the supply was manufactured in the United States.[61]

By January 2006, profound repercussions were already being felt from Fox's phoney war and the United States' inexplicable apathy towards El Chapo and his partners. The Mexican drug gangs grew apace, as if fatted on bloodshed; that year they controlled the distribution of cocaine and methamphetamine in most of the United States. They were now the main distributors in five of the seven regions: Great Lakes, Pacific, South East, South West, and Midwest. Although Colombians still dominated in Florida and the Caribbean, the presence of Mexican traffickers was on the rise in this coveted zone. And, at least in New York, the Mexicans had displaced the Colombians as the main distributors and retailers of cocaine.[62]

When Vicente Fox completed his term in office, the toll from the drugs war was 9,000 dead. The rivers of blood were shifting their course, and destroying everything in their path.

In December 2006 the next president of Mexico, Felipe Calderón, was sworn in. He came from the same party as Fox, the National Action Party (PAN). Within days he announced the beginning of a supposed "war" on the drug trade, and chose none other than Genaro García Luna and his boys to lead it. The worst was yet to come.

CHAPTER TEN

Freedom Is Priceless

It was early in 2008 when General X, disciplined, tenacious, and daring as he was, traveled to the home territory of Mexico's most powerful drug lord to speak to him face to face.[1] El Chapo Guzmán was expecting the messenger from Los Pinos. Now more than sixty-five, the military man still exudes the vitality and verve of his best years. He'd been working with Juan Camilo Mouriño in the Presidential Office since 2007—an adviser in the shadows, as he had been through most of his forty-five years in the Mexican army, serving in the White Brigade, the Federal Security Directorate, and the National Security Coordination. Mouriño, one of President Calderón's closest confidants, had given the general an impossible task: to broker peace between the drug cartels. In January 2008, Mouriño was made Interior Secretary, but the mission still stood, and coming from a man so close to the president it was not to be taken lightly.

If the general couldn't succeed, with all the guile he had acquired over the years, then nobody could. He had spent seven years in prison, accused of links with Amado Carrillo Fuentes, El Señor de los Cielos. A number of witnesses testified against him, but there remained an element of doubt, as happens so often in these labyrinthine cases involving the military. He still had seven years of his sentence to go, but in the first year of Calderón's government he was set free. Those in the know say his imprisonment was a political affair, as was his release.

Nine months after he left prison, to the astonishment of his colleagues, he was decorated by the secretary of defense, General Guillermo Galván, for his "patriotism, loyalty, and self-sacrifice." The government had to make him visible and credible to his interlocutors: the drug traffickers. General X has said that the secretary of defense also knew of the mission entrusted to him by Mouriño.

He'd never been too fussy about the tasks he took on. Many of them had required building relationships with different groups of traffickers. So in 2008, when he started knocking on the doors of the different groups involved in the narco war, most of them swung open. That's what happened with El Chapo.

"Freedom is priceless," El Chapo Guzmán told the general when they met. It sounded very cynical, even coming from a cynic like El Chapo. The remark was a cue for General X to inquire how he had managed to get out of the Puente Grande maximum security jail on that January day back in 2001. Guzmán was quite candid about it. They had begun to help him in 1995, when he was transferred from La Palma to Puente Grande on the orders of the Interior Secretariat. El Chapo named three men as being responsible for the "escape" itself. All were prominent figures in Mexico's political and security establishment.

One was the former governor of Quintana Roo, Lieutenant Colonel Joaquín Hendricks. El Chapo said he helped him when he worked in the Interior Secretariat. The only post Hendricks occupied in that ministry was as director of sentence implementation in the prison service, from 1996 to 1997, when Francisco Labastida was the secretary.

In 1999, Hendricks became governor of one of the states with the highest intake of drug shipments in Mexico, a key operational base for both the Sinaloa and Juárez cartels. His predecessor had been Mario Villanueva, who was extradited in 2010 for his alleged links to the Amado Carrillo Fuentes organization, which El Chapo had belonged to.

In February 2001, just after El Chapo's "escape" and without any particular prompting, the head of the Specialized Organized Crime Unit (UEDO), José Luis Trinidad, announced that he was not carrying out any investigation "into the alleged involvement of the elected governor of Quintana Roo, Joaquín Hendricks Díaz, in the case of the drug trafficker Joaquín El Chapo Guzmán." Indeed, "no member of UEDO is carrying out such an investigation, in that state or in any other."[2] After leaving Puente Grande, Guzmán hid out mainly in the states of Nayarit and Quintana Roo.

The second man implicated by El Chapo in his escape was the then attorney general, Rafael Macedo de la Concha. It was his office that was in charge of the operation carried out after the escape and which put Genaro García Luna at the helm of the subsequent investigation—one that was carried out with striking negligence.

At the beginning of 2005, Macedo resigned as attorney general and was sent by President Fox as military attaché to the Mexican embassy in Rome, where he remained in exile until the end of the sexennial. When Felipe Calderón assumed the presidency, Macedo returned to Mexico and was made a judge in the Military Tribunal, where he kept a rigorously low profile.

The third accomplice named by El Chapo to General X was Jorge Tello Peón, the then deputy secretary in the Secretariat of Public Security (SSP). Tello, as we saw, visited the Puente Grande prison the very day of El Chapo's escape, as if to finalize some of the details. From 2008 to 2009, this man, explicitly fingered by the drug baron as the man who set him free, was President Calderón's chief adviser on public security, working with García in the SSP as executive secretary of the National Security System. In January 2010 he moved to the National Security Council, apparently because of disagreements with his erstwhile protégé. García Luna now had more power, and wanted to show his teacher that the pupil had outgrown him. Tello didn't last long in that job either, and ended up simply as an adviser to Calderón.[3]

There is no doubt El Chapo is a perverse individual, capable of flipping his own destiny inside out. On June 9, 1993, he was delivered to General Carrillo Olea, the anti-drugs coordinator, in the back of a clapped-out old pickup truck, bent double with his hands and feet tied, on a remote roadside in Chiapas. Eight years later, it was Carrillo's alter ego, Tello Peón, his anointed son, fashioned in his own likeness, who would seemingly set him free.

El Chapo told General X that all the "turfs" in Mexico, that's to say all the states where organized crime operates, "have been sold." The trouble was that some national officials, as well as some local government officials, had sold them more than once to different groups, resulting in chaos among the gangs.

When the envoy from Los Pinos met Guzmán, the drug lord had already joined open battle with the Beltrán Leyvas, his cousins and long-time partners. Maybe that was why El Chapo informed the general, in a tone of wounded complaint, that Juan Camilo Mouriño and his then chief adviser at the Secretariat of the Interior, Ulises Ramírez, had sold the rights to the State of Mexico to the Beltrán Leyva brothers for $10 million. The point was, this transaction took place *after* operations in that state had been promised to El Chapo Guzmán. Mouriño had been talked into it by Ramírez, who El Chapo described as a "crook." "Ramírez must have kept at least a million for himself," the general thought.

Sources close to Mouriño confirmed this story, but said the secretary was apparently unaware of the deal done in his name by Ramírez.

El Chapo Guzmán told the presidential envoy that he and his clan had already agreed with the federal government that the latter would combat his old partners, the Beltrán Leyvas. General X must have felt very uncomfortable at hearing this. It put him on the spot because there was no way, when he came to report back to Mouriño, that he would be able to repeat El Chapo's complaint. He had worked long enough inside the system to know that it could cost him his life.

For obvious reasons, General X's meeting with the drug baron was brief, and for his own safety he hasn't said where it took place. By the time they said goodbye, the envoy from Los Pinos was sure of one thing: El Chapo did whatever he wanted, and he was not prepared to give up his freedom, whatever it might cost.

The uncomfortable truth

On December 1, 2006, the second president from the National Action Party (PAN), Felipe Calderón, delivered his maiden speech and announced that his government's number one priority would be to restore public security. Four days later, he formally declared "war" on organized crime. This would become the main weapon in his government's desperate bid to win support and legitimacy,[4] in a society that was equally desperate for the rule of law.

"Rest assured that my government is working hard to win the war on crime, to ensure that the rights of all are protected and respected, with the right to property and investment; and fighting relentlessly against corruption and to safeguard the right to life, liberty, and heritage,"[5] declared Calderón emphatically. He didn't deliver. Either he couldn't, or he wouldn't.

What nobody could explain was why he decided to fight organized crime with the same officials that had so singularly failed in the task already, the one because he was inept, the other because he was corrupt: Eduardo Medina Mora and Genaro García Luna.

Medina was a colorless secretary of public security during the last year of the Fox government; under Calderón he served as a vacillating attorney general, who never managed to get out from under the thumb of García Luna. So much so that for the first two years his own secretariat's police force, the AFI, was still controlled by García Luna rather than himself.

In spite of his somber record in the Fox administration, García Luna was made secretary of public security with backing from Tello Peón and from Mexico's (and the world's) richest man, Carlos Slim, who had been persuaded to support him. The United States embassy was soon keeping a close eye on him and his team. In a confidential cable dated December 11, 2006, the embassy describes García Luna as an "intense" character, and notes his "mumbled" Spanish which is "hard to understand even for native speakers." Their overall view of him was positive, because several US Agencies like the DEA had worked with him in the past, and he had been very cooperative. But not all of his team were regarded in the same light.[6]

In charge of the SSP, he rapidly became a feared member of cabinet. Nobody could look him in the eye. Nobody trusted him. He has been publicly questioned over his sudden personal wealth, including more than 40 million pesos' worth ($2.8 million in 2010) of real estate in Mexico City and Morelos. He has so far been unable to explain how he grew so affluent on a civil servant's salary.[7] In a letter sent to the Mexican Congress in 2008, a group of federal agents who had worked with him accused him of being connected to the drug trade, and said he had been directly threatened by drug barons like Arturo Beltrán Leyva to make him fulfil his agreements.[8] Many legends have been written about him, like the existence of rooms full of money and lavish properties in the Dominican Republic.

His front companies include two restaurants called Café Los Cedros, registered in the name of his wife, Linda Pereyra Gálvez: one in a lower-middle-class neighborhood in the south of Mexico City, the other in Cuernavaca. These establishments function as operational centers separate from his official activities as a public servant. In 2010, Café Los Cedros was recruiting polygraphists, specialists in applying lie detector tests, to work throughout Mexico. An unusual skill for a restaurant employee.

US government sources say their intelligence services have monitored García Luna's properties and carried out satellite scans in search of money. They claim that $15 million were identified in one of the houses.

Since December 2010, many civic leaders have accused him of links to drug traffickers, and of making death threats against those who question his integrity or imperil his interests.

Of course, García Luna did not come to the Secretariat of Public Security alone. His unholy band from the AFI came with him. He made Luis Cárdenas Palomino, El Pollo, first director general of private security and then Intelligence Coordinator for the Federal Police. Javier Garza Palacios came to the SSP as coordinator of regional security, but he didn't last there even a year. In May 2007, eleven truckloads of hit men from the Sinaloa Cartel drove 200 miles along a federal highway to Cananea, in Sonora state, to execute twenty-two local policemen in the mining town. There was a public outcry, because no one in Garza's department had been able to spot the monstrous convoy.

A few days later, García Luna sacked the entire Regional Security command, and appointed Edgar Millán in Garza's place. However, García owed too much to Garza, so he sent him as SSP attaché to the Mexican embassy in Colombia. Some say that in fact Garza never went, and that he continued to do the clan's business away from the spotlight. There is documentary evidence that Garza Palacios remained on the SSP payroll until early in 2009, although the Secretariat has denied it.

Igor Labastida was given the key job of director of traffic and contraband at the Federal Police. Like him, Facundo Rosas Rosas,

Gerardo Garay Cadena, Rafael Avilés, Armando Espinosa de Benito, Luis Jafet Jasso, and other members of the "inner circle" were simply reshuffled.

García Luna also recruited fresh talent for his new tasks as head of the SSP. When he was director of the AFI, he had always boasted that one day he would have more power than a president; in this new job, he was closer than ever to making the dream come true. Marco Tulio López, a lawyer with a history of human rights abuses in Oaxaca and minor posts in district courts, was named legal director of the SSP, his only merit being that he had helped to get García Luna off the hook when he was accused by the Auditor of mismanagement in 2000. Another new signing was Edgar Enrique Bayardo, former judicial policeman and more lately the deputy attorney in Tlaxcala state, where he was reputed to be involved in a kidnapping gang allegedly run by his brother. García Luna named him deputy director of crime investigation with the Federal Police.

There was a rotten smell in the Secretariat of Public Security. Soon the stink would waft out onto the streets, and cause a public scandal.

The phoney war on drugs

From the beginning of his government, the phrase "war on drugs" became Calderón's great buzzword. The first troop movement began on December 11, 2006, with the Michoacán Joint Operation. Seven thousand troops and police officers from the army, the navy, the AFI, and the PFP were deployed in the state of Michoacán, which was then controlled by the Gulf Cartel.

The military commander of that first battle was General Manuel García Ruiz, assigned by the secretary of defense, Guillermo Galván. In charge of the civilian forces was Gerardo Garay, appointed by García Luna. A year later Garay and other senior SSP officials were denounced after appearing in videos taking instructions from members of El Chapo Guzmán's organization.

In the months that followed, Calderón continued to speak about the "war":

I have said it before, and I'll say it again: this is a deep-seated problem in our country, with such profound roots that it will take time, a lot of time, and money, a great deal of money, as a war on this scale does. And regrettably it will continue to cost, as it has already cost in the last two years, human lives.

But rest assured, my friends, the Mexican state, and your government, are absolutely determined to fight this battle, without respite, until we win back the streets, the squares, the cities, for all of Mexico's citizens.[9]

Up to August 2010, the cost in human lives referred to by the president amounted to 28,000 people killed. By July 2011, this terrifying figure had risen to more than 40,000. To the sound of gunfights and grenades going off, Mexico was turning into a graveyard.

Throughout his six years in government, Felipe Calderón refused to change one iota of his anti-drug strategy. And when you look in detail at the operations undertaken, it raises all manner of suspicions about the president. When questioned on the direction taken by his "war," Calderón bristled: either you were with him, unconditionally and without question, or you were against him. His critics were made out to be anti-patriotic.

Throughout this presidency, the enemies of El Chapo and his closest allies fell like flies, while he basked in his impunity.

On February 24, 2010, President Calderón was asked at a press conference whether his government had protected Joaquín Guzmán Loera. He exploded: "That is absolutely false!" and went on to explain:

We have fought all of them. And to all of them we have dealt serious blows, to their operational and financial structure, and to their leadership. This is a false and malicious accusation, I don't know what the intention behind it is, but it just doesn't stand up. We have attacked in the same way both the Gulf and the Pacific cartels.

What's more, we've hit almost the same number of big drug barons and criminal bosses on both sides. It's incredible to me that when we are catching criminals as important as El Teo, for example, who is from El Chapo's organization, from the Pacific Cartel, the government is

accused of protecting that cartel. Or when we are extraditing someone like Vicente Zambada,[10] we are accused of covering up for them.
At best it's pure ignorance.

Once again, the president was repeating a series of myths about his
policy for fighting Mexico's drug gangs. His supposed war on the
drugs trade was as "real" as that waged by Ronald Reagan twenty
years earlier, with the results that are only too well known. From
the beginning of his government, Calderón's strategy against the
drug barons was designed to favour El Chapo Guzmán and his
main partners: El Mayo Zambada, El Nacho Coronel, and El Azul
Esparragoza.

There is firm documentary evidence that Calderón's war was overwhelmingly aimed against those drug traffickers who are El Chapo's
enemies or represent a threat to his leadership. Since 2007, the
government has known the exact addresses of Mexico's main drug
traffickers and their relatives. In some cases they have the telephone
numbers, bank accounts, and other valuable details that would allow
them to take successful, targeted action against them. This is evident
from the files on each drug baron drawn up by the SSP with the
support of the intelligence agency, Cisen.[11] In fact, what Mexico has
experienced in the last decade is not a "war on drug traffickers," but
a war between drug traffickers, with the government taking sides for
the Sinaloa Cartel.

The people responsible for designing President Calderón's war
strategy and setting its main priorities were Genaro García Luna and
his team, with their long and reliable history of service to the same
cartel. This strategy put forward by the SSP was based on certain
"lines of inquiry" which identified as "strategic priority no. 1" the
capture of the leader of the Gulf Cartel, Ezequiel Cárdenas—brother
of Osiel Cárdenas—and of Jorge Costilla, El Coss, his second in
command. The only leaders of The Federation labeled "strategic
priority no. 1" were Alfredo Beltrán Leyva, El Mochomo, Arturo
Beltrán Leyva, El Barbas, and Edgar Valdés, La Barbie.[12]

Of all El Chapo's partners, the one who represented the greatest
threat to him in terms of power was Arturo Beltrán Leyva and his
group. El Barbas was beginning to get too much power of his own.

Nor did Guzmán appreciate the fact that his cousin's loyalties to Vicente Carrillo Fuentes seemed stronger than they were to him. The murder of the Golden Boy, Rodolfo Carrillo Fuentes, ordered by El Mayo and approved by El Chapo, was a wound that never healed. Relations between these two leaders of the Sinaloa Cartel and Vicente El Viceroy were hanging by a thread, and the former were disturbed by El Barbas's close relation with the latter. Although the Beltrán Leyvas were still part of The Federation in 2007, it's clear that from the beginning of Calderón's term, the stench of betrayal hung in the air. It was just a matter of time.

By contrast, Joaquín Guzmán, Ismael Zambada, Ignacio Coronel, and Juan José Esparragoza were only classified as "strategic priority no. 2,"[13] in spite of the fact that they were leading the most powerful drug trafficking organization in the Americas, and the one with the strongest presence in the United States.

A declassified document from the US Northern Command, drawn up in 2009, states categorically that the Sinaloa Cartel is the most dangerous of the Mexican drug trafficking organizations, and blames this "rogue cartel" for the violence along the border. The authors note with concern that the Sinaloa Cartel controls the Pacific corridor, and there is little or nothing to stop it taking over the corridor that was in the hands of the Arellano Félix organization.[14]

The government's dubious strategy has helped to strengthen El Chapo Guzmán, since most of the drug traffickers arrested belong to groups that oppose him. Edgardo Buscaglia,[15] one of the main critics of the Calderón government's failed war, has done the math: of the 53,174 arrests made in the four years to 2010, for either involvement in organized crime or criminal association, he says that only 941 were connected with El Chapo Guzmán's cartel.

What is more, most of the arrests that did take place came to nothing. Buscaglia points out that when you look for consequences after the arrest of the son, or the grandfather, or whatever, of El Mayo Zambada, there are none to be found: "Was somebody sent to prison? Did they reveal the details of the fortunes belonging to El Chapo, El Mayo, or El Azul Esparragoza?" The facts back up this troublesome UN adviser.

The protection given by the Mexican government to Joaquín Guzmán is palpable. And the drug lord himself makes a show of it.

At the beginning of July 2007, El Chapo decided to "get married" in broad daylight, with Mexican army soldiers as minders, and drug traffickers and politicians from both the PRI and the PAN as his guests.

El Chapo's wedding

That July day in 2007, in the municipality of Canelas, in Durango state, the band Los Canelos suddenly stopped playing. The ranch was surrounded by soldiers in olive green. For a few seconds at least, the couple celebrating their nuptials with this sumptuous fiesta ceased to be the center of attention: The King of Crystal had arrived. Ignacio Coronel was the regional big shot and guest of honor on a day when "royalty" were sealing such an important union. The bridegroom, at fifty-three, was undoubtedly the king of Mexican drug traffickers. The bride, at just eighteen, was the recently crowned Queen of the annual Canelas Coffee and Guava Fair. Canelas is a heavenly spot, surrounded by waterfalls, woods and all manner of wild flowers, but Emma Coronel was the loveliest flower of them all.[16]

In the course of his life, El Chapo has had quite a collection of women. Now, it seems he has eyes only for Emma. The name she adopted after her coronation suits her well: Emma I. Slim and child-like, she has long, brown, curly hair that reaches halfway down her back, white skin, an oval face and brown, melancholy eyes. But the union was not really a wedding, says the daughter of one drug baron who knows the situation well. "El Chapo cannot marry because he never divorced his first wife, Alejandrina." What he did was to formalize his relationship and commitment to Emma.

When El Chapo saw his friend and partner Nacho arrive, he hurried over and gave him a bear hug, the kind you give to a brother. They were having a party. It had been a long time since El Chapo had felt at peace. That wasn't because he feared arrest by the government, but because of the war The Federation had started against the Gulf Cartel four years ago. Now, at last, he could spare a few moments for his personal life.

El Chapo enjoyed considerable freedom of movement in Canelas, where the mayor was Francisco Cárdenas Gamboa, of the PAN. In

May of 2007 the mayor had been involved in a scandal after local police officers were caught by the army carrying several kilos of opium gum with a permit signed by him.

Apart from the star guest, Nacho Coronel, El Chapo had invited all his nearest and dearest. After all, it was a day to celebrate in style. El Mayo, El Azul, the Beltrán Leyva brothers and La Barbie were all there. People in the know say that one of the politicians present was the young PAN senator, Rodolfo Dorador, who is close to President Felipe Calderón. He would stand unsuccessfully for mayor in Durango in 2010 as the candidate of the "Durango Unites Us" coalition, made up of the PAN, the left-of-center PRD, and Convergencia. When asked whether he really was at the wedding, Dorador doesn't deny it. And if a party colleague reproaches him for it, he replies testily: "So what? Fox hung out with El Chapo, too."

Some of those who attended say the Sinaloa state district attorney, Alfredo Higuera Bernal, was also there. When the magazine *Proceso* reported this, Higuera called a press conference to deny it. In fact he said he had never been to Durango, although other guests still insist he was present.

El Chapo also invited Jesús Aguilar, the governor of Sinaloa, and he apparently accepted, although the former governor of Durango state, Ismael Hernández, did not, preferring to avoid trouble. People in Durango claim he was so closely involved with El Chapo that the latter once went around to his house and tell him off, reminding him that he had to answer his calls whenever he phoned, and not to forget it again.

The party went on long into the night. In times of truce, El Chapo could allow himself such a luxury. However, not everything went his way. The celebration soon became public knowledge, and that infuriated him. The repercussions of the leak were severe. Cárdenas Gamboa, who completed his term as mayor of Canelas in August 2007, was shot by two gunmen on September 22 in downtown Durango city. The following day, Reynaldo Jiménez, the leader of the PAN in Canelas and a former municipal secretary, was kidnapped and never seen again. The last thing El Chapo needed right then was the glare of publicity. Only weeks before his "marriage" to the Queen of the Coffee and Guava Fair, he had attended a less agreeable gathering.

The Valle Hermoso pact

In June 2007, various drug barons from The Federation and the Gulf Cartel held a series of meetings in different parts of the country. The aim was to put an end to the war between the two organizations that had lasted almost four years (since 2003) and caused thousands of deaths. One of the meetings took place in Tamaulipas, on Zetas territory,[17] at a property belonging to Heriberto Lazcano, near the junction of the Valle Hermoso and Matamoros highways. Since the members of The Federation were the "aggressors" and those of the Gulf Cartel the "aggrieved," the latter set the terms for the encounter.

Many grudges had been piling up, but what the Zetas most resented was that while they had conquered their territory in battle, "fairly and squarely," The Federation had relied on "the support of the government and of people at the top of the AFI and the Secretariat of Public Security." The fact that the Zetas had managed without "official support" made them feel invincible. A little ingenuously, they even thought they could snatch back from The Federation its traditional strongholds in Jalisco and Sinaloa.

The Federation was represented at the meeting by Joaquín Guzmán, Vicente Carrillo Fuentes, Juan José Esparragoza, Ismael Zambada, Ignacio Coronel, Arturo and Héctor Beltrán Leyva, and their chief enforcer, Edgar Valdez, La Barbie, who had started the war in Nuevo Laredo on the orders of the cartel.

Although in 2002, it was Esparragoza, El Azul, who had urged his partners to begin hostilities against the Gulf Cartel, now the high cost for both sides had convinced him to be one of the main promoters of the truce meeting. It is said he was encouraged by a senior government official, who promised nobody would be harassed if there were a ceasefire. At the beginning of 2007, El Azul had already made one attempt at a pact, through an official in the Public Prosecutor's Office.[18] But the Gulf Cartel, and especially the Zetas leader, El Verdugo Lazcano, had refused. He didn't trust his adversaries an inch, and didn't want to fall into the same trap as his boss, Osiel Cárdenas. "We'll never make a pact with them," had been Lazcano's response. In the end, The Executioner was forced to sit down with his enemies after the Beltrán Leyva brothers kidnapped one of his cousins. El Azul intervened to secure his safe return before the meeting, as a token of peace.

The Gulf Cartel was represented by Ezequiel Cárdenas and Heriberto Lazcano. Humberto García Ábrego, regarded as the honorary leader of the Gulf Cartel, was not present; the brother of Juan García Ábrego had not been directly involved in the drug business for some time, though he still took his cut of the profits.

Such a meeting between Mexico's top drug traffickers, in the middle of one of the bloodiest wars ever, seemed unthinkable. But business is business. The hostilities between the organizations was costing them dearly, in terms of both cash and casualties. Even their respective contacts in Colombia were beginning to wonder if the Mexicans could still be trusted. Intelligence reports indicate that cocaine shipments from Colombia had noticeably fallen off around that time.

It was just after midday when Joaquín Guzmán arrived at the meeting place. The tension rose. There were so many grievances on both sides. All the men were armed to the teeth, but there were no fingers on the triggers. When El Chapo Guzmán stood face to face with Heriberto Lazcano, the room fell silent. "If I was queer, I'd have fucked you already", said Guzmán, looking the Zeta leader's youthful, athletic figure up and down with a face of surprise. Then he gave him the sort of hug only a mafioso can give one of his rivals. The ice was broken. Everybody burst out laughing. It wasn't for nothing that El Chapo was who he was; his ability to charm, even at moments of life and death, was scarily impressive.

The first agreement they came to was to stop the violence. They decided to respect the territorial advances made by each cartel during the war, and not to attack the authorities in the areas where they were operating. The Gulf Cartel would keep Tamaulipas, Coahuila, Veracruz, Tabasco, Campeche, and Quintana Roo. The Federation would have Sonora, Sinaloa, Durango, Chihuahua, Nayarit, Jalisco, Guerrero, Guanajuato, Querétaro, and Oaxaca. In states like Nuevo León, Michoacán, the Federal District, and the State of Mexico, each group would keep the areas it had conquered, sharing the territory as a whole. Aguascalientes, San Luis Potosí, Zacatecas, and Puebla would be left as "neutral" states. They also agreed, at the request of the government, to try to put a stop to retail drug dealing, and to ensure that most of the product left Mexico. Of all the agreements, that would be the most difficult to fulfill. Furthermore, it was agreed that the two organizations would join together to pay for state protection, on the understanding that this would henceforth be provided to all the groups, not just El Chapo's.

The Valle Hermoso pact was in fact an opium dream, a fleeting illusion. Two factors made it only too easy for the truce to break down. The first was the difficulty of sharing territory, especially between drug traffickers who had been at one another's throats for years. It was one thing for the generals to reach an agreement, quite another for the rank and file to obey. The second factor was, strange to say, the United States government—very fond of making pacts itself, but not so keen on others making them behind its back.

In typical narco style, the meeting in Valle Hermoso ended with a wild party. Heriberto Lazcano and his colleague went to bed, while the guests enjoyed an abundance of alcohol, music, and prostitutes. Other meetings followed, in Cuernavaca and the Polanco neighborhood of Mexico City, to wrap up the final details of the accord. A fragile calm descended on the country's streets. The death rate fell sharply, from ten executions a day to an average of eight a week.

For his part, Heriberto Lazcano got on famously with Arturo Beltrán Leyva. Their violent personalities were a perfect match. It is said that around this time El Verdugo had a plane accident and that Arturo, El Barbas, came to rescue him in a helicopter. As a sign of his friendship, El Barbas began to share with the Zetas leader all the protection The Federation enjoyed from officials in the SSP. Those who had been hunting the Zetas like dogs were now helping them collect their bribes. At the same time the Mexican government, rotten to the core, in speech after presidential speech continued to extol its phoney "war on drugs."

The truce could not last. Betrayal is the only constant among drug traffickers. If El Chapo had foreseen that this pact would turn out to mark not the end, but the beginning of the worst phase of the war, he would never have held out his hand to El Verdugo.

The reek of betrayal

It was the beginning of 2008, and Alfredo Beltrán Leyva, El Mochomo, was feeling wound up. By nature he was a cautious man, but that day he was in a hurry to visit one of his women, who it is said was a relative of Joaquín Guzmán's. He usually carried a Colt .38, and moved around with a group of bodyguards, but in matters of the heart he preferred privacy. His rendezvous was to be in Culiacán, at no. 1970 Juan de la Barrera, in the Burócratas neighborhood. Very few people knew where the couple would meet, much less at what time.

On Sunday, January 20, two AFI officers traveled to Culiacán to follow up a supposed anonymous phone call, giving advance notice of where El Mochomo would be that day.

In 2007, the PGR and the SSP had signed an agreement to place the AFI under the jurisdiction of the Secretariat, together with its assets, weapons, offices, and files. Genaro García Luna aspired to create a single police force, bringing together the Federal Preventive Police (PFP) and the Federal Investigation Agency (AFI) under a single command: his own. The agreement was a first step towards what would be known as the Federal Police.

The AFI officers, following orders from García Luna's team, checked out the address they had been given at 4:30 p.m.[19] They could be sure that El Mochomo would spend a good few hours there with his lady friend, maybe for the last time. At 2 a.m. the officers returned, with reinforcements from the Mexican army. Something, or someone, caused El Mochomo to leave the premises at precisely that time. The property's electric gate swung open for Alfredo Beltrán Leyva to depart in a chunky white BMW, accompanied by just three bodyguards.

The trafficker, sitting in the back seat behind the driver, was livid when the police officers ordered him to stop. But he and his men were so convinced it was a mistake that they all got out without their guns. The last to alight was El Mochomo, who confidently gave his real name and never thought of using his pistol. It could only be a mix-up, or else one of those pointless pantomimes they put on from time to time. Alfredo was the one who paid the bribes to the former

AFI chiefs who now ran the SSP, as well to the army chiefs. Like the rest of The Federation, he took it for granted that he was untouchable.

The officers showed him a summons. El Mochomo couldn't understand what was happening; suddenly everything was going wrong. Then they confiscated an AK-47, five handguns, magazines and ammunition of various calibers, a bullet-proof vest, and three travel cases whose contents added up to $950,000—not a lot for a drug baron of his stature. They also found in the car valuables worth five million pesos (about $450,000 in 2008), including eighteen Rolex, Dior, and Chopard watches, made of platinum or gold and set with precious stones, as well as emerald and diamond rings, and five spectacular rosaries. Drug traffickers often use religious images or objects as talismans. These rosaries were of gold, with black pearls for beads and diamond-encrusted crucifixes, but they didn't bring El Mochomo any luck on that occasion.

The situation reeked of betrayal. El Mochomo's arrest had little to do with justice and much more with the envy of his cousin, El Chapo Guzmán. And it didn't take long for his brother, Arturo, to figure that out. The Beltrán Leyva brothers had been climbing the ladder inside The Federation way too fast for El Chapo's taste. They owed their rise to the fact that, through them, the organization was developing many new contacts with local, regional, and national authorities in its operational zones. To some extent El Chapo had been sidelined: he was no longer the cartel's only means of getting close to the government, as he had been since his escape.

The truce agreed in 2007 had also strengthened the Beltrán Leyvas. It was Arturo, El Barbas, who had the contact with Los Zetas, with whom he began to arrange his own shipments without consulting anyone. This made El Barbas feel more powerful, and encouraged him to throw his weight about. The straw that broke the camel's back was a clash between El Chapo and El Barbas over the handling of Mexico City airport, where thanks to García Luna's team they could fly in all the drugs and dollars they wanted.

All the members of the cartel had long known that it was El Mayo Zambada who controlled Mexico City International Airport. That was his quota of power, and the source of much of his influence in the organization. In 2007, the Federal District as a whole was a territory run by Reynaldo Zambada, El Rey, El Mayo's brother, with help from the Beltrán Leyva brothers and from Sergio Villarreal, El Grande, who had moved to Mexico City from Durango.

Once El Grande became operational boss he started executing people left, right, and center. A violent and taciturn man, he carried out the killings himself, with little in the way of explanation. In December 2007, when a shipment of pseudoephedrine belonging to El Chapo Guzmán arrived at the airport, Villarreal refused to release it, claiming it needed authorization from El Barbas. El Chapo was furious, and called a meeting in Culiacán with El Mayo Zambada and El Barbas to sort things out.

Strangely, Zambada backed Beltrán, and told Guzmán not to worry, he only had to let them know when he wanted to shift any merchandise. Arturo explained that his people hadn't recognized El Chapo's men, and of course they couldn't let just anyone in; but as long they were forewarned, they'd always be happy to help out. El Chapo felt like a fool, and was not at all mollified, but he held his tongue, as is his way. The incident became common knowledge within The Federation when El Mochomo, Arturo's younger brother, started bragging about it. El Chapo soon convinced El Mayo that it had been a mistake to support his cousin; the two of them agreed to teach the Beltrán Leyva brothers a lesson that would serve as a warning to other members of the organization.

On the same day that Alfredo was arrested, the PFP—which came under García Luna as Secretary of Public Security—carried out surprise raids on three of Arturo's houses in Mexico City. Things were happening very fast. Arturo barely avoided capture, slipping away minutes before the police arrived. He had already guessed that El Chapo was behind his brother's arrest. Apart from his obvious anger, something else must have pained Arturo Beltrán. It seemed his cousin had forgotten that he was the one who had sent him money in Puente Grande, enabling him to live like a king; he'd also forgotten that their family ties had become even closer since the marriage of his daughter to one of Guzmán's sons.

"El Chapo is a big traitor, he'd betray his own mother if he could." That's what Pablo Tostado, the erstwhile aide to Esparragoza, was always saying; his words must have been echoing in El Barbas's head.

At that moment of crisis and definition, the Beltrán Leyva clan had one unconditional ally: Heriberto Lazcano, The Executioner, the head of Los Zetas. Lazcano immediately provided Arturo with his most trusted lawyer to take on Alfredo's case, thereby sealing the bond between them. The strength of the Zetas helped El Barbas to make a drastic decision: he would break with The Federation, and take revenge for his younger brother's capture.

Vicente Carrillo Fuentes, Sergio Villarreal, Edgar Valdez, and the Gulf Cartel sided with the head of the Beltrán Leyva clan. They realized that if El Chapo and El Mayo were capable of handing over Alfredo and trying to get El Barbas arrested, then they could be next. La Barbie and El Verdugo, the two "military" chiefs, had never gotten along very well. But they were now together in the same boat, with the same objective: to put an end to El Chapo Guzmán and his clan. Thus two big blocs of drug traffickers emerged in Mexico: the Sinaloa Cartel headed by El Chapo and El Mayo, and the Beltrán Leyvas' organization, united with the Juárez and Gulf cartels, and with what was left of the Tijuana Cartel. The split at the core of The Federation would trigger a war such as the country had never seen, a merciless struggle to the death, from which nobody would be safe.[20]

For seven years The Federation had been protected en bloc by the main public bodies in the judicial and security sectors: the army, the navy, the PGR, the AFI, and the SSP at federal level. Its rupture produced another, equally violent rupture among these state institutions. Public officials who worked for The Federation, at local, regional, or national level, now faced an acid test. They were like the children of a marriage that has suddenly broken down, and have to decide if they want to live with Mom or Dad. Many corrupt officials found themselves trapped between the two sides, and unable to dodge the bullets.

The warnings were explicit. At the end of May 2008, a banner appeared in Culiacán with a chilling message on it: "THIS IS FOR YOU AGUILAR PADILLA [THE STATE GOVERNOR], EITHER YOU MAKE AN ARRANGEMENT OR I'LL ARRANGE YOU. THIS WHOLE GOVERNMENT WORKING FOR EL CHAPO AND EL MAYO IS GOING TO DIE." A few days earlier, the governor had already received an anonymous phone call falsely claiming that one of his sons had been murdered. Arturo Beltrán Leyva began to leave dozens of banners in the streets of Culiacán that became a sort of criminal mural newspaper: "LITTLE LEAD SOLDIERS AND STRAW POLICEMEN, THIS TERRITORY BELONGS TO ARTURO BELTRÁN." No one does more certain damage than a friend who becomes a foe. The fight between El Chapo and El Barbas was to the death. In this battle of titans, the first victims were from García Luna's ranks. They began to fall like flies, dead or captured.

García Luna's casualties

The first of García's men to fall was Roberto Velasco, a recent appointee to the Federal Police who had previously worked in a department store. On the afternoon of May 1, 2008, he was returning to his home in the Irrigación district of Mexico City. Close to the house, two men intercepted his vehicle and shot him three times in the head. He died a few hours later. The US embassy in Mexico was quick to condemn the "brutal" murder, and paid tribute to Velasco for his "outstanding work in the front line of the battle against drug trafficking." The truth is he had a bad reputation, and was accused by several people of links with the drug business.

That same day, Francisco Hernández, who had just been moved from Cancún to a new post as deputy representative of the AFI in Victoria, Tamaulipas, was kidnapped by a group of heavily armed men in AFI uniforms. The following day his body was found dumped outside a stadium in Culiacán, on the other side of the country. However, by a bureaucratic mix-up not uncommon in Mexico, the body was handed over to the wrong family. Since his own family and the authorities continued to search for him, seven days later someone hung a banner on the stadium railings which read: "STOP LOOKING FOR ME IN TAMAULIPAS, BECAUSE I WAS BETRAYED AND KILLED OUTSIDE THE BANORTE STADIUM IN CULIACÁN ON MAY 2."

For at least a year, Hernández had been working for The Federation enabling planes full of drugs or money to land at Cancún international airport. His second-in-command, José Luis Soledana, another García Luna man, had already been murdered in November 2007.

The third member of García's team to be murdered was Aristeo Gómez, aged thirty-four. On May 2, 2008, he was talking to a woman colleague in a parked vehicle in the Romero de Terreros neighborhood of Mexico City, when two men pulled him out of the car and tried to force him into a van. His companion moved to intervene but they warned her off, shouting, "The problem isn't with you!" When Aristeo resisted, they shot him at point-blank range.

The fourth to die was Commander Igor Labastida. On June 26, 2008, he was shot down in a cheap diner near the AFI offices where he still worked, even though by then he was employed in the Federal Preventive Police. A lone assassin emptied two weapons, a 9mm Uzi and a .380 caliber, into him and his bodyguard. Outside the restaurant Labastida's Cadillac was parked with $1 million in the trunk, according to unofficial information from the Defense Secretariat.

The previous month, Labastida, who was then director of Traffic and Contraband at the PFP, revealed a delicate secret to an attorney friend in Nuevo León: he was trying to contact the US authorities with a view to becoming a protected witness, and revealing all he knew about the corruption in the AFI and the SSP. He was the one who had complained that García Luna and Cárdenas Palomino gave him all the dirty work.[21]

The two Edgars

Hardest of all for García Luna, however, was an earlier killing. At dawn on May 8, at 132 Camelia Street, in a densely populated and notorious part of Mexico City called Tepito, nine shots felled Edgar Millán, García Luna's close friend and one of his most trusted and powerful subordinates. As well as being reputedly among the most highly trained and educated of the commanders, Millán had specialized as a police observer for United Nations missions, and was the SSP's contact person with the US Government for the exchange of sensitive information. Days earlier he had been the target of an attack at Federal Police headquarters by a sniper with poor aim. His death was a shocker. Millán was ranked third in the hierarchy of the SSP, behind Secretary García Luna and Under Secretary for Police Intelligence Facundo Rosas.

In Tepito, where he was killed, Millán had been a familiar figure ever since his family moved there ten years earlier. Camelia is one of the most dangerous streets in the area, because of the amount of drug peddling that takes place there. It's said there is a small store where they sell drugs right in front of the building where Millán's parents owned several apartments.[22] A few doors further down is a well-known brothel. The federal police commissioner, however, was very respectful towards his dodgy neighbors, and his frequent presence did nothing to deter them from lawlessness.

Everyone made it their job to turn Commander Millán into a hero. In his public tribute, Calderón declared: "The Mexican government expresses its profound grief at the cowardly murder of an exemplary official like Edgar Millán, who was committed to keeping Mexican families safe." García Luna lamented the death of his friend and colleague in rousing terms: "The country has lost one of its most valiant men, a true professional at the service of the nation. . . . Rest in peace, Edgar Millán, with the honor of knowing you did your duty."

The death of Edgar Millán was treated like an occasion for national mourning. The US ambassador himself, Tony Garza, joined the emotive chorus:

> I am deeply saddened by the murder of Edgar Millán Gómez, Coordinator of Regional Security at the Preventive Federal Police. Struck down by criminals in the prime of his life, Mr. Millán was an example of the highest professional standards and a broad dedication to public service. . . . Mexico has lost another hero. Another life has been lost, and this is a cause of indignation to all of us who admire and respect the thousands of officials who selflessly devote their lives to the betterment of their country.

Judging by what the authorities said of Millán, it seemed that all the negative reports about him, all the accusations of corruption and complicity with criminals, were nothing but idle gossip. Now the press room in the SSP headquarters bears the name of Edgar Eusebio Millán, following the example of the DEA in calling its El Paso building after the agent killed in 1985, Enrique Camarena.

Also on May 8, 2008, at 8 p.m. in the parking lot of the Culiacán's City Club shopping mall, a barrage of AK-47 rifles and a bazooka riddled dozens of vehicles, according to press reports, and killed Edgar Guzmán López—the twenty-two-year-old son of El Chapo and Griselda López. With him died Arturo Meza Cázares, the son of Blanca Cázares, known as The Empress, who handled finances for El Mayo Zambada.

The body of the apprentice drug baron lay face down on the tarmac, covered in blood, outside the Bridgestone Tyre Center. A month later an iron cross was erected on that spot, above a stone plinth with the inscription: "We will always love you." El Chapo Guzmán's pain was real, and ran deep. He was certain that Arturo Beltrán had ordered his son's killing as revenge.

The US government was growing increasingly alarmed at the violence in Mexico. It feared the gangs might start targeting members of President Calderón's cabinet. Within weeks, those fears would become reality. Meanwhile, the paranoia at the SSP intensified. They had upset a lot of people.

The narco-hero

On May 9, 2008, six federal policemen dressed in navy blue carried the weighty casket of Edgar Millán past the luxurious SSP offices on Mexico City's Avenida Constituyentes. The casket was draped in the national flag, for a hero's send-off. President Felipe Calderón, Genaro García Luna, Interior Secretary Juan Camilo Mouriño, Defense Secretary Guillermo Galván, Navy Secretary Mariano Saynez, and Attorney General Eduardo Medina Mora, lined up in a guard of honor for the fallen commander. This image will be remembered as one of the most emblematic of what was really going on in the "war on drugs" launched by the Mexican government, this theater where nothing is what it seems. The true story of Edgar Millán is a far cry from all those honors bestowed at his death.

*   *   *

Back in June 2007, Arturo Beltrán Leyva had summoned two senior SSP officials to receive their instructions. The meeting took place at one of his houses in Cuernavaca, where he spent most of his time. He asked his brother Alfredo to join them. The purpose of the meeting was to inform the federal police chiefs of the conciliatory agreements reached between The Federation and the Gulf Cartel. Joaquín Guzmán and his partners had a new brief for the SSP: they were to stop arresting members of the Gulf Cartel, and instead give them the same protection already being provided to themselves.

Arturo Beltrán Leyva recorded the whole meeting on audio and video. On the tapes you can clearly see the faces of Edgar Millán, who at the time was acting commissioner of the Preventive Federal Police (PFP) and general coordinator of regional security, and Gerardo Garay Cadena, the supervisory chief of the central region of the PFP. According to the SSP, Garay had "triple anti-corruption credentials," having been vetted by the DEA, the FBI, and the SSP (in the form of the PFP) itself. This account is contained in the sworn statement of a protected witness, José Puga, who the PGR gave the code name of Pitufo.[23]

Neither Millán nor Garay were aware of El Barbas's habit of photographing and recording his meetings with government officials, which went back to 2005. Millán, Garay, and Igor Labastida all appear receiving bribes in a number of such recordings, according to Pitufo. The tapes were made, he said, so that if the officials ever went back on their agreements, they could be shown to the media.

Later in 2007, the recordings of Millán and Garay negotiating with members of The Federation fell into the hands of Los Zetas. In fact they were given to Miguel Treviño, El Z40, by Arturo Beltrán himself, as proof that they had already told the SSP to lay off the Gulf Cartel.

Everything indicates that Millán was not killed for his valiant stand against the drugs trade, but because he betrayed the drug barons he had been protecting, and from whom he had presumably received millions of dollars in bribes for himself, his colleagues, and his superiors. It was he who was in charge of the Federal Police when the operation was mounted to capture Alfredo Beltrán, in January 2008.

But Millán's was not the only corpse that now disturbed García Luna and his team. On July 31, in a car trunk in the south of Mexico City, they found the lifeless body of a fourteen-year-old named Fernando Martí. The boy had been snatched a few weeks before.

Crime and punishment

By 2007, Mexico City's fearsome kidnapper, Sergio Ortiz, El Apá, was once more on the job. He sent the family of one kidnapped woman a video of the moment when she was being sexually abused. Then, as proof of life, he sent them her ears. And once the $5-million ransom had been paid, the only thing the family got back was her head. Emboldened by the protection he apparently received from the AFI during Vicente Fox's government, Ortiz now decided to look for bigger fish.

To this end, El Apá became interested in a group of businessmen who liked to race cars. During the week they'd meet at the Hermanos Rodríguez circuit and show off their ability to drive very expensive sports cars, very fast. Among the habitués of these get-togethers were the main proprietor of Televisa, Emilio Azcárraga, the owner of a sports chain, Alejandro Martí, and his friend, Óscar Paredes. Early in 2008 El Apá kidnapped Óscar's son, Javier Paredes. Months after, he kidnapped Alejandro's son, Fernando Martí.[24] Javier was freed after a sum of millions of dollars was paid; Fernando was murdered, even though his father had paid the ransom. But the matter of the boy soon became a nightmare for El Apá, García Luna, and his crooked team.

The grief and indignation of Alejandro Martí was contagious. Mexican public opinion was moved as seldom before. The PGJDF arrested El Apá in September 2008. At almost the same time, they arrested a woman called Lorena González, who had been named in previous investigations as an active accomplice of El Apá and the La Flor group. They accused her of being a member of the gang, and of putting up a roadblock with AFI signs on it to facilitate the kidnapping of Fernando. The boy's chauffeur identified González by sight.

Lorena González was no ordinary kidnapper. In fact, she was the deputy head of the Federal Police's anti-kidnapping unit when she set up that roadblock, and was still in the post the day she was arrested.[25] Her bosses were Luis Cárdenas Palomino and Facundo Rosas, and she was so close to their cabal that she was a regular guest at their select parties. After she was arrested, the SSP tried to wash its hands of her. Rosas announced that she had worked in the AFI, but never in the Secretariat. García Luna said the same, incriminating himself even further. It was untrue. Thus a war began between the SSP and the PGJDF.

From prison, González sent greetings and a message to her pals in the Secretariat: either they got her off the hook, or she would tell everything. García's team jumped to it, but they were working against the clock. They had at all costs to separate El Apá and González from the case of Fernando Martí. But the deputy head of the anti-kidnapping unit was in a tight spot. Back in 2007, an accomplice of El Apá's gang had testified to the PGJDF that Lorena—La Comandante Lore, as she was known—and another federal officer, Gerardo Colín Reyes, El Colín, had been in the gang since the time of the Fox administration, when both of them were serving in the AFI. The witness stated that they had not only provided protection, but had taken active part in the kidnappings. However, as the case was turned over to the Federal Police's Department of Kidnappings and Theft, where La Comandante was section head, naturally the investigations went nowhere.

In July 2009, Lorena's former boss, Cárdenas Palomino, himself an expert in kidnappings and not precisely because he'd investigated many of them, announced the arrest of one Noé Robles and presented him to the media as a member of the Petriciolet gang, led by Abel Silva Petriciolet, which in reality had been a branch of El Apá's organization for several years. At the press conference, Cárdenas showed one of his famous videos—many of which were recorded under torture, and have no legal validity—where Robles states that he killed Fernando Martí, and that El Apá and Lorena were not part of the gang.

People close to Alejandro Martí say he obtained permission to speak to Robles in the prison where he was being held.

"Why did you kill my son?" he demanded.

"Because you didn't pay what we asked for."

"But I did pay," said Martí desperately.

"Well, the Federal Police only gave us some of it," shrugged the hired crook.

On July 20, 2009, Javier Paredes's chauffeur, who had been kidnapped along with Martí's friend's son, declared before the Mexico City authorities that he recognized Noé as the person who had guarded them during their captivity. And he recognized El Apá, without a shadow of a doubt, as the man who had gone to visit them in the safe house during their captivity. He confirmed that both were members of the same gang.

The SSP were feeling cornered. On September 2 they arrested José Jiménez, El Niño, and accused him of belonging to the Beltrán Leyva organization and of taking part in the kidnappings of Fernando Martí and another boy, Marco Antonio Equihua. Later in the month they arrested Abel Silva himself, who also "confessed" to the kidnappings, and declared that neither El Apá nor Lorena were involved. This refrain was no longer credible, and his testimony was soon contested by Alejandro Martí, who was becoming ever more of a nuisance for the SSP. Martí exposed every one of Silva's contradictory assertions, so that despite García Luna and his cronies' best efforts, the case against El Apá and La Comandante Lore was beginning to look solid.

In September 2009 the SSP once more detained George Khouri Layón, El Koki, the yuppie businessman from Polanco who in 2005 had boasted of his connections in both the criminal and police worlds. But the arrest was surreptitious: his friends thought he might have been kidnapped. The SSP was only pre-empting the PGJDF, to prevent the Federal District authorities from questioning him. They announced the arrest in late November, when they accused him of attempting to murder an unspecified member of the force. Later, the PGJDF found witnesses who would link El Koki to El Apá.

The fact is that El Apá and his various kidnapping cells were all part of the same organization, and all have been linked to Joaquín El Chapo Guzmán.

Igor Labastida, Edgar Millán, and Comandante Lore were behind the kidnappings, torture and unimaginable abuse committed against youngsters like Fernando Martí, Marco Antonio Equihua, and numerous others. An internal document from the Mexico City

Attorney's Office (PGJDF) directly accuses Millán and Labastida of protecting Sergio Ortiz, El Apá.[26] Ortiz died in jail in November 2009, of respiratory failure. Two other cells of the organization, as well as El Apá's sons who have been directly accused by some kidnap victims, remain at large. In January 2013, Comandante Lore was still pleading her innocence in jail. Other arrests have been made. The case continues.

The search for justice has cost Alejandro Martí dearly. It is said he received death threats from the heads of the SSP, before it was dissolved under Peña Nieto. At the time of the kidnapping, the avalanche of mud loosened by the García team's foul deeds was only just beginning to pour down.

From Monterrey to the Desierto de Leones

After the Valle Hermoso pact, Garay Cadena was sent by García Luna to Nuevo León state, where he began to protect The Federation's new "friends." At the time the Public Prosecutors, attached to the PGR, were about to carry out a series of raids on warehouses and homes, and arrest members of the Gulf Cartel they had already identified. Following his new orders, Garay contacted Jaime González, El Hummer, one of Heriberto Lazcano and Miguel Treviño's main associates, told him what was going to happen, and proposed a deal. The proposal seemed reasonable to the drug trafficker, who told him sort out the details with another Zeta, Sigifredo Talamantes, El Canicón. The PFP commander, with his "triple anti-corruption vetting," asked El Canicón for a million dollars. Permission was sought from Treviño, El Z40, who agreed, not without misgivings. "Goddam Feds," thought José Puga Quintanilla, Pitufo, who was working for the Gulf Cartel and would be the one to hand over the bribe.

Pitufo met a representative of Garay's at the Gonzalitos fire station in Monterrey, and showed him the money. However, his instructions were to give it to nobody but the prosecutor they were meant to be buying off. Z40 had told Pitufo to take advantage of the meeting to fix future deals with Garay as well. But the appointment with the prosecutor, supposedly arranged by Garay, never materialized. The man sent by Commander Garay had to tell Pitufo that in fact there was no arrangement with the prosecutor, and that his boss was like that sometimes.

El Hummer immediately called Garay, who tried to explain that although the prosecutor had backed out, they should give him and his people the money anyway: they would simply refuse to accompany the prosecutor on his projected raids, and "there's no way he's going to arrest anyone on his own." But El Hummer wasn't stupid. He ordered El Canicón to fetch Commander Garay from the hotel where he was staying, and take him to Tampico. Garay didn't want to come out, and ordered his men to resist. Two of them were seized, and tortured to death; the other three were shot dead in the hotel doorway.

El Canicón's phone soon rang. It was Garay Cadena, quaking in his boots. "I'm sorry, I'm sorry, please don't kill me, I only did it because the guys lied to me, they said they were going to raid warehouses and arrest people, but they were really investigating things that didn't matter," whimpered the police chief, fully aware that he had tried to cheat the Gulf Cartel by charging for a non-existent favor, and that it had gone badly wrong.

After Millán's death in May 2008, García Luna made Garay acting commissioner of the PFP. After all, he already knew what the orders were and who was giving them. But the more untouchable Garay felt, the more unruly he became.

After the split in The Federation, Garay received a counter-order from El Chapo Guzmán and El Mayo Zambada's organization. He had to stop protecting the Gulf Cartel and the Beltrán Leyva brothers, who he'd been dealing with since 2005.

In October 2008, Commissioner Garay Cadena, Senior Commander Edgar Bayardo, and Francisco Navarro, director general of the Federal Support Forces Coordination at the Federal Police, led an operation that covered them in glory, and soon after in shame. It took place in the early hours of October 16, at a mansion in Desierto de los Leones, on the edge of Mexico City. The police chiefs burst into the ornate building—which had its own zoo with white tigers, panthers, gorillas, and lions—during a party organized by their target, the Colombian Harold Poveda, one of the main suppliers of cocaine to the Beltrán Leyva organization. Poveda got away. The police managed to capture eleven other suspect guests, including Teodoro Fino Restrepo, alias La Gaviota, The Seagull—a Colombian with links to the Valle del Norte Cartel.

On October 19, the under secretary for police strategy and intelligence, Facundo Rosas, announced the "successful" operation. He said it was the result of at least two years' painstaking intelligence work. Marisela Morales, then head of SIEDO (the specialized organized crime investigations unit) before becoming President Calderón's last Attorney General, assured the press that this was one of the most important operations carried out in recent times.

Days later, a number of García Luna's principal aides were exhibited to the press in the same SIEDO office, accused of links with drug traffickers. They included Gerardo Garay, Edgar Bayardo, and Francisco Navarro, as well as Luis Cárdenas Palomino and Mario Arturo Velarde (another veteran member of the inner circle).[27]

It turned out that the operation in Desierto de los Leones hadn't been quite as impeccable as was made out. The four days it lasted were an orgy of sex and violence. Thanks to the testimony of two Colombian women arrested, Ángela María Quintero[28] and Juliana López, believed to be Poveda's partner, the truth came out. That night Garay Cadena decided to forget his responsibilities as a lawman; he chose four women from the thirty alleged prostitutes present, ordered cocaine for them and shut himself in the jacuzzi. While that was going on, Bayardo and Navarro tortured several of the men at the party, plunging them in a tub full of ice. After that, they went with other police officers to rob the homes of four of those detained, taking both money and jewellery.[29] Eye-witnesses say that during those four outrageous days, Luis Cárdenas Palomino called in on the house, but did nothing to check the abuses. At the end of it all, $500,000 had disappeared from the "war chest" stolen from the drug barons; it seems Garay and Bayardo fought over who was to keep it.

The war of extermination between former members of The Federation turned out to be much more efficient than that of the government, perhaps because it was more deeply felt. The police operation in Desierto de los Leones was not the fruit of patient intelligence work, as Rosas had claimed: it happened because El Chapo and El Mayo's camp tipped them off. And the murkiest part of the affair was still to emerge. The following week, in response to the police attack on the Beltrán Leyvas's friends and suppliers, something happened that would give a sudden new twist to the story of drug trafficking in Mexico.

The king in check

According to the AFI agents, it all began with an anonymous call to the PGR, reporting that at number 430, Calle Wilfrido Massieu, in the San Bartolo Atepehuacán area of Mexico City, they would find armed men from El Mayo Zambada's group. AFI agents attached to the PGR went to check it out. Nearby they spotted a Volkswagen Polo carrying two men with rifles. When challenged, the car veered into the driveway of the reported address, and more men began to fire from inside the house.

A month earlier, on September 23, 2008, a group of AFI officers had demonstrated in the street against García Luna's proposal to unify the police forces. As they marched along Reforma, the main avenue in the center of Mexico City, the agents carried banners that read: "Out with corrupt PF commanders from the AFI," and "Out with Genaro, he favors the bandits." Far from owning up to the deep reasons for the protest of these men who had been working for him for six years, García Luna insulted them, in many cases unfairly, claiming they didn't want to submit to trustworthiness tests. He never imagined that the officers would pay back the affront by bringing his pact with El Chapo to the verge of collapse.

In the gunfight in San Bartolo Atepehuacán, the federal agents stood their ground and managed to capture four of the shooters. The others were about to escape when reinforcements arrived from the Mexico City security department, three of whom were wounded. The battle continued for some time.

The drug baron who had his base in that bourgeois neighbourhood was not Ismael El Mayo Zambada but another, almost as sizable, fish: Jesús Zambada, alias El Rey (The King), his younger brother. As we saw, El Rey controlled the capital's airport for El Mayo and El Chapo's group. For an hour and a half, as the bullets flew, nearby residents cowered in their homes. It was impossible to tell the goodies from the baddies. On one side, in the street, were federal agents and Mexico City police officers trying to detain a drug boss; on the other, on the roof of the house, were police officers on the drug trafficker's payroll, trying to cover his escape.[30]

El Rey, in despair at the firefight raging around him, sought help. He called Commander Bayardo, who only a few days earlier had been up to his pranks in Desierto de los Leones. "I'll be right over, godfather,"[31] answered Bayardo, giving him to understand that he was riding to the rescue. But time passed, and nothing happened. Terrified that he was about to be captured, El Mayo's brother called again.

"Where are you, godson? We're getting screwed to hell, we're about to be taken by the others," cried the drug baron, possibly referring to authorities who hadn't been bribed by them or were answering to the Beltrán Leyvas.

"Hang in there, I'm on my way," replied Bayardo.

El Rey and his son Jesús, aged twenty-two, were on the roof of the surrounded house. Zambada made another call, this time to the Mexico City security department, and without saying the name of the person he was talking to, begged urgently: "Listen son, you've got to send in the *pitufos*,[32] because I don't know if these guys are the others or the government."

About eight minutes later a detachment of Mexico City police officers did arrive, but because officers from the same force were already in combat on the scene; they could do nothing to help their man. "Call him again, get him to come and help us," pleaded young Jesús, from behind the water tank. El Rey phoned Bayardo again: "What's going on, godson? What's going on?" As a helicopter circled overhead, the drug trafficker, beside himself, told Bayardo: "Okay, you take care of my kids, I'm through, I'm not going to let them catch me, I'll kill myself first." El Rey took his pistol and raised it to his head, but his son jumped out from his hiding place and stopped him committing suicide.

In the end, Jesús El Rey Zambada was arrested along with his son, his stepson Richard Arroyo—the son of his Colombian partner, Patricia Guízar—and thirteen other members of the organization.

That same day the PGR issued a news release informing that sixteen people had been arrested. Four of them were being held at the SIEDO, and the others were in medium security detention in the PGJDF building. Neither institution revealed that one of them was Jesús Zambada; instead he was presented under the name Víctor Rosas Montes. Nor did they say that two of his sons had been captured. These hours were precious. As long as the public didn't know the importance of one of the prisoners, there was still a chance to set him free. It is said that the US government started pressing the Mexicans to reveal that Víctor Rosas was in fact El Rey Zambada, one of the most prolific traffickers of cocaine and methamphetamine from South America.

On October 22, the attorney general, Eduardo Medina Mora, officially announced the arrest of the drug baron and his son. Warning lights started flashing in the SSP. That same day Federal Police agents burst in on the search that the SIEDO was carrying out at the house in San Bartolo. At about 2 p.m., five police pickup trucks, each carrying about ten men, and three private vehicles arrived and went through the perimeter barrier that the investigators had set up.[33] Four armed men got out of one of the vehicles and tried to break through a fence, but the AFI agents working with the SIEDO stopped them.

An unidentified individual in a bullet-proof vest, alighting from a black sports car with no license plates, said he was in charge of the contingent. He went to speak to one of the women officers responsible for the SIEDO investigation.

"I'm here on superior orders," the man said, while conferring with someone else on his walkie-talkie.

"You'll have to tell me whose," the officer responded curtly.

Minutes later, the intrusive convoy of federal agents withdrew.

El Rey Zambada's hideout contained evidence of his links to senior figures in the Secretariat of Public Security. And they didn't want that getting into the hands of the PGR.

On Saturday 25 and Sunday 26 October, identical banners attributed to the Gulf Cartel appeared in ten Mexican states, rubbing salt into the wound. As the saying goes, the truth is the truth, even when told by a liar. The message read:

With the highest respect for your office, Mr. President, we ask you to open your eyes and realize what kind of people are in the PFP. We know you are not aware of the deal that Gerardo [*sic*] García Luna has had since the Fox government with the Sinaloa Cartel, protecting El Mayo Zambada, the Valencias, Nacho Coronel, and El Chapo.

As citizens we ask you to take a look at the following people who we are 100 percent certain are protecting the drug traffickers: Luis Cárdenas Palomino, Edgar Enrique Bayardo, Gerardo Garay Cadena. And we ask you to put people into the PFP who fight drug trafficking in a neutral way, without leaning on one side of the scale, and to investigate using the intelligence services of the Mexican army and the PGR, which are neutral independencies [*sic*]. You know that the PFP did not take part in the arrest of El Rey Zambada; if they had, he would have been tipped off in advance.

El Rey Zambada's son and stepson, inexperienced and frightened young men, soon blurted out all they knew and began ratting right and left. The first card to fall was Edgar Bayardo, who was arrested on October 29, along with two other members of the PFP accused of helping El Mayo. One of them, Jorge Cruz, had taken part in the operation in Desierto de los Leones, and had a long story of his own to tell.

Of course, Bayardo had no intention of going down on his own. Among those he dragged down with him was Garay Cadena, exposing the corruption in the SSP that García Luna tried to conceal. In the last days of October, Garay and Francisco Navarro were summoned for questioning by SIEDO.

Some of those arrested in the operation against El Rey had already stated that both Bayardo and Garay received monthly stipends of up to $500,000 in exchange for protection. PFP officers who had been under the command of Acting Commissioner Garay further accused him of taking money, jewelry, and weapons—gold-plated, diamond-studded AK-47s—during operations against El Chapo's adversaries, to be sold on to El Rey as war trophies. In this last operation in the Desierto, he had even stolen a pet bulldog.

The legal case against Garay was very serious, meaning the police chief would have to appear before a judge for a preliminary hearing.

This was very worrying for García Luna and Rosas, as the only two officials ranked above Garay in the chain of command. So, at 2 p.m. on October 30, they called an emergency meeting in García Luna's offices in the SSP on Avenida Constituyentes. In attendance were the secretary himself, the four under secretaries, and the coordinators of the Secretariat's various departments.

In his intervention, the coordinator of regional security, Ramón Pequeño, argued that under no circumstances should they allow Garay to appear in court, "because regardless of the truth of these allegations, they would cause irreparable damage to our plans for the Federal Police, at a time when both houses of Congress are precisely debating the new Security Law." This was the bill in which García Luna was seeking to create a unified police force. The majority agreed.

García Luna spoke to Attorney General Medina Mora—with whom his relationship had been poor for some time—to request support in getting Garay freed. When Medina refused to commit, he went to see his friend, Interior Secretary Mouriño. They hacked out an agreement whereby Garay, after giving evidence for several hours in the PGR, would be released. The plan was that the PFP chief would resign the following day, enabling him be charged merely with theft and other minor offenses, of which he could later be acquitted. On this condition, Garay Cadena agreed to hand in his valuable police badge.

His release on "orders from above" caused a storm of protest within Calderón's administration, in particular from the PGR and Sedena, who argued that it would ultimately be impossible to protect him. On October 31, 2008, minutes before Garay announced his resignation at a brief press conference, the under secretary of public security, Facundo Rosas (later Commissioner of the unified Federal Police) was rumored to have suffered an attempt on his life in Mexico City. The SSP was being rocked by a schism that was barely perceptible to ordinary citizens. Rosas was not seen in public for several days, and his staff say he did not go to the office. It added fuel to the rumors of an attack, one presumably carried out by the Sinaloa Cartel, in reprisal for their "employees" not doing their job.

Two other close associates of García Luna's were also subpoenaed: Mario Velarde, García's private secretary during the Fox years, and

Luis Cárdenas Palomino, both suspected of links to the Beltrán Leyvas when these were allied with the Sinaloans. Medina Mora was not going to miss this golden opportunity to show the secretary who was attorney general. Nevertheless, after intense pressure from García Luna, Velarde and Cárdenas walked free. Velarde, who knew what he knew, resigned quietly in November 2008. Cárdenas Palomino kept his job.

CHAPTER ELEVEN

The President of Death

The day that twenty-two-year-old Jesús Zambada Reyes and thirty-one-year-old Richard Arroyo Guízar were arrested, they at once began to relate stories worthy of a crime thriller, whose central characters were senior figures in the Secretariat of Public Security (SSP). The Colombians' reports of abuse by federal officers during the operation in Desierto de los Leones were merely the tip of the iceberg: now, the great submerged bulk came into view.

Jesús and Richard, respectively the son and stepson of Jesús Zambada García, El Rey, enrolled in the protected witness program run by the Attorney General's Office (PGR), still led by Eduardo Medina Mora. Jesús took the pseudonym Rambo III, and Richard, whose role had been in intelligence work and delivering bribes to the authorities who protected El Rey,[1] called himself María Fernanda.

One of those most incriminated by their testimony was Edgar Bayardo. The Federal Preventive Police (PFP) commander tried to deny to prosecutors that he knew or had worked for El Rey Zambada, but the evidence against him was so strong that he too opted to become a protected witness, using the cover name Tigre, Tiger. His testimony, consistent with that of Pitufo,[2] unmasked the systematic corruption of top officials in the SSP, and especially their collusion with the organization of El Chapo and El Mayo. When you read these hair-raising statements you begin to understand why that institution has been unable to fight crime effectively, and why, wherever its representatives go, disaster follows.

This is how María Fernanda told his tale, on October 22, 2008:

> I met Edgar Bayardo, alias El Jumex, two years ago. He was attached
> to the PGR, I don't know his exact post, and I met him through El
> Pelón, who like I said is part of the organization led by my father,
> Jesús Zambada. Well, my father and Bayardo knew each other from
> way back, when they worked for Amado Carrillo Fuentes, I don't
> exactly know what Bayardo was doing there, but then they lost touch.

In 2006, Bayardo had tried to resume contact with El Rey, and they
fixed up a meeting in Mexico City. At the last minute the drug baron
had to leave the capital, and sent his stepson to represent him.
Bayardo and Richard Arroyo met in a fast-food restaurant in the
luxury development of Bosques de las Lomas, where El Rey Zambada
had one of his safe houses.

> We greeted each other and he offered to work for the organization.
> From then on we were giving him money to get him promoted to
> more senior posts in the PGR, so that he'd be more useful to us. I
> should clarify that the amount we gave him at the time [2006] was
> $100,000 every time he told us he was going to be promoted, and
> the money was to pay the people who were helping him. . . . About
> a year and a half ago, Bayardo moved to the Federal Preventive
> Police, so we began paying him $25,000 a month for his services,
> which included warning us of any raids that were going to take
> place.

At the age of forty-one, Bayardo was already an old policeman. From
1997 to 1999 he was in the Federal Judicial Police (PJF), where he
met El Señor de los Cielos, Amado Carrillo Fuentes. Then he became
Deputy Attorney for Specialized Organized Crime Investigations in
the state of Tlaxcala. On July 1, 2007 he became a deputy head of
department at the PFP; Facundo Rosas, who appointed him, was
acting commissioner of the PFP at the time. Under his auspices,
Bayardo rose rapidly.

Early in 2008, at the beginning of the war against the Beltrán
Leyvas, Bayardo brought more recruits from the SSP to help El

Rey, gathering information and supporting operations against the enemy gangs.

In María Fernanda's words:

> From November last year, when [Bayardo] was made commissioner or chief inspector in the PFP, he began to provide us with security, of a purely logistical kind . . . And when we raided houses belonging to the enemy, the Zetas, Vicente Carrillo, or the Beltrán Leyvas, he'd come with us to provide security, bringing people from his own force.
>
> In January and February 2008, Bayardo went to a safe house in Las Lomas along with two people who worked with him in the PFP, called Jorge and Fidel . . . Jorge often went on these operations, to break into houses, like my father or I would give him the addresses and he'd go search them. While Fidel is the PFP man in charge of bugging the enemy's telephones, so when he found out anything he used to pass it straight on to me.

Jorge Cruz Méndez, who María Fernanda refers to above, was no newcomer. He'd worked for García Luna since 1998, following him from Cisen to the PFP and the AFI, with Facundo Rosas; Fidel Hernández, the other policeman mentioned by María Fernanda, worked under Cruz, and like him had experience under Rosas.

According to El Rey's stepson, Bayardo, Cruz, Hernández, and a certain Giovanni who has not been fully identified, carried out a string of operations for El Mayo against Arturo Beltrán Leyva, in Cuernavaca, Morelos, and Huixquilucan, State of Mexico. "We descended on the Beltrán Leyvas houses and if there was anybody in they were arrested and taken into custody," boasted María Fernanda, hinting that Rosas was acquiescent:

> Bayardo split the twenty-five thousand dollars he was paid a month with his assistants, including Fidel and Jorge, and I also know they shared some with Commander Facundo. As far as he is concerned, I remember that in May or June Bayardo mentioned to me that Commander Facundo was also helping to supply us with information.

The only "Commander Facundo" above Bayardo was Facundo Rosas, then under secretary in the SSP. He was Bayardo, Hernández, and Cruz's boss, and had appointed them to the positions in which they served El Mayo's group. So it seems almost certain that there was tacit approval by Rosas of the collaboration with El Rey Zambada's people, as his stepson said. On the basis of much less substantial testimony, numerous national and local authorities have been subpoenaed or subjected to travel bans. Commander Facundo, it seems, remained untouchable to the end.[3]

For his part, Bayardo said in his statement to the PGR that he had begun to work directly with Gerardo Garay Cadena in 2007, when the latter was made head of the Anti-Drug Division of the PFP's Third Section. Garay told him that if, in the course of his investigations, he ever came across specific references to Arturo or Héctor Beltrán Leyva, he shouldn't tell anyone else but should let Garay himself know, in person or by telephone. "It seemed strange," Bayardo recalled.[4] Those were the days when the Beltrán Leyva group was part of The Federation, and the SSP's protection extended to all of its members.

Bayardo told the PGR that on one occasion he and two other officers spotted Harold Poveda in Santa Fe, a then new development in Mexico City. The Colombian cocaine trafficker, who at the time was supplying all of The Federation, was accompanied by twenty or thirty men wearing uniforms from the State of Mexico State Security Agency (ASE), so Bayardo called for reinforcements. Garay assured him he was dispatching a patrol that was just approaching the Mexico City–Toluca highway, so they'd be there in ten minutes. The back-up arrived three and a half hours later, by which time the suspects were long gone.

Another time, the US embassy informed Bayardo that the Mexican-American Edgar Valdez, La Barbie, would be outside the Ángeles de Interlomas Hospital. Bayardo mobilized 150 officers and a Black Hawk helicopter, but Garay ordered them not to begin the operation until he got there, which he did at 7 p.m. Later, Bayardo heard—it's not clear if from the Zambada clan or from the embassy again—that La Barbie and his people were still near the hospital. But Garay declined to carry out aerial reconnaissance, and sent the officers home.

Garay Cadena's behavior became clear thanks to María Fernanda's evidence. The witness explained that Garay was also on the payroll of El Mayo Zambada's organization, and had previously been briefed to attack the clan's new enemies—the Beltrán Leyvas and their enforcers such as La Barbie. But in March 2008, after a vacation in Acapulco, Garay had done a deal with Arturo Beltrán not to serve the Sinaloa cartel anymore.

"When did you discover that Commander Garay was in league with the Beltrán Leyvas?" asked the prosecutor questioning María Fernanda.

"I suppose it was after his vacation in Acapulco that he made the arrangement with Arturo Beltrán, because from March 2008 onwards it became more difficult to get raids launched on Beltrán's houses."

"What do you mean by 'made the arrangement with Arturo Beltrán'?"

"I mean that from then on, Commander Garay had a deal with the Betrán Leyva organization not to act on the tip-offs we gave him via Commander Bayardo."

In the end, Garay bowed to superior orders and in October 2008 carried out the operation against the Beltrán Leyvas's main cocaine supplier, Harold Poveda. His triple certificate of trustworthiness, bestowed by the DEA, the FBI, and the SSP, had gone down the plughole a long time ago.

Edgar Bayardo was richly rewarded for all the information he gave to the PGR. He was given complete freedom of movement and a bodyguard, and continued to enjoy the good life. He didn't live in a safe house, as protected witnesses usually must, but in a luxury block at 86 Calle Tres Picos, in Polanco. It's said he owned two apartments there, each worth $800,000, with no visible security. Among the narco-cop's illustrious neighbors were the foreign secretary, Patricia Espinoza, and a former foreign secretary, Jorge Castañeda.

The US Embassy's mounting suspicions

This whole investigation, conducted in secrecy by the PGR with the declarations of El Rey Zambada's sons, sent tremors of anxiety through the SSP. In the US embassy they were beginning to worry that Genaro García Luna, their servile ally in the Mexican government, might not be useful for much longer if his reputation continued to take a battering.

On November 25, 2008, the embassy sent a confidential cable to the main government departments in Washington: Justice, Treasury, Homeland Security, the DEA, and others.[5] The message focussed on the corruption in the police and justice areas of the Calderón administration, and how officials close to García Luna were being investigated by the PGR.

The embassy had not failed to note President Calderón's obstinate defense of García Luna during a state visit to Peru. In the context of the storm of criticisms leveled at the top team in the SSP by protected witnesses in their statements to the public prosecutors, the president had declared that the investigations into his government's infiltration by drug traffickers were not directed at García, of whose abilities he had no doubt. The US cable went on to remark: "Nevertheless, some perceive the investigations into the behavior of so many of Garcia Luna's close colleagues and subordinates as potentially undermining his authority as an effective Public Security Secretary." The SSP "appears to be less an active agent in an anti-corruption campaign and more a passive participant as the PGR is investigating and prosecuting corruption cases in the Secretariat."

A political and security adviser at the Embassy, quoted in the cable, suggests that "the number of corrupted officials surrounding García Luna points to either negligence or tolerance on his part, even if thus far evidence has not been presented to publicly implicate García Luna in corrupt activities." The embassy notes that there has been speculation in Mexico that Calderón might ask García to step down, although such rumors have been rife in press and political circles "practically since García Luna assumed his current post." "Concerns about Garcia Luna's ability to manage his subordinates may complicate Mexico's ability to work bilaterally on sensitive security issues," the cable cautions. And points out that the international police corps, Interpol, was worried that international data might have been leaked in Mexico to organized crime groups by García Luna's team:

Interpol announced November 20 that it sent a team to Mexico to investigate the possibility that its communication systems and data-bases are not being used for legitimate law enforcement purposes, even while the Mexican government sought to assure Interpol that no sensitive information from the international police agency's system was leaked to cartels.

Added to this were the misgivings of the Colombian government: "Colombia also is worried about the levels of corruption in Mexican law enforcement," the cable noted. On November 19, a diplomat at the Colombian embassy in Mexico told a political officer at the US embassy that the director of Colombia's National Police had given García Luna an ultimatum. He warned him that if he couldn't demonstrate that the vetting process for Mexican Federal Police officers receiving training from Colombia was "thorough," Bogotá would have to consider closing the program.

These were difficult days for García Luna. The last thing he wanted was to increase the distrust of the US government. That could mean dismissal, or worse, imprisonment—the fate of General Jesús Gutiér-rez Rebollo, who quickly went from being an intimate collaborator of the US Government to becoming an outcast.

In the end, García's growing influence over President Calderón won the day. In September 2009, Attorney General Eduardo Medina Mora—García's rival and the only man who had managed to act as a counterweight to him—was relieved of his duties and sent as ambassador to London. Far enough away from García Luna. Things immediately got better for the secretary of public security and his team. On November 20 that year, protected witness Rambo III, the foolishly garrulous Jesús Zambada Reyes, was found dead in the PGR safe house where the authorities of Calderón's govern-ment were supposed to be watching over him. The scandal of his convenient death quickly subsided. The official version was that he committed suicide.

On December 1, 2009, Edgar Bayardo, the other key witness against SSP officials, was executed in broad daylight in a busy Star-bucks coffee shop in a smart district of Mexico City. Just after eleven in the morning, an Isuzu 4x4 suddenly pulled up outside. One person stayed inside with the motor running. Another, with a machine gun, burst through the door and shot Bayardo at point-blank range. He knew who his target was. They disappeared as quickly as they'd arrived, leaving the protected witness spread on the ground, his body slightly bent.

The person responsible for the witnesses' security was Marisela Morales, the deputy attorney in charge of SIEDO, and an obliging collaborator of García Luna and his team. As noted, she later became President Calderón's last attorney general.

In most countries, such a series of blunders would have spelled disaster for a whole raft of public officials. In Mexico, they had no consequences at all. Luckily for the secretary of public security, there was something else in the air that was weighing on President Calderón's mind.

The assassination of Juan Camilo Mouriño

When the government arrested El Rey Zambada, his brother, El Mayo, felt betrayed. He thought he'd been stabbed in the back. The "lord of the mountains," as he also liked to be called, complained to his subordinates that he had already paid this presidency so that he could work in peace, and "a pact is a pact."[6] United States government sources have said, off the record, that after the arrest of El Rey Zambada they detected threats and warnings made to Los Pinos presidential palace.[7] They go as far as suggesting that El Mayo phoned Los Pinos to demand the release of his dear brother. He was told this wasn't possible, because the US government was exerting a lot of pressure. But Ismael Zambada is not a man to be toyed with. So, it's said, he decided not to wait any longer.

On November 4, 2008, just before 7 p.m., a Learjet 45, flying from San Luis Potosí, crashed in Mexico City close to the intersection of the Periférico ring road and Paseo de la Reforma, only a few miles from Los Pinos itself. On board were the secretary of the interior, Juan Camilo Mouriño, the secretary of the Penal Reform Commission, José Luis Santiago, then an adviser to the president on organized crime, and seven others, including the crew and other government officials.

Many witnesses told the media, both on the night of the crash and the next day, that the plane was already ablaze before it hit the ground: "We suddenly saw this ball of fire that fell from the sky and destroyed everything in the street," said businessman Sergio Lebrija. Some said they felt the force of a blast, others even claimed to have seen a "mushroom cloud."[8]

It was an appalling scene: men and women wrapped in flames, running or trapped inside their burning cars, buildings half destroyed, billowing smoke, and body parts strewn everywhere, amid a stink of fuel. The body of José Luis Santiago—who had once held key posts in the PGR—was left hanging in a meeting room on the second floor of an office building, on the corner of Montes Urales and Monte Pelvoux. It had been thrown out of the plane with terrible force. Only pieces were found of Mouriño; his hand was identified by the wedding ring engraved with the name of his wife, Marigely. The popular verdict on that infernal night was that the drug traffickers had done it.

That day Felipe Calderón was in Atotonilco el Alto, Jalisco. It was after seven when the president left the podium at the end of his visit. Suddenly his private secretary, Aitza Aguilar, approached looking shaken, but Calderón paid no attention and kept walking towards the helicopter that would take him to the airbase in Zapopan and the presidential jet. "Felipe, Juan Camilo is dead," Aitza finally said. Calderón's face crumpled. The president of the Republic put up a hand to hide his pain, vulnerable, helpless, in a word, human. Aitza told him briefly what had happened as they walked on. The short time it took before he got into the plane and could give in to tears must have seemed an eternity.

That unhappy night, Calderón gave a short speech in the presidential hangar: "My government, in coordination with the relevant authorities, will carry out all the investigations necessary to get to the bottom of what caused this tragedy."

Members of Mouriño's family say it was organized crime that killed the young politician with presidential aspirations. A few days after the crash, Carlos Mouriño, his brother, went to see the president in hopes of an explanation. "Tell us who killed Juan Camilo, we just want to know who it was," he insisted, with the frankness that went with being the brother of Calderón's best friend.[9] The president merely repeated the official version that had been given to the media: the accident was the result of pilot error. Later it became known that the crew were, to say the least, highly experienced professionals. Carlos Mouriño left the president's office in high dudgeon.[10]

Juan Camilo's family asked Calderón several more times to tell them what had really happened. The president stuck to the official line. On Thursday, November 6, the president bade farewell to Juan Camilo at a somber funeral ceremony at the Campo Marte military base. His heartfelt words expressed pain and affection for his friend, but his expression and demeanor conveyed something deeper, a visible aura of fear. When the funeral was over, a troubled-looking president went over to the Mouriño family. "Do you really want to know who killed him?" From the look on his face, the family understood that it was better not to know.[11]

People in the drug trafficking world say that El Mayo claimed responsibility for the death of Juan Camilo Mouriño, and that he let the president know it. "I have absolutely no doubt of that," said a source close to the drug baron.

On November 9, 2008, Carlos Mouriño Atanes, Juan Camilo's father, published an emotive letter in the Campeche newspapers insinuating much more clearly that his son's death had not been an accident, and that the enemy had been identified as the drug gangs. After the letter the family spent a long time in Spain, and only returned in 2011.

Iván [as they called Juan Camilo in Campeche], your accident must not alter our path. We must be clear that your struggle and that of the authorities has to continue with equal or greater strength than before, in the conviction that we will defeat them, that there is an army of citizens behind us all, behind the president, the Congress, the parties, the authorities and the institutions, which urges us forward.

We know that in the present pass there are thousands of resolute and energetic citizens who have said enough is enough, for we are always more, and more determined. We will drive them into a corner, push them over the edge, and when they are defeated we will be able to smile and say to all those who struggled for the same ideals: Mission accomplished. Now may you rest in peace.

El Mayo's people say that powerful C4 explosives were put in the plane. Several military intelligence informants say they noticed "unusual movements" at the airport in San Luis Potosí, where the aircraft waited while Mouriño signed a cooperation agreement with the state government.

In 2009 there were two arrests that shook the world of organized crime. On March 18, in Lomas de Pedregal in Mexico City, the Mexican army captured Vicente Zambada, El Mayo's son; he looked and dressed like a rich kid, but he was his father's right-hand man and the natural heir to his empire. A couple of weeks later, on April 1, Vicente Carrillo, the son of Amado Carrillo Fuentes, was also arrested. His PGR file describes him as a very active member of the Juárez cartel.

The death of El Barbas

Not even Juan Camilo's death would change the deadly and absurd course of the narco war. After that, García Luna became the person closest to Calderón. They used to play paintball together in the gardens of Los Pinos, that game where nobody actually dies like they do in real life. The government's actions against organized crime followed the same pattern as before: attacking the enemies of El Chapo, whatever the price.

Arturo Beltrán Leyva died on December 16, 2009. His body lay as cold as the marble floor of the luxury apartment in Cuernavaca that he used as a safe house. He was executed in an operation carried out by the Navy Secretariat, with guidance from the United States. The Mexican Navy had information—provided by the DEA—that Arturo Beltrán was in the Altitude apartment blocks, but they didn't know in which unit. At about 5:30 p.m. the marines began to search the towers, securing three apartments: numbers 201 and 202 in Tower Four, and 1001 in Tower Five. The result was three suspected drug traffickers arrested and seven killed, among them El Barbas, according to the military report. Some photographs of the place where the eldest of the Beltrán Leyva brothers died show a bed soaked in blood, but it was never made clear who had died there.

The powerful drug baron had been savagely blasted, so savagely that the right side of his chest was a pulp, and the arm had almost come off. It was as if they had either used dumdum bullets or fired repeated rounds into the same spot. The following day the press published gory photos of the body, covered in dollar and peso bills, with the pants pulled down, showing blood-stained underwear, and the shirt pulled up. The scene had been ghoulishly stage-managed.

The autopsies showed that all seven had either been drinking heavily or were drugged, which makes it difficult to imagine they put up much of a fight when the Navy attacked.

Arturo Beltrán Leyva's corpse, even before it was manipulated for the photos, was found with the tee-shirt rolled up over the arms and the pants pulled down, a common technique for immobilizing a suspect during arrest. This led the forensic team carrying out the autopsy to believe he had already been subdued before he was killed. It didn't suit anyone for El Barbas, in captivity, to reveal the secrets of the last twenty years of organized crime in Mexico.

Concerns over a possible summary execution were raised by Arturo Chávez, the newly appointed attorney general, at a meeting of the national security cabinet a few days after the operation. Chávez made it clear that he was against summary executions, and expected any alleged criminals to be taken alive so that they could be put on trial.

On December 18, 2009, El Barbas's body was collected by his sister, Felícitas Beltrán Leyva, Erika Beltrán Martínez, his half-sister, and Araceli Flores, a family friend. Next day the remains of the celebrity drug baron were flown to Culiacán and buried, surrounded by wreaths of red, red roses, in the Jardines de Lumaya cemetery. He had reached his last resting place, from where he would continue to inflict much damage on the country.

Even in death, El Barbas was trouble. In the search after he was killed, they found a list of beneficiaries on his narco-payroll—officials in the Morelos state attorney's office, in the SSP at federal and state levels, and police chiefs in five of the state's municipalities, including Cuernavaca. According to the papers found, the Beltrán Leyvas paid monthly bribes of between $5,000 and $10,000 to federal and state officials, and of 10,000 pesos ($760 in 2009) to municipal authorities. As we say in Mexico, you pick your stone according to the toad you're aiming at: depending on the rank of the official being bought, the bribes were paid in pesos or in dollars.

It also turned out that the Beltrán Leyvas were paying 1.8 million pesos per month ($136,800) to journalists and the media in Morelos state. There was also a wide network of informants listed at two thousand pesos apiece ($152), without specifying whether this was per day, per week, or per month.

The information recovered in the operation showed that El Barbas wanted to turn Cuernavaca into "the Switzerland of Mexico, where calm reigns and their families can live in peace. To this end they had begun a clean-up operation." Among the documents an inventory of weapons was also found, 112 items in all, including five rocket launchers. But only forty-three guns and grenades were actually recovered.[12] The rest, including the rocket launchers, are still out there, in a Mexico that is ablaze.

The fall of El Barbas intensified the struggle between Mexican cartels for territorial control. His death severely weakened the group led by Vicente Carrillo in Ciudad Juárez. In the face of an unrelenting offensive by the Sinaloa cartel, El Viceroy gradually lost organizational and military capability. He is said to have abandoned the territory at the beginning of 2010. In his place, Sergio Villarreal, El Grande, was left to defend the historic and much coveted bastion of the Juárez cartel, using a group of fighters known as La Línea, who El Chapo was intent on defeating. Meanwhile Edgar Valdez, La Barbie, and Gerardo Álvarez, El Indio, two of Arturo Beltrán's chief enforcers, sought to create their own cartel: El Indio had the contacts with Colombia, and La Barbie the brute force, to embark on such a project.

The Sinaloa cartel suggested to Vicente Carrillo that he sign a peace deal and form a new alliance with them. But El Viceroy refused, because his family still wasn't ready to pardon the murder of his brother, Rodolfo. Instead he maintained his alliance with Héctor Beltrán Leyva, who took over the leadership from his late brother. The ones who did sign a truce with the Sinaloa cartel were the leaders of the Gulf Cartel. Apparently with the consent of the government, the two organizations set as their joint main target the elimination of

Los Zetas, who, according to US official reports, went from being the armed wing of the Gulf Cartel to forming a new cartel in their own right. The feared Zetas were now the best allies of the Beltrán Leyva clan. Together they turned the flourishing city of Monterrey, capital of Nuevo León state and internationally famed for its industry and economic strength, into a carnival of horrors, where the spectacle of tortured bodies hanging half-dismembered from footbridges is an everyday occurrence.

All these shifting alliances led to a savage increase in violence in Chihuahua, Coahuila, Nuevo León, Tamaulipas, Michoacán, Guerrero, and Morelos. In all of these states, body parts from one side or the other turn up on an almost daily basis—not to mention the many innocent individuals who perish in the crossfire.

After more than twenty years of domination by the Carrillo Fuentes gang in Ciudad Juárez, and nearly fourteen years after El Viceroy inherited the Juárez cartel from his brother, El Señor de los Cielos, El Chapo Guzmán had virtually taken over the prized territory. He achieved it at the cost of an immense bloodbath: 1,500 people executed in the border city in 2008; 2,660 in 2009; and by 2010 the figure was 3,116, or about eight murders a day.

On April 9, 2010, Andrea Simmons, the FBI spokesperson in El Paso, Texas, said that after two years of war between the gangs for control of Juárez, the Sinaloa cartel had virtually won. Ironically, the announcement of this "victory" coincided with the withdrawal of the Mexican army and its replacement on the streets of Ciudad Juárez by the SSP's Federal Police. After the arrival of García Luna's sturdy cops, the violence in that part of the country rose to unprecedented levels. The earlier suspicions of complicity between the Sinaloa cartel and the institutions answering to García Luna can only add to speculation that this move to put the Federal Police in charge of Ciudad Juárez was also designed to favor that particular criminal organization.

El Mayo's air fleet

During its so-called war on drugs, the Calderón government dealt some much-publicized blows to members of the Sinaloa cartel, in an attempt to distract public attention from the many clues to its complicity with that organization. These blows were always aimed at middle-level personnel. They never struck at the heart of the cartel: its top leaders and its core business.

The Sinaloa cartel's main artery runs through Mexico City airport. It remains intact and fully operational, pumping money to the leaders, money which in turn empowers them to continue their criminal enterprise. Inside Mexico City International Airport (AICM), on the inner road from Terminal 1 to Terminal 2, are the offices and hangars of Aviones, S.A., a company that officially does aircraft repairs.[13] It's a good location. It has hangars, maintenance and repair sheds, a spare parts center, and 50,000 square feet of apron that connects directly to the runways. The company has branches at several other airports in the center of the country, in the State of Mexico, in Puebla, and in Cuernavaca. It also hires out airplanes, according to the brochure.

In his sworn statement of 2008, the PGR's protected witness Richard Arroyo, code name María Fernanda, insisted that in this firm's AICM hangar, drugs and cash belonging to El Mayo and El Chapo's Sinaloa cartel are loaded and unloaded every day.

> I wish to state that next to Terminal 2 in the AICM, although I don't remember the exact address, we have a company called Aviones which is right next to the AESA [ASESA] hangar, with direct access to the airport, and you can see the name from outside, blue lettering on a white façade, and you can make out its offices, on two floors, employing around thirty people.
>
> To get in, there is a security barrier manned by a policeman. Inside there's this blue cargo plane we never had a chance to use, but which was bought with illicit money. At least it was blue last time I saw it, they paint it every month. We also have two helicopters in there, one of them hired out to the municipality of Ecatapec, the other is getting a propeller fixed. Both were bought with illicit money. We also use these helicopters to spot enemy positions and for leisure trips. There are three fuel tanks of ours, too, two small ones and one large. They are white with the name "Aviafuel" written on them.

María Fernanda's description of the building and how to get there was accurate. What's more, this was not the first time that Aviones

S.A. had come to the PGR's attention. The file from a previous investigation (siedo/ueicc s/132/2008) states that on March 30, 2008, police officers from the PFP—then headed by Edgar Millán—used official vehicles to escort a shipment of chemical precursors to the Aviones hangar. The container was carrying 600 kilograms of ephedrine, which had come in from the Netherlands on KLM flight 685.[14]

On December 1, 2008, the PGR recognized that "there is sufficient evidence to say for certain that the accused [the Zambada clan] were active in operations such as drug trafficking at Mexico City International Airport."

The company Aviones, S.A. was founded in Mexico City in 1948. Its original registered owners were Héctor Mariscal, Benjamín Burillo, Raúl Esponda, and Aarón Sáenz Garza, who appeared as the only shareholders. According to its constitution, the company provided a range of services pertaining to the purchase and rehabilitation of aircraft—a broad enough brief to enable El Mayo Zambada and his henchmen, years later, to acquire the necessary narco-planes, as well as assure secondary services such as maintenance and refueling. The firm has been ensconced in AICM since at least 1978.

It seems that Benjamín Burillo is uncle to Alejandro Burillo Azcárraga, the cousin of Emilio Azcárraga, the chairman of Mexico's biggest TV empire, Televisa. Aarón Sáenz was a politician and military man who held posts in several post-revolutionary governments, before founding key companies like the airline Mexicana de Aviación, the bank Banca Confía, Seguros Atlas insurance company, and a number of sugar mills. Today the official owners of this company, that El Mayo's stepson insisted was linked to the Sinaloa cartel, are another company, Consan (the majority shareholder), plus various members of the Sáenz Couret and Sáenz Hirschfeld families, who in turn also own Consan. The business history of the "official" owners of Aviones S.A. is itself controversial. Several of the shareholders have been implicated in financial scandals, including the Banca Confía and Atlas Insurance affairs.[15]

Complicity and negligence at Mexico City airport

Indeed, everything to do with this company, Aviones, is murky. From January 2005 to the end of 2012, the director general of Mexico City International Airport was Héctor Velázquez Corona, a man close to Felipe Calderón.[16] In spite of the scandals over what seem to be the Sinaloa cartel's operations in the airport, he was not replaced by Calderón. In June 2012, *Proceso* magazine reported allegations in El *Universal* that the US Justice Department regarded Velázquez Corona as linked to organized crime, along with the PGR's swift denial of it in a communiqué on the same day: the PGR claimed it had no data justifying such a link, and had never heard of one from its regular contacts in the US.[17] Velázquez Corona did not last into a third presidency: the current AICM director is Alfonso Sarabia de la Garza.

The AICM management refuses to give any explanation of since when, how, and why a company apparently controlled by El Mayo Zambada has a strategically placed hangar in the country's principal airport. The only thing that is known for certain is that on August 1, 1994, five months before the end of Carlos Salinas's presidency, it was granted a contract to occupy the hangar, valid until July 31, 2008. On November 17, 2005, during the government of Vicente Fox, and with Velázquez now head of the airport administration, the company was given an extension.

The airport administration did reveal in 2010 that Aviones was paying to the AICM the modest sum of 41,030 pesos ($3,200 at the time) per month in rent for the hangar, excluding value added tax. This is absurdly little compared with the millions of dollars in profit it can bring in every week. Although the airport administration admits that Aviones no longer has a valid rental contract, they are unable or unwilling to take the space away from the company, regardless of its alleged drug links.[18]

Another serious irregularity that ought to be enough to stop Aviones from using the hangar is the fact that it has agreed to share this space with another company, MTC Aviación, in clear contravention of AICM rules. This other company, founded in 1997, also provides aircraft repair services, as well as running an air taxi service. In fact, private flights have been banned from Mexico City airport since 1994; but for some reason that doesn't apply in this case. It seems to be the only one allowed to fly private planes in and out of the capital's prized airport.

The official response of the airport administration to this firm was evasive, and suggests complicity. Although they said that Aviones was illegally sharing its hangar, they claimed not to know the name of the company it shares it with, even though it is clearly the administration's responsibility to know. And although AICM accepted that this constituted grounds to evict, the company continues to operate unhindered—four years after the direct accusations made by El Rey Zambada's stepson.[19]

If it is true that Aviones S.A. is owned by members of the Sinaloa cartel, as Richard María Fernanda Arroyo testified, then this would surely constitute the biggest scandal of corruption and collusion with the drug cartels in recent decades—one which would necessarily implicate authorities at the highest levels in the Secretariat of Communications and Transport, the Mexico City Airport administration, the Secretariat of Public Security, and even the Secretariat of Defense.

Sedena contracts a drug-related company

Aviones S.A., a company allegedly controlled by El Mayo Zambada, had thirty-two contracts with the Secretariat of Defense between 2001 and 2008, for the maintenance of planes belonging to the Mexican Army and Air Force. In the words of El Mayo's nephew, the government put its planes literally in the hands of the enemy. But were they really the enemy?

Twenty-two of these contracts were signed by Sedena during the Fox administration, and ten during Calderón's. The concessions were granted by General Fausto Zamorano, in the former case, and by General Augusto García Ochoa in the latter. (García Ochoa, one of the closest associates of the then Defense Secretary, General Galván, was hoping to take over that very post in the next government, even though questions have hung over his career ever since he

THE PRESIDENT OF DEATH 287

was accused by his colleague Gutiérrez Rebollo of protecting Amado Carrillo Fuentes, back in the 1990s.)

The majority of the contracts with Aviones were granted directly or by invitation to two or three companies; that is to say, they were not put out to tender. They include the purchase of spare parts, repairs and routine maintenance. They show that at different times Sedena handed over to the alleged narco-company everything from its Bell 206 helicopters, to a Boeing 727, and a giant Hercules C-130, as well as an array of light aircraft including no fewer than sixty-seven Cessna 182 Skylanes. Some of the contracts explicitly give Aviones the right to take the military planes on test flights after they've been repaired. For the delivery of spare parts purchased by Sedena from Aviones, they also make available the military airbase of Santa Lucía, in the State of Mexico, as well as the Lester Industries airstrip in San Antonio, Texas.[20] Other contracts, like the maintenance policy for the Cessnas, signed in August 2003, allow for Aviones to "take the defective planes to a suitable place for their repair."

In 2009, the Navy Secretariat likewise signed two contracts with Aviones for the purchase of spare parts. The National Institute of Geography and Information Technology signed twelve contracts between 2004 and 2009. Eleven were for the repair of its Cessnas and one was for "air transport," even though Aviones has no license to offer this kind of service.

One other public security institution that used Aviones was the Preventive Federal Police (PFP), with contracts signed in 1999, when the head was Wilfrido Robledo and Genaro García Luna was coordinator of intelligence for crime prevention.

On September 19, 2000, the PFP bought five Cessna 182s from Aviones for $1.18 million. Public auditors criticized that contract, saying it was tweaked to suit the company's interests, including the provision for the planes to be delivered at Cessna Aircraft's installations in Independence, Kansas. It also noted that although the Aviones offer had supposedly been the cheapest, it ended up being more expensive.[21]

AFI and SSP help unload drugs at airports

In addition to Aviones S.A., María Fernanda said that since 2007 they had been able to count on a whole network of SSP and AFI officials who would help them to bring in planes and get the merchandise out. It's worth recalling that until the beginning of 2010, the AFI and the SSP were both controlled, simultaneously, by García Luna.

María Fernanda specifically identified the regional delegate of the AFI in the Metropolitan Attorney General's Office, Roberto Sánchez, who was appointed by García Luna. They paid him $75,000 a month to work for the Sinaloa cartel, $50,000 of which were for him and $25,000 for his second-in-command, identified only by the code X1.[22]

María Fernanda also mentioned another AFI agent who worked for them, Edwin González, who was attached to the airport from the metropolitan PGR. Apparently he helped them bring in suitcases full of cocaine, for which service he was paid $10,000 a month. "He carried out arrests in the airport for us, and helped provide us with security as far as the exit when we brought in a plane loaded with cocaine," said El Mayo's talkative nephew.

Rambo III, the son of El Rey Zambada, also recognized González as the policeman who one afternoon in February 2008 went to see his father at a house in Bosques de las Lomas. On that occasion, he added, the AFI agent was accompanied by the agency's regional head, Roberto Sánchez, himself.

For his part, Edgar Bayardo remembered González recruiting "mules" to carry drugs or money for the organization, often to other countries. He described one occasion, before the split in The Federation, when Sergio Villarreal, El Grande, who ran the airport operations for El Mayo, sent one of the people recruited by González to Venezuela, where he was supposedly received by some government authorities. He didn't say who they were or what posts they held, only that they received money from the drug traffickers.

After the testimony against him, Edwin González was arrested on December 13, 2008 when he went to make a statement. Three days later he was given a conditional release, on the grounds of changed legal circumstances, suggesting he too has become a protected witness. Sánchez, however, in spite of the accusations against him, continued in his same job at least until May 2009.

Another PGR witness, codenamed Jennifer, who claimed to have worked for Edgar Valdez and his boss, El Barbas, stated that Mexico City was not the only airport used by The Federation. They also favored Cancún, on the Caribbean coast. According to Jennifer, Arturo Beltrán Leyva controlled that airport on behalf of the whole Federation, giving orders to let all the associates freely move their merchandise by plane, as though he owned the place. Between March 2007 and February 2008, for an outlay of just over $19 million, The Federation apparently unloaded thirteen planes at Cancún airport, with the complicity of authorities at all levels.

The split in The Federation forced the officials who worked for it to negotiate with one side or the other to save their lives. When AFI agent Edgar Ramos, El Chuta, the organization's contact at Cancún airport, heard about the quarrel between the bosses, he got González to arrange for him to meet El Rey Zambada in Mexico City. María Fernanda tells the story:

> He wanted to persuade the organization not to take reprisals against him for belonging to the Beltrán Leyva group, and promised in advance he wouldn't support Arturo Beltrán against us. . . . They met in the middle of July that year [2008] at one of the offices in that city, specifically a building in Calle Río Bamba . . . Jesús Zambada García told him they wouldn't take any reprisals, he'd just have to make sure he didn't interfere with them and undertake not to handle any merchandise from Arturo at the airport, because that region was now controlled by the Zambadas's organization.

Later El Chuta was transferred to Mexico City, where he continued to help El Mayo and his clan. From there he served the Sinaloa cartel by "unloading suitcases of cocaine and loading money into planes, together with the Preventive Federal Police," recalled protected witness Jennifer.

In the midst of this web of complicity around Mexico City airport, on the morning of June 25, 2012, the country awoke to shocking news: a shoot-out in Terminal 2 of the International Airport between two sets of Federal Police officers when the force was under the command of Luis Cárdenas Palomino, who is alleged to be a drug lord disguised as a police chief. The dispute was over another cargo of drugs being handled by the PF. Two of the officers involved in the firefight publicly identified Cárdenas as the person who coordinated these drug shipments in the AICM. But despite the scandal, the police chiefs kept their jobs.

Inside a drug baron's head

The drug barons are unsophisticated people. Most can hardly read. They are little given to reflection, except upon matters of business and their particular cut of the profits. The rest of the time they are guided by the extremely aggressive instincts which, according to them, keep them alive.

In their world, anyone who gets a university education is to be admired, as if a degree were synonymous with intelligence. One anecdote illustrates this attitude. In jail a group of prisoners from the Pacific cartel joined a group from the Gulf Cartel for a game of volleyball. The captain of one side was a veteran drug baron from Sinaloa, his counterpart a young trafficker from the Gulf. On seeing this younger man fluff a pass, the old narco murmured to one of his team:

"It's hard to believe he plays so badly!"

"What do you mean?" asked the other.

"Well, he went to university, didn't he!"

But when a drug trafficker is forced to choose between intelligence and loyalty, he won't hesitate to choose loyalty—an invaluable quality, but one that's in danger of extinction. These days they try to have it both ways, by sending their sons to university or by directly recruiting more educated people. Yet it will take several generations for drug bosses to become any kind of educated, professional caste, given the nature of their day-to-day activities.

For example, El Chapo's children have graduated with degrees, or diplomas in administration. Many thought that Iván Guzmán Salazar, El Chapito, was the closest to his father within the cartel, but it appears that it is rather Alfredo, Alfredillo, the youngest of the sons from his marriage to Alejandrina, who is following most closely in his footsteps. The US authorities say he coordinates the logistics for multi-ton shipments of cocaine and heroin into the United States, together with one of El Mayo's sons.[23]

The only laws governing the battles of the drug kingpins are that of the vendetta and that of business. If one group slaughters a member of another, the offended group will respond by slaughtering two. The violence spirals on, until nobody can remember who started it. Volatile, capricious, and contradictory, with a keen survival instinct, these men talk a lot about loyalty, but in reality they have none. The motto of their existence is: "I win, everybody else loses." Their weakness for drugs and drink, allied to the stresses of the trade, renders them paranoid and quick to panic; someone can be a boon companion one minute, and a mortal threat the next, with inevitable consequences.

Roles are clearly demarcated. For them, the businessmen who launder their money are allies, genuine partners, to be regarded with respect as fine fellows who work hard and take risks—not like those cops and politicians who simply hold out the begging bowl. When asked who approached who, the narcos affirm: "The entrepreneurs come to us. They want our money in order to make more money." As far as one can tell, there have been very few instances of deals gone sour between businessmen and drug traffickers.

The drug trade is armor-plated by these networks of money-laundering moguls. For they are not small businessmen, but big-time entrepreneurs. And if there is one criminal organization that throughout its history has known how to handle such people, it is the Sinaloa cartel. Of all the drug groups, the Sinaloa cartel has for many years had the most stable leadership. El Mayo Zambada has never been in prison, and he's been trafficking drugs for more than forty years. That stability gives greater confidence to the producers in Colombia and Peru, and is one reason why the Sinaloa cartel has grown so much more than any other in the continent.

Edgardo Buscaglia, a senior research scholar in law and economics at Columbia Law School in New York, has thoroughly researched this aspect of the story, in Mexico and elsewhere. His conclusion is that the Mexican government treats the narco-tycoons as untouchable.[24]

They are not doing the most important thing, which is to attack the basic reason why organized crime groups exist. And that is to increase the wealth they get from unlawful activities, so that someday they can enjoy *la dolce vita*. The aim of these groups is to legalize their wealth, integrate it into the legal economy, and pay taxes. I always tell friends and colleagues that El Chapo's goal is to pay taxes. When the criminal groups legalize their wealth—which derives from twenty-two different kinds of crime—and pay taxes, their success is complete. Their crowning achievement comes when they manage to hide in the mainstream economy and legitimize the income generated by crimes ranging from people trafficking, smuggling, and piracy, to extortion, kidnapping, and drug trafficking. As a matter of fact, drugs are only in second place in terms of capital generation; in first place come piracy and smuggling.

This is why there is a problem with the way the Mexican president [Calderón] understands this; unfortunately he is very poorly advised. The Mexican government already possesses the legal instruments to identify and confiscate this wealth, once it enters the legal economy. But they aren't being used, so organized crime continues to expand—both Mexican organized crime, and that of twelve other countries that operate in Mexico.

We tend to focus only on home-grown groups, but Mexico has also become a haven for the assets of criminals from China, Japan, Ukraine, or Russia, who buy real estate and generate returns by investing in construction, trust funds, chemicals, and so on. The government hasn't touched any of this. So, the likelihood of a criminal group that launders money and assets in Mexico being identified, investigated, and tried, is less than one percent.

But reform is hindered by inertia and vested interests. Buscaglia continues:

Obviously, the legal businessmen, who in part benefit from these assets, feel that the flow of capital which has been so advantageous for decades is what has fostered their expansion and enabled high rates of return from their activities in the legal economy. This is why the Mexican business elite—legally constituted companies—have resisted measures to fight organized crime, measures without which the cancer of corruption and violence can only continue to spread. The purchase of arms, the logistics of transport—trucks, boats, submarines—are paid for with these assets hidden in the legal economy. So the hand that throws a grenade at Mexican soldiers or civilians, the hand of the hit man, is also that of the above-board businessman who finances all this. Therefore we have to hold these businessmen criminally responsible.

The world of drug trafficking disposes of well-oiled mechanisms for laundering money, mainly through the Mexican banking system, according to sources involved in the process. Almost any bank will accept huge deposits in cash, wherever in the world they come from, in exchange for a commission that varies between 3 and 7 percent. None of this is reported anywhere. The amount involved determines how high up in the bank the decisions are taken. Sometimes it reaches as high as the board, according to witnesses of such negotiations. The measure taken in 2010 by the Calderón government to increase the tax levied on cash deposits will only mean fatter commissions for the banks. It will not stop money laundering.[25]

For Buscaglia, the lack of action against big companies involved in money laundering also has political and tactical motives.

> The political reason is that many of these companies are ultimately the ones that finance election campaigns. So the politicians are reluctant to do what they see as shooting themselves in the foot.
>
> The tactical reason is that the Mexican authorities fear that if they begin to attack and dismantle these fortunes, it will damage the formal economy. This is a major conceptual error. When I talk to people in the Finance Secretariat, they assume that if you begin to confiscate assets in the legal economy, economic growth will suffer. I always tell them it's the reverse. At the moment there is a lot of capital that doesn't get invested in Mexico, because many foreign investors are terrified their pension fund and mutual fund assets will get mixed up with criminal funds that have been laundered. So if you don't clean up the economy in the way we suggest, that has a negative impact.

The Mexican government sends increasing numbers of soldiers and police here and there, but the criminals' wealth remains intact. Meanwhile the gangs react by spending more and more on corruption and violence. The only way to break this vicious circle of more soldiers, more policemen, more violence, more corruption, is to remove thousands of millions of dollars of drug traffickers' money from the legal economy. That is the only way of undermining their logistics, their transport, their arms deals. And the Calderón government is not doing this because, I repeat, at best they have the mistaken view that it might damage economic growth; at worst, it would mean treading on the toes of the companies that provide the campaign finance for Mexico's political parties.

The drug traffickers see politicians, public officials, policemen, and soldiers as mere appendages of their own existence. They seek them out, seduce them, put them forward as candidates, and pay for their campaigns or their publicity once they're in office. But ultimately they regard them as employees, and will always treat them as such—even though they know that sooner or later, someone will betray them. That is why the execution of public servants is becoming more and more frequent in Mexico, at every level of the administration. Once they've accepted a bribe, they won't ever be allowed to back out.

There are politicians, policemen, soldiers, and businessmen who have acquired immense fortunes by teaming up with the drug barons who now have the country on the rack. Their impunity only feeds the cycle of blood. Yet without these sustaining pillars—businessmen, politicians and public officials—the drug business would simply collapse. Buscaglia warns:

Political protection is one of the pillars of the growth of these criminal groups. Colombia has already confronted this problem of corruption [at one time, 32 percent of the members of the Colombian congress were facing trial], as have the judges and prosecutors in Italy, the United States, of course, and most of the European countries. But we do not see Mexico following suit. There's no serious attack on corruption here. All we see are isolated spasms, like the "Michoacanazo,"[26] which rather than form part of a systematic operation nationwide was just a show, in which most of the prosecutions eventually collapsed.

There's no easy way out for the political and entrepreneurial elite: they would have to fight corruption in their own milieus, to stop the laundering that fuels the murder of ordinary people in this country. They have to put a stop to the capital flows that have ensured decades of good times for Mexico's biggest tycoons. The politicians have to start by cleaning out their own sewers. No more campaign finance from criminal groups, no more party members collaborating with money launderers.

There is a pact of impunity and corruption which prevents any such measures. It is not out of ignorance, or lack of money, or lack of trained personnel. And in the meantime, as I said, this inexcusable negligence is causing thousands of homicides a month. History will not forgive this.

The disease of Mexican narco-rule (narcotics traffickers, narco-businessmen and narco-politicians) is contagious, and has begun to make Mexico a security problem for the rest of the region.

When Mexican criminal groups like Los Zetas arrive in Guatemala, the first thing they do is buy up the local authorities. That's nothing new. Criminal groups everywhere do the same. But in this case it's not just local authorities. Because it's a politically unstable country, they get as far as Álvaro Colom [president of Guatemala 2008–12], buying up advisers and officials close to him. They even put microphones in the president's office. This creates still more political instability. Colom has been the target of coup attempts by different political factions in the pay of either the Zetas or the Sinaloa cartel.

In Paraguay, a country with serious problems of governance and terrible poverty, worse than in Mexico, the drug traffickers have already infiltrated Congress and some licit business sectors. They have also been financing attempts to impeach President Fernando Lugo, to put a puppet of their own in his place.[27]

The saying we quoted in chapter 3, "The gringos build you up and the gringos knock you down," points back to the origin of it all. What would the architects of the Iran-Contra scheme think now, if they looked at the small-time traffickers of those days, who worked with the CIA, converted into the authentic monsters of today? Those junior partners of Pablo Escobar, who in the 1980s helped him get his drugs into the States, have now become a living nightmare.

The "National Drug Threat Assessment 2010" report gives us the measure of the beast:

> Mexican DTOs [drug trafficking organizations] continue to represent the single greatest drug trafficking threat to the United States. Mexican DTOs, already the predominant wholesale suppliers of illicit drugs in the United States, are gaining even greater strength in eastern drug markets where Colombian DTO strength is diminishing. . . . Mexican DTOs were the only DTOs operating in every region of the country.[28]

Mexican cartels control the bulk of the sale and distribution of cocaine, heroin, methamphetamine, and marijuana in the United States, ahead of the Colombians and the Chinese and Russian mafias. The US Justice Department observed an exponential growth in these activities:

> Mexican DTOs increased their cooperation with US-based street and prison gangs to distribute drugs. . . . In 2009, midlevel and retail drug distribution in the United States was dominated by more than 900,000 criminally active gang members representing approximately 20,000 street gangs in more than 2,500 cities.[29]

Quite an army. From this angle, the so-called "war on drug trafficking" launched by Calderón seems purely rhetorical. Although in public the Mexican president maintained that no battle between the government and the drug barons had yet been lost, it is said that in private a troubled Calderón admitted halfway into his presidency that the war was hopeless. He knew it; the rest was political propaganda.

The truth is that not so much as a scratch has been inflicted on the massive business empires of organized crime in Mexico. According

to the "National Drug Threat Assessment 2010," the increased avail-
ability of heroin, methamphetamine, and marijuana in the US is
largely the result of "higher production in Mexico." There are
numbers to back up these assertions. Buscaglia says:

> One calculation links the Sinaloa Cartel to 3,007 legally constituted
> companies, inside and outside of Mexico. Obviously these are esti-
> mates. It would be up to the prosecutors to investigate and bring
> charges. But the Mexican authorities have done nothing.
>
> In any advanced, civilized country in the world, when you appre-
> hend a member of a criminal group you would expect her or him to
> provide evidence that could help identify companies, trust funds,
> bank accounts. That doesn't happen here in Mexico. The arrests are a
> performance put on by the Secretariat of Public Security. . . . It's an
> insult to the Mexican people. They make out that by arresting thou-
> sands of people, organized crime will diminish in Mexico. They
> pretend that by sending in valiant soldiers or marines, the violence
> will decrease. But it won't. Sending the troops or the police will only
> produce results if at the same time you're dismantling the billion-
> dollar fortunes of the seven main criminal organizations in Mexico; if
> the criminals begin to worry that their companies and trust funds are
> being decommissioned, and that they no longer have the resources to
> finance more corruption and more violence.

A new and disturbing trend has emerged. According to official
figures, since 2004 the market for drug consumption in the United
States has stagnated. It hasn't got smaller, but nor has it grown.
Consumption in Mexico, on the other hand, has increased, and this
is directly linked to the increase in violence.

According to the drug organizations' own information, many of
Mexico's street brawls are now down to the strife between gangs of dealers for control of the burgeoning local market. Many such small-time
outfits already have the resources to acquire high-powered weapons,
and have been able to build effective organizational structures.

The violence of these local territorial disputes escalates when
middle-level, "wholesale" drug gangs intervene, trying to force
dealers to sell their product rather than their rivals'. While

President Calderón pushed on with his "war," there was a complete lack of serious social policies to tackle drug use. In the absence of such a strategy, the local market is looking increasingly attractive for the drug traffickers, in contrast with the US market which, although much bigger in terms of population, proportionally tends to decline.

DRUG CONSUMPTION IN MEXICO		
	2002	2008
Number of people who have taken drugs	3.5 million	4.5 million
Proportion of population who have used marijuana	3.8%	4.4%
Proportion of population who have used cocaine	1.3%	2.5%
Source: National Addiction Survey 2008. National Anti-Addiction Council		

Nevertheless, billions of dollars still flow into Mexico from drug profits in the US. The growth of organized "Mexican mafias" in the United States is a result of the impunity they enjoy on both sides of the border—particularly the Sinaloa cartel. This is why some people, both inside the cartels and in Mexican intelligence, believe that Washington prefers to deal with just one criminal organization. Edgardo Buscaglia puts it like this:

When [North American] agencies talk about concentrating and consolidating the criminal market, it's that they think it's always more feasible to control a single, consolidated organization, rather than hundreds of atoms that don't really hook up, producing a situation of chaos and instability. Nobody in the United States is talking about negotiating. But they do want to impose the rules of the game, and give these criminal groups a way out through amnesties, plea bargaining, or parole, as provided for in Mexican law. Or like what Vladimir Putin did in Russia, imposing tacit rules that criminal groups had to follow, remaining within certain bounds.

However, the big question is whether Mexico's fragile system of governance and democratic deficit can withstand the consolidation of a single cartel and the "narcocracy" that might go with it. Based on his experience, Buscaglia thinks not:

No, with this weak state the country's institutions would collapse and give way to a mafiocracy. That's why the United States is not a failed state, because it sets out to impose the rules of the game. The very expression "impose the rules" implies that the state is not dysfunctional. Right now, Mexico is in no position to impose anything. Various figures on the left and right of the Mexican elite, from the PRD and the PAN, keep talking about negotiating with organized crime, because they want an easy solution. But they don't realize that the easy solution, the one attempted by [César] Gaviria or [Ernesto] Samper [former presidents of Colombia], will lead to the total collapse of the Mexican state.

As long as the State prevaricates, and drug lords continue to earn multi-million dollar profits at little cost and less risk, the dreadful trade will continue. The profit margins are astonishing. Today [2010] you can buy a kilo of quality cocaine in Colombia for $2,500. It sells in New York for $28,000 and in Spain for €33,000. The big drug barons share some of the pie with smaller dealers who move maybe a quarter of a ton of cocaine a week, but make enormous profits and go quite undetected. Two hundred and fifty kilos of cocaine fit easily into a couple of suitcases, and drug traffickers on that scale are two a penny in our country.

The political rhetoric lurches this way and that. But when it comes to the crunch, the government fails us time after time.

The "death" of Nacho Coronel

On the afternoon of July 29, 2010, General Edgar Villegas, deputy head of operations at the Secretariat of Defense Chiefs of Staff, confirmed that Ignacio Nacho Coronel had died in an operation carried out in Guadalajara. He had been killed trying to resist arrest.

Nacho Coronel was at the height of his criminal career. The King of Crystal, as he was known, controlled the entire methamphetamine market, and had begun to produce it in Mexico. Personally, however, he had taken a hit. Weeks earlier, a death squad working for Héctor Beltrán Leyva had kidnapped and murdered his sixteen-year-old son. They say the drug baron was devastated.

At 5:30 a.m. on Friday, July 30, the military asked public prosecutors and the Jalisco Institute of Forensic Science to examine the body of Ignacio Coronel. Those who saw the body reported it was clean, with no signs of torture or mistreatment, apart from six bullet holes. It was that of a white man of medium height, slim, with perhaps some fat around the belly. His beard was neatly trimmed. He was the spitting image of a photo recently published in *Proceso* magazine, which showed him as a young man. But he bore little or no resemblance to another photo, also published by *Proceso*, showing Coronel much older.

While the national media published conflicting accounts of how this partner of El Mayo Zambada and El Chapo Guzmán had died, the autopsy came up with some disquieting results: "Corpse of masculine sex, probable age between 40 and 45, closer to the former." That couldn't be. According to his files in the SSP, Cisen, and the FBI, Nacho Coronel was born on February 1, 1954. They differ only on whether the place of birth was Veracruz or Durango. That means that in July 2010 he would have been fifty-six. How could his body then appear to have a biological age of forty?

Fingerprint tests came up with no match in the Jalisco state archives, so they were sent to Mexico City. A positive match was then found in the Sinaloa state archives, with one Dagoberto Rodríguez, born on January 1, 1964. Another positive match was apparently found in police records in Culiacán, corresponding to "Dagoberto Rodríguez Jiménez, date of birth July 31, 1964."[30] This information was never made public, so it is not known how the authorities identified the corpse.

Back in 1993, PGR Bulletin 492 reported that on November 2 the Sinaloa Judicial Police had captured a person calling himself Dagoberto Rodríguez, aged twenty-nine, along with eleven other suspects who were his bodyguards. The PGR identified Dagoberto Rodríguez as being really Ignacio Coronel. This information was taken to be true, which is why the name Dagoberto continued to feature as a pseudonym for Nacho Coronel in his SSP file drawn up in 2007.

However, a day after his supposed demise, two newspapers, El *Noroeste* in Culiacán and La *Jornada*, made an important discovery.

Nacho Coronel had indeed been arrested with those eleven people in November 1993. But he was booked by the police under the pseudonym César Barrios, not Dagoberto Rodríguez; Dagoberto was actually one of the other men detained with him.[31] In other words, if Nacho Coronel's finger prints were indeed on file in Sinaloa or anywhere else, they would have come up as belonging to César Barrios, not to Dagoberto Rodríguez.

It seems clear that the person killed by the Mexican army, who the government trumpeted was Nacho Coronel, was not in fact him. Either they didn't analyze the fingerprint evidence, because they already knew the body was someone else's; or the deceased really was Dagoberto Rodríguez, whose age would match the estimated age of the corpse. People close to the Coronel family say the drug baron is still alive.

Nacho Coronel's alleged body spent three long days laid out on the cold slab at the forensic center. Apparently his sister went to collect it on August 1. It was released without a DNA test, because the PGR saw no need for one, and was subsequently buried in the Jardines de Humaya cemetery in Culiacán, where Arturo Beltrán Leyva also lies.

The Zetas' messages

El Chapo, El Mayo, and El Azul are firmly in control of an empire. Between them they have achieved a virtual monopoly of narcotics trafficking in Mexico and the United States, a dominion based on blood, sweat, and tears. Their men know the price of betrayal or desertion: in the last ten years, the Sinaloan leaders have seen off most of their enemies, including the Arellano Félix brothers, Osiel Cárdenas, Arturo Beltrán Leyva, Edgar Valdez, Sergio Villarreal, and Heriberto Lazcano.

But they haven't won yet, and the war will surely cost countless more lives. Lazcano's killing by Mexican marines on October 9, 2012, may have altered the balance of forces in favor of the Sinaloa Cartel and to the detriment of the Zetas. But just as Lazcano's body immediately disappeared, stolen by a Zetas commando from the funeral parlor, and is thought by many not to be his body at all, so the shape of future struggles is uncertain. Now led by Miguel Treviño, Los Zetas have not ceased to constitute a "global threat," as the White House described them in 2011.[32] Meanwhile Héctor Beltrán Leyva, El Ingeniero, continues making blood sacrifices and consulting santería priests whose magic formulas convince him of imminent victory over his enemies.

General X got a glimpse into the Zetas world when, on his mission from Juan Camilo Mouriño to pacify the country, he met with them in March 2009. He was appalled when the delegation saluted him in smart military style. Yet it was not a mockery, for although they have lost all sense of right and wrong, these renegades continue to regard themselves, deep down, as part of the Mexican Army. The general formally requested Heriberto Lazcano to moderate the violence. Z3's reply confirmed the envoy's worst fears: while the Zetas controlled twenty-two states, it had spawned many "satellite" groups that didn't take orders from them.

According to US government sources, one of their agencies possesses a lengthy video of the encounter between General X and Z3, presumably mailed to that agency by the Zetas as documentary proof of government complicity with the Sinaloa cartel. When they parted, the soldier turned narcoterrorist gave General X two messages for President Calderón.

Following Mouriño's death in the plane crash, the general was never again received in Los Pinos or any other government office. Defense Secretary Galván stopped taking his calls. What did those messages from the Zetas leader to Calderón say? General X never told another soul.

Fallen Angels

The balance of Genaro García Luna's time as a secretary speaks for itself. From December 2006, when he was put in charge of the Secretariat of Public Security, to August 2011, of his sixteen closest collaborators, twelve were killed, forced to resign, taken to court, or jailed. That's over two thirds. The ones who were meant to be fighting the "war on drug trafficking" were accused of being in league with the traffickers. Maybe that's why García Luna and his controversial team failed from the start, and became part of the problem rather than the solution.

The frequent fall of people working for García Luna shows that the corruption surrounding the secretary was not an isolated circumstance, nor was it accidental. In fact, it was systemic. The charges against the members of his team were never initiated by the SSP, and on several occasions the secretary stepped in to try to prevent his people going to prison.

After the removal of Medina Mora, another attorney general was appointed who García soon fell out with: Arturo Chávez, the protégé of a prominent PAN leader and one-time presidential candidate, Diego Fernández de Cevallos, who never liked García Luna.

In May 2010 the Mexico City Attorney's Office arrested Luis Jafet Jasso—who worked in the operational command center of the Federal Police (PF) and was one of García Luna's men—for car theft on behalf of the Beltrán Leyvas. In March 2010, the flashy Rafael Avilés, coordinator of Federal Support Forces, long rumored to lead a secret group of corrupt policemen known as The Brotherhood, got a fresh stain on his record: his director of operations, Roberto Cruz, was caught in possession of drugs and weapons.

In August 2010, Avilés had a further problem. Four hundred federal policemen, sent to fight the drug traffickers in Ciudad Juárez, turned around and accused their own bosses of being the criminals. In a public revolt, the officers claimed that the commanders assigned by Avilés and García Luna kept stashes of drugs and arms, which they used to incriminate and extort innocent people.

At last, after putting up for years with the terror and impunity of García Luna and his team, in January 2011 various social and civil organizations broke their silence, denouncing the links between the SSP cabal and the criminal gangs. A priest in Oaxaca, Alejandro Solalinde, director of the Hermanos en Camino shelter that assists Central American migrants, accused García Luna and his team of protecting the cruel gangs that kidnap migrants, and in some cases of actually taking part in the kidnappings. Solalinde says he has received death threats from García Luna, as do other social leaders who have criticized the police chief. In July 2011, as he led a protest march of citizens and migrants, the "Step by Step towards Peace Caravan," the priest was arrested and held for several hours by García's police. He was charged with carrying firearms, but freed when he showed that these belonged to his bodyguards, and had all the necessary licenses. Of course, the reason he had bodyguards in the first place was because of the threats from García Luna.

In May 2011, Javier Sicilia, a respected poet living in Cuernavaca, called a National March for Peace when his son became one more casualty of the bogus war on drugs. On May 8, 2011, in the Zócalo square in the heart of the capital, Sicilia demanded on behalf of Mexican society the sacking of Genaro García Luna. He urged President Calderón to ask for his resignation.

Although the crowd shouted all together, "Out, out, out!" Calderón has remained a silent witness to the crimes of those who captain his real war, not against but between drug traffickers. He didn't fire García Luna, nor ask for his resignation. What he did do was institute a Federal Police Day to be held every June 2, so people could celebrate his misdeeds year after year. And on that first occasion in 2011, Calderón presided over a ceremony to decorate eminent policemen like Luis Cárdenas Palomino.

García Luna contributed with a peculiar speech, boasting that in record time they had succeeded in building an institution—the unified police force—to the highest international standards, with all the strength and the tactical-strategic intelligence capabilities needed to take on organized crime. The facts suggest that what they managed in record time was exactly the opposite.

Every two years at most, all SSP officials are meant to undergo a test of trustworthiness. This includes drug dependency tests, a session with a lie detector, and a psychological evaluation. The tests on García Luna's team, carried out in-house, cannot be challenged. The SSP consistently refused to reveal either the content of the tests or the results.[33]

Nobody evaluated García Luna himself. He never took any trustworthiness tests during the Calderón presidency, because supposedly he held an administrative job, not an operational one— yet he was the man President Calderón chose to design and oversee his "war on drugs."

The surrender of La Barbie and El Grande

In the current climate of violence, some narcos prefer to surrender to their friends rather than remain exposed to their foes. After the death of Arturo Beltrán Leyva, his brother Héctor moved to divest Arturo's chief henchmen— Edgar Valdez Villarreal, La Barbie, and Sergio Villarreal, El Grande—of everything they had. With help from the Zetas, a ruthless hunt began.

La Barbie was described by the US State Department in 2007 as Arturo El Barbas's closest lieutenant, and one of the main promoters of the slaughter resulting from the discord between the gangs. His love of speed almost did for him in 2010, when he was badly injured in a motorcycle accident. At the time, as we've seen, he and El Indio Álvarez were thinking of setting up their own organization.

Then, on August 30, 2010, Valdez was captured in what was portrayed as a PF operation in the State of Mexico. In reality La Barbie decided to give himself up, because he felt safer in the custody of the federal government than on the run from the Zetas and Héctor Beltrán. The deal was that Valdez would grass on other members of his former gang. As a bonus, he would also point the finger at politicians who threatened the ruling PAN, such as the then governor of the State of Mexico and current president of the Republic, Enrique Peña Nieto, of the PRI. In return he would get an easy ride in court, and permission to keep his ill-gotten gains—which are, after all, the most important things to a narco.

Friends of La Barbie report that he spends little time in his cell, and is even free to roam the city in the interests of his unlawful businesses.

Sergio Villarreal, El Grande, was arrested shortly after La Barbie, on September 12, 2011, in the city of Puebla, and promptly signed up to the PGR's witness protection program under the name of Mateo. His statements blackened the late hero Edgar Millán, as well as men still alive and in office at the time, such as Cárdenas Palomino and Armando Espinosa de Benito, both members of García Luna's inner circle. Villarreal accused them both of collusion with the Sinaloa Federation of El Chapo and El Mayo.[34]

The privileges and obligations of traffickers who agree to become informants are set out in documents amounting to contracts signed with the PGR; privileges include protection of the witness's immediate family. For his part, El Grande undertook to reveal everything about the Beltrán Leyvas' organizational structure and activities in various states.[35]

The President of death

Felipe Calderón stepped down as president of Mexico in December 2012. His time in office will be engraved in collective memory as an era of death and corruption. Josefina Vázquez Mota, the valiant PAN member who sought to succeed him, lost the election to the PRI's Peña Nieto. Calderón's trusted confidant, Genaro García Luna, the tainted secretary of public security, did not after all run for president. And he may not remain immune for ever. In December 2012, an anonymous DEA agent told *Proceso* magazine that they had only kept quiet about García Luna "out of respect for Mexican institutions and because he was the direct contact with the United States, assigned by the Mexican president. No other reason."[36] Diplomatic sources say that he sold up his many assets in Mexico before joining his family in Florida—with a time bomb in his luggage.

The future, however, is uncertain, and the present is complex. The United States government is on red alert at the possibility the mounting violence might spill over its border. In 2011 the former Mexican president Vicente Fox spoke up in favor of "dialogue" with the criminal organizations, and legalization of the production, distribution, and sale of currently illegal drugs. Maybe this is one of the promises made to organized crime during his time in office.

President Calderón's popularity plummeted well before his departure. Thousands protested against the absurd strategy of "war" and its non-existent victories. For although some drug barons opposed to El Chapo have been captured, many of the groups they controlled continue to grow, and could themselves become new cartels. It is estimated that over 80,000 people were killed by drug-related violence during Calderón's sexennial. By comparison, during the dictatorship of Augusto Pinochet in Chile, some 40,000 people died. And that is seen as one of the most bloody and shameful periods in Latin American history. How will Mexico's president of death go down in history?

The only clear winners in this disaster are El Chapo Guzmán and El Mayo Zambada, who grow more powerful by the day. El Chapo's reign will last as long as he wants it to. Inside his clan some say he is already preparing his retirement, so no one should be surprised if he were to turn up "dead" in some "successful" operation, like his friend Nacho Coronel. On the other hand, like it or not, business might demand he stay on a little longer, while any successor gains the trust of partners and accomplices on both sides of the border.

Among the ranks of organized crime they say the rules of the game are getting stricter. Nowadays the drug barons kill their own henchmen at the least sign of hesitation, ever fearful they might be betrayed. And as some frighteningly prescient criminal sources pointed out in August 2010, many of the dead will be public officials.

The men who feed on blood and pain are redeploying. The indictment of the State made by Edgardo Buscaglia in 2010 is as pertinent as ever, while we await the policies of the new president:

> I have no proof that [Calderón] personally protects El Chapo Guzmán, but the system he presides over certainly does. Nobody is accusing the president of criminal responsibility for the protection of El Chapo Guzmán. But his system, the SSP, and sectors of an Army that remains contaminated by this ill-conceived battle, do indeed adopt a position that shields some groups and attacks others.
>
> One way or another, the president and his policies are causing, by omission, the deaths of soldiers, policemen, and ordinary citizens. All as a result of failing to follow the best practices exemplified by Colombia and Italy. There is no excuse for such neglect. History, and the Mexican people, will never forgive him.

It has got to stop, and the only ones who can stop it are ordinary citizens. As the lords of the drug trade—callous traffickers, ambitious politicians, greedy businessmen—continue to bump up their profits in the midst of this desolate, deathly landscape that is slowly replacing Mexico's beautiful scenery, someone has got to tell them that they are not invincible. What makes them invincible are their networks of political and business protection. It will only end when Mexican society unites against this immense mafia. That means overcoming fear and apathy, and above all the tacit assumption that things cannot be any different.

Similarly, those countries with more developed economic and political systems than Mexico, that look on in horror as if it were all a third-world movie, must not be indifferent. If the Mexican drug cartels are able to export their drugs, their money, and their corruption, what makes anyone think they might not do the same with their violence? According to an official US report published in 2011, the war between El Chapo Guzmán and the Beltrán Leyva brothers has already pushed the latter into expanding their operations in Spain.

To the south, the violence from Mexico's drug wars has spilled into Central America. At the same time, a dirty secret is beginning to come out across Mexico's border to the north, where there are also lords of the drugs trade, and hands that feed them.

During Calderón's sexennial, in what he called his "war on drugs," more than 80,000 people were killed, over 20,000 disappeared, and 200,000 thousand people were driven from their homes. Calderón himself is off to Harvard, to give classes at the John F. Kennedy School of Government, leaving a wake of blood, corruption, and impunity. Genaro García Luna has taken refuge in Miami Beach. And the PRI, the party that launched the Mexican model of corruption and protection for drug traffickers, is back in power.

The Drug Lords are getting ready for the next era. Some are reorganizing their narcotics business, while others retire from the public stage for a rest. As long as they go unpunished, Mexico will continue to be Narcoland.

La Barbie Strikes Back

Four days before the end of President Felipe Calderón's presidency, drug trafficker Edgar Valdez Villarreal, alias La Barbie, decided to break his silence. The thirty-six-year-old US citizen is accused in Mexico of being part of the Beltrán Leyva cartel, and of managing groups of professional killers like Los Números and Los Maras. He faces three indictments in the United States, filed in Texas, Louisiana, and Georgia.

From the Altiplano maximum-security prison in the State of Mexico, where he was being held, he dropped a real bombshell for the Calderón government. Mexico's violent drug barons have embraced the new fashion for car bombs. La Barbie preferred something more subtle: a letter.

Never before in the history of Mexico had a drug trafficker publicly broken the pact of complicity. With the end of Calderón's deadly administration just days away, and his own extradition to the US also imminent, the time was right for La Barbie's unexpected confession.

On November 26, I received an unusual call from his lawyer, Eréndira Joselyn Guerra. She wanted to see me regarding a matter of public interest which her client had instructed her to raise with me. It was the first time I had spoken to her, and, for obvious journalistic reasons, I accepted.

As the time of our meeting approached, my heart was racing. I had waited seven years for this moment. In the course of my research I had spoken to many people inside and outside of the law, but never had a drug baron or one of their employees wanted to make a direct, public confession—apart from those who had made statements to public prosecutors which were then kept secret, to avoid implicating public figures and businessmen.

The reason the lawyer, Guerra, wanted to see me was to hand over a letter that her client had dictated to her in prison. They had worked on the text together for several weeks before settling on the final document, just one page long, that he signed and wanted me to publish. The letter was handed to me on November 27, 2012.

In it he accused Felipe Calderón of personally presiding over several meetings with criminal groups to reach a deal with them. He said he had been singled out for persecution because he had refused to make a pact with the other organizations. And he stated that the US government was informed of these events.

"Subsequently there were various meetings with General Mario Arturo Acosta Chaparro who had orders from the president and Juan Camilo Mouriño to meet with two of the leaders of the Micho-acán Family.[1] After that the general met with Heriberto Lazcano and Miguel Ángel Treviño, Z40, in Matamoros. And later Acosta Chaparro and Mouriño spoke to Arturo Beltrán Leyva, El Barbas, and the general also spoke to El Chapo Guzmán, the leader of the Sinaloa cartel. Calderón wanted an agreement with all the cartels: the Zetas, the Gulf Cartel, myself, the Juárez Cartel with Vicente, as well as Mayo and Chapo," Valdez writes.

"Because I didn't respond to this and didn't want to have links with any of the criminal organizations, an intense persecution began against me, to the point where several of my homes were raided without a warrant, from which they stole money, valuables, cars, and other belongings," the letter continues.

The drug baron revealed the bribes he said Calderón's secretary of public security, Genaro García Luna, had received from the drug cartels and from himself since 2002, when García Luna was director of the Federal Investigations Agency (AFI) during the Fox adminis-tration. The payments the traffickers made to the policemen also bought access to DEA information.

"Genaro García Luna, the head of the Secretariat of Public Secu-rity (SSP), has since 2002, first in the AFI and later in the PFP, I know received money from me, from drug trafficking, and from organized crime, along with a select group of corrupt policemen that includes

Armando Espinosa de Benito who worked for the DEA and passed information on to me.

"Among other things they were given the task of 'arresting me in some operation,' although in fact they had orders to kill me, so that when I was arrested in the house that was mentioned in the media, where I was alone, they say that no shots were reported, but in fact there was shooting. A federal police officer who brought me to the place where I am now, tried to get me to run away so he could shoot me. Then they could say I had been killed resisting arrest," La Barbie wrote in his letter.

He went on to denounce the impunity of García Luna:

"It is worth mentioning that in spite of Genaro García Luna's record, which is contained in various case files, of which the American government is well aware, and which even came up in the Merida Initiative, and which I have had access to, most recently in the testimony of the witness known as Mateo (Sergio Villarreal), still President Felipe Calderón keeps him in his post and no legal action is taken against him.

"Another fact worth noting is that however many arrests the Federal Police make, they do not confiscate anything, everything gets lost (money, watches, vehicles, drugs, etc.). On the other hand it should be pointed out that both the Mexican Army and the Navy are more honest, they arrest people and hand them over with all their possessions," alleges Valdez in the letter his lawyer handed to me.

The last lines of the letter demolish anything still standing: "I may have done whatever I have done, but the public servants I mention, they too are part of the criminal structure in this country."

This letter was published in *Reforma*, Mexico's most prestigious newspaper, on November 28, 2012, two days before Felipe Calderón left office.

Throughout Calderón's sexennial, the main cases against drug traffickers and public officials who protected groups other than El Chapo's were based on the testimony of other criminals. Such testimony was treated as entirely credible, as long as it served the right political interests. Now that the accusations of a drug trafficker are directed at the president himself and his police chief, this approach has blown up in their faces. García Luna immediately responded that the accusations were false, and that a judge should rule on their admissibility. The president's office maintained a deafening silence. They did not deny what La Barbie said.

The drug baron's lawyer says that when her client is extradited to the United States, he will testify further, and provide proof of the accusations made in his letter.

FULL TEXT OF LETTER:

I wish to state firstly that I have not joined any protected witness program, and I categorically deny the account given by those who apprehended me of how my arrest happened. The truth of the matter is as follows:

My arrest was the result of political persecution by C. Felipe Calderón Hinojosa, who began to harass me because the undersigned refused to be party to an agreement that Calderón Hinojosa wanted to make with all the organized crime groups, for the purpose of which he personally convened various meetings in order to hold talks with the criminal organizations.

Subsequently there were various meetings with General Mario Arturo Acosta Chaparro who had orders from the president and Juan Camilo Mouriño to meet with two of the leaders of the Michoacán Family. After that the general met Heriberto Lazcano and Miguel Ángel Treviño, Z40, in Matamoros. And later Acosta Chaparro and Mouriño spoke to Arturo Beltrán Leyva, El Barbas, and the general also spoke to El Chapo Guzmán, the leader of the Sinaloa cartel.

Calderón wanted an agreement with all the cartels: the Zetas, the Gulf Cartel, myself, the Juárez Cartel with Vicente, as well as Mayo and Chapo (Sinaloa Cartel). Because I didn't respond to this and didn't want to have links with any of the criminal organizations, an intense persecution began against me, to the point where several of my homes were raided without any warrant, from which they stole money, valuables, cars, and other belongings.

Genaro García Luna, the head of the Secretariat of Public Security (SSP), has since 2002, first in the AFI and later in the PFP, I know received money from me, from drug trafficking and from organized crime, along with a select group of corrupt policemen that includes

Armando Espinosa de Benito who worked for the DEA and passed information on to me, Luis Cárdenas Palomino, Edgar Eusebio Millán, Francisco Garza Palacios (Colombian Federal Police), Igor Labastida Calderón, Facundo Rosas Rosas, Ramón Eduardo Pequeño García and Gerardo Garay Cadena, who were also part of this and received money from organized crime and from me.

Among other things they were given the task of "arresting me in some operation," although in fact they had orders to kill me, so that when I was arrested in the house that was mentioned in the media, where I was alone, they say that no shots were reported, but in fact there was shooting. A federal police officer who brought me to the place where I am now, tried to get me to run away so he could shoot me. Then they could say I had been killed resisting arrest, as they did with Arón Gines Becerril who they killed near the Perisur shopping mall. He was shot in the back on the same day I was arrested. But it was all covered up by the PF.

It is worth mentioning that in spite of Genaro García's record, which is contained in various case files, of which the American government is well aware, and which even came up in the Merida Initiative,[2] and which I have had access to, most recently in the testimony of the witness known as Mateo (Sergio Villarreal), still President Felipe Calderón keeps him in his post and no legal action is taken against him.

Another fact worth noting is that however many arrests the Federal Police make, they do not confiscate anything, everything gets lost (money, watches, vehicles, drugs, etc.). On the other hand it should be pointed out that both the Mexican Army and the Navy are more honest, they arrest people and hand them over with all their posssessions.

I may have done whatever I have done, but the public servants I mention, they too are part of the criminal structure in this country.

EDGAR VALDEZ VILLARREAL

The truth will out, as they say, even if via an unexpected path. The drug trafficker's account is the same as the one I heard directly from General X, in 2010. And it so happens that General X, whose identity

I carefully concealed for two years, is none other than Mario Arturo Acosta, named by La Barbie in his letter.

The general was silenced by a lone gunman in Mexico City, in April 2012, months before Calderón's government came to an end. He would have been one of the chief witnesses to the now ex-president's shameful agreements, were Calderón ever to be brought to trial, in Mexico or abroad. But his testimony died with him.

Notes

1. A POOR DEVIL

1. Jorge Carrillo Olea agreed to give the author an extensive interview for this book on October 16, 2009, at his home in Cuernavaca. The conversation was recorded. The general stated that Mexico has the fourth biggest army in the world with the largest number of generals, after the United States, China, and Russia.

2. José Alfredo Andrade Bojorges is the author of *Historia secreta del narco. Desde Navolato vengo* (Mexico City: Océano, 1999). It is an investigation into Amado Carrillo Fuentes and his network of associates in the drugs business, as well as his protectors in the sphere of politics, the police, and the judiciary. For this study I obtained a copy of the original draft of his book, before it was edited and published.

3. Several years after leading the National Anti-Drugs Institute (INCD), Gutiérrez Rebollo was arrested and convicted for his links with Carrillo Fuentes.

4. On September 29, 1999, *Reforma* newspaper published an account of Andrade Bojorges's book launch. According to some of those interviewed, he had disappeared on July 20 of that year.

5. In May 2011, the author interviewed the lawyer for the Guadalajara archdiocese, José Antonio Ortega, who gave her a copy of Benjamín Arellano Félix's statement.

2. LIFE OR DEATH

1. *Proceso* magazine, no. 166, January 1980.

2. In Vallarta's former Sheraton Bugambilias Hotel, they still remember how the drug trafficker used to rent an entire floor for his stay. That is where he created the scandals that so annoyed his boss, Amado Carrillo Fuentes.

3. National Action Party, the party of former presidents Vicente Fox and Felipe Calderón.

4. *Milenio* magazine, July 8, 2002.

5. The author lodged a complaint with the IFAI (Freedom of Information Institute) over Sedena's reponse. In June 2010, IFAI ordered the Secretariat to look again for the document. But the commissioner, a former security adviser to President Calderón, Sigrid Artz, refused to sign the order for three and a half months, holding up the search. In October 2010, the author lodged a complaint against Artz in the IFAI's internal affairs office.

6. Both the governor of Baja California, Ernesto Ruffo Appel, and his brother Claudio, had been linked with the Arellano Félix gang by El Chapo in his original statement.

3. A PERVERSE PACT

1. This section is a reconstruction of the kidnapping and murder of Enrique Camarena, based on the sworn statements of Ernesto Fonseca Carrillo and Rafael Caro Quintero, which were obtained by the author.

2. Information taken from justice.gov/dea/pubs/history/1985-1990.pdf.

3. Henry Weinstein, "Witness Who Tied CIA to Traffickers Must Testify Anew," Los *AngEles Times*, July 6, 1990.

4. The author has a copy of the complete document.

5. Information taken from the "Final Report of the Independent Counsel for Iran/Contra Matters," better known as the Walsh Commission Report, archives.gov.

6. From an article published in the electronic magazine, *Salon.com*, on 25 October 2004 by journalist Robert Parry, who was responsible for many reports in the 1980s on the Iran-Contra affair for outlets like Associated Press and *Newsweek*. Kerry Report consulted on whatreallyhappened.com, January 14, 2013.

7. Manuel Buendía was killed on May 30, 1984, in Mexico City. The only person imprisoned for his murder was the then head of the DFS, José Antonio Zorrilla.

8. Given his close relations with the then president, Miguel de la Madrid, it was thought that del Mazo had a good chance of being nominated as PRI candidate for the 1988 presidential election. In the end, to his surprise and disappointment, the ruling-party candidate was Carlos Salinas. Today, del Mazo backs the former governor of the State of Mexico, Enrique Peña Nieto, who won the disputed presidential election of July 2012. Ironically and not by chance, Salinas also backs Peña Nieto.

9. Javier Juárez Vásquez, another Veracruz journalist, was also killed around that time; some have wrongly identified him with Velasco.

10. Edén Pastora, or El Comandante Cero, was one of the leaders of the armed movement against the Somoza regime at the end of the 1970s. After the revolution won, Pastora split from the FSLN and turned against the Sandinista government, becoming a Contra leader.

11. For this investigation the author was in touch with many sources linked to different drug organizations.

12. The author obtained a copy of Rafael Caro Quintero's written statement, which has not been published before.

13. Information published in the Los *AngEles Times*, June 8, 1990, by journalist Henry Weinstein, who covered the Camarena murder trial.

14. Los *AngEles Times*, August 1, 1990.

15. William R. Doerner *et al.*, "Latin America Flames of Anger," *Time*, January 18, 1988.

16. "Crime of the Century: CIA – Cocaine International Agency," *USA Today*, June 1999.

17. Jefferson Morley, "LITEMPO: The CIA's Eyes on Tlatelolco," *National Security Archive Electronic Briefing Book, no. 204*, October 18, 2006.

18. Information obtained by Leslie Cockburn and Andrew Cockburn, "Guns, Drugs, and the CIA," *Frontline*, PBS, May 17, 1988; see also John Kerry's report, published in 1989.

4. RAISING CROWS

1. The Mexican army divides the country into military regions and zones. The first are commanded by Major Generals, the highest rank, and the second by Brigadier Generals.

2. Peter Dale Scott and Jonathan Marshall, *Cocaine Politics: Drugs, Armies, and the CIA in Central America*, Berkeley and Los Angelos: University of California Press, 1991.

3. Ibid.

4. Diego Enrique Osorno, "Memorias de un capo," *Gatopardo*, Mexico City, May 2009.

5. Seal's story is so fascinating that in 1991 HBO made a TV film out of it called *Doublecrossed*.

6. The author has a copy of a CIA document which mentions Seal's existence and his activities.

7. Daniel Hopsicker, *Barry and "the Boys,"* Oregon: TrineDay, 2001.

8. Ambrose Evans-Pritchard, *The Secret Life of Bill Clinton*, Washington: Regnery Publishing, 1997.

9. "Report of Investigation, Volume I: The California Story," cia.gov/library.

10. Evans-Pritchard, *The Secret Life of Bill Clinton*.

11. "DEA History Book," 1985-1990, justice.gov/dea/pubs/history/1985-1990. html

12. Villa Coca was the name given to the case of the Peruvian drug baron Reynaldo Rodríguez López, El Padrino, after his cocaine laboratory exploded in a residential area of Lima on July 24, 1985.

13. "DEA History Book," 1985–1990, justice.gov/dea.

14. "El fin de El Mexicano," *Semana*, Colombia, June 8, 1992.

5. EL CHAPO'S PROTECTORS

1. Marc Lacey, "Mexican Leader to Visit U.S. as Woes Mount," *New York Times*, May 17, 2010.

2. Details taken from a copy of the police report dated September 5, 1992.

3. The author has a copy of Cristina Sánchez's statement.

4. "News Release," DEA, December 20, 2004.

5. *Wall Street Journal*, June 13, 2009.

6. "El contador de El Chapo," *Milenio Semanal*, January 31, 2010.

7. Details from a copy, in the author's possession, of the police report dated September 22 and October 2, 1992.

8. Information from the initial inquiry into the Iguala murders.

9. Thomas A. Constantine, DEA Congressional Testimony, "Drug Trafficking in Mexico," March 28, 1996, justice.gov/dea.

10. Information borne out by the police report and, verbally, by people directly involved in the operation, including former Attorney General Morales. Aero Abastos still operates, benefitting from some fuel privileges, as was confirmed to us by the Transport Secretariat for this investigation, though they said they could not find the original documents.

11. Morales said as much in several interviews he gave in 1998, talking about his hopes of standing for governor of Veracruz state for an opposition party.

12. Sam Dillon, "A Fugitive Lawman Speaks," *New York Times*, December 23, 1996.

13. "Drug Wars," Part 2, *Frontline*, aired October 10, 2000, pbs.org.

6. THE LORD OF PUENTE GRANDE

1. *Reforma*, December 5, 2000.
2. The information on the state in which El Chapo's cell was found after his escape is contained in the Visual Inspection Report of January 21, 2001, part of penal case 16/2001-III carried out by the federal public prosecutors attached to the Specialized Unit against Organized Crime (UEDO).
3. "Congressional Testimony Statement by Donnie Marshall," DEA, March 19, 1998. In 1993 the Customs Service confiscated from Eduardo González two cargos of cocaine weighing 2.9 tons (El *Norte*, September 10, 1997). This information must have been communicated to the relevant authorities, so it cannot have been a surprise to anyone that the wealthy Jalisco businessmen were in fact drug traffickers.
4. Formal statement by Division General Jesús Gutiérrez Rebollo, December 29, 1997.
5. Ibid.
6. Sworn statements of Juan Galván Lara (February 19, 1997) and Jesús Gutiérrez Rebollo (December 29, 1997).
7. "Trends in Resource Utilization on Major Cases," declassified FBI report, September 2003.
8. *Reforma*, July 7, 1997.
9. Ibid., July 10, 1997.
10. The officer, whose name cannot be given for reasons of security, was consulted as a professional expert for this book.
11. *Milenio*, May 8, 2010
12. Or maybe his wife, Celia Quevedo, told the truth in her statement: she insisted that Vicente was dragged out of their apartment in his pyjamas, and that "the sports gear in which he was presented to the press was a fabrication" (*Proceso*, no. 1711, August 16, 2009).
13. *Proceso*, no. 1732, January 9, 2010.
14. Ibid.
15. Ibid.
16. Antonio Toledo Corro, Labastida's predecessor, was from 1986 mentioned in DEA reports as a probable collaborator with the Pacific organization.
17. PGR Bulletin 1237/09. In 2008 a war began between El Chapo and the Beltrán Leyvas, which explains why the latter at once became the target of federal pursuits and arrests.
18. Sworn statement by Antonio Aguilar Garzón, February 9, 2001, penal case 16/2001-III.

19. Sworn statement by José de Jesús Carlos Cortés Ortiz, January 25, 2001, penal case 16/2001-III.

20. Statement by Miguel Ángel Leal, January 22, 2001. The dialogue here has been reconstructed from that statement.

21. Additional statement by Juan José Pérez Díaz, January 30, 2001, penal case 16/2001-III.

22. Sworn statement by Salvador Moreno Chávez, February 17, 2001. Additional statement by José Salvador Hernández Quiroz, February 9, 2001, penal case 16/2001-III. Sworn statement by Margarita Ramírez Gutiérrez, January 24, 2001.

23. Ibid.

24. Sworn statement of Antonio Aguilar Garzón.

25. The Oaxaca Center for Human Rights promptly requested the National Human Rights Commission to ensure the physical and psychological safety of the female guerrillas.

26. Sworn statement by Salvador Moreno Chávez, February 17, 2001, penal case 16/2001-III.

27. Sworn statement by Felipe de Jesús Díaz, January 24, 2001, penal case 16/2001-III.

28. Sworn statement by María Guadalupe Morfín Otero, January 20, 2001, penal case 16/2001-III.

29. Sworn statement by Antonio Aguilar Garzón, February 9, 2001, penal case 16/2001-III. The dialogues that follow have been reconstructed from that statement.

30. Additional sworn statement by Juan Gerardo López Hernández, January 27, 2001; sworn statement by Carlos Uribe, January 27, 2001; additional sworn statement by Juan Carlos Sánchez, February 9, 2001. All are in penal case 16/2001-III.

31. Sworn statement by Juan Gerardo López, January 25, 2001.

32. García Luna's declaration of interests, SFP, May 24, 2010.

33. Alegre told various people what Guzmán said in his statement to General Álvarez Nahara on that flight. At the end of 2009, one of them was interviewed for this book.

34. Sworn statement by Luis Francisco Ruiz, January 27, 2001.

35. Sworn statement by Joel Villalobos Anzaldo, penal case 16/2001-III.

36. Additional statement by Juan José Pérez Díaz, January 24, 2001, penal case 16/2001-III.

7. THE GREAT ESCAPE

1. *La Jornada*, January 20, 2001.
2. Sworn statement by Miguel Ángel Leal Amador, January 22, 2010.
3. Ibid.
4. One of Mexico's foremost banks, Banamex was taken over by Citigroup in August 2001, in the largest ever US-Mexican corporate merger. [*Translator's note*]
5. Additional statement by Guillermo Paredes Torres, February 9, 2001, penal case 16/2001-III.
6. Sworn statement by Juan Carlos Sánchez Castillo, January 26, 2001.
7. Ibid.; sworn statement by Margarita Ramírez Gutiérrez, January 24, 2001, penal case 16/2001-III.
8. Sworn statement by Juan Carlos Sánchez Castillo, January 26, 2001, penal case 16/2001-III.
9. Additional statement by José Salvador Hernández Quiroz, January 22, 2001, penal case 16/2001-III.
10. Sworn statement by Jaime Sánchez Flores, January 20, 2001; additional statement by Juan Gerardo López Hernández, January 29, 2001, penal case 16/2001-III.
11. Sworn statement by Ernesto Ramos Aguilar, January 21, 2001.
12. Sworn statement by María Mercedes Fajardo Cantero, January 20, 2001, penal case 16/2001-III.
13. Additional statement by José Salvador Hernández Quiroz, January 22, 2001, penal case 16/2001-III.
14. Sworn statement by Juan Carlos Sánchez Castillo, January 26, 2001; additional statement by Guillermo Paredes Torres, February 9, 2001, penal case 16/2001-III.
15. Visual inspection of the visitors' register for Puente Grande Federal Rehabilitation Center No. 2, carried out on January 22, 2001. The book contains visitors' movements from October 30, 2000, to January 21, 2001.
16. Sworn statement by Juan Carlos Sánchez Castillo, January 26, 2001.
17. Additional statement by José Salvador Hernández Quiroz, February 10, 2001, penal case 16/2001-III.
18. Sworn statement by José de Jesús Briseño Martínez, January 21, 2011.
19. Sworn statement by Ernesto Ramos Aguilar, January 21, 2011.
20. Sworn statement by José de Jesús Carlos Cortés Ortiz, January 24, 2001, penal case 16/2001-III.
21. Criminal investigation notes, Sheet 1007, penal case 16/2001-III.

22. This was confirmed by some who toured the maximum security prisons with Juan Pablo de Tavira.

23. Sworn statement by José de Jesús Carlos Cortés Ortiz, January 24, 2001, penal case 16/2001-III.

24. Criminal investigation notes, Sheet 1008, penal case 16/2001-III.

25. Sworn statement by José de Jesús Carlos Cortés Ortiz, January 24, 2001, penal case 16/2001-III.

26. The author has a copy of these still unpublished files.

27. Additional sworn statement by Juan Gerardo López Hernández, January 27, 2001, penal case 16/2001-III; sheet 2339 of penal case 2339.

28. Sworn statement by Antonio Díaz Hernández, January 21, 2001, penal case 16/2001-III.

29. Additional statement by Juan José Pérez Díaz, January 25, 2001.

30. Sworn statement by Leonardo Beltrán Santana, January 20, 2001, Penal case 16/2001-III.

31. Sworn statement by Víctor Manuel Godoy Rodríguez, January 26, 2001.

32. *La Jornada*, January 21, 2001.

33. Additional statement by Juan Carlos Sánchez Castillo, February 9, 2001. Sworn statement by Guillermo Paredes Torres, January 27, 2001, Penal Case 16/2001-III.

34. El *Universal*, October 22, 2011.

35. *Reforma*, January 5, 2002.

36. Ibid., July 18, 2002.

37. Ibid.

38. The interview was conducted by the author.

39. Ibid.

40. According to official regulations, published on May 6, 2002, in the *Diario Oficial*, this body depends on the Secretariat of Public Security and it is the secretary who appoints and dismisses the commissioner in charge.

41. The author spoke to one of the DEA's coordinators in Mexico at the time.

42. *Forbes*, March 30, 2009.

8. BLOOD TIES

1. *New York Times*, March 4, 2000.

2. *Reforma*, May 1, 1999.

3. *Actual*, April 1, 1999.

4. Santería: an Afro-Cuban cult to which many drug traffickers subscribe, partly for divine protection. Another marginal or outlaws' cult is *La Santa Muerte*, Holy Death. *[Trans. note]*

5. Sworn statement by José Javier Bargueño Urías under the protected witness codename of César, November 14, 2000, sheet 91 of penal case 16/2001-III, of which the author has a copy.

6. *La Jornada*, January 8, 2006.

7. Sworn statement by Albino Quintero Meraz, April 22, 2003, penal case 15/2008-IV, of which the author has a copy.

8. US State Department, Bureau of International Narcotics and Law Enforcement Affairs.

9. Ibid.

10. The author has a copy of case 15/2008-IV, which gives details of Héctor Beltrán Leyva's activities.

11. *Reforma*, June 18, 2010.

12. "Héctor" written backwards.

13. *Reforma*, June 18, 2010.

14. Bulletin no. 6466 of the Federal District Arbitration and Conciliation Board, June 24, 1999.

15. Bulletin no. 317/06 of the PGR, March 15, 2006.

16. US State Department, Bureau of International Narcotics and Law Enforcement Affairs.

17. "Mochomo" is used in Sinaloa to refer to a large red ant with an irritating but not poisonous bite. [*Trans. note*]

18. *Río Doce*, December 21, 2009.

19. Several names were supplied in the sworn statement of José Javier Bargüeño Urías, November 14, 2000, penal case 16/2001-III.

20. *La Jornada*, June 14, 2001.

21. Sworn statement by José Javier Bargueño Urías, November 14, 2000, penal case 16/2001-III.

22. *The New York Times*, April 8, 1995.

23. PRI presidential candidate Colosio was assassinated in Tijuana during a campaign rally. Mario Aburto confessed, but the ballistics, the forces behind the murder, and many other aspects are widely regarded as suspicious. The replacement candidate would be Ernesto Zedillo. [*Trans. note*]

24. *Proceso*, no. 1057, February 1, 1997.

25. Ibid.

26. *Semana*, August 18, 2007.

27. "National Drug Threat Assessment 2010," United States Department of Justice, National Drug Intelligence Center.

28. Narco-corridos are a version of that Northern Mexican form, with lyrics celebrating the lives and deeds of drug traffickers instead of the traditional heroic bandits. [*Trans. note*]

29. *Palabra*, March 29, 2004.

30. Bulletin no. 099 , PGR, March 18, 1999.

31. *La Jornada*, October 26, 1997.

32. *Mural*, May 29, 1999

33. This information and that which follows comes from intelligence reports and oral accounts made available for this book.

34. Sworn statement by Albino Quintero Meraz, April 22, 2010, penal case 15/2008-IV.

35. Sworn statement by José Javier Bargueño Urías, November 14, 2000, penal case 16/2001-III.

36. Penal case 15/2008-IV.

37. This information was provided for this book by one of the DEA agents directly involved in these investigations.

38. US District Court, Eastern District of New York, F. no. 2009R01065/ OCDETF # NYNYE-616, known by the US Justice Department as the "Indictment against The Federation."

39. Ibid.

40. *Proceso*, no. 1744, April 4, 2010.

41. *Milenio Semanal*, July 16, 2000.

42. *Milenio*, November 16, 2008.

43. Author's interview with Mario López Valdez, *Reporte Índigo*, July 8, 2010.

44. Syndicated column by Jesús Blancornelas, May 30, 2006.

45. *Noroeste*, July 10, 2009.

46. *Noroeste*, July 7, 2008.

47. El *Norte*, May 19, 2007.

48. Ibid.

49. Conagua, concession no. 03SIN116508/10ABGR02.

50. *Proceso*, no. 1744, April 4, 2010.

51. "Godmother," or unofficial assistant to a corrupt member of the judicial police; see chapter 4. [*Trans. note*]

52. Intelligence reports obtained for this book.

53. It was in this capacity that General Álvarez accompanied the handover of El Chapo by Guatemala in 1993, and heard his first, now vanished, statement on that flight from Tapachula. See Chapter 1. [*Trans. note*]

54. SSP/Cisen file on Ignacio Coronel Villarreal, of which the author has a copy.

55. Information confirmed directly by one of the DEA officers in charge, in May 2006.

56. US State Department Narcotics Rewards Program file.

57. Ibid.

58. SSP/Cisen file on Juan José Esparragoza Moreno, of which the author has a copy.
59. SSP/Cisen file on Juan José Esparragoza Moreno.
60. *Proceso*, no. 1746, April 18, 2010.
61. El *Universal*, June 6, 2005.
62. Case filed in the New York Eastern District Court, F. no. 2009RO1035/NYNYE614.24/07/2009.
63. *Proceso*, no. 1682, January 25, 2009.
64. Alfredo Corchado, "Cartel figure lashes out," *Dallas Morning News*, October 15, 2006.
65. Ibid.
66. Ibid.
67. Ibid.
68. Declarations given to the author by a senior DEA officer in Mexico.
69. Corchado, "Cartel figure lashes out."
70. US Court of Appeals for the Eighth Circuit, case no. 08-2657, March 10, 2009.
71. Ibid.

9. NARCO WARS

1. "Zeta" is the Spanish word for the letter "Z." *[Trans. note]*
2. SSP/Cisen file on Heriberto Lazcano, of which the author has a copy.
3. This information was requested of Sedena on September 4, 2009. The Secretariat replied on October 5 that it had found no record of Heriberto Lazcano's enrolment in the Heroico Colegio Militar.
4. This information was provided directly by Irma Pérez Ochoa's lawyer.
5. Secretariat of National Defense, public information request no. 0000700083405, December 22, 2005.
6. SSP/Cisen file on Heriberto Lazcano.
7. FBI Report drawn up by the Criminal Investigative Division & San Antonio Field Intelligence Group, July 15, 2005, of which the author has a copy.
8. SSP/Cisen file on Heriberto Lazcano.
9. This information comes from interviews with staff attached to the PJF who witnessed these measures.
10. SSP/Cisen file on Heriberto Lazcano.
11. Ibid.
12. Ibid.
13. Ibid.

14. FBI Report drawn up by the Criminal Investigative Division & San Antonio Field Intelligence Group, July 15, 2005.

15. Ibid.

16. Ibid.

17. Ibid.

18. Ibid.

19. Ibid.

20. Revealed by members of the Centro de Derechos Humanos Fray Francisco in Victoria, at the meeting "Construyendo acciones: presente y futuro de las víctimas de la delincuencia organizada," held on July 30, 2011 in Mexico City.

21. *Proceso*, no. 1746, April 18, 2010.

22. Sworn statement by Miguel Ángel Beltrán Olguín, preliminary investigation pgr/siedo/ueidcs/111/2004.

23. The Zetas recount this in a letter they sent to a senior government official at the beginning of the Calderón presidency, of which the author has a copy.

24. Ricardo Ravelo, *OsiEl. Vida y tragedia de un capo*, Mexico City: Grijalbo, 2009.

25. SSP/Cisen file on Edgar Valdez Villarreal, of which the author has a copy.

26. Star protected witness for the PGR in the case known as Operation Cleanup, against officials of the PGR itself accused of links to the Beltrán Leyva clan, Jennifer was also La Barbie's attorney.

27. This story features in a confidential report entitled "The Footballer Case," of which the author has a copy. It was corroborated directly by people who worked in the AFI at the time.

28. Sworn statement by the protected witness called *Karen*, October 5, 2005, penal case 15/2008-IV, of which the author has a copy. Thanks to this statement, it has been possible to reconstruct an account of what happened in Acapulco and Ixtapa-Zihuatanejo.

29. *Proceso*, no. 1763, August 15, 2010.

30. El *Universal*, December 8, 2005.

31. Communiqué from the Presidential Office, June 11, 2005.

32. Ibid.

33. See Chapter 8.

34. This version was given by The Zetas in a letter sent to a senior government official at the beginning of Felipe Calderón's presidency, of which the author has a copy.

35. The initial investigation into the executions in Acapulco was recorded as pgr/siedo/ueidcs/106/2005.

36. Bulletin no. 071 of the Sistema Penitenciario del Distrito Federal.

37. Information obtained from the Civil Service Secretariat.

38. Anabel Hernández, *Fin de fiesta en* Los *Pinos*, Mexico City, Grijalbo, 2007.

39. In 2008 a request was made through the Federal Law on Transparency and Access to Public Information to reveal the number of initial investigations opened against García Luna between 1990 and 2008. In January 2009 the IFAI ruled on our complaint that the PGR had refused to supply the information. It ordered the Attorney General's Office to hand over the list. But by the time this book went to press, the PGR had still not complied with the order.

40. Based on direct testimony from sources with first-hand experience of these events.

41. Confidential AFI internal affairs report, of which the author has a copy.

42. Ibid.

43. Ibid.

44. Ibid.

45. Ibid.

46. El *Universal*, December 22, 2012.

47. Confidential AFI internal affairs report, of which the author has a copy.

48. Ibid.

49. Ibid.; the author was also able to talk directly to Igor Labastida's lawyer.

50. Confidential AFI internal affairs report, of which the author has a copy. The information was corroborated by first-hand sources, the testimony of one of whom is on tape.

51. Anabel Hernández, Los *cómplices d*El *presidente*, Mexico City: Grijalbo, 2008.

52. In December 2008 the author revealed the content of these case files in *Reporte Índigo*.

53. Information based on an official document of the Federal District Public Security Department on Khouri's arrest, of which the author has a copy.

54. Information from sources involved in the investigation, who confirmed these details.

55. Testimony related by their attorney, José Antonio Ortega, in Hernández, Los *cómplices d*El *presidente*.

56. *Reporte Índigo*, September 25, 2009, researched by Isela Lagunas.

57. Bulletin no. 438/05 of the PGR, May 3, 2005.

58. Classified FBI report, July 15, 2005.

59. FBI report drawn up by the Criminal Investigative Division and San Antonio Field Intelligence Group, July 15, 2005, of which the author has a copy.

60. The Obama administration closed down the NDIC in June 2012. [*Trans. note*]

61. "National Drug Threat Assessment," NDIC, April 2004.

62. "National Drug Threat Assessment," NDIC, January 2006.

10. FREEDOM IS PRICELESS

1. Given the implications of this first-hand account we have decided to leave out the general's name.
2. Bulletin no. 058/01 of the PGR, February 1, 2001.
3. Today Tello works for the Mexican cement giant, Cemex.
4. The 2006 elections were won by the PAN amid widespread accusations of fraud. *[Trans. note]*
5. Communiqué of the Presidential Office, December 4, 2006.
6. Wikileaks Cable 06, Mexico 6871.
7. The author carried out an extensive investigation of García Luna's properties, published in *Reporte Índigo* in 2009 and 2010, which demonstrated wealth that is difficult to explain for a public servant. These reports led to the illegal detention of two journalists from the TVC television company in 2009, and of three employees of *Reporte Índigo* in 2010. To try to make the origin of his property appear legitimate, García threatened to sue *Reporte Índigo* and the journalist, but he never did.
8. Letter sent on November 18, 2008, by a group of AFI officers to the then President of the Public Security Committee of the lower house of congress, and to forty-nine other lawmakers.
9. Communiqué of the Mexican Presidential Office, April 27, 2007.
10. The son of Ismael El Mayo Zambada.
11. The author has copies of the files from both institutions, which show they were drawn up in Cisen, the Interior Secretariat, and the Public Security Secretariat.
12. Information obtained from the files drawn up by the SSP, of which the author has copies.
13. Ibid.
14. The author has a copy of this document.
15. Edgardo Buscaglia, in his capacity as Adviser to the UN on Corruption and Organized Crime, has taken part in missions to Colombia, Italy, and Afghanistan. In February 2010, he gave the author an exclusive interview for this book.
16. From the beginning of July 2007, the author heard accounts of the union between El Chapo Guzmán and Emma Coronel from some of those present. At the same time, the magazine *Proceso* published a report of the event by journalist Patricia Dávila on September 3, 2007. All the accounts have much in common. It remains uncertain whether she is a relative of Nacho Coronel.

17. These events are recounted by Los Zetas in a letter sent to a senior government official at the beginning of Felipe Calderón's presidency, of which the author has a copy.

18. On April 27, 2007, the author wrote an exclusive report in *Reporte Índigo* on the attempts to negotiate a truce between the two cartels.

19. Dispatch of January 21, penal case 15/2008-IV, of which the author has a copy.

20. *Reporte Índigo*, February 7, 2008, researched by the author.

21. The author spoke directly to Igor Labastida's attorney after his execution.

22. The author met tradespeople and community leaders in Tepito to learn more about the background to Edgar Millán and his family.

23. Pitufo, a former member of the Gulf Cartel, gave his statement on March 9, 2009. The author has a copy.

24. The PGJDF has published the findings of its investigations into these kidnappings, which it attributes to Sergio Ortiz.

25. *Reporte Índigo*, September 10, 2008. The author documented with payslips and other civil service documents that Lorena occupied a senior post in the SSP, one day after Rosas and García Luna denied it.

26. Document of the Federal District SSP on the characteristics of the kidnap gang led by Sergio Ortiz.

27. *Reporte Índigo*, October 2, 2008. The author exposed in an exclusive report the investigation carried out by the SIEDO into these officials for alleged protection of the Sinaloa Cartel.

28. The lawyer Raquenel Villanueva told the author that Ángela Quintero, a surgeon, was close to former Colombian president Álvaro Uribe. It seems she did not know whose party this was.

29. *Reforma*, December 13, 2008.

30. At the scene were four men among others who opened fire to defend the Zambadas. They were serving policemen, connected to the SSP and to García Luna: Marco Valadez, assistant inspector of the PFP assigned to the international airport; Carlos Castillo, from the AFI's Regional Deployment Directorate; José Báez, from the Intelligence Department; and Francisco Montaño, of the State of Mexico police.

31. "Godfather" and "godson" signify intimate bonds, much like compadre, rather than a literal ceremonial kinship. *[Trans. note]*

32. Colloquial name for the Mexico City police force: "smurfs."

33. *Reforma*, September 23, 2008.

11. THE PRESIDENT OF DEATH

1. Sworn statement by Richard Arroyo Guízar, October 28, 2010, of which the author has a copy.
2. The code name of José Salvador Puga Quintanilla, the former member of the Gulf Cartel who had also become a protected witness.
3. He moved between the PF and posts elsewhere in the SSP until the end of Calderón's mandate in 2012.
4. Sworn statement by Edgar Enrique Bayardo del Villar, March 9, 2009.
5. Information from Wikileaks which appeared after the first edition of this book (November 2010), cable 08, Mexico 3498.
6. The author had access to sources who witnessed these events.
7. The author had access to sources connected to the US government.
8. *Reforma*, November 5, 2008.
9. The author had access to several sources that recounted the version that drug boss Ismael Zambada gave to his people, and also spoke to a member of Mouriño's family.
10. The author spoke directly to Mouriño's relatives.
11. After the first edition of this book, the author had contact with a close friend of the Mouriño family, who told her this part of the story.
12. The author has copies of the military reports on the operation.
13. The address is 425, Calle Fuerza Aérea Mexicana.
14. *Reforma*, December 15, 2008.
15. Information from the National Commission for the Defense of Financial Services Users (CONDUSEF).
16. Héctor Velázquez was secretary of administrative financial services at Congress when Felipe Calderón was leader of the parliamentary PAN group. Later Velázquez would be remembered as the official who allowed Calderón, just after the latter became director of Banobras, the state development bank, to lend himself the money to buy a house in 2006.
17. *Proceso*, no. 1896, June 26, 2012.
18. Information provided to the author officially by the AICM.
19. The author made a formal request in 2010 for information on how Aviones S. A. operates in the AICM, how much rent it pays, with which companies it shares its hangar space, etc. For its continued operation in the airport, see its website: avionessa.net (accessed March 15, 2013).
20. Specifications of contract FAM 973/2007.
21. Auditoría Superior de la Federación, public accounts audit for fiscal year 1999-2000, Volume 2.

22. Sworn statement by Richard Arroyo Guízar, November 21, 2008.

23. United States District Court, Northern District of Illinois, Eastern Division, no. 09 CR 383.

24. Edgardo Buscaglia was interviewed by the author in February 2010.

25. In December 2012, the British bank HSBC was fined $1.9 billion for turning a blind eye to money laundering at its Mexican affiliate, HSMX. $7 billion in US bank notes had been unquestioningly transferred to its US affiliates between 2007 and 2008, according to a Senate report.

26. In 2009, twenty-eight officials in Michoacán state, including eleven municipal presidents, were arrested on suspicion of links to organized crime. [Trans. note]

27. President Lugo was impeached and ousted by a right-wing Congress in June 2012.

28. "National Drug Threat Assessment 2010," US Department of Justice, NDIC, February 2010.

29. Ibid.

30. Information obtained by the author from sources directly involved in the case of Ignacio Coronel's supposed death.

31. El Noroeste, July 31, 2010, and La Jornada, August 1, 2010.

32. "Strategy to Combat Transnational Organized Crime," July 19, 2011.

33. In June 2011, the author requested copies and results of the tests to which those closest to García Luna were subjected. The SSP refused to hand them over. The classification put on these documents by the SSP itself means that we will not be able to discover for another twelve years whether the senior SSP staff were "trustworthy."

34. Proceso, no. 1777, November 21, 2010.

35. The author has a copy of the agreement signed by the PGR and El Grande.

36. Proceso, no. 1883, December 2, 2012.

EPILOGUE

1. La Familia Michoacana was a quasi-religious, extremely savage group in Michoacán state that developed from vigilantism to working with the Zetas for the Gulf Cartel during the 1990s. They formed their own group in 2006, but have now disbanded; an offshoot is Los Caballeros Templarios, the Knights Templar. [Trans. note]

2. A controversial security cooperation agreement between the US and Mexican governments, 2008.

Glossary of Acronyms

AFI (Agencia Federal de Investigación): Federal Investigation Agency, attached to the Ministerio Público (Public Prosecutors' Office, under the PGR), created in 2001, replaced PJF in 2002; its functions were planned to be divided between the PFM and the PF in reform project of 2009. Only officially disbanded in 2012.

AICM (Aeropuerto Internacional de la Ciudad de México): Mexico City International Airport.

AUC: United Self-Defense of Colombia, right-wing paramilitary group founded by the Castaño brothers, accused of drug trafficking.

Cendro (Centro de Planeación para el Control de Drogas): Center for Drug Control Planning, created in 1991.

Cisen (Centro de Investigación y Seguridad Nacional): Center for Investigation and National Security, replaced DFS in 1985 as main intelligence agency.

CNDH (Comisión Nacional de Derechos Humanos): National Human Rights Commission.

GAFE (Grupo Aeromóvil de Fuerzas Especiales): the Mexican army's Special Forces Airmobile Group.

DEA: Drug Enforcement Administration, the US anti-drug agency.

DFS (Dirección Federal de Seguridad): Federal Security Directorate, the Mexican intelligence agency before 1985.

ICE: Immigration and Customs Enforcement, a US government agency.

INCD (Instituto Nacional para el Combate a las Drogas): National Anti-Drug Institute.

PAN (Partido de Acción Nacional): National Action Party. Traditionally the right-wing party of opposition to the PRI, in 2000 the PAN became the first party to defeat the PRI in a presidential election. Many hoped its victory would sweep out the old, institutionalized corruption.

PF (Policía Federal): Federal Police, projected June 1, 2009, in plan to amalgamate AFI and PFP. Currently designates non-investigative police force.

PFM (Policía Federal Ministerial): Federal Ministerial Police, projected in 2009 to replace the AFI. Attached to the PGR's Public Prosecutors' Office, with investigative functions. Officially inaugurated in July 2012.

PFP (Policía Federal Preventiva) Federal Preventive Police, created in January 1999, under the Interior Secretariat. In 2000 it was attached to the newly created SSP, and in 2009 subsumed into PF.

PGJDF (Procuraduría General de Justicia del Distrito Federal): Mexico City Attorney General's Office.

PGR (Procuraduría General de la República): Attorney General's Office.

PJF (Policía Judicial Federal): Federal Judicial Police. Predecessor of AFI, as an investigative force attached to the PGR.

PRI (Partido Revolucionario Institucional): Institutional Revolutionary Party. Coming out of the the last phase of the Mexican Revolution and initially called the Partido Nacional Revolucionario (PNR), the PRI ruled continuously for seventy-one years, from 1929 to 2000. Its networks of control spread throughout the state apparatus, the economy, and the trade union movement. The party and many of its leading members were frequently accused of corruption and electoral fraud.

Sedena (Secretaría de la Defensa Nacional): Secretariat of Defense.

SIEDO (Subprocuraduría de Investigación Especializada en Delincuencia Organizada): Organized Crime Special Investigations Unit, a department of the PGR.

SSP (Secretaría de Seguridad Pública): Secretariat of Public Security, instituted in 2000 by President Fox and dissolved in 2013 by President Peña Nieto, its functions transferred to the Interior Secretariat.

UEDO (Unidad Especializada contra la Delincuencia Organizada): Special Organized Crime Unit, part of the PGR, an earlier name for what became SIEDO.

Glossary of Persons

A note on names

This glossary of names is organized alphabetically according to the main, that is the first, family name.

The use of names in Mexico can be confusing for English-speaking readers. In general, Spanish-speaking countries use two surnames or family names. The father's surname or patronym, officially regarded as the main surname, comes first, then the mother's, or matronym. So in the case of Joaquín Guzmán Loera, his father's patronym was Guzmán and his mother's was Loera.

In many countries the matronym is usually omitted, except in formal situations. Mexicans, however, are more inclined to use both, and the two surnames used together, without any first or given name, sometimes becomes the most common way of referring to a person. There is no absolute rule. President Salinas, for example, was familiarly known by just the patronym, but President López Portillo was never referred to as plain López. Drug barons seem to be particularly given to using both surnames: Miguel Ángel Félix Gallardo, Amado Carrillo Fuentes, the Arellano Félix brothers and the Beltrán Leyva brothers, for example, are hardly ever shortened.

In this book, we have used the full name the first time someone is mentioned, or for reminders when they have dropped out of the story for a while. After that, we have either omitted the second surname, if that seems clear and common practice for that individual, or we have used both surnames as if they were a double-barreled family name.

Two other factors should be noted. Many people have compound first or given names, and many of these usually use both: José Francisco, Juan Camilo, Miguel Ángel, etc. There is also a widespread use of nicknames, especially common in the criminal underworld.

Mexican Presidents

The narrative of Mexican politics is shaped by the single, six-year terms (sexennials) of successive presidents. In the period covered by this book, they were:

Luis Echeverría Álvarez, Institutional Revolutionary Party (PRI), 1970–76
José López Portillo, PRI, 1976–82
Miguel de la Madrid Hurtado, PRI, 1982–88
Carlos Salinas de Gortari, PRI, 1988–94
Ernesto Zedillo, PRI, 1994–2000
Vicente Fox, National Action Party (PAN), 2000–06
Felipe Calderón, PAN, 2006–12
Enrique Peña Nieto, PRI, from December 2012. He was previously governor of the State of Mexico, and features in this book mainly in that role.

The rest of the cast

Acosta Chaparro, General Mario Arturo. Initially referred to in the book as "General X," was entrusted by President Felipe Calderón and Interior Secretary Juan Camilo Mouriño with the task of meeting the top drug barons and seeking a peace deal between them. It was unsuccessful. He was murdered in April 2012.

Aguilar Garzón, Antonio. Became a supervisor in the prison service in 2000, then assistant warden of Puente Grande prison later that year, where he lasted just two months. In both posts he denounced corruption in the prison and later gave testimony against his own bosses, including Enrique Pérez Rodríguez, the director of the prison service. Aguilar died in a car accident shortly after testifying.

Álvarez Nahara, General Guillermo. Head of the Military Judicial Police during the presidency of Carlos Salinas, and took part in the capture of El Chapo Guzmán in 1993.

Arellano Félix, Benjamín. Leader of the Tijuana Cartel along with his brother, Ramón. In 2001, they became the first target of El Chapo's Federation and of President Fox's war on drugs.

Arroyo Guízar, Richard. Stepson of the Sinaloa Cartel's Jesús Reynaldo Zambada García. Turned protected witness for the PGR, with the code name María Fernanda, after being arrested with his stepfather and half-brother in 2008.

Avilés Pérez, Pedro, alias León de la Sierra (Mountain Lion). First Mexican drug baron to smuggle cocaine into the US. He was murdered in 1978, and Miguel Ángel Félix Gallardo took his place.

Bayardo del Villar, Edgar Enrique, known as El Jumex (The Fruit Juice). As a policeman, allegedly worked for Amado Carrillo Fuentes and later for El Rey Zambada. After being incriminated by the sons of the latter, like them he became a protected witness and gave information about corruption and collusion in García Luna's SSP.

Beltrán Arredondo, Manuel. Businessman in the mining sector, allegedly a leading member of the Sinaloa Cartel and a close friend of El Chapo Guzmán's. Sent Dámaso López to Puente Grande. Shot dead by Mexican navy forces in November 2007.

Beltrán Leyva, Marcos Arturo (the Marcos is usually left out), alias El Barbas (The Beard). Eldest of the Beltrán Leyva brothers (Arturo, Héctor, and Alfredo, collectively "The Three Knights"). Helped Amado Carrillo Fuentes build his empire in the 1990s, then backed El Chapo in his rise. They turned on each other in 2008, after El Chapo orchestrated the arrest of his brother, Alfredo. Shot dead by forces of the Mexican navy in December 2009, in a raid on one of his luxury flats in Cuernavaca.

Beltrán Leyva, Héctor, alias El H, El Ingeniero, or El Elegante. In charge of developing the organization's relations with senior public officials.

Beltrán Leyva, Alfredo, alias El Mochomo (The Ant). The youngest of the brothers, arrested in January 2008.

Beltrán Santana, Leonardo. Warden of the Puente Grande maximum security prison when El Chapo "escaped," and oversaw the period when the drug baron controlled most of what went on there. He spent nine years in prison and was released in 2010 on the orders of Genaro García Luna.

Beltrones, Manlio Fabio. Senior PRI politician, governor of Sonora 1991–97, and, since 2012, leader of the PRI in the lower house. Has been accused of links to drug traffickers and providing protection to the Pacific organization, as well as involvement in the murder of Cardinal Posadas Ocampo, and diverting the investigation into the killing of PRI presidential candidate Luis Donaldo Colosio in 1994.

Berrellez, Hector. DEA special agent who led the investigation into the murder of Enrique Camarena, known as Operation Leyenda.

Bribiesca Sahagún, Manuel. Son of Marta Sahagún, the second wife of President Fox. Allegedly developed business links with Ignacio Coronel of the Sinaloa Cartel.

Buendía Tellezgirón, Manuel. Mexican journalist murdered in 1984.

Camarena, Enrique, known as El Kiki. DEA special agent, murdered by the Guadalajara Cartel in 1985. His death caused friction between the US and Mexico, but also between the DEA and the CIA.

Camberos Rivera, Francisco Javier, alias El Chito. While El Chapo was in Puente Grande, El Chito acted as his fixer on the outside.

Camil Garza, Jaime. Businessman and friend of President Zedillo, father of soap star Jaime Camil, and allegedly a front person for Amado Carrillo Fuentes.

Cárdenas Guillén, Osiel. Leader of the Gulf Cartel, captured in March 2003 and extradited to the US in January 2007.

Cárdenas Guillén, Antonio Ezequiel. As Osiel's brother, took charge of the Gulf Cartel after his brother's arrest in 2003. Killed in November 2010, along with a number of his bodyguards, in a shootout with federal forces.

Cárdenas Palomino, Luis, also known as El Pollo (The Chicken). AFI Director General of Police Investigations in 2003, when he was part of a group that briefly "arrested" El Chapo Guzmán, inaugurating the lucrative relationship between the drug baron and García Luna. Held a series of senior posts in the Federal Police under García Luna, during the Calderón administration.

Caro Quintero, Rafael, alias El Príncipe (The Prince). He and Amado Carrillo Fuentes were the two main protégés of Ernesto Fonseca Carrillo in the early phase of the Pacific organization, which would later give rise to El Chapo's Sinaloa Cartel.

Carpizo McGregor, Jorge. Attorney general 1993–94, the third of five to hold that post under President Salinas.

Carrillo Fuentes, Amado, alias El Señor de los Cielos (The Lord of the Skies). At the head of the Juárez Cartel, became the most powerful of all Mexican drug traffickers in the 1990s, and in many respects took over from the Colombian Medellín Cartel. Allegedly died in July 1997 as a result of botched plastic surgery.

Carrillo Fuentes, Rodolfo. Youngest brother of Amado. Shot dead with his wife in 2004, apparently on orders of El Chapo or El Mayo, for not toeing the line of The Federation. His death almost led to a split between El Chapo and Vicente Carrillo Fuentes and the Beltrán Leyvas, but in fact this did not occur until 2008.

Carrillo Fuentes, Vicente, alias El Viceroy. Younger brother of Amado and elder brother of Rodolfo, took over the Juárez Cartel on Amado's supposed death in 1997.

Carrillo Leyva, Vicente, alias El Ingeniero (The Engineer). Son of Amado Carrillo Fuentes.

Carrillo Olea, General Jorge. Key figure in the Mexican political and security establishment for many years. Under President de la Madrid, in 1985, set up the intelligence agency Cisen. As anti–drug coordinator for Salinas, he set up Cendro in 1992, took charge of the capture of El Chapo in 1993, and effectively ran the Attorney General's Office. As governor of Morelos state from 1994–98, was accused of protecting drug traffickers and of being close to Amado Carrillo Fuentes.

Castaño Gil, José Vicente, alias El Profe (The Professor). Colombian paramilitary and drug trafficker. Founded the far-right paramilitary group AUC with his brother, Carlos.

Cervantes Aguirre, Brigadier General Enrique. Secretary of Defense under President Zedillo.

Coello Trejo, Javier. Drug czar under Enrique Álvarez del Castillo, President Salinas's first attorney general. Allegedly in the pay of Amado Carrillo Fuentes, prevailing on him to hand over Guzmán as the scapegoat for the cardinal's murder in 1993.

Coronel Villarreal, Ignacio, known as Nacho. Also known as El Rey del Cristal for pioneering the traffic in the synthetic drug, methamphetamine. Leading figure in the Sinaloa Cartel and close associate of El Chapo. Shot dead by the Mexican army in July 2010.

Costilla, Jorge Eduardo, alias El Coss. Right-hand man to Osiel and then

Ezequiel Cárdenas. Took charge of a divided Gulf Cartel after death of Ezequiel in 2010, and was himself arrested in September 2012.

Escobar, Pablo. Head of the Medellín Cartel, and the most powerful Colombian drug trafficker in the 1980s. Shot dead in 1993.

Esparragoza Moreno, Juan José, alias El Azul (Blue). Leader of the Sinaloa cartel. Like a number of drug traffickers, began his career as an agent of the DFS intelligence service in the 1970s. Became a key aide to Amado Carrillo Fuentes, then to El Chapo Guzmán. Known by US agencies as "The Peace Maker" for his repeated attempts to broker peace deals between different drug factions.

Félix Gallardo, Miguel Ángel. One of the early leaders of the Guadalajara Cartel, or Pacific organization, which gave rise to the Sinaloa Cartel. Arrested in April 1989.

Fernández Ruiz, Luis Francisco. Assistant warden of the Puente Grande maximum security prison when El Chapo "escaped" on January 19, 2001. One of sixty-eight members of the prison staff charged in connection with that event, spent five years in prison before being released on appeal.

Fonseca Carrillo, Ernesto, known as Don Neto. Early leader of the Pacific Cartel, uncle of Amado Carrillo. Currently in jail for Camarena murder.

Gallardo, José Luis, alias El Güero (Blondie). Kidnapped DEA agent Camarena for Caro Quintero and Don Neto in 1985. Thought by some to be a nephew of Miguel Ángel Félix Gallardo; this book suggests he may have been a CIA agent.

Garay Cadena, Víctor Gerardo. García Luna put him in charge of civilian forces at the beginning of Calderón's "war on drugs" at the end of 2006. A year later videos emerged showing him and other SSP officials taking orders from members of the Sinaloa Cartel. After Edgar Millán was killed in May 2008, García Luna made Garay acting commissioner of the PFP.

García Ábrego, Juan. With brother Humberto, became leader of the Gulf Cartel when their uncle, Juan Nepomuceno, retired. Arrested in 1996 and extradited to the United States.

García Luna, Genaro. Secretary of public security under Calderón and one of the central figures in the "war on drugs," which he is accused of using to benefit El Chapo and the Sinaloa Cartel. In 2001, under President Fox, founded and became director general of the AFI. Previous to that held posts in the PJF and Cisen.

Garza Palacios, Javier, alias El Frutilupis. AFI director of special operations in 2003, when he was part of the group that usefully "arrested" El Chapo Guzmán. García Luna made him coordinator of regional security in the Calderón government, but was forced to "sack" him after a scandal in 2007.

Gertz Manero, Alejandro. First secretary of public security, appointed by Fox. Had been a senior PGR official 30 years earlier, the heyday of the "suitcase ritual," which collected bribes from drug traffickers and channeled them up to higher echelons in the Mexican state.

González Calderoni, Guillermo. Head of the PJF in Guadalajara in 1987, and allegedly represented the Salinas family before the Gulf and Juárez cartels.

Gutiérrez Rebollo, General Jesús. From 1989 chief of 5th Military Region, including Jalisco and Sinaloa, when the Pacific organization was consolidating its dominance in that region and beyond. President Zedillo made him head of the INCD in 1996. In February 1997 he was arrested and sentenced for links to Amado Carrillo Fuentes.

Guzmán Loera, Joaquín, alias El Chapo (Shorty). Leader of the Sinaloa Cartel, the largest Mexican crime group and the most powerful drug trafficking organization in the world.

Harrison, Lawrence Victor, alias Torre Blanca (White Tower). US communications specialist who installed radio systems for Mexican drug cartels in the 1980s. Entered a protected witness program in 1989, testified in a Los Angeles court in 1990, and again in 1992.

Higuera Bernal, Alfredo. Sinaloa district attorney, allegedly a guest at El Chapo's "wedding" in 2007.

Higuera Bernal, Gilberto. Deputy attorney general under President Fox and close ally of García Luna. Accused of making appointments to favor Joaquín El Chapo Guzmán and The Federation.

Kerry, John. Democratic Senator, currently US Secretary of State. Chaired the Kerry Committee hearings into the Iran-Contra affair (1986–89).

Labastida Calderón, Igor. AFI director of federal investigations in 2003, when he was part of the group that "arrested" El Chapo Guzmán. Shot dead in June 2008, when head of Traffic and Contraband at the PFP, and reportedly preparing to turn protected witness for the US Government against corruption in the AFI and SSP.

Labastida Ochoa, Francisco. Former governor of Sinaloa state and PRI candidate for president in 2000. As secretary of the interior in 1999, made a number of appointments that favored El Chapo.

Laborín Archuleta, Clara Elena. Wife of Hector Beltrán Leyva and would-be society hostess.

Lazcano, Heriberto, alias Z3 or El Verdugo (The Executioner). One of the founders and subsequent leader of Los Zetas, a breakaway group originally comprised of former Mexican Special Forces recruited by the Gulf Cartel. Reportedly killed by government forces in October 2012; the body was stolen by an armed commando a few days later.

Leaños Rivera, Felipe. Guard at Puente Grande who denounced the corruption leading up to El Chapo's escape. He was reportedly found dead in a sack, after disappearing from the prison, in 2007.

Lehder, Carlos. Founder of Colombia's Medellín Cartel alongside Pablo Escobar.

León Aragón, Rodolfo, alias El Chino. Named head of PFJ by Carrillo Olea in 1991. He has been accused of direct responsibility for the killing of Cardinal Posadas Ocampo in 1993, and of being involved with Amado Carrillo Fuentes.

López Núñez, Dámaso. Took over as assistant warden of Puente Grande in April 1999, bringing with him a whole team from Sinaloa. Allegedly in the employ of El Mayo Zambada and the Sinaloa Cartel.

Macedo de la Concha, Rafael. Attorney general under President Fox.

Martínez Herrera, Arturo, alias El Texas. Member of the Gulf cartel and associate of El Chapo Guzmán and El Güero Palma in Puente Grande.

Matta Ballesteros, Juan Ramón, alias El Negro. Honduran drug trafficker, partner of Medellín Cartel and of Miguel Ángel Félix Gallardo.

Medina Mora, Eduardo. Former Televisa board member, appointed head of Cisen by President Fox, then secretary of public security during the last year of that adminstration. Became attorney general under Calderón

Milián Rodríguez, Ramón. Chief accountant of the Medellín Cartel.

Millán Gómez, Edgar Eusebio. Subordinate and close friend of García Luna. Replaced Javier Garza as coordinator of regional security in 2007. Shot dead in May 2008.

Morfín Otero, María Guadalupe, known as Lupita. President of the Jalisco State Human Rights Commission, she tried to take action against the abuse of women and overall corruption in Puente Grande.

Mouriño, Juan Camilo. Interior secretary under President Calderón, killed in an air crash on November 4, 2008, along with eight others. El Mayo Zambada is widely suspected of ordering his killing.

Nepomuceno, Juan. Historic leader of the Gulf Cartel.

Ochoa, Jorge Luis. Prominent member of Colombia's Medellín Cartel, along with brothers Fabio and Juan David.

Ortiz, Sergio Humberto, alias El Apá (Daddy). Former policeman and chief of Mexico's biggest kidnap gang, La Flor, allegedly protected by García Luna and his cronies. Died in prison in 2009.

Palma, Héctor, alias El Güero. A close associate of El Chapo Guzmán in the Guadalajara and Pacific organizations.

Pérez Díaz, Juan José. Prison guard at Puente Grande who resisted being recruited by the drug traffickers.

Pérez Rodríguez, Enrique. Became deputy director of the prison service in the SSP in 1999. Closely involved in the corruption that characterized the system.

Posadas Ocampo, Cardinal Juan Jesús. Killed in a shootout in the car park of Guadalajara airport on May 24, 1993. His death was a national scandal. The official version, that he was caught in the crossfire during a clash between El Chapo and the Arrellano Félix brothers, was rewritten several times. This book suggests he was murdered by the security services because he knew too much about their connections with the drug trade.

Puga Quintanilla, José Salvador. Former member of the Gulf Cartel, given the code name Pitufo when he made a sworn statement to public prosecutors on March 9, 2009.

Rodríguez Gacha, José Gonzalo, alias El Mexicano. Another founder of the Medellín Cartel, who pioneered close dealings with the Mexican drug traffickers in the late 1970s.

Rodríguez Orejuela, Gilberto and Miguel. Colombian drug traffickers.

Rosas Rosas, Facundo. Under secretary for Police Strategy and Intelligence under García Luna during the Calderón administration.

Sahagún, Marta. Spokesperson for, then second wife of, President Fox.

Salcido, Manuel, alias El Cochiloco. Leader of the Guadalajara Cartel, killed in October 1991.

Salinas de Gortari, Raúl. Brother of President Carlos Salinas. Arrested in 1995 on murder and corruption charges. Acquitted of murder in 2005, but still on trial for illicit enrichment.

Santiago Vasconcelos, José Luis. Deputy attorney general for SIEDO, responsible for investigations into García Luna and his staff.

Seal, Adler Berriman, better known as Barry Seal. Pilot for the Medellín Cartel in the 1980s and a CIA agent.

Tello Peón, Jorge Enrique. An aide to Carrillo Olea in the early 1990s, he became under secretary for public security in May 1999, and continued in that post under President Fox. After a spell in business at Pemex, he returned in 2008 as Calderón's adviser in the "war on drugs." El Chapo identified him as one of three officials who facilitated his escape from Puente Grande.

Tostado Félix, Pablo. Aide to Esparragoza and others in the Sinaloa Cartel. In 2005, questioned in prison by lawyers for the Guadalajara archdiocese seeking to clarify the killing of Cardinal Posadas, gave abundant details about the organization and its links to government. Found shot and hung in his cell in May 2009.

Treviño, Miguel Ángel, alias El Muerto or Z40. Lazcano's second-in-command and current successor as Zetas leader.

Valdez Villarreal, Edgar, alias La Barbie. Sent by The Federation to Nuevo Laredo in 2002 to begin the war on the Gulf Cartel and the Zetas. Became the organization's most violent enforcer, working mainly for Arturo Beltrán Leyva. After the latter's death, began to develop own drug business. Was "captured," or gave himself up, in 2010, apparently to save himself from Héctor Beltrán Leyva.

Valencia Fontes, Jaime. El Chapo's "private secretary" in Puente Grande prison. Organized a group of inmates as enforcers, known as The Plumbers.

Villanueva, Mario. Former governor of Quintana Roo state, extradited to US in May 2010 on drug charges.

Villarreal, Sergio, alias El Grande. Former policeman who began to work under Arturo Beltrán Leyva in 2000 and joined La Barbie in leading The Federation's war on the Gulf Cartel. For a time he ran the organization's operations at Mexico City Airport. After the split in The Federation and the death of Arturo Beltrán Leyva, was left defending the bastion of the Juárez Cartel against El Chapo.

Vizcaíno Medina, Jesús. One of the Sinaloas, or police commanders linked to the Sinaloa Cartel who accompanied López Núñez when he became assistant warden at Puente Grande.

Hernández, Zulema Yulia. one of the women El Chapo took as a partner while in Puente Grande prison.

Yunes Linares, Miguel Ángel. Adviser in the SSP, then director of the prison service. In July 2000 became chief adviser to Gertz Manero, the first secretary of public security, while his friend Pérez Rodríguez took over as director of the prison service.

Zambada García, Ismael, known as El Mayo. Leader of the Sinaloa cartel, regarded by some as the man behind El Chapo's throne.

Zambada García, Jesús Reynaldo, alias El Rey (The King). Brother of Ismael, helped run operations for El Mayo and El Chapo in the capital, especially the airport. Arrested along with his son and stepson after a confused shootout in Mexico City in October 2008 between different groups of policemen, some of them his bodyguards.

Zambada Reyes, Jesús. Son of Jesús Zambada, turned protected witness for the PGR, with the code name Rambo III, after being arrested with his father in 2008.

Zuno Arce, Rubén. Businessman and brother-in-law of former president Luis Echeverría. Accused of drug trafficking from the 1970s, and convicted by a Los Angeles court in 1990 of involvement in the murder of DEA agent Camarena.

Index

Page numbers in **bold** indicate glossary location.

Persons with nicknames or pseudonyms are listed under both names.

The Informer on, 69–70
on Posadas murder, 15–17
mentioned, 89, 105, 159, 170, 176, 179, 188, 193, 205, 234, 282, 287
Carrillo Fuentes, Rodolfo (El Niño de Oro), 192–4, 242, **339**
Carrillo Fuentes, Vicente (El Viceroy), **339**
after Amado's leadership, 110–11
after El Barbas death, Beltrán Leyva alliance, 281–2
and Amado's son, 113
background, 192–4
El Chapo on, 242
in The Federation, 180
and Lalo Ramírez Peyro, 194–6
at traffickers meeting, 176–8
Carrillo Leyva, Vicente (Amado's son) (El Ingeniero), 112–13, 279, 319n12, **339**
Carrillo Olea, General Jorge, **339**
and Alegre, Cisen in Puente Grande, 133
on Carrillo Fuentes, 16
El Chapo arrested (1993), 9–14, 23–8, 235
on El Chapo's confessions, 29–31, 37–9
on El Chapo's narco-payroll, 92
and Coello, 20
on González Calderoni, 97–8
interviewed by author, 5, 23, 37–9, 315n1
on Mexican army generals, 315n1
in planning meeting, 40
under Salinas, Investigation and Security, 20–1, 93
mentioned, 68, 114
"cartel," term origin, 63–4
Carter, Jimmy, and Tower Commission, 50
Cash, Theodore, 55
Castañeda, Jorge, 273
Castaño Gil, Carlos (AUC), 172–3
Castaño Gil, José Vicente (El Profe), 170, 172–3, **339**
Castillejos, Marcos, 221
Castillo Alonso, Juan, 102
Castro, Fidel, 110
Ceja, Justo, 109–110
Cemex, 152
Cendro (Center for Drug Control Planning), 11–12, 14, 25, 30, **333**
Central American migrants, 303
Cervantes, Hector, 57
Cervantes Aguirre, Brigadier General Enrique, 106–9, 202, **339**
César (El Chapo's son), 34, 146
El Chacho (García, Dionicio), 205–6
Los Chachos (armed detachment), 207
El Chapo. *See* Guzmán Loera, Joaquín
Chávez, Arturo, 280, 303
El Chino (León Aragón, Rodolfo), 39, 64, 85–9, 92, 98, **342**

El Chipilón (García Gaxiola, Rodolfo), 171–2, 174
El Chiquilín (Hernández Nájar, Roberto), 96, 99
El Chito (Camberos Rivera, Francisco Javier), 146–7, 152–3, 176, **338**
Christine Discotheque, 10, 30, 36, 85
El Chuta (Ramos, Edgar), 289
CIA
arms smugglers/traffickers relations, 51–6, 78–9
Berrellez on drug trade of, 58
and Boland Amendment, 49
as Camarena's murderers, 55
drug trade as political weapon for, 181
on Guatemalan guerrilla training, 47–8
and Iran Contra, 5, 48–50, 70–4, 296, 316n3
and Medellín Cartel links, 77
and Miguel Nazar (DFS), 56, 67
and narcos of Veracruz, x
1956–68, in Mexico, 59–61
on Seal, 74, 317n6
and Setco airline, 71
spokesman Mansfield on non-involvement, 48
Torre Blanca's testimony, 73
See also DEA; Harrison, Lawrence; US government Commissions
Cisen (Center for Investigation and National Security), **333**
files on traffickers, 241, 328n11
during Fox administration, 138
monitoring Puente Grande prison, 133, 154
officers join AFI, 210
set up by Carrillo Olea, 20–1, 93
Citigroup, and Banamex merger, 138, 321n4
Ciudad Juárez, 93, 281–2
Clinton, Bill, 72, 99
Clouthier, Manuel (PAN politician), 183
CNDH (National Human Rights Commission), 66, 142–3, 320n25, **333**
Cocaine Politics (Scott and Marshall), 317n2
El Cochiloco (Salcido, Manuel), 35, 53, **343**
Cockburn, Leslie and Andrew, 317n18
Coello Trejo, Javier, 16–17, 19–20, 23, 105, **339**
Cohen Bisu, Abraham, 88
El Colín (Reyes, Gerardo Colín), 258
El Coloche (Laija, Ramón), 87
Colom, Álvaro, 295
Colombia
Arturo and Castaño Gil links, 172–3
AUC, 172–3, 192, **333**
Cali Cartel, 30, 94, 111
diplomat from, on García ultimatum, 275
US cable on, 265
Valle del Norte Cartel, 168, 262
Colombians, raids on, 261–2
Colosio, Luis Donaldo, 172, 174, 323n23
Commandante Lore, 257–8, 259–60, 329n25

Monterrey, Nuevo León state, 282
Montes, Virginia, 126
Moraila, Julio (PJF), 175
Morales, Marisela (SIEDO), 262, 276
Morales Lechuga, Ignacio (AG)
  acting on Coello's crimes, 20
  and Carrillo Olea, 31
  El Chapo link, via Ponce, 30–1
  Echeverría's house search, 91
  resignation of, 12
  and Salinas, 93, 96–9, 318nn10–11
  as Special Affairs Prosecutor, 86
  and Vázquez Raña hangar case, 95
Moreno, Martin, 87
Moreno, Salvador (guard), 142–3
Moreno, Yves Eréndira, 125, 127–9
Morfín Otero, María Guadalupe (Lupita), 126,
  129, 142–4, 150–1, 154, **342**
Morley, Jefferson (journalist), 59
Morton, John T., 98
Moss, Frank, 72
Mouriño, Carlos (Juan's brother), 277–8
Mouriño Atanes, Carlos (Juan's father), 278
Moya Palencia, Mario, 64
MTC Aviación, and Aviones, 285–6
Mucel Luna, General Luis, 109
El Muerto. See Treviño, Miguel Ángel
"mules" recruitment, 288
La Muñeca. See Valdez Villareal, Edgar
Muñoz, Ramón, 146
Murder of a Cardinal (Carpizo and Andrade), 38
Muskie, Edmund, 50

Nacho. See Coronel Villarreal, Ignacio
El Nalo (Gutiérrez, Leonardo), 183
narco-corrido(s), 173, 193, 199–200, 323n28
"narcocracy," 295, 298
narco-payroll (El Chapo's), 89–92
National Anti-Drugs Institute (INCD), 105,
  315n3, **333**
National Drug Intelligence Center (NDIC),
  231–2
"National Drug Threat Assessment 2010" (US),
  296–9
National Human Rights Commission (CNDH),
  66, 142–3, 320n25, **333**
National March for Peace, 304
National Public Radio, 194
National Water Board (Conagua), 186
Navarro, Francisco, 262
Nazar Haro, Miguel, 56, 67
Ndrangheta of Calabria, Italy (group), 203
El Negro (Matta Ballesteros, Juan Ramón), 48,
  55, 57, 70–1, 74, **342**
Los Negros (Zeta group), 207
Nepomuceno, Juan, 19, 21, 96–7, **343**
Don Neto. See Fonseca Carrillo, Ernesto
New Alliance Party, 158

New York Times (newspaper), 83, 99
Niebla Cardoza, Rosario (Doña Rosario), 180,
  181
El Niño (Jiménez, José), 259
El Niño de Oro. See Carrillo Fuentes, Rodolfo
Noé Robles, 258
Noroeste, El (newspaper), 300–1
Norte, El (newspaper), 95
Norte del Valle Cartel, 192
North, Oliver, 49
"The Northern Peace," negotiated by El Azul,
  191
Los Números (hitmen), 309
Núñez, Jorge, 88, 92

Oaxaca, and cocaine transport, 70
Oaxaca Center for Human Rights, 320n25
Ocaña, Guillermo (Ocañita), 162, 167–9, 215
Ochoa, Commander Carlos, 114, 118, 131, 145
Ochoa, Jorge Luis, 54, 71, 74, **343**
Ochoa brothers, 71, 77–8
officials
  as employees, to traffickers, 294
  trapped between warring Cartels, 251
Ojeda Paullada, Pedro, 64
"old guard," executions of, 93–4
Operation Casablanca scandal, 111–14
Operation Cleanup, 326n26
Operation Condor, 67–8
Operation Leyenda, 47, 51–2, 56, 58
Ortega, Daniel, 76, 78
Ortega Sánchez, José Antonio (lawyer), 116,
  315n5
Ortiz, Sergio Humberto (El Apá), 222, 228–30,
  257–60, **343**
Osorno, Diego Enrique (journalist), 157

Los Pachangos (airport police), 170
Pacific Cartel, consolidation of, 175, 178
pact (Valle Hermoso), 245–7, 248–52
Padierna, Dolores (PRD), 168
Palma, Héctor (El Güero), **343**
  Aguilar's sanctions on, 130–1
  air shipments of, 6, 94–5
  ambition of, 21–3
  arrest of, 188
  and Camarena, 44, 54–5
  and Carrillo Fuentes, 15–18, 78, 109
  and El Chapo, 10, 15, 30, 33, 36, 83
  and Iguala massacre, 87–8
  indicted and acquitted, 152, 153
  in Puente Grande, 101, 104–5, 114, 118–21,
    124–5
  Puente Grande's last days, 140, 144, 146
  Segoviano on, 89–90
PAN (Partido de Acción Nacional), 99, 181, 232,
  243, 299, 305, **334**. See also PRI
Paraguay, 295

10/13